Sexual Compu

A Program of Recovery

3rd Edition – Revised and Expanded

Sexual Compulsives Anonymous
International Service Organization

P.O. Box 1585
Old Chelsea Station
New York, NY 10011

USA (800) 977-HEAL (toll-free)
International +1 (212) 606-3778

http://www.sca-recovery.org

ISBN 978-1-949225-06-8

Table of Contents

Sexual Compulsives Anonymous (SCA)
A Program of Recovery

Preface to the Third Edition

This book contains more than four decades of experience, strength, and hope in recovery from sexual compulsion. It begins by addressing the individual in recovery and then discusses how we recover together in groups and as a fellowship. The latter part of the book contains personal stories of our recovery written by SCA members.

This volume's creation and production required a multi-year process. Many of the chapters previously existed as separate SCA literature pieces, including the first two editions of SCA: A Program of Recovery. They have been reviewed and updated for this edition. The Twelve Steps commentaries and those of the Traditions and the Characteristics are more recent and are the product of many hours of labor, debate, and consensus. Additional chapters, such as those on sexual anorexia and pornography, apps, & internet addiction, have also been recently developed to address the fellowship's changing needs.

A group of gay men founded the SCA Fellowship because they needed a place to share honestly, openly, and without judgment to recover from their sexual compulsion. Society has changed over the last few decades, and so has our fellowship. Our program is more diverse today than at any time in our history. SCA is open to everyone per our Third Tradition, which states that "the only requirement for membership is a desire to stop having compulsive sex." What initially began as a safe meeting space for gay men to recover is today a safe space for all, but we always remember and value our roots.

In the pursuit of our recovery, we abstain from those sexual behaviors we deem harmful to our mental, physical, or spiritual health. In SCA, we seek to integrate sex as a healthy element into our new, more joyful lives of love, compassion, and service. We hope that this book will help make recovery a vital part of your life, seeking the honesty, openness, and willingness to say "yes" to a new way of living.

May you find the same freedom, happiness, and serenity that we have found in SCA.

Foreword by Alexandra Katehakis, Ph.D.

As far back as the 1800s, western medicine has continuously examined excessive sexual behavior, arguing over how to categorize it and giving it different labels along the way. While the field of psychotherapy continues to debate whether the excessive use of sex can be an addiction and what the definition of "excessive" is, millions of people who struggle with the issue find their way to healing through 12-Step programs like Sexual Compulsives Anonymous (SCA).

In 1983, Patrick Carnes introduced the term "sexual addiction" in his groundbreaking book, *Out of the Shadows: Understanding Sexual Addiction*. The term "sex addiction" was soon popularized by the media and increasingly recognized in clinical settings. Therapists continued to see their patients struggling with compulsive sexual behaviors, yet researchers argued that the literature relied on theory and subjective clinical observation. Without sufficient empirical evidence to support the problem's existence, academics and researchers continued to invalidate the problem. Meanwhile, 12-Step programs devoted to assisting the sexual compulsive proliferated. Almost forty years later, the World Health Organization announced Compulsive Sexual Behavior Disorder (CSBD) as a new diagnosis into the eleventh edition of the *International Classification of Diseases* (ICD-11). This addition was a major "win" for those who struggle with sexual addiction and compulsivity the world over.

Sexual compulsivity, also known as sexual addiction, has its genesis in childhood neglect or emotional, physical (including bullying), and sexual abuse. The ensuing wounds bequeath the sexual compulsive a shame-based sense of self that attempts to right itself through the distorted mime language of sex. In other words, the sexual compulsive desperately seeks validation, love, and a place to belong through multiple disconnecting and emotionally harmful sexual experiences, further traumatizing and damaging their very sense of self.

Shame accompanies all forms of abuse and is considered a barrier emotion that blocks all other vitality states from being experienced. Chronic and unrepaired shame in early childhood prevents the healthy development of a sense of self. It has devastating effects on being relational. Emotional contact, or attachment to others, can't be met due to the shame and even terror that human contact can bring. When the self suffers in this manner, the sexual compulsive feels tormented, as if their very soul is sick. Even worse, shame can become dissociated or repressed for a long time without awareness. Sexually "acting out" then, is the manifestation of unconscious, unresolved shame. Sadly, it leads the sexual compulsive into a vicious cycle of self-loathing, self-destruction, and self-sabotage when things are going well, making shame the cause and effect of their sex addiction.

Sexual addiction and compulsivity are also thought of as an intimacy disorder, with fantasy often being the counterpoint to shame. Shame resides deep in the gut, while fantasy is a neural pathway in the brain that allows the person to dissociate. Pathological dissociation is a disconnection between the cortical (intellect) and subcortical (emotional) parts of the brain. In effect, this means that due to neural circuitry that has uncoupled, the brain and body have lost communication with each other. This disconnection accounts for why addicts report feeling inadequate, unbearably lonely, and internally numb. It also allows them to drift into a fantasy world, never grounded in the reality of their lives. This elegant system that provided them a necessary escape in childhood – often when there was no other escape – now serves to protect them from the psychic pain they cannot bear to acknowledge, let alone feel. Even though the sexual compulsive intellectually knows they're hurting themself, this dysfunctional neurobiological organization leaves them struggling mightily to form and forge relationships and stop their destructive behaviors.

When an addict "hits bottom" or "gets sick and tired of being sick and tired," they're ready to ask for help. The human organism always seeks to heal itself, so it's often a matter of time before a newcomer walks into the rooms of SCA. This first step is crucial to becoming affiliated with a community of concern and coming out of isolation. No longer having to do it alone, the program becomes a stand-in for a healthy family.

Studies show that over time, the social relationships intrinsic in the program change participants' attachment styles. Relying on others to get their needs met leads people to experience themselves more accurately. Many see their anxious and avoidant attachments decrease, and a sense of being secure in relationship to others increases. Participants begin to take comfort in connection, expand their ability to trust others, and experience less fear of being close or of others wanting to leave.

Defining and making contact with a Higher Power is an essential component to the restoration of the self, whether the recovering person locates it in the actual meetings or comes to experience it as a universal divinity within. Regardless, working through the 12 Steps helps participants organize the emotional, physical, and psychological pains of the past into a coherent narrative that helps them make meaning of the present and stay healthy. A new capacity for self-regulation and self-reflection and the inner peace those skills bring may be an early gift of recovery that grows with continued sobriety and neural integration.

Through their affiliation with others and eventual spiritual awakening, the recovering person can earn a secure attachment, laying the foundation to move toward healthy sexuality. By diligently working the program, recovering addicts experience an emotionally and spiritually intimate relationship with other fellows and with themselves - sometimes for the first time. This foundation of affiliation is the bedrock on which a healthy sexual self can emerge. Sex is no longer a source of shame, dissociated from the self, dismissive of others, and devoid of meaning.

Instead, sex is a manifestation of vital energy that is awake in the body. The expression of that energy represents the love recovering people feel for themselves and others. Emotional connection and bodily pleasure are the necessary combination for robust and healthy sexuality.

In these pages, you will hear the lived experience of recovering people. They describe not expert opinion, theory, or speculation, but transformation born out of hard work through dedication to the program. By attending meetings and workshops, working the Steps, taking service commitments, and regularly connecting to the fellowship, recovering people find a roadmap to healing.

Brave SCA members have put their minds and hearts together to write this comprehensive and valuable book to guide the reader through the recovery process. If you're reading this, you've already begun to change your life. Within these pages, you will find the experience, strength, and hope you've been seeking. SCA changes people's lives. There is hope; *you* are the one you've been waiting to discover!

~~~

Alexandra Katehakis, Ph.D., is a Clinical Sexologist and Founder of Center for Healthy Sex. She is the author of numerous books on sex addiction and intimacy issues.
~~~

Chapter 1: SCA Statement of Purpose

SEXUAL COMPULSIVES ANONYMOUS is a fellowship of people who share their experience, strength and hope with each other, that they may solve their common problem and help others to recover from sexual compulsion. The only requirement for membership is a desire to stop having compulsive sex. There are no dues or fees for SCA membership; we are self-supporting through our own contributions. SCA is not allied with any sect, denomination, politics, organization, or institution; does not wish to engage in any controversy; neither endorses nor opposes any causes.

Our primary purpose is to stay sexually sober and to help others to achieve sexual sobriety. Members are encouraged to develop their own sexual recovery plan, and to define sexual sobriety for themselves. We are not here to repress our God-given sexuality, but to learn how to express it in ways that will not make unreasonable demands on our time and energy, place us in legal jeopardy, or endanger our mental, physical or spiritual health.

Chapter 2: Twenty Questions

1. Do you frequently experience remorse, depression, or guilt about your sexual activity?
2. Do you feel your sexual drive and activity are getting out of control? Have you repeatedly tried to stop or reduce certain sexual behaviors but inevitably found that you could not?
3. Are you unable to resist sexual advances or turn down sexual propositions when offered?
4. Do you use sex to escape from uncomfortable feelings such as anxiety, fear, anger, resentment, guilt, etc., which seem to disappear when the sexual obsession starts?
5. Do you spend excessive time obsessing about sex or engaged in sexual activity?
6. Have you neglected your family, friends, spouse, or relationship because of the time you spend on sexual activity?
7. Do your sexual pursuits interfere with your work or professional development?
8. Is your sexual life secretive, a source of shame, and not in keeping with your values? Do you lie to others to cover up your sexual activity?
9. Are you afraid of sex? Do you avoid romantic and sexual relationships with others and restrict your sexual activity to fantasy, masturbation, and solitary or anonymous online activity?
10. Are you increasingly unable to perform sexually without other stimuli such as pornography, videos, “poppers,” drugs/alcohol, “toys,” etc.?

11. Do you have to increasingly resort to abusive, humiliating, or painful sexual fantasies or behaviors to get sexually aroused?
12. Has your sexual activity prevented you from developing a close, loving relationship with a partner? Or have you developed a pattern of intense romantic or sexual relationships that never seem to last once the excitement wears off?
13. Do you only have anonymous sex or one-night stands? Do you usually want to get away from your sex partner after the encounter?
14. Do you have sex with people with whom you normally would not associate?
15. Do you frequent apps, websites, clubs, bars, adult bookstores, restrooms, parks, and other public places searching for sex partners?
16. Have you ever been arrested or placed yourself in legal jeopardy for your sexual activity?
17. Have you ever risked your physical health with exposure to sexually transmitted diseases by engaging in "unsafe" sexual activity?
18. Has the money you spent on pornography, videos, web-camming, apps, phone sex, or hustlers/prostitutes strained your financial resources?
19. Have people you trust expressed concern about your sexual activity?
20. Does life seem meaningless and hopeless without a romantic or sexual relationship?

Chapter 3: The Characteristics Most of Us Seem to Have in Common

1. As adolescents, we used fantasy and compulsive masturbation to avoid feelings, and continued this tendency into our adult lives with compulsive sex.
2. Compulsive sex became a drug, which we used to escape from feelings such as anxiety, loneliness, anger and self-hatred, as well as joy.
3. We tended to become immobilized by romantic obsessions. We became addicted to the search for sex and love; as a result, we neglected our lives.
4. We sought oblivion in fantasy and masturbation, and lost ourselves in compulsive sex. Sex became a reward, punishment, distraction and time-killer.
5. Because of our low self-esteem, we used sex to feel validated and complete.
6. We tried to bring intensity and excitement into our lives through sex, but felt ourselves growing steadily emptier.
7. Sex was compartmentalized instead of integrated into our lives as a healthy element.
8. We became addicted to people, and were unable to distinguish among sex, love and affection.
9. We searched for some "magical" quality in others to make us feel complete. Other people were idealized and endowed with a powerful symbolism, which often disappeared after we had sex with them.

10. We were drawn to people who were not available to us, or who would reject or abuse us.

11. We feared relationships, but continually searched for them. In a relationship, we feared abandonment and rejection, but out of one, we felt empty and incomplete.

12. While constantly seeking intimacy with another person, we found that the desperate quality of our need made true intimacy with anyone impossible, and we often developed unhealthy dependency relationships that eventually became unbearable.

13. Even when we got the love of another person, it never seemed enough, and we were unable to stop lusting after others.

14. Trying to conceal our dependency demands, we grew more isolated from ourselves, from God and from the very people we longed to be close to.

INTRODUCTION

WHERE WE'VE BEEN

In its early years, Sexual Compulsives Anonymous (SCA) sought to identify what traits its members had in common. In 1983, the SCA New York fellowship sponsored a series of workshops to facilitate a group inventory. Bob R. and Rob F., early members of SCA, refined the output of these sessions[1]. These efforts resulted in an early draft of *The Characteristics Most of Us Seem to Have in Common* during the latter half of the 1980s. These individual characteristics were reordered and further edited before their publication in SCA: A Program of Recovery in 1996.

Many newcomers to our fellowship have described their experiences of hearing *The Characteristics* read at meetings. While it might have been uncomfortable to hear the unmanageability reflected in these descriptions, they also heard hope. If others understood the pain these newcomers had experienced, there was a sense that they were finally in the right place to get help. Many described their identification with *The Characteristics* as a feeling of belonging. Meetings became a place where there was the potential for the healing process to begin and a move toward spiritual growth.

While writing commentaries on these characteristics, some common themes emerged. There was an overwhelming sense of *powerlessness*. The compulsive behaviors and fantasies were so addictive that we seemed doomed to repeat them no matter how

---

[1] Frank H., a founding member of SCA, provided this information in a telephone conversation on September 25, 2020.

destructive these patterns became. The feeling of shame, the absence of self-esteem, and the unquenchable thirst for validation were common denominators in the collective experience *The Characteristics* outlined. In writing about them, we remembered that these descriptions reflected what life was like *before* recovery. As dark, dreary, and sometimes hopeless as these patterns of behavior appeared, we realized that help and hope were available once the process of recovery began.

The commentaries on *The Characteristics* provide a reference point based on the collective experience of others who have come before. Following these commentaries, we share a perspective on how 12-Step recovery opened the door to a new way of living.

Characteristic One

"As adolescents, we used fantasy and compulsive masturbation to avoid feelings, and continued this tendency into our adult lives with compulsive sex."

For many of us, masturbation began in childhood as a temporary escape for anything and everything that ailed us. Masturbation may have started as an exercise in self-discovery, but the pleasurable sensation we experienced made us want to repeat it, again and again. During these early days of exploration, most of us remained sexually innocent. We masturbated to distract ourselves from stress caused by family, school, or other issues. We masked our painful feelings with a pleasurable activity we could control. It was something we might have done alone, although some of us may have experimented by masturbating with others.

As our bodies developed, we became more sexually aware. We began to associate masturbation with sexuality and to fantasize about people and sexual activities we found appealing. Images we encountered through TV, movies, or pornography, often at an early age, became part of our masturbation ritual. The reward of receiving physical and emotional pleasure from our self-stimulation and fantasies made masturbation a habitual and repetitive activity.

Such behavior helped many of us cope with the daily struggles and emotional turbulence of dysfunctional families. Some of us experienced neglect during our childhood. Others had families that discouraged emotional expression. We needed a way to suppress or avoid the feelings we were not allowed to express or found difficult to process. We sought refuge from such empty or repressive environments by resorting to masturbation, which brought us immediate, intense pleasure and temporary relief. This relief and the need to avoid our feelings made it our default option to deal with stress. Our masturbation habits had little or nothing to do with intimacy. They were secretive and often became a hindrance to engaging in healthy sexual activities with others.

Our persistent reliance on masturbation led to feelings of shame and low self-esteem. These feelings may have begun in childhood and intensified during our adolescence. For many, masturbation became associated with antisocial or "bad" behavior, accompanied by the fear of being caught by someone, especially a family member. Yet we couldn't stop, which made us even more ashamed. We may have masturbated at inappropriate times and places, careless of our privacy, and to the point of causing ourselves physical pain or damage. Our parents, teachers, or religious leaders might have told us of the terrible things that would happen to us if we continued to masturbate. This scolding shamed us and made us see ourselves as defective. In response to this humiliation, we may have masturbated even more, and so the cycle intensified. These repetitive efforts to avoid our feelings and escape our reality only made us feel worse.

As young adults, conflicting feelings often accompanied this new stage of life, and our sexual and romantic fantasies evolved as we imagined new possibilities. Our compulsive masturbation ultimately made our lives unmanageable. Using a coping mechanism that had "worked" for us in our youth kept us from learning how to deal with our feelings as adults. Our masturbation and sexual fantasies interfered with organizing our time and planning for the future. Many of us failed to learn other ways of dealing with our feelings and everyday life stresses.

The qualities of our compulsive masturbation often translated into similar patterns when we had sex with others. We used sex to numb ourselves in stressful situations and to convert unpleasant feelings to more pleasant ones. We used compulsive masturbation, casual sex, anonymous sex, and other activities to avoid feelings. These behaviors provided the means to escape from reality into a fantasy world. The pain of life prompted us to seek the relief that compulsive sex seemed to bring, even as we came to understand that our behaviors were problematic, harmful, and self-defeating.

Characteristic Two

"Compulsive sex became a drug, which we used to escape from feelings such as anxiety, loneliness, anger and self-hatred, as well as joy."

As adolescents and young adults, many of us tried to avoid our feelings by masturbating, later turning compulsively to various forms of sex or pornography. Some of us believed that feelings would hurt us, embarrass us, or remind us of past shame or abandonment. With no healthy means to manage our feelings, we saw them as unpredictable and out of our control. When these emotions surfaced, we often felt an urgent, nearly overwhelming need to numb them. We turned to sex, which may have worked for a while, until fresh feelings surfaced, driving us back out for more sex to deaden them.

Sex became our drug of choice, and like many other drugs, it was highly habit-forming. The more we got, the more we needed, putting us on a seemingly endless quest for the next "fix." If we felt shame after our compulsive sexual activities, the only remedy seemed to be more sex. On and on we went, from one acting out session to the next, turning to compulsive sex during good times as well as bad. Eventually, any strong feelings led us to our drug.

When anxiety gripped us and wouldn't let go, we frequently turned to sex as a means of escape. And while sex seemed like the perfect potion for these anxious feelings, it couldn't address the underlying conditions that made us anxious in the first place – insecurity, trauma, pain, and fear. Sex shielded us for the moment from life's challenges and frustrations. Inevitably, though, when we came down from the high of compulsive sex, our pain and anxiety were still there, often more powerful and unmanageable than before.

A general sense of loneliness plagued many of us. We may have felt ignored, forgotten, or dismissed by others as uninteresting or just not good enough. This feeling of inadequacy often led us to self-isolate to protect ourselves from others hurting us in these ways. This behavior compounded our unhappiness because we couldn't stand being alone. Compulsive sex became the only relief from this unbearable sense of loneliness.

Sometimes feelings of anger - at ourselves or toward others, became overwhelming. Often, as children, we had caregivers who never let us express anger. This pattern made it difficult for many of us to express our anger constructively as adults. Instead, we turned it inward, where it took the form of self-hatred. These feelings were overpowering at times, and we sought the numbness and escape we found in ever more extreme compulsive behaviors.

As our acting out behaviors increased and intensified, they made our sense of isolation and loneliness more acute and painful. We couldn't see the paradox – that the more physical contact we had, the less connected to others we felt. We grappled with low self-esteem, and our feelings of worthlessness could make the search for sex even more desperate. We longed for validation to soothe our raw feelings through sexual encounters with others. Many of us thought so little of ourselves that we would do almost anything, with anyone, to get the validation we craved.

We desperately needed to evade our emotions, and this need intensified and began to overwhelm us. Yet the more we pursued the high of escape and oblivion, the more it seemed to elude us. Recklessly, we chased our fix, ignoring the ever-worsening consequences. For some of us, risk fueled the high, so we put ourselves in jeopardy - physically, emotionally, financially, or legally. We may have acted out compulsively for entire days or weekends at a time. Sometimes we acted out in public places, risking arrest. Some of us invited strangers into our homes, disregarding our physical safety. Safe sex became an afterthought or even purposely avoided to increase the danger and amplify the high.

Ironically, it wasn't just negative feelings that we tried to avoid or could not process. We were equally ill-equipped to handle positive ones. A celebration, some recognition, or even a gesture of affection could compel us to act out. Self-loathing often crept in, telling us we didn't deserve the accolade or attention – that we had no right to feel good and happy. Every situation in which we found ourselves, and every feeling that accompanied it, could send us fleeing to our drug of choice. However, despite our attempts to medicate our feelings, we became lonelier, angrier, and sadder.

Characteristic Three

"We tended to become immobilized by romantic obsessions. We became addicted to the search for sex and love; as a result, we neglected our lives."

As sexual compulsives, our notions of sex, romance, and relationships often became distorted. Romance and the prospect of romance exerted a mysterious and powerful pull over many of us, as did the allure of sex and love. Our feelings of shame and unworthiness increased our fear of physical or emotional intimacy. We continually searched for ways to get out of ourselves, to escape from these feelings. Fantasy provided an escape to distract us from what was going on in our own lives. We often allowed the world of fantasy to spiral into obsessive thinking, leading us to project "ideal" values onto situations or people. The situations or people could be real or imagined. This obsessive behavior provided temporary relief from the pain of real life.

These obsessions became a coping strategy that allowed us to forget what was lacking in our lives. This false reality sometimes developed consciously, but often it was a pattern we weren't aware of initially. Ultimately, our tendency to objectify and romanticize others became habitual. We began to lose ourselves in fantasies involving people we envied, admired, or found physically attractive. We may have seen someone at a distance, or perhaps we met them at a social or work event. Sometimes, it was a colleague we worked with every day. A look, a word, a touch, and we felt captivated, feeling a sense of exhilaration. If we had a chance to spend some time with them, our fantasies intensified. But whatever the level of our involvement, that exhilaration we initially experienced began to permeate our consciousness, and we became obsessed. We were often rejected by those we desired, and our euphoria vanished, leaving us with our stress and anxiety and feeling abandoned.

If we lacked another person to obsess over, we focused our energies on finding one. We hunted for that idealized person whose attentions would validate us. The hunt itself became compulsive, with its potential to create an escape. While we were searching, we were sometimes numb to the everyday problems in our lives, including painful feelings. However, with our experience of seeking sexual gratification compulsively, we often found ourselves looking for these people in all the wrong places. Some of us genuinely believed the same behaviors we had used to seek out objectifying sexual encounters would result in finding "the one" who could magically relieve our pain.

During periods of romantic obsession, many of us set aside or even ignored our other relationships. Our inability to be present made us unavailable to our friends and families. It may have led us to neglect our careers or other aspects of our daily lives. This intense infatuation became our top priority: endlessly fascinating, often painful, and always urgent.

Sometimes, we stopped taking care of ourselves altogether; our everyday routines became less important to us. We put our energy into doing what we hoped would make our obsession respond to us. In some cases, our obsession with another person may have driven us to violate their boundaries. Our emotional development may have suffered as a result of our focus on winning the attention of others. We lost track of ourselves and reality, molding our personalities to fit our obsession.

The intensity of our fixation and the stress of maintaining it often led to severe anxiety. We feared that we would never get what we wanted from our obsession. This fear of rejection or abandonment might trigger us to seek out other avenues of compulsive sex. Alternatively, some of us abstained from sex because others never lived up to our fantasy expectations. Even while obsessed, some of us continued “the hunt,” using compulsive sex to cover up our emotions. It became addictive; we could never put aside the obsession for long.

Characteristic Four

"We sought oblivion in fantasy and masturbation, and lost ourselves in compulsive sex. Sex became a reward, punishment, distraction and time-killer."

Many of us used fantasy early in our lives as a way to escape painful situations over which we had little or no control. We wanted to "check out" – to become oblivious to our thoughts, feelings, and surroundings. We fled into a fantasy world - a world where we were in control. A place where no one could hurt us and our lives were idyllic. Losing ourselves in this fantasy world was often our first addiction.

Once sex entered our lives, many of us quickly integrated it into our fantasy world. Thoughts of being sexual or romantic with others became an exhilarating new way of escaping our reality. Masturbation was often the first sexual experience we had. We used it as a "security blanket" when we felt anxious or upset. The surge of physical pleasure was a great payoff and enhanced the euphoria we felt in fantasy.

Sexual activity created a powerful combination of pleasure, pain, and remorse and was a source of shame for many of us. We craved the physical pleasure of masturbation, but after engaging in it, we felt a deep sense of guilt. This guilt often brought up other painful feelings: a loss of innocence, a loss of integrity, and the sense that we had lost our true selves. Diving deeper into our fantasies seemed like the only action we could take.

However, all our efforts to escape were ineffective and fleeting. We may have escalated our sexual behaviors in frequency and intensity to find oblivion. We found ourselves in a deepening downward spiral of compulsivity and illusion. These efforts frequently created drama in our lives, distracting us from our problems, and deferring any constructive actions to address them. We wasted time indulging our fantasies that we could have spent working on ourselves. We found that once this pattern was in place, we had truly lost our way, with every turn we took leading back to where we began.

Initially, our sexual experiences with other people may have provided some relief. We got an adrenaline rush from acting out that strengthened our desire for more sex. As that desire increased, we began to believe that sex, alone or with someone else, was something we just had to do – that we had no choice in the matter. We felt more and more shame until we reached the point of just giving up - we desperately and urgently needed the relief that sex provided.

We felt powerless over our behavior, and our lives became unmanageable. We sometimes neglected everything else in our lives, avoiding friends and family, social events, even work assignments. We didn't care if we put ourselves at risk or harmed others with our acting out. Many of us were so self-absorbed that we failed to connect our actions with their consequences. We only wanted to satisfy our urge for more and to find the oblivion we desperately sought.

For some, our view of the world narrowed until compulsive sex was all we could see. We lost sight of our true selves and any hopes we once had for the future. In our fantasies, we may have imagined ourselves with a better job, better relationships – a better life. However, they were just that – fantasies – and our compulsive pursuits made us incapable of taking any concrete action to improve our lives.

As addicts, we often had difficulty processing our feelings in the extreme, whether positive or negative, and turned to compulsive sex as a coping mechanism. If something went right, we rewarded ourselves with sex. When we judged ourselves harshly, we may have engaged in harmful sexual behavior, telling ourselves it was all we deserved. Sex was our universal response to everything. When we were bored or had time on our hands, we often indulged in fantasy and masturbation to lose ourselves.

Many of us used any available sexual behavior to distract us. We filled any time we had with compulsive sexual activity, searching for sex, or fantasizing about sex. Sex and fantasy were our anesthetics, numbing our pain, and sheltering us from the realities we didn't want to face. Some of us spent entire nights, weekends, even workdays lost in binges of fantasy, masturbation, and compulsive sex.

Eventually, for most of us, sex became devoid of pleasure or any real feeling. It became an overused and ineffective tool to help us deal with life's ups and downs. It became automatic, a repetitive act, and we forgot or gave up on other ways of living. The worst realization of all was that our sexual acting out no longer stopped our pain but instead became the source of it. The more we escaped into compulsive sex and fantasy, the more we left behind things that once gave us real pleasure. We had built up a tolerance for these compulsive behaviors, and our repeated use of them began to render life meaningless.

Characteristic Five

"Because of our low self-esteem, we used sex to feel validated and complete."

For most of us, our compulsive behavior and its anesthetic qualities served as a way to shield us from feelings of shame and low self-esteem. Although individual circumstances varied, the source of our pain included family-shaming, sexual abuse, secrecy, emotional exploitation, isolation, or rejection by the very people we expected to support us. The message we received from these experiences told us that we were somehow defective and not worthy of love.

Some of us learned that we were unforgivable and incomplete, with little or no value as human beings. In some cases, we were worthy only if we suppressed our emotions or performed sexually. Others may have manipulated us, convincing us that our value was conditional. The message was clear: we were judged and found wanting.

We discovered power and pleasure in manipulative seduction, sexual prowess, and our growing list of conquests in our search for esteem. We soon discovered that sex provided a short reprieve from our low self-esteem by allowing us to feel powerful. This short-term strategy worked well to convince others to validate us, even if it was only as a sexual object. When we experienced rejection, this strategy fell apart, reinforcing our worst feelings about ourselves.

Our lives often seemed empty, except when we thought about, sought out, or had sex. We sought attention in sexual situations, or conversely, retreated into a world of fantasy and isolation.

Emotional scars from our upbringing compounded feelings of unworthiness, and we sought to fill the void where our self-esteem should have been. Many of us shied away from friendships or relationships altogether because contact with our peers threatened us. We were sure that others could see our lack of value. We felt intensely lonely, often left out, ignored, or even excluded completely.

Besides physical contact, we avoided being close to others because we were afraid to be vulnerable or uncomfortable. This pattern presented a significant barrier to intimacy. Instead, some of us engaged in empty, meaningless sex that reinforced our core belief about ourselves as undeserving of love and respect or as a substitute for real intimacy. We tried hard to be attractive to strangers, spending considerable time, energy, and money trying to make ourselves look desirable. We often abandoned our sense of self and objectified ourselves, ceding all power to others. We became people-pleasers, often compromising our integrity or dignity to maintain a connection.

The validation we received from being sexually desired allowed us to feel we had real worth, however briefly. We rarely had sex with anyone for reasons of mutual liking or respect. It was primarily about the affirmation we received, and we could never get enough. Most of us believed our self-worth depended on our ability to please others sexually. Sex for us was serious business. Sex gave us a temporary euphoria, a false sense of satisfaction. However, after the effects wore off, the shame around our behaviors compounded our feeling of low self-worth. Our search for someone who would validate us and make us "whole" became all the more desperate.

This pattern stopped providing any lasting relief to our feeling of being "less than." Afterward, we usually felt a heightened sense of shame for acting out, which affirmed our degradation. When these feelings intensified, we eventually went back for the quick fix. We received instant gratification when we resorted to sex that masked what we believed was lacking in our lives. Subconsciously, we knew that these behaviors were increasing our core of shame and unworthiness. This cycle drove us to seek others to use sexually, to relieve our continual need for affirmation. The more we relied on this temporary infusion of validation, the less worthy and more incomplete we felt.

Characteristic Six

"We tried to bring intensity and excitement into our lives through sex, but felt ourselves growing steadily emptier."

Many of us experienced dissatisfaction with our lives. Especially when compared to others, we may have found our lives dull and frustrating. As addicts, we often formed resentments against others or our circumstances. We had a sense that we were inadequate, that our lives were empty, or lacked adventure. Whatever the source of our discontent, we began to develop an intense craving for excitement to dull its pain. At some point, we discovered that sexually acting out could provide a temporary escape.

We often remembered times in our past when sex and fantasy brought us excitement. Some experienced euphoric recall of past sexual exploits. Many of us began to look for ways to experience this excitement again, to fill the void we felt within us.

Some of us used online dating sites or apps to connect with others. We loved the excitement of being wanted and desired without having to be physically involved. We may have used other ways of finding sexual connection by frequenting bars, clubs, or any place where sex was available. We jumped from one relationship to the next – seeking connection but ultimately unable to sustain it. We may have cheated on our partner, craving the rush of a clandestine encounter.

Some of us paid for sex, used objects, experimented with drugs, or engaged in voyeuristic activities. Some used pornography to fill what seemed to be a growing void. The list of possible sexual activities was as diverse as our imagination. Many of us already had a history of using sex in compulsive ways, so choosing it was familiar. No matter which of these we chose, its purpose was to bring excitement and intensity into our lives through sex. However, we soon found that the intensity and excitement of our sexual behaviors began to fade.

No matter how much we engaged in these activities, the disappointment with our lives often remained. The rewards became intermittent. By repeating the same behaviors without any further benefit of excitement, we felt a sense of emptiness and futility. The sex failed to relieve the disappointment and unhappiness we experienced in our everyday lives. We still felt incredibly empty. Some chose to stop seeking sex or intrigue completely as the answer to these feelings. However, most of us found ourselves unwilling or unable to make that choice. For us, it wasn't a choice at all. The emptiness we felt compelled us to seek more intensity.

Many of us doubled down and tried to find more intense sexual activities. The hookups became more dangerous, as more risk temporarily increased the adrenaline-high we experienced. The "vanilla" pornography no longer worked, so we searched for something edgier. Our pornography use might have included underaged images, or perhaps we looked at graphic or violent scenes. No matter how much we got, we had to keep chasing the next "high" – hoping to find that elusive "perfect" sexual experience. As the compulsion deepened, many of us escalated our activities to the point of violating our values, morals, and integrity. The hookups became sessions filled with humiliation, unsafe sex, and other physical dangers.

Eventually, these sexual activities stopped working altogether. We had run out of options. Our sexual behavior had reached the point where it was making unreasonable demands on our time and energy, placing us in legal jeopardy or endangering our mental, physical or spiritual health. Perhaps we lost jobs or sabotaged relationships by introducing an intensity that others couldn't tolerate. Many of us suffered physical health consequences, sometimes contracting sexually transmitted infections. Some experienced arrest, possibly becoming labeled as a sex offender or a sexual predator.

The deepening spiral of injecting intensity and excitement into our lives through sex had left us emotionally and spiritually drained. The emptiness of our lives was still there and, in fact, had deepened with shame. We had trapped ourselves into a spirit-breaking ritual. We realized that no amount of sex would fill the emptiness we felt or make our lives magically free from the everyday irritations. We needed to find a new source of spiritual energy to rejuvenate our lives.

Characteristic Seven

"Sex was compartmentalized instead of integrated into our lives as a healthy element."

Discovering how we wanted to express our sexuality and setting boundaries was an essential part of growing up. However, those who struggled with sexual compulsion often explored their sexuality using behaviors inconsistent with their values and had poor boundaries. Very few of us had solid role models to demonstrate how to integrate sex into our lives and were negatively affected by images of sex we saw in pornography and the media. Many used sexual acts to acquire attention and validation instead of finding affirmations of our worth in healthier ways.

We were often in denial about our behaviors' harmful effects on our lives – we lied to ourselves about the destructive nature of our actions. We tried to protect ourselves from the painful reality we had created. We often felt an intense need to hide these behaviors from ourselves and others: we believed if others saw us as we were, they would have judged us defective, perverse, and unworthy of love and respect. This belief created a conflict within us: we had shame about our sexual activity and had few positive experiences. We often separated these activities and feelings into discrete "boxes" to contain and conceal them from ourselves and others. The more our sexual activities diverged from our values, the more effort we put into separating and hiding them.

Our hidden sexual life made our everyday existence increasingly uncomfortable for most of us, eventually becoming unmanageable. The feeling that our sexuality was different from others may have started with trauma or even our identity:

perhaps we had been victims of sexual abuse; perhaps we agonized over body image issues. Some of us struggled to accept our sexual orientation. Keeping our sex lives secret and lying about our activities required some mental acrobatics – we had to keep track of the lies we told to keep the stories straight. This need to separate our sexual behaviors from the rest of our lives kept us from being honest with others in matters both great and small. Our dependence on secrecy increased our stress and contributed to our belief that we were manipulative, deceitful, and unlovable.

Some of us even developed "double lives" by creating an alternate persona for our acting out fantasies and compulsive sex. This split in our identity helped us hide our sexual activity and made it easier to deny its impact on our lives. Since we now had an alter ego, whose behaviors were somehow separate from our own, we compromised any sense of integrity we may have had. We reinforced barriers between our acting out and our "real" life to keep our guilt and shame from contaminating the image we presented to others.

Living a double life became painful and complicated, especially in our relationships with family, friends, or potential romantic partners. Most of us did not believe that anyone could love and accept us as we were. We could not allow anyone to know us intimately for fear that they would discover our secrets. The fragmentation of our identity often accelerated if we engaged with a partner. The possible discovery of our acting out life created tremendous anxiety and fear. We feared exposure and humiliation. We worried we would lose the connections we had if our web of lies unraveled. If we had agreed to a monogamous relationship, our secret life increased our feelings of fear, anxiety, regret, or resentment. Our promises were empty.

Deception and secrecy became a way of life, and keeping it up only increased our guilt and shame. We found that whatever aspect of integrated sexuality we imagined, our compartmentalized life usually put it out of our reach. Others showed us by their example that healthy sexuality included honesty, openness, willingness, acceptance, compassion, affection, and physical aspects. However, as long as we engaged in meaningless objectifying sex and spent our energies hiding our sexual behavior from those who mattered most, it was almost impossible to see ourselves as whole people capable of healthy sexuality.

The more separate we kept our identities, the less available any integrated sexuality seemed to be. Sex had become a ritual, something we could dissociate from even while engaging in it. We often had a sense of ourselves as hypersexual, entitled to have more sex than others. We imagined ourselves as superior to the average person whose sexual needs and abilities could not rival ours. For many of us, healthy sexuality sounded boring or an ideal that we could never achieve. The integration of sex as a healthy element seemed foreign, entirely at odds with our sexual activities. Sexual intimacy, genuine affection, and emotional closeness were far from where we found ourselves – most had no idea what those experiences looked or felt like, nor what actions might help us move toward them.

Characteristic Eight

"We became addicted to people, and were unable to distinguish among sex, love and affection."

For many of us, romantic obsession and love addiction are among the more subtle and insidious forms of our disease. When we were younger, we often found it hard to distinguish an innocent crush from an intoxicating attraction that triggered us. We might have convinced ourselves that our latest infatuation had to be "the one" and confused obsession with love. We craved the overwhelming feeling of being in love as we imagined it – the racing pulse, the cold sweat, and the extreme focus on another person. Eventually, a pattern emerged, and we developed destructive behaviors around these infatuations. We struggled to win the targeted person's attention, but we were often disappointed even if we succeeded. Sometimes the alluring qualities that attracted us to these people vanished when we eventually saw them as human, instead of a romantic ideal. Ultimately, these emotional highs and lows made our lives unmanageable.

Often, trauma and stress from our childhood were the foundation for these unhealthy obsessions. A range of issues – alcoholism in the family, neglect, physical and emotional abuse, incest – contributed to experiences in which our needs were ignored or belittled. Some of us came from families incapable or unwilling to give us affection. In extreme cases, we didn't receive hugs, kisses, or even a smile at home. Still, we naturally needed affirmation, attention, and affection. When we didn't receive these things in our formative years, our self-esteem frequently suffered. Our families confirmed our worst fears – that we were indeed unlovable.

We began trying to fill the void where self-esteem and acceptance should have been. If we failed to learn healthy boundaries as children, we had difficulty setting them as adults. If another person paid attention to us or showed the slightest affection, it could trigger us to obsess about them. Many times, we ignored the actual signals we received from the other person. Instead, we projected our fantasies onto them. We wanted them to conform to our image of what they should be.

We often sent mixed messages and misinterpreted responses. We blurred the lines between sexual and non-sexual relationships, often mistaking sex for love, and affection for sexual attraction. We needed sex or romantic intrigue to feel loved. These exaggerated ideas continued into adulthood. We sought love and affection, the only way we knew how, through an all-consuming focus on another person, wanting to "own" them and consummate our fantasies with sexual activity. When we violated sexual boundaries with our friends, they often withdrew from us, and the relationships suffered or disintegrated entirely, leaving us feeling rejected. People rotated in and out of our lives. Sometimes it seemed that the only friends we had were the people with whom we were sexually involved.

Some of us developed a well-worn habit of engaging in sexual activity as a means of finding love and affection. Yet, the very act of casual or anonymous sex thwarted our efforts to build intimate relationships. We found ourselves repeatedly frustrated and let down, blind to the fact that the sex act itself was transactional and not genuinely intimate. We were often confused – unable to see the difference between what we wanted and what we were getting. Our sexual encounters often left us with a feeling of emptiness and the need to fill ourselves with something better, but we didn't know what or how.

If we tried dating, many of us found it difficult to establish any real connection. Often, we chose to be sexual right away, but doing so seemed to stall any further momentum in building an intimate relationship. It became yet another transactional experience, and we were discouraged; we still seemed to be missing out on a deeper, more intimate connection. Still, our addiction told us to do it again – convincing us that the next sex partner was our best hope for fulfillment.

Some of us became obsessed with strangers or people we barely knew. We could quickly become "hooked" on another person and build an intricately conceived fantasy life about our future with them. These fantasies felt real and possible for us, regardless of whether we knew the person. We objectified them, putting them on a pedestal, convincing ourselves that only *they* had the qualities that would make us happy and solve all our problems. Sometimes these obsessive thoughts remained only fantasies, but they distracted us and made it difficult for us to function well. At other times, we pursued the objects of our fantasies to possess them. Some of us saw these people merely as conquests – trophies to add to our collection.

In some cases, our perception of such a person's overwhelming attractiveness led us to suppress our personality. We idealized the object of our obsession, and they held power over us much as an addictive substance does. We found ourselves compelled to pursue our targets to all extremes, even violating our dignity if necessary. Moral values, integrity, and prior commitments fell to the wayside during our relentless quest. If we achieved our goal and connected with them, we immediately and compulsively immersed ourselves in their lives – only to discard them when we became obsessed with the next one. As this pattern repeated, we grew more confused about sex, love, and affection: these "wires" became intertwined, and we didn't know how to separate them.

Characteristic Nine

"We searched for some 'magical' quality in others to make us feel complete. Other people were idealized and endowed with a powerful symbolism, which often disappeared after we had sex with them."

For some of us, our need for validation often drove our hunt for people who would make us feel like we mattered. We desperately looked for a way to feel better about ourselves through others. Instead of building up our sense of self-worth by focusing on our problems and possible solutions, we directed our attention and energy outward, developing fantasies about people and idolizing them.

For some of us, these fantasies began in adolescence and accelerated as we grew older. We often imagined fictional romantic partners whom we idealized and endowed with magical qualities. We believed that if we could somehow merge with these "perfect" figures and get their attention, their power would be ours as well, and we would feel complete.

We sought out others who had some mystique, a hidden power, almost entirely of our making. We often fantasized about these people while acting out, wishing that we could be with them instead of our current sex partner. The more we focused on other people, the more attractive they seemed to us. This fixation blinded us to any possibilities we had with available people – people who genuinely wanted to connect with us – and we continued our search for a fantasy person who could make us feel whole.

Many of us had spent years feeling incomplete as human beings. The reasons for this varied, but the result was the same - we felt inadequate, defective, and unlovable. Once we discovered that sex and fantasy could bring temporary relief from these feelings, it became a way to escape them.

As our addiction escalated, we often found we needed more compelling sexual adventures and all-encompassing fantasies to fill the increasing emptiness we felt. We directed more and more energy into the dream of a perfect partner who would complete us. While we waited for our dream, we settled for what we could get: ordinary sex with people who didn't matter to us, who were ultimately disposable, but whose attention temporarily eased our pain.

We often believed that if only we could spend time with the object of our fantasy and ultimately have sex with them, their magical qualities would fill the emptiness we felt. We also hoped this would help us escape from our negative feelings about ourselves, even believing that others would view us in a more favorable light. We focused, not on reality, but on the fantasy that we associated with this person. We imagined they would rescue us from the repetitive, meaningless cycle of sex we pursued. Sex with "ordinary" people who lacked power and symbolic qualities became a filler while we waited for our "rescuer." Sometimes we found ourselves in a relationship with someone who was using us as we were using them. Our actual sex life could never measure up as long as we held on to the fantasy. Sexual activity with others felt like settling for less, reinforcing how undeserving we were of what we truly wanted.

If we eventually had sex with someone we idolized, our image of them frequently shattered as reality set in. Our idol's imperfections and the sex act itself were at odds with the unattainable fulfillment we sought. We were dismayed to discover that they were not perfect. When we touched our idols, their luster faded. That "trophy" we had won wasn't worth having after all. The anticipated reflected glow from them quickly disappeared. Any spiritual uplift we hoped to find did not materialize or failed to last. Our negative feelings of resentment and self-recrimination were still there. They often increased as we felt disillusioned and humiliated by our previous idealization of that person. We felt cheated out of the time and energy we had spent pursuing them. For most of us, sex with our idol had not changed our feelings of emptiness and isolation: if anything, our need to find a new idol became more desperate.

Characteristic Ten

"We were drawn to people who were not available to us, or who would reject or abuse us."

For many of us, low self-esteem and a deep-rooted sense of unworthiness were familiar aspects of our lives. We sought validation from others and were often rejected, ultimately feeling worse about ourselves than before. Our response to this pain and emptiness - "the hole in our soul" - varied but had a common theme: we needed to find a way to escape from these feelings, if only temporarily. Some of us continued to seek out sexual encounters with strangers. However, observing others connecting in relationships, many of us decided to pursue a relationship ourselves. We looked for someone who might tolerate us since we felt we deserved very little. We may have had no experience with healthy relationships and few positive role models, so when we engaged with others and attempted a meaningful connection, we often made poor choices.

For some, these choices seemed comfortable since we felt that we were defective and should settle for whatever we could get. For others, it was more subconscious. We may have found ourselves drawn to those who symbolized someone from our past, who had threatened or hurt us, hoping it would be different this time. Regardless, we often gravitated toward people who affirmed our unworthiness by demeaning, ignoring, or abusing us.

Finding a relationship became a kind of quest, a mission. We believed the other person would somehow "fix" or "rescue" us or that we would do the same for them. Many of us felt a powerful attraction to people who were inappropriate in one way or another. If we saw their character flaws, we ignored them. We often felt that only someone with defects would accept us, inadequate as we believed ourselves to be. Perhaps they had visible problems: drug or alcohol use, aggressive tendencies, sexual addiction, a history of infidelities. Those of us who were accustomed to being treated poorly may have found comfort in being abused. Part of our fantasy life enabled us to deny these flaws, glossing over them as just part of the price we were willing to pay to be in a relationship.

Another type of inappropriate attraction included people in committed relationships who were therefore unavailable to us. The fact that this person was married or otherwise in a relationship only added to the allure. The hidden nature of the affair may have fed our desire for risk and excitement. It also left us free to pursue other sexual activities or to avoid committing ourselves. We derived validation from these clandestine affairs – convincing ourselves that if the object of our attraction was willing to endanger their relationship for us, then surely it meant we were worth something. These situations could turn abusive if the "committed" person strung us along, promising commitment but not delivering.

Sometimes, the object of our desire ignored us and seemed to be unaware of how much they meant to us. That person's unavailability gnawed at us, made us yearn for them all the more, and led to our creating fantasies about them. If they responded to us, especially if we had sex with them, our sense of self-worth immediately soared. We also became anxious to hold onto what we had gained. We felt unworthy of anyone's affection, love, and respect. We often convinced ourselves we did not deserve these things, and we may have secretly believed the other person either already knew or would soon discover it.

Nevertheless, our need to possess the other person drove us to overlook any of their character traits that made us feel uncomfortable. Sometimes, we found ourselves allowing the person to behave in ways that crossed our weak or non-existent boundaries. We would make allowances or pretend to ignore their behavior, hoping that by doing so, we were showing our devotion and commitment, thereby strengthening our connection.

However, we often found that no matter how many concessions we made, that person only became more demanding, abusive, or dismissive. Perhaps they behaved unreliably or became aggressive: physically or emotionally. Sometimes they seemed uncaring, distant, or even absent. Our need to hold onto them gave them power over us - a license to mistreat us, in private and public. This abuse hurt us, but we became used to it and somehow felt it was no more than we deserved. Ultimately most of these relationships imploded: in some measure because their foundations were unstable.

Eventually, we began to resent these people for mistreating us. Often, we blamed ourselves for ignoring the warning signs and our lack of boundaries in our desperate quest for connection. This pattern of desperately seeking unavailable people, then being rejected or abused by them, fueled a cycle of shame that added to our sense of unworthiness. Instead of learning from our mistakes, we found ourselves continuing to pursue unavailable people. We didn't know how to let go of the need for this idealized connection, and we couldn't accept ourselves as worthy of being treated with respect, honesty, and kindness. If we did find a "normal" relationship with another, it seldom lasted. We sabotaged it when our sexual compulsion resurfaced, convincing us to take the next risk or find someone better. Deep down, we believed we did not deserve happiness.

Characteristic Eleven

"We feared relationships, but continually searched for them. In a relationship, we feared abandonment and rejection, but out of one, we felt empty and incomplete."

We eventually became weary of the repetitive cycle of compulsive sex. Many of us began to feel that having a relationship might provide the continual validation that had eluded us. We may have chosen this path to avoid confronting our fear of loneliness. However, we often had little experience in finding and sustaining healthy bonds with another person. Those experiences we had mostly involved a romantic obsession or perhaps an inappropriate person whose abuse we tolerated. We settled for scraps of attention, fearing abandonment if we asked for more. We had deep-rooted issues around our shame, self-esteem, and acting out behaviors. We struggled with the feeling that we did not deserve a lasting connection. The alternative of seeking out temporary connections for sex or having magical fantasies about a fictional love no longer seemed like satisfying options.

We were frequently conflicted: we desperately wanted a connection that would supply our need for validation and fill our emptiness, but our fear of rejection was ever-present. Often, childhood trauma or neglect made us fear abandonment, and we brought this fear into any relationship we began. We may have felt defective and unlovable, and our fear seemed justified. Parental neglect sometimes resulted in our need for approval and the fear of rejection, which shaped how we acted within relationships. Our desperate need often drove us to seek those relationships despite our fear. We hunted relentlessly for another person whose attentions would fill our emptiness.

We assumed that connecting with another person would somehow make us feel whole, relieving our isolation and self-doubt. But we also had fears which limited closeness with another person; fully sharing our lives felt threatening to our need for control. We feared that by revealing our true selves, we might lose any chance of getting the love and respect we imagined others having, which had only been a fantasy for us. We still wanted these people to cherish us and hold us in high esteem, so we tried desperately to please them, hoping to win their approval.

Often, this need to control and conceal our feelings made us reluctant to cultivate anything but casual relationships. For many of us, searching for sex or retreating into isolation became a way of life. We kept our distance from others, even as we were having sex with them. We often lied about ourselves, always trying to hide the details of our lives or possibly creating a fictional fantasy persona. Many of us had minimal experience with being honest and present in a sexual encounter, and we were equally unprepared for a relationship. We were afraid to share any more of ourselves than necessary to get what we wanted from them. These conditions made it nearly impossible to maintain any close bond. Often, these relationships ended, leaving us feeling more desolate and defective than before.

Many of us accepted a relationship as the ultimate goal of our search for a meaningful expression of love, affection, and sexuality. We wanted to believe that such a connection would protect us and keep our secrets safe. However, our issues with trust and low self-esteem interfered. How would we share our lives with another person while continuing to project our fantasy of self-worth? We wanted them to like us, even while we had doubts about whether we deserved it. We felt like an imposter, a hollow shell with some physical attractions, having nothing but negative qualities at its center. We felt that if the other person began to share these doubts, they would quickly reject us.

We wanted the other person's attention and affection but often found we could not reciprocate, other than superficially. We felt that we had nothing to bring to the relationship; we took more than we had to give. This lopsided arrangement created a strain. We had grasped for a connection with another, and we didn't want to let go. We tried to make them happy, but we feared that they would soon abandon us after becoming tired of our emotional unavailability. Our need to hold onto this relationship sometimes forced us to compromise our values to satisfy their demands. We often felt humiliated by ignoring our boundaries, but we didn't know how to stop. We often settled into a pattern where our desire for closeness collided with our fear and anxiety about exposure and the risk of losing what we had.

We generally avoided commitment since this would intensify all of our feelings of neediness, fear, and self-loathing. Often these relationships ended painfully. No matter how involved the connection had been, we felt its absence as a big hole in our lives, leaving us with a renewed sense of emptiness. We were no longer half of a couple: facing that void, we often searched for another relationship. We might go back to chasing casual sex again, building barriers to closeness with another person. Many of us began the cycle again: isolating while we searched for just the right person – not too distant, not too close; the discomfort of needing to give when we wanted to take; the constant fear and anxiety. If we were outside of a relationship, it meant no one wanted us. "Empty and incomplete" turned out to be the same as abandoned and rejected. If not to us, our deficiencies became apparent to others: we lacked the self-esteem, openness, and other intimacy skills we needed to support an honest relationship.

Characteristic Twelve

> "While constantly seeking intimacy with another person, we found that the desperate quality of our need made true intimacy with anyone impossible, and we often developed unhealthy dependency relationships that eventually became unbearable."

Many of us subconsciously recognized that our need for validation was a driving force in our lives. We had become obsessed with finding another person who might "complete" us or cure what ailed us by providing their approval. Our feelings of inadequacy tormented us: we felt we were undeserving of real love or affection. Our fantasies about ourselves and others were at odds with our reality but provided temporary relief. Eventually, we set our sights on finding a source of affirmation and acceptance that we believed would always be there for us.

We rarely knew what such a source might look like since our experience had primarily involved fleeting sexual encounters and superficial relationships. We often saw others who appeared to have what we thought we wanted: however, the openness and honesty they seemed to express filled us with fear about the consequences of exposing our true selves. If revealing ourselves to another person was required for "intimacy," it seemed beyond our reach. However, we continued to crave it, with its possibility of wholeness, something to fill the emptiness at the core of our being.

In seeking to fill this void, we found meaningless sex and unhealthy relationships. We may have developed elaborate fantasies and obsessions about others, real or imagined. When these tactics failed us, many of us realized that we had run out of options. If we wanted the intimate closeness that others had, we needed to risk exposure of our fundamental unworthiness. It was hard to believe that anyone would accept us as we were: yet we had tried everything else and had failed to become whole. Our pain had become more intense and escaping it using the old methods required more effort than we could spare. The inescapable pain drove us to take more drastic measures and risks, including exposing our secrets, lies, and character defects. Our need for some healing connection had become genuinely desperate.

We repeatedly sought a healthy relationship but lacked the emotional courage to be open about ourselves. We had long-standing issues of low self-esteem and sexual compulsion that we feared to disclose. There was always the driving need to be wanted, appreciated, and valued behind our interactions with the other person. This situation created a paradox – we wanted to be loved unconditionally, like a child, but respected on our merits as a partner, always knowing that we were deceiving ourselves. As a fallback, we often hoped that we could trade sex for a sense of closeness that would make up for what we lacked emotionally.

We had little understanding of what it took to sustain a relationship based on honest and open communication, affectionate closeness, and seeing the other as a real person, not a fantasy. We may have covered ourselves in protective armor in response to previous rejections and disappointing sexual connections. Our sexual relationships rarely developed emotional intimacy, which would require honesty, acceptance, respect, and openness. No matter how much we wanted to be close with another person, our defenses made us wary and withholding.

For some of us, our insecurities kept us from revealing things about our lives we were ashamed of, including aspects of our sexual desires or embarrassments about past sexual experiences. To protect ourselves from exposure, we carefully controlled information within any relationship, only giving of ourselves what we felt safe in revealing. And yet, we were afraid they would lose interest in us if we didn't satisfy their needs, sexually and emotionally. Fearing their disapproval often made us suppress our desires and feelings, which led to resentments and distrust.

Our compulsive need to please others often drove us to do things we didn't want to do to stay in a relationship. Sometimes this involved financial and domestic arrangements we might otherwise have rejected. We would make concessions to various requests we found disturbing but were willing to overlook for the sake of maintaining the appearance of closeness. Often, we felt so pressured by our need for "belonging" that we sacrificed what few values we had left to maintain just the appearance of it.

Such pressures made us want to cut our dependency ties, but our fears held us back. We felt we had too much to lose by ending the relationship. We were dependent upon the other person. The prospect of losing our domestic arrangements, rupturing our finances, and giving up the physical connection kept us trapped. We could not stand the prospect of another failed relationship, no matter how dysfunctional. If we were the financial provider, we feared we would bear the blame for our partner's hardship. Our already low self-esteem heightened our anxieties about appearing insensitive, selfish, and ungrateful.

Our co-dependency began to consume us: we felt trapped, but we were afraid to let go of what little we had. We needed the other person to keep our emptiness at bay. However, the price we paid for this was an escalating demand to perform our dependency role in the relationship. The strains caused by these conflicts made any semblance of intimacy unsustainable.

Characteristic Thirteen

> "Even when we got the love of another person, it never seemed enough, and we were unable to stop lusting after others."

Our sexual compulsions, obsessive fantasies, secrecy, and low self-esteem had many consequences in our everyday lives. One of the most damaging was the reinforcement of the feeling that we were unlovable. Some of us had decided to pursue intimacy because it seemed to offer more lasting relief from the pain we felt about being inadequate, flawed, and unworthy. However, believing no one would or could love us increased our shame, isolation, and hopelessness. We often used our compulsive behaviors and fantasies as a means of getting validation, sexual gratification, and conquest, but we still could not escape our feelings of emptiness and unworthiness. For most of us, the ability to love and accept love in return seemed entirely removed from our well-worn habit of using people as disposable objects.

Despite our behavior, there were times when our current object of desire "turned the tables" and began to respond to us lovingly. Perhaps the other person fell in love with the enhanced image we had worked so hard to project. In other cases, they may have seen through our pain and recognized our vulnerability, despite our attempts to hide any signs of weakness. They found qualities in us that we were unaware we had. Sometimes this came as a surprise since many of us had convinced ourselves that we had no intrinsic value as people. We only needed to examine how we manipulated relationships and sexual conquests to find evidence of how flawed we were.

Some of us were uncomfortable with these expressions of affection, caring, and love since we believed that anyone who felt these things for us must be defective in some way. They had to be emotionally blind since they could not – or would not – see us as we knew ourselves to be.

Many of us were uncomfortable with this change in the relationship dynamic. We had become accustomed to using deception and misrepresentation to get what we wanted and distrusted others' motives. Some of us were excited to experience the satisfaction we had sought; however, this feeling eventually faded. Most of us felt more familiar with a "horse-trade" type of relationship, where sex was a commodity, possibly exchanged for validation: this new freely given expression was disturbing. We didn't seem to recognize the value of what they were offering – the love of another. We knew it wasn't enough; we wanted more.

Some of us were terrified at the prospect of real closeness and began to pull away when we felt vulnerable, sometimes sabotaging the relationship with more casual sex. Some of us expected that having "won" the love of another, we would be free of our emptiness and finally become whole. When this failed to happen, we were disillusioned and looked for something or someone to blame. Whether we blamed ourselves or our partner, we did everything we could to extricate ourselves from the relationship that was no longer happening on our terms, under our control.

Our need for control of any relationship conflicted with the equal exchange that most intimate relationships share. We craved the closeness but also feared the possible exposure of all our lies and compulsive behaviors. In a committed relationship, we often found, to our frustration, that we no longer sexually desired our partner. Intimacy caused anxiety, which often led us to act out with others to escape our feelings. We were uncomfortable within ourselves, spiritually and emotionally empty, and believed that another person might fill the void within us. The idea that we had to love and accept ourselves first before truly bonding with someone else had never occurred to us.

Many of us suspected that *we* were not enough, and we sought to fill our emptiness in ways we felt might work. We continued to lust after and fantasize about others, even when we had a relationship. We divided our attention between the person we were with and our next prospective conquest. We got validation and excitement from the hunt *itself.* Most of us had poor boundaries and continued to have sex with others, even when doing so was most inappropriate and hurtful, sometimes with people known to our partner. We became proficient in deceiving ourselves and others. We felt entitled to have the sex we wanted, even as we tried to achieve the appearance of intimacy with our partner. We often failed to recognize that in trying to have everyone, we ultimately had no one.

For many of us, nothing and no one was ever enough. No amount of casual sex, no supply of validation, not even the love of another, would relieve our pain and emptiness. Yet we carried on, returning to old patterns that had worked for us in the past. No matter which way we turned, we eventually found ourselves seeking our next fix, knowing almost from the start it would never satisfy our dependency needs. In this process, we often tried to break off our current relationship, so we would be free to pursue the greener grass we always hoped would be on the other side of the fence. There was pain involved in these breakups, but we persuaded ourselves that we needed them to move on with our lives. However, with every connection we turned our backs on, some portion of shame stuck to us, adding to our feeling of unworthiness, emptiness, and hopelessness.

Characteristic Fourteen

"Trying to conceal our dependency demands, we grew more isolated from ourselves, from God and from the very people we longed to be close to."

Our urgent need for validation made us dependent on others for our temporary self-esteem. This need drove many of us into a familiar way of life that was habitual but seldom satisfying. We had become adept at concealing our sexual activities from others. Hiding our behaviors and lying about them had become second nature to most of us. The rest of the world might see one side of us, but only the side we chose to show. We felt the need to conceal anything we thought might cause us embarrassment or shame. Most of all, we feared that if others saw our character defects, it would lead to humiliation and rejection.

Many of us went to great lengths to conceal our sexual behaviors, sometimes even disguising our daily activities. We tried to cover our tracks, hiding our activities from partners, family, friends, and work colleagues. Some of us created false personas, or fabricated identities, trying to convince others that we were mysterious and fascinating. Perhaps we became social butterflies seeking to become the person everyone wanted to know. We hid behind this curtain, sure that nobody knew who we truly were. These defense mechanisms developed gradually and supported our sexual compulsion. Many of us failed to understand that concealing our true nature from others would isolate us from ourselves. We played different roles with different people and often forgot who we were at our core. We had no way to retrace our steps or return to our former selves.

Many of us compartmentalized our lives in our search for sex, concealing our deficiencies and compulsive demands. Projecting a false image and the maintenance required to sustain it increased our separation from ourselves and others. We often constructed barriers that allowed us to disguise our behaviors, showing one side of us to the world while veiling our secret life. We spent more time and energy searching for fleeting excitement by acting out sexually. Those moments, however brief, provided temporary validation that soon disappeared after the sex was over.

We often felt shame about our compulsive behaviors, but we were powerless to stop them. We had no skills to help us resolve this conflict. Our fears made us afraid to admit the truth, especially to ourselves. We chose to hide things from ourselves - things we subconsciously knew we couldn't face. The notion of taking a self-inventory - a reality check - was too painful to contemplate. Yet, we lived in fear that something or someone would expose us.

Our search for sexual validation and connection often became more of a ritual and less a choice. As long as friends and family weren't aware of what we were doing, we felt we could continue our deception and manage our lives. We may have pushed other people away, whether they were a long-time friend, a parent, or a partner. We became unresponsive and unreliable; we would arrive hours late for previously planned visits or social events, with an improbable excuse, or maybe not arrive at all. We would sometimes fail to return calls or messages or do so after extended, inexplicable delays. We might be deliberately vague with the information we gave to partners or spouses about where we were going or where we had been.

This perpetual vagueness eventually led to the breakdown of our friendships and connections to our community. The demands of friendship got in the way of our having sex whenever we wanted. Making a connection to have sex was second nature to us, but we became less interested in non-sexual relationships. The people, places, and things that once brought us joy, no longer did. Our isolation continued to increase, separating us from our family and friends. Any belief we may have had in God or a Higher Power diminished as we grew more self-absorbed. Many of us instinctively felt that our acting out was taking us further away from any spiritual connection. This void in our lives contributed to our shame and made us more likely to dismiss the value of any spiritual way of life. We may have told ourselves we were too far gone, and we didn't believe anyone could help us, not even a Higher Power.

The focus on meeting our dependency demands and fear of being exposed as a fraud kept us trapped in a repetitive cycle of acting out. No matter how much sex we had, we felt a growing emptiness, a "hole in the soul." Most of us failed to recognize that we had few boundaries regarding our sexual activities. We had created barriers that separated us from our family, friends, and community. In short, we had orchestrated our abandonment. We were subconsciously aware that as long as we were acting out and lying to everyone in our lives, we would never attain the connection, love, and acceptance we so desperately needed.

AFTERWORD

WHERE WE'RE GOING – OUR JOURNEY OF RECOVERY

The preceding commentaries reflect the effects of excessive neediness, longing, obsession, emptiness, and hopelessness that often accompany sexual compulsion. Something finally happened that made our lives so unbearable that we were willing to try anything that offered some hope of freedom. The circumstances varied from person to person: arrest, incarceration, divorce, humiliation, lost jobs and relationships were just a few. No one can say what it means to "hit bottom" for every person. Some have suggested that we hit bottom when we stop digging: we finally realize how deep the hole in us had become. Some of us who suffered the kind of pain described in these pages eventually found our way into 12-Step recovery.

When we attended our first SCA meeting, many of us heard *The Characteristics* read aloud and had moments of insight. We identified with many of the patterns of behavior and related to their effect on our lives. In the early days of recovery, it was reassuring to know that we were not alone, that others had been through similar experiences. As our trust in this group of recovering sexual compulsives grew, we found acceptance, safety, and community. We began to see ourselves as part of this fellowship.

By attending meetings and working the program one day at a time, we gradually found freedom from our most destructive behaviors and toxic shame. For some, meetings and the support they provided was enough for us to stop acting out. However, sexual compulsion is a spiritual problem, requiring a spiritual solution. Some of us realized that we needed to have a spiritual awakening if we wanted to recover what we had lost as active sexual compulsives. This awakening is one of the program's promises, provided that we work the Steps and improve our relationship with a Higher Power of our choosing. Our ability to do, feel, and believe things that were previously impossible for us was a sure sign that our spiritual life was expanding.

By working the Twelve Steps and utilizing the program's tools, we began to transform our lives: not overnight, not in a straight line, but gradually our attitude and outlook on life began to change. Our lives became more than the compelling need for our next sexual encounter, fix of validation, or the distraction of a new obsession. We were finally able to focus on our personal growth and set goals and boundaries for how we wanted to live in recovery.

While recovery works differently for everyone, many of us began to build new coping skills instead of falling back into the ways of our addiction. We took care of ourselves as adults, building self-respect, self-worth, and self-liking, where we previously had only shame and self-loathing. We experienced our feelings fully, without the compelling, urgent need to escape from them. We learned to separate fantasy from reality in life and intimate relationships. We developed healthy boundaries with others. We practiced intimacy skills while remaining secure in our right to be ourselves, independent of others' control. We no longer needed to continue finding false comfort and release in acts that came back to torment and humiliate us. We found the courage to turn toward a new way of living. We learned to trust that, over time, the process of recovery would restore our integrity, dignity, and clarity.

Working the Twelve Steps is a spiritual process of growth, being, and becoming. It is finding what works for us, asking for what we need, and accepting who we are. We might not be the brightest star in the sky as we sometimes fantasized, but neither are we a black hole of infinite need, as we might have once believed. Our lives will never be free of all stress. We will never be "perfect" people, nor do we aspire to be so.

Through working our program and the Steps, we become "right-sized," neither grandiose nor self-deprecating. With our Higher Power and our community of recovering sexual compulsives, we will live more fully and use our energies well.

Chapter 4: The Twelve Suggested Steps of Sexual Compulsives Anonymous (SCA)

THE TWELVE SUGGESTED STEPS OF SCA[2]

1. We admitted we were powerless over sexual compulsion — that our lives had become unmanageable.
2. Came to believe that a Power greater than ourselves could restore us to sanity.
3. Made a decision to turn our will and our lives over to the care of God as *we understood God.*
4. Made a searching and fearless moral inventory of ourselves.
5. Admitted to God, to ourselves, and to another human being the exact nature of our wrongs.
6. Were entirely ready to have God remove all these defects of character.
7. Humbly asked God to remove our shortcomings.
8. Made a list of all persons we had harmed, and became willing to make amends to them all.
9. Made direct amends to such people wherever possible, except when to do so would injure them or others.
10. Continued to take personal inventory, and when we were wrong promptly admitted it.
11. Sought through prayer and meditation to improve our conscious contact with God *as we understood God,* praying only for knowledge of God's will for us and the power to carry that out.
12. Having had a spiritual awakening as the result of these steps, we tried to carry this message to sexually compulsive people and to practice these principles in all our affairs.

[2] The Twelve Steps and Twelve Traditions are reprinted and adapted with permission of Alcoholics Anonymous World Services, Inc. Permission to reprint and adapt does not mean that Alcoholics Anonymous is in any way affiliated with this program. AA is a program of recovery from alcoholism. The use of the Twelve Steps and Twelve Traditions in connection with other programs which are patterned after AA, but address other problems, does not imply otherwise.

Step One

> "We admitted we were powerless over sexual compulsion — that our lives had become unmanageable."

A sense of defeat was common for us before we even decided to go to our first meeting. It might have come after being caught having an affair, feeling the shame of being arrested, or being fired for viewing porn. The decision to come was sometimes ours alone. However, many of us chose to go at the insistence of loved ones, therapists, or the courts.

As we approached the meeting, our anxiety level rose. We feared entering a room where we were sure every seat would belong to some kind of "pervert" or sexual predator. *There is no way I belong here!* We just needed to get through this one meeting so we could tell our therapist, loved one, or probation officer we had given it a try.

Once we overcame the fear of opening the door, we usually saw what so many of us see in meeting spaces across the world. There were folding chairs, sparse decorations, and harsh lighting. People were chatting with each other and expressing pleasantries. The feeling in the room seemed calm and as pleasing as any such room could be.

Some of us may have had a strategy of where we would sit in our first meeting. We may have chosen the seat with the best view of the most attractive person in the room. On the other hand, it could have been the seat with the most obstructed view of the most desirable person. Perhaps we chose the chair closest to the door for a quick escape. Whatever reasoning we used, we took our seat and started to hear about Sexual Compulsives Anonymous (SCA).

Powerless? Unmanageable? We had difficulty with these terms and concepts. *Powerless can't possibly apply to me! I am not an animal! I don't walk down the street like a drooling lunatic ready to grab anyone to have sex! I have standards and morals. My life works just fine most of the time. I pay the bills. I take care of my errands. My house isn't a complete sty. I get to work. Things get a little crazy once in a while, but whose life doesn't?*

Maybe the light bulb went on right away, or perhaps it took some time. The stories we started to hear began hitting close to home. The guy who lost his job for having porn on his work computer. A woman who lost her marriage because of an online romance that she told herself would never be consummated in real life, until it was. The person who felt imprisoned by their use of hookup apps. Those few questionable images of young people on someone's computer. The person arrested for trying to have sex with someone underage. The fear in the voice of that man anticipating the result of an HIV test. Stories about abortions, abuse, and the secrets about children conceived through affairs. The stories started to sound like our own. Not every detail resonated with us, but enough to know that we were in the right place.

Once we admitted to ourselves that we needed the help of an SCA program, others in the program suggested that we find a sponsor. Many of us initially rejected the idea outright. *I'm an adult. I can do this myself. Nobody's going to tell me what to do.* Whether we found one right away or after some time in recovery, most of us eventually learned the benefits of working with a sponsor. To find one, we asked someone who was in the program long enough to have completed some of the Steps and who maintained some sexual sobriety.

Sponsors may take different approaches to this work. They may recommend that we read and begin working the 12 Steps from the Alcoholics Anonymous "big book." Another might suggest various other 12-Step workbooks or authored works focusing on recovery. Others might have the sponsee write about powerlessness, unmanageability, *The 20 Questions*, or *The Characteristics* of SCA.

Often, our sponsors ask us to write a sexual history. "Acting out" is used to describe the behaviors that brought about the unmanageability and powerlessness in our lives. "Acting out" can also refer to actions used to escape from our feelings. This sexual history is a list of these activities. Writing our stories exposed how much time and money we spent on "acting out." It might have been on prostitutes, pornography, massage parlors, strippers, drugs, sex toys, bathhouses, treatments for sexually transmitted diseases, internet-based sex, or legal consequences. We can see how many hours, days, years we spent in obsessive thinking about sex: either compulsively seeking or avoiding sex.

The SCA program suggests that members develop a Sexual Recovery Plan (SRP). Suggested SRP formats contain elements using different names: e.g., "bottom line," "gray area," "inner circle," or "first column." The SCA program strongly encourages new members to ask for assistance from a sponsor or others in the program when writing a plan. The written sexual history can be a useful tool in the development of a Sexual Recovery Plan. Every member's sexually compulsive activities are different. One person may struggle with sex in public places, another with online pornography, and still another with romantic intrigue. Because sexuality is such a personal part of a member's life, SCA believes the definition of sobriety is individual as well. We are rigorously honest about behaviors we want to stop, one day at a time. Those prohibitions give us a start on our SRP and help define our abstinence from people, places, and things that we consider harmful.

Sexual compulsion is a progressive disease. We were mostly in denial, especially in its earlier stages. As the disease progressed, we began to bargain with ourselves, hoping to find ways of controlling our behaviors. Whatever rules we set, we eventually broke. *I will only do this once a month. I will only spend this much money. These activities will only happen outside of my home.* No matter how hard we tried to keep them, we always broke our promises. We felt confused and frustrated, wondering how it could happen yet again.

It took more attempts at trying to stop our sexually compulsive behaviors than we cared to admit. Time after time after time, we found ourselves in that bewildered state. Nobody could tell us we were powerless; we had to come to that realization on our own. That moment of pain and desperation is what the program calls "hitting bottom…"

The SCA program asks us to be rigorously honest. Without honesty, we remain in denial. Denial tells us that our lives are manageable, that our sexuality is under control. Honesty begins to break that bubble. Living outside the bubble feels very uncomfortable, even foreign, at times. The wisdom of the program tells us to keep coming back to meetings. We find it possible to survive the transition to living outside the bubble of denial when we come to meetings and talk about our dis-ease.

A simple acronym, HOW, **H**onest, **O**pen, and **W**illing, tells us how the program works. Writing our sexual history is an act of honesty. Sharing parts of it with another person or at a meeting demonstrates openness. And trying to follow the program of SCA shows a willingness to live life differently.

The actions of Step One begin to rebuild trust, something most of us lost in our active addiction. Even with the smallest amount of trust, we can now turn our focus toward Step Two - a Step that connects us to hope. If we stay in Step One, we miss the experience of the healing power of the program. So, we bravely look ahead.

Step Two

> "Came to believe that a Power greater than ourselves could restore us to sanity."

With Step One, we began to learn about powerlessness and unmanageability and their ties to our acting out behaviors. But those behaviors did not have to control our lives. There is hope, and we find it in Step Two.

"A Power greater than ourselves" sounds like a veiled attempt to avoid saying the word God while meaning just that. We came to accept our powerlessness and unmanageability: now, we had to embrace the concept of God. Was this the God who let us suffer in active addiction, who failed us time and time again? The very God who judged us as unworthy of love? Fellow members told us that this was not a religious program, and yet here was God. The center of religion and all its piety.

But the term mentioned in this Step is a Power greater than ourselves. For some, this might evoke an image of God. However, our newfound willingness helps us focus on the simple concept of a Higher Power. This Higher Power may equate to a "traditional" understanding of God, a newfound conception of God, or even the collective wisdom of the group. Some program members focus on finding a Higher Power that has a positive attitude toward sex and sexuality.

The most significant notion to grasp is that <u>we</u> are not that Higher Power. Self-will was useless in the face of our compulsion. Step One and our endless experiences taught us that. No, we need to go beyond ourselves. If we are to have any hope at all, we find a power stronger than self-will. Do we dare believe that such a power exists? That we let this power be of our understanding, and not that of an unknowable God?

What is that power supposed to do for us anyway? Restore us to sanity? That is a lot to believe. *I've accepted that I am powerless over my acting out. I can see some unmanageability in my life: but labeling me insane just won't fly! I don't need a straitjacket! I don't see imaginary people or hear voices in my head! How can insanity possibly describe me?*

One definition of insanity is "doing the same thing over and over again and expecting different results." This pattern sounded familiar. How many times did we expect that the next sexual experience would be the best of our lives? That the next pornographic image would fulfill all our desires? The next romantic entanglement, the next obsession, the next relationship? Our addiction always told us that what we really wanted was just around the corner. If we could endure the soul-crushing journey a little longer, the magic would happen.

Continuing to listen to our compulsive thoughts was insane. Hadn't we collected enough evidence to know that our addiction was lying to us? Yet despite all the evidence, we still wanted to act out. We forgot about the consequences. In our insanity, they did not matter. *I want what I want when I want it – even if it kills me.*

Being restored to sanity means we do something different to get different results. We acknowledge our powerlessness, unmanageability, and insanity. We talk about our lives in meetings, on the phone, or with another sexual compulsive. Compulsion thrives in secrecy; we take action to break that cycle.

Shattering the wall of isolation takes time and effort. Admitting our powerlessness and unmanageability begins to open cracks in this wall that surrounds us. To help support this opening process, we find a way to connect to hope - a hope that our lives can be different.

"A Power greater than ourselves" becomes the bridge out of isolation and into hope. Creating a practical understanding of a Higher Power can be useful. Some sponsors suggest writing down the qualities we want in a Higher Power: for example, friendly, compassionate, directive, strong, funny, forgiving, gentle. Describing the qualities we find most desirable in a Higher Power may help overcome the harsh attributes some of us previously associated with God, like judgmental, stern, authoritative, damning, or severe. We look for a Higher Power - someone or something - we can trust. Step Two leads us to build trust in a Power greater than ourselves.

With the seed of trust planted, we begin to believe our lives can be different. As we continue to work Step Two, our faith in a Higher Power grows. We start to see that we might be able to let go of the need to control our addiction. That will be an act of courage. We will find that courage in Step Three.

Step Three

"Made a decision to turn our will and our lives over to the care of God *as we understood God*."

We looked at our powerlessness and the unmanageability in our lives in Step One. We started to form a concept of a "Power greater than ourselves" in Step Two. All that Step Three asks us to do is to make a decision. A decision to start trusting the Higher Power we came to understand in Step Two.

We take some actions in working Step Three that seem odd or counterintuitive. It was hard to believe anyone in their right mind would do these things. It is easy to lose trust and not to believe what we were being told. Step Three asks us to do something that we never imagined doing. But we looked to others in our meetings and listened to them describe the things they did to maintain their sobriety. They spoke about making phone calls, doing Step work, going to more meetings, and doing service work, and they seemed to be in a better space. We see that others have taken the actions we fear, and they survive and even thrive. Their testimony provides evidence that trusting in a Higher Power works.

And so we begin, sometimes slowly, to build trust. Many of us find it in witnessing consistency in other program members. We see the same people showing up at meetings. Members are showing up to do service work to keep the doors open; members are expressing concern for others, doing the same readings. We hear the consistency in the shares. This consistency leads us to start trusting that these people will do what they say. That is a big leap for us since many of us grew up in households where people said one thing and did another, laughing one minute and yelling at us the next. There was no consistency, therefore, little trust.

We build trust over time. Consistency allows us to predict what others are likely to do. While we recognize that no one is entirely consistent in their actions and mood, eventually, we gravitate toward those who are most dependable.

The concept of a caring God is an essential part of the Third Step. For many of us, control mistakenly replaces the word "care" in our minds when we read this Step. Growing up, "care" might have been said, but the actions spoke "control." In SCA, we mean care. No one likes being under the thumb of someone else's control. The relationship with a Power greater than ourselves is a partnership based on being cared for throughout our lives.

At first, the phrase "turn our will and our lives over" can create images of giving up everything we hold dear. Some of us have found it helpful to think of this in simple terms. As we gain trust and actively surrender control, we turn our thoughts and actions over to the care of the God of our understanding. These actions help build our faith by trusting our Higher Power to take care of us. Our fears do not vanish – we simply develop a faith slightly deeper than our fears.

Can we believe that we will be taken care of if we live our lives differently? If we let go and trust that the world is an abundant place, will our needs be met? We find that we do not need to take action based on the fear of scarcity. Our world is full of abundance for everyone.

Once we build up some trust that the God of our understanding cares for us, we start taking actions to change our lives. We go to more meetings, make phone calls to people we do not know, share our stories more openly, and do service work to help meetings thrive. These are all actions that may have once felt like "punishment" or "chores" that our sponsors told us to do. After some time in Twelve Step recovery, the benefits of taking these actions become apparent. We start to feel more comfortable with ourselves and others. The process of recovery opens us up to be stronger advocates for ourselves and gives us compassion for others. That sense of being alone in the world, of being unlovable, starts to fade.

We know we are making progress when honesty feels like the best response, rather than yet another lie. Our interactions with people rely on openness instead of shutting down. We respond with a willingness to say yes to the program.

Grounded by the first three Steps, we are ready to go out on a limb. We are willing to begin an honest self-examination and decide to start working on our Fourth Step.

Step Four

> "Made a searching and fearless moral inventory of ourselves."

Working the first three Steps took courage, acceptance, and willingness. We had the energy to move forward into our new lives of recovery. However, in our honest sharing and reflections, it quickly becomes apparent to us that there is past wreckage blocking us from moving forward. There are damaged relationships, self-sabotaged careers, significant debts, and a bundle of resentments, hurts, and regrets of every variety. Any of these can block us from making progress inside and out. If we are to become happy, joyous, and free, we deal with this baggage. We don't want to return to our acting out behaviors. We set out to do a searching and fearless moral inventory.

When we hear the words "moral inventory," it can stir flashbacks of negative experiences or religious dogmas from the past. The "moral inventory" referred to in Step Four is about facing the truth – helping to clean out the cycle of shame that fuels our obsessive thinking and compulsive behavior. It is not about becoming "pure" or being worthy of a deity's praise. The SCA program asks us to do this because experience has shown that the spiritual principle of cleaning house will help us stay away from our sexually compulsive behaviors.

The culture we live in might discourage introspection; the idea of writing down all this personal information may seem risky, too hard, or just plain crazy. Procrastination leads many of us to do an "addict's waltz," where we work the first three Steps, then act out, repeating indefinitely: 1-2-3, 1-2-3, 1-2-3....

How do we muster the courage and willingness to do a Fourth Step? There is no need to do any part of the SCA program of recovery alone. In Step Two, we learned to ask for help, and now we seek guidance, usually from a sponsor. Reaching out to other members of the fellowship who have completed a Fourth Step encourages us and bolsters our willingness. Meeting in a group with other members working the Fourth Step may also provide mutual support.

We do not expect to finish an entire inventory in one sitting. We work the Fourth Step at our own pace, but the idea is to keep working at it. We ask our Higher Power to support us with the strength and initiative to move forward.

One tried-and-true method of doing a Fourth Step comes from the book Alcoholics Anonymous. This method asks us to write out our Fourth Step using several columns. We start by focusing on resentments. In the first column, we write down each of our resentments. We list them all, leaving nothing out. Their "size" does not matter. If it comes to mind, it is meant to be written down. We may have resentments against ourselves, other people, an institution, a place, a disease, an act of nature, or a conception of God. These feelings are part of life, but writing them down is a crucial element of the Step. We may be surprised at how many we have been holding onto.

Once we complete the first column, we think through each resentment. In the second column, we write down why we have that resentment. The reasons will vary. However, as we go through each one, patterns may start to come into focus. These revelations can be very painful. Bringing emotions to the surface can send many of us back to acting out, so we stay in contact with our sponsor and other trusted members of SCA during this process.

We then fill in a third column, listing how the resentment affects us. What aspects of our lives are being hurt or threatened? Here are some possibilities:

- Our self-esteem
- Our sense of pride
- Our finances
- Our ambitions
- Our relationships
- Our sexual relations
- Our emotional security
- Our physical security

We write down all that apply.

It is easy to conclude that we are simply a victim of this insane world. *Everyone is out for themselves: they don't care who they hurt*. The spiritual program of SCA asks us at this point to stop. Take a deep breath. Shift our focus from being a victim. We start a fourth column, which challenges us to look at *our* part in the resentments. Were we selfish, dishonest, self-seeking, or frightened?

If we are rigorously honest with ourselves, we find that we had a role to play in most of these resentments, even if it was merely allowing ourselves to feel hurt. If our resentments arose from childhood trauma, our only role might have been to allow them to block us from moving forward with our lives as adults. This process does not ask us to take the blame for what occurred.

The process of acknowledging our part in these resentments is a hard pill to swallow. We have become comfortable holding onto them. They are close friends, and we can't imagine a life without them. We certainly struggle to recognize our part in them while completing the fourth column.

After we complete the inventory of our resentments, we begin to examine our fears. We write down a simple list of our fears, large and small. Once the list is complete, we return to each and write precisely why we have that fear and the purpose it serves. Maybe something occurred in our lives that cemented the fear in place. There may be some that have no basis in actual events, that seem to exist with no cause. Completing our inventory may reveal the basis for these fears.

The next part of a moral inventory is to look at our sexual behaviors. An accounting like this may seem like a big task for us sexual compulsives. We attempt to write down every person with whom we had sex. For those of us with long histories of anonymous sex, we may not remember every person's name, so perhaps we list them by a physical feature. In some cases, we group them, like "men in a certain park," "women from a particular app," "people we met at bars," or "men in that bathhouse." The essential point is to be thorough and rigorously honest with ourselves.

Some sexual compulsives have a history with fantasy-based acting out, rather than physically acting out. In these cases, writing down the object of our fantasy can be helpful. We may have the name of a person we know. There are other cases where the person is simply an image in pornographic material. Whatever the case, we write down all that we can recall.

We now look at each incident and ask ourselves if it was selfish, dishonest, inconsiderate, or hurtful? In some cases, all will apply: in other cases, none will. Even as active sexual compulsives, sometimes our sex was not addictive. We still need to take responsibility for our actions and remember that honesty is key to any inventory.

Next, we ask ourselves this: did our sexual activity arouse jealousy? Suspicion? Bitterness? If so, what part did we play in it? We contemplate if there was a better way to approach the situation. Was there a healthy way to have engaged in the activity without bringing about harm to ourselves or others? Should we have engaged in the activity at all?

The sexual inventory ends the approach to a moral inventory we have been discussing. This can be a good time, as sexual compulsives, to stop and review our Sexual Recovery Plan. Many of us had only listed the things we *could not* do to stay sober. It can be a valuable exercise to start considering healthy sexual activities for ourselves. Just as every member defines their acting out behaviors, we also define our ideal sexuality. It is not uncommon that this ideal definition changes over time as we grow and change. Working with a sponsor may give us more insight and support throughout this process.

There are other methods of working the Fourth Step. We can look at other areas in our lives, areas where we were not powerless, but where we experienced unmanageability to one degree or another. This unmanageability could have involved money, alcohol, food, or any number of other potential pitfalls. The important aspect is to consider when we have been selfish, dishonest, inconsiderate, or hurtful in that area of our lives.

Focusing just on resentments, fears, and wrongs for some of us is not a complete picture of our "moral inventory." We also look at our strengths. An inventory, after all, involves taking stock: counting the stock, good and bad, assets and liabilities. Indeed, some of our actions resulted from being self-centered, but not all.

We find that our moral inventories are most effective when written out. The *act* of writing helps us to be honest and makes our Fourth Step searching and fearless. Many of us unduly worry that we might leave something out. Connecting with our Higher Power in these moments helps create the trust that everything necessary for us to consider will find its way into "this" inventory.

When we stop thinking of this being "the inventory to end all inventories," we relax, knowing we can return to this Step when we have new revelations.

Our fellow sexual compulsives warn us not to dally at this point. We have unearthed a motherlode of shame, which can drive us to act out. We want to unload what we have dug up. We move on to Step Five.

Step Five

"Admitted to God, to ourselves, and to another human being the exact nature of our wrongs."

Many of us grew up in households that taught us never to show weakness. Weakness was exploited and used against us time after time. Are we now supposed to bare all only to have it thrown in our faces once more? Our inventories, after all, include things we swore we would take to our graves with us.

SCA is a spiritual program that asks us to take actions that might feel uncomfortable or seem counterintuitive. We are not undergoing this process to punish ourselves but to heal ourselves. Our goal is to integrate healthy sexuality and to become the people we have longed to become - living useful lives, happy, joyous, and free. The process of admitting our wrongs begins to unburden us from the wreckage of our past. Facing these patterns of behavior requires honesty, humility, courage, self-love, and compassion.

"The exact nature of our wrongs" are those patterns of behavior that became clear in our Fourth Step. They stem from the resentments, guilt, shame, and fears that fuel our sexual compulsion.

The God mentioned in this Step is the concept of a "Power greater than ourselves" from Step Two and the "God *as we understood God*" from Step Three. The spiritual program of SCA asks us to admit the exact nature of our wrongs to this understanding of God. Some may find a prayer practice from their religious background helpful. Others might find writing a letter to their Higher Power admitting the exact nature of their wrongs useful. If the collective experience, strength, and hope of the fellowship is our Higher Power, we can share honestly at meetings about the patterns of our behavior revealed in our Fourth Step.

Admitting to ourselves the exact nature of our wrongs can be done in a letter to ourselves. We also might read aloud our Fourth Step in front of a mirror, where we are face-to-face with ourselves. We do not undertake this Step to make us feel bad about ourselves. When we honestly admit to ourselves the exact nature of our wrongs, we begin to develop humility, honesty, and integrity, so we can become the people we wish to be.

The idea of telling another human being the exact nature of our wrongs might arouse fear and shame and trigger us to act out. Those who have taken this Step reassure us that we will not face ridicule or rejection from the person who hears our Fifth Step. The solidity of our Third Step helps us trust the process, even if we fear its outcome. We don't need to take any part of our SCA journey alone.

We want to find someone with whom we feel safe to hear our deepest secrets. We find someone we can trust not to repeat what we say and who will not judge us. If our behavior was illegal, we might seek out someone with whom we can be entirely honest without fear of consequences. Usually, however, we choose our sponsor, who already knows much of our story and our motives.

We choose a place and a time where distractions and interruptions will be unlikely. The person hearing our Fifth Step can offer support and understanding, while also pointing out blind spots to our patterns of behavior, of which we might be unaware. This person can also share their own experience, strength, and hope. Sometimes taking our Fifth Step requires more than one session. Thoroughness counts more than speed.

When we complete our Fifth Step, we feel that a heavy burden has been lifted from our shoulders. It may be wise to decompress for a time or process whatever feelings arose. In any case, we feel gratitude for the opportunity our Higher Power gave us to delve into how our personalities led us to commit wrongs. We can now explore a different path.

The work of the Fourth and Fifth Steps eases the burdens of our resentments and fears. This process prepares us to focus on those traits which keep us from growing spiritually. We are ready to begin Step Six.

Step Six

"Were entirely ready to have God remove all these defects of character."

We bared our souls in Steps Four and Five. It took a lot of energy to engage in all that honesty. Nothing was left unsaid. There are now people in the world who know everything about us, yet these people don't run away or abandon us. *Surely the program isn't going to ask more of us!*

At first glance, Step Six looks like it might be simple and easy. We can sit back, relax, maybe pray, and perhaps meditate. *This will be easy!*

This Step certainly requires self-examination, prayer, and meditation. First, we define the phrase "character defects." It is easy to get caught up in the negative connotation of the word "defect." It sounds like we are somehow broken people. The program uses the phrase "character defects" to call attention to behaviors we engage in that no longer serve us. They prevent us from growing spiritually.

For many of us, it takes time to realize that there are parts of our personality that prevent us from moving forward. Our problems do not just revolve around the sexual behaviors that brought us to SCA. Those behaviors are but symptoms of the underlying spiritual disease. On some level, we felt entitled to these behaviors. They had come to define who we were. *Nobody knows what I have been through. I have a right to be angry. Look how many idiots roam the earth. Success means taking what I deserve without worrying about others.*

A variety of defects may show up for us: arrogance, perfectionism, anger, self-pity, dishonesty, impatience, bigotry, blaming others, and more. The central theme of our defects is fear. Fear is a basic human survival mechanism. It's instinctual for us as humans to be afraid of things that will hurt us. This mechanism is core to our being, but the ways we interpret it sometimes make us adopt a "survival mindset" when dealing with everyday life. Although some of us do face physically violent circumstances, the majority of us live in relative physical safety. Yet fear persists, telling us that the universe is a dangerous place, and we are on our own.

Fear takes on many forms. We may see an authority figure correcting us as a threat to our intelligence. Someone cutting in front of us is taking advantage of us. *Rules are a way to oppress me. Successful people always break the rules anyway. People of another culture don't respect my ways and only want to hurt me.*

Writing down our defects of character is essential to working this Step. We have a written list so we can refer to it in those times when we would rather forget these defects. As we progress through the program, this list changes. New defects become apparent, and old ones are removed through the grace of our Higher Power.

We consult our sponsors or trusted program friends, who provide us insight on the accuracy of our lists. Those who heard our Fifth Step may have gained a special perspective on what defects might be getting in our way. They point out times when these defects show up. We add these instances to our lists.

Once we feel we have a thorough list of character defects, we observe how they affect our lives. We take note of what happens when the defects come to the forefront. What are the rewards and unwanted consequences? How do we feel, and who else is affected? Does a resentment develop? Do we want to act out?

Taking all this into account, we focus on a character defect and begin to see the negative impact. We come to understand that life would be better without this defect. It may happen quickly. It might take time for the pain to reach the tipping point. Eventually, we reach the point of becoming entirely ready for our Higher Power to remove the defect.

God doesn't always remove a character defect in the way we might anticipate. Sometimes the character defect is removed by providing us the opportunity to be confronted with it head-on. Financial insecurity is a common character defect. In a "worst-case" scenario, we might lose our job, triggering this defect. Could we survive? Would the God of our understanding continue to take care of our will and our lives?

The sexually compulsive behaviors, the romantic obsessions, and the fantasies begin to subside. Even with these subsiding, though, we can see that our character defects still have the ability to make our lives unmanageable. Are we ready? Maybe we are simply in a state of willingness. Willing does not necessarily mean ready. We may be willing to have our character defects lifted, but we may not have done the work to allow this to happen. We can be willing to climb Mount Everest, but to become ready for the task means we endure physical training, hire expert guides, and purchase specialized equipment. Becoming ready for the task of Step Six means we develop a trust that the Higher Power of our understanding is capable of removing the defect.

Removing the defect isn't just exercising self-discipline or self-help. We had tried those many times before, and they did not work. This Step tells us the defect is not ours to remove; that God will remove it. The evidence becomes more apparent as we work the Steps, listen to others, pray, and meditate. These are all actions that help us gain this trust.

We come to understand that this Step is not reached at a single point in time. All we need to do is be as ready as we can. Maybe we can only focus on one or two defects at a particular moment. Like all the Steps, this is a process, not a one-time event. Slowly, with the help of our Higher Power, we become ready to see our lives transformed. We are ready for Step Seven.

Step Seven

"Humbly asked God to remove our shortcomings."

If we were honest in writing down our inventory in Step Four, we became able to address our character defects in Steps Five and Six. Step Seven asks us to be in a state of humility when asking God to remove our shortcomings. Humility is not humiliation.

Humiliation is about being shamed or being made to feel foolish. Our past may be filled with episodes of being humiliated, harangued, belittled, and made to feel we were "wrong." Sometimes this happened in front of others, making us feel embarrassed and small. Admitting we had aspects of our character that were defective could seem like giving in to the bullies, opening ourselves up for more ridicule.

Humility is a state of realizing we are not in control, that we do not have all the answers. It is a state of being fully prepared to accept the "how, what, why, and where" of what happens rather than believing we can control the outcome.

Working Step Six helped us to build a strong foundation of humility. In this state, we took our list of character defects and wrote ways we could counter the defect. Although humility does ask us to be vulnerable, it gives us an opportunity for real growth. Some think of this as learning to take contrary action to our learned impulses. Doing so is one way to humble ourselves and meet our Higher Power halfway in removing our character defects. For example, instead of retaliating against someone who cuts in front of us, we take a deep breath and count to five to center ourselves. Rather than reacting with the anger welling up inside, we take a moment to let the anger pass. One of the hardest contrary actions to take is to pray for those people or institutions we resent.

When we get stuck, we ask others for help. Consulting with our sponsors and other trusted program friends provides new perspectives as they share their experiences with similar character defects.

Sometimes we are confronted by a particularly tough character defect. Self-will exerts itself, and we reject all suggestions to take contrary action. We dig in our heels and return to feeling entitled to behaviors that we have determined to be objectionable. This behavior is not unusual for us as sexual compulsives. Talking to others, writing, and praying helps us become "entirely ready" once again. Some of us continue to experience this struggle indefinitely to varying degrees. We realize that we are not the only ones to struggle with character defects. However, in those moments when our character defects are lifted through the grace of our Higher Power, we feel a great sense of peace and serenity.

The more we experience this sense of peace, the more we grow spiritually. We learn that our character defects keep us self-centered and apart from others. When our character defects are removed, we feel "right-sized" – neither better nor worse than our fellows. We learn to feel compassion for ourselves, and most importantly, compassion for others. The more we work this Step, the greater compassion we feel. This growth helps prepare us for the remaining Steps.

We begin to see the miracle of having our shortcomings transformed into character assets, which we can put to use in service to others. We learn the importance of taking actions to enrich these character assets, confirming faith in the God of our understanding who removes our character defects. If we are stubborn, for example, we learn that this behavior is a shortcoming when it leads us to refuse to work the Steps. Instead, this same behavior can be transformed into persistence when used to carry the message of recovery to the sexual compulsive who still suffers. Witnessing this process inspires us to move forward, as we wonder how the next Steps can enhance these miraculous feelings.

Steps Four and Five helps us deal with resentments and fear. Steps Six and Seven helps us deal with character traits that prevented us from growing spiritually. We are now ready to rebuild fractured relationships by moving forward and beginning Step Eight.

Step Eight

"Made a list of all persons we had harmed, and became willing to make amends to them all."

Step Eight seems simple enough. We just make a list. We have already had some advice: *First Things First*. We begin by writing our name at the top of the list because we have done grave damage to ourselves as a result of our compulsion.

In working Step Four, we had created a list of people and institutions we resented. Now we start a new list with these names, and next to each name, we write down what harm we have done. Next to that harm, if there is a way we can make an amend, we write it down and describe it. Reviewing our Fourth Step helps fill this list out.

Although this is a good start, the simplicity seems to slip away. A thousand urgencies begin crowding into our life. We take our list out of the desk drawer, look at it, and put it back. Occasionally we might add a name to it, but this Step seems to recede in importance as compared with all the other demands we face. After all, the rent is due, or there is another meeting to attend, or yet another stressful relationship demands time and effort.

Step Eight is again asking us to take a counterintuitive action. It feels as if we are being asked to show weakness to those with whom we already have difficult relationships. Saving face and keeping up appearances had been a habitual coping mechanism in our active addiction. *What is this going to accomplish? These people don't care about me.*

A fog descends over our program. Everything had seemed so clear just a short time ago. Where had our vision gone? It seems as if we are slogging through the mud. Putting one foot in front of the other seems enormously challenging. How can we possibly figure out how to reach our goal of completing this list?

Many of us didn't realize it at the time, but we have hit a roadblock, a spiritual desert. Our thirst for the program has dried up. Some of us stop going to meetings, or go only occasionally, fed up with hearing the same sob stories over and over again. *What's going on? Why is there such resistance to moving forward?*

Using the principles from the preceding Steps, we learn to ask God to remove our resistance. Bringing our Higher Power into our consciousness increases our willingness to take the next right action. The next right action often is in calling our sponsors and telling them what is going on, holding nothing back. They offer a sympathetic ear, and occasionally some advice, but mostly all they can do for us is bear witness to our struggle. They cannot take on the task of completing the Eighth Step list for us.

Often, we are blocked by our fear of having to make face-to-face amends in Step Nine. Maybe there is a lingering feeling of resentment that those on our list are the ones who harmed us, so they should be making amends to us! Our faith in the spiritual program of SCA is being tested. Resisting and procrastinating on this Step denies us spiritual growth. Hiding out in the spiritual desert feels easier than moving forward.

Even so, the spiritual desert we now occupy feels scary and uncomfortable. Many of our old tried-and-true methods we used before program were stripped away doing the work in the preceding seven Steps. But really, what had been stripped away? Not our comforts, not our reliance on others, not even the basics of life. No, what had been stripped away were our false beliefs.

Exploring those false beliefs is one way to move forward - a way to break the resistance and to continue with Step Eight. We can discover false beliefs by filling in the blanks in this sentence: "If only I have enough ____________, I can _________."

We write it in two columns:

If only I have enough	**I can**
Money	Pay the rent Live in luxury Travel the world Help the poor
Sex	Satisfy my desires Have lasting relationships Gain power over others
Healthy food	Avoid fatal diseases Live a long life Lose weight

How do the above examples reflect false beliefs? We commonly accept money, food, sex, and the accumulation and abundance of these as measures of success. Upon reflection, we can see this misses the point. As we review these measures of success in the reflected light of our Higher Power, we can see how false they are. All the medicine in the world won't keep us healthy if we get an incurable disease. Our beliefs about sex may be thoroughly distorted, even if unconscious.

We then add a new column, one that brings us back to some of the self-examination we did in our Fourth Step: "How this false belief worked in my life..." We may have adopted these beliefs as our truths, or way of living, which often led to conflicts, frustrations, and unhappiness. For example, our beliefs about money might have produced workaholism. We sometimes put our career ahead of our closest relationships, including those with our Higher Power and ourselves. Our beliefs about food as a source of comfort and escape rather than nourishment might have led to health problems. Our beliefs about sex led us to disaster, time and time again. Other false beliefs also had devastating consequences.

Next came a fourth column, "How acting on this false belief harmed others." Now we are on our way to completing the list of people we had harmed. It flows like water, or more like tears. It becomes easy - painfully easy - to see how we had caused harm, sometimes grievous harm, in pursuing our false beliefs.

There is an underlying principle of Step Eight. That principle is one of forgiveness. Expecting or demanding perfection from ourselves and others often led to wrongs and resentments that have burdened us. Most of us find the notion of forgiveness frightening, if we feel we have to ask for it, or condescending, if we feel obliged to forgive others. Allowing our Higher Power to be part of the process can change our awareness and attitude. It becomes so much clearer that to be forgiven, we forgive.

Reviewing our list of resentments that many of us compiled in our Fourth Step is another place to look for harms we have done to others. Resentments often create a sense of entitlement. In this entitled state of mind, with our sexual compulsion activated, we may have caused harm to others, which seemed perfectly justifiable. In trying to make amends rather than confronting them, we could write a letter of forgiveness to the person or entity that we resented. We don't need to send this letter to anyone, though we might read it to our sponsor or a trusted friend. The letter writing itself can be very revealing. While writing the details of our specific resentments, we often learn more about the part we played in the story, and this gave us more clarity about how to make our amends, both generally and specifically.

Making it a "forgiveness letter," rather than a litany of complaints against past hurts, also helps to focus on an integral part of recovery. We can't change the past. While we may have real, justified resentments and even lasting damage that we may have suffered, our willingness to forgive can help free us from some of the burdens of past baggage. It is one way of opening ourselves up to accepting the present. Also, the actual process of writing such a letter, along with reading it out to someone, often allows us to "right-size" the resentment. Forgiving can be difficult, perhaps impossible for major traumas, but writing down the resentments can give us clarity about their real impact. We may even find that some of our grievances now seem petty as we begin to accept who we are today.

There are various approaches to completing an Eighth Step. Each of us encounters varying degrees of resistance and struggle with working this Step. The important thing is to focus on our actions and how they caused harm. The spiritual program of SCA tells us that we ought to attempt to make things right whenever possible. This process is not a punishment. We have a spiritual malady that will continue to thrive if we do not remove the "fuel" it feeds on. These harms stoke the fire of addiction. If we do not make things right, our addiction will continue to burn, causing us to act out.

The mess is ours alone, and ours to clean up. We become willing to make amends to all those we have harmed. We move on to Step Nine.

Step Nine

> "Made direct amends to such people wherever possible, except when to do so would injure them or others."

When we first understood the meaning of the Steps, the Ninth seemed the most daunting. It tells us to make direct amends for the things we may have kept hidden for years. Just the notion of making ourselves vulnerable to imagined negative reactions - or attacks - from others can make us feel uneasy.

Step Nine is not about apologizing. It is about making amends. While there is often nothing wrong with apologizing, and apologies are sometimes appropriate, making amends is a different process altogether.

Our Fourth Step brought up shame, which our Fifth Step helped relieve. But those Steps did not free us from our negative feelings such as guilt, anxiety, and shame. Working the Eighth Step brought these feelings to the forefront. Before beginning recovery, how many times did we apologize to assuage our guilt? Did we buy flowers for our loved ones? Did we tell people that we were sorry and would never do it again? And did those people learn, time and time again, that our apologies meant nothing? We need more than apologies to work Step Nine.

Making amends is a process of change. The entire spiritual process of recovery allows us to be open to change. Step Nine comes relatively late in the process for a good reason. Until we have made significant changes in our behavior, our amends mean nothing. In taking Step Three, we turned our will and lives over to the God of our understanding and began the process of making changes. With Step Six, we became ready. In Step Seven, we trusted our Higher Power to put these changes into practice, converting our shortcomings into assets. Step Eight helped show us specifically how our behavior had hurt ourselves and others. And now, in Step Nine, we take what we have learned and confront our pasts.

From experience, we know that we need to work closely with our sponsors or other trusted spiritual advisors. We are long past trying and failing to work the Steps on our own. Our sponsors and others help us to decide when direct amends might cause harm. They help us determine what appropriate amends might look like for each person on our Eighth Step list. We try to imagine what effect our amends might have on the other person, not in a codependent way, but with compassion and insight. At the same time, we remember the phrase "wherever possible," working this Step each time the opportunity arises and not making excuses based on an unwarranted fear of causing harm.

Direct amends can take a variety of forms, each one tailored to the circumstances under which we harmed others. Sometimes the opportunity presents itself by chance, but in most cases making amends requires careful deliberation and planning. We often begin without going into specifics by asking to meet to discuss our past behavior. The other party's response can be unpredictable. Sometimes we are told to get lost; in that case, we respect their boundary.

Often, the other person wants to know details before agreeing to a meeting; in such a case, it is appropriate to say that we have changed our behavior based on a new outlook on life and that we want to make amends. Rarely, when the other person is in recovery, they might ask if this is a Ninth Step amends? In that case, our joyful reply is: yes indeed.

It is important to determine if approaching someone after a long time of being absent from their life is appropriate. Such a request might seem odd or even threatening to the other person. Social media makes it easier to find old flames, friends, and acquaintances. Popping up in their life after 25 years of no contact can be shocking. It can be disingenuous to reach out to them to say we wish to make amends when there is no intention of wanting to be acquainted with them other than the amends. Receiving guidance from sponsors and trusted program friends is critical.

When we meet the other person, we avoid speechifying. We are brief and to the point. We lay out what we did and why. We don't try to explain addiction since, in the majority of cases, this is a person outside of recovery, more interested in our behavior than our spiritual wellbeing. Explaining addiction can seem like an excuse not to take ownership of our past behavior. We explain how our behavior has changed. Sometimes our amends is about living our lives differently one day at a time. In referring to such "living amends," we do not promise what we cannot deliver. We simply share our own experience, strength, and hope.

After we say what we feel the need to say, we ask, "Have I left anything out?" This question gives the person receiving the amends an opportunity to speak from their perspective. This process ensures we obtain a better understanding of the actual harm we have caused, rather than merely making amends we feel comfortable making. It matters little whether they praise us, harshly criticize us, or do something in between. We have no power over how others react. The purpose of the amends is about our wreckage. It is not about the other person's reaction. We are not asking for their forgiveness, which may or may not be forthcoming. Instead, we rely on God as we understand God to take care of the situation, and we avoid interjecting our ego. A good practice is to talk to our sponsor before and after making amends. This practice of bookending our actions gives us another person's perspective and can provide us with support in the case of unexpected consequences. It is important not to be alone in doing this difficult work.

In some cases, direct amends are impossible. We might have no idea how to reach the other person. They might have died. In those cases, we take appropriate actions to remember those we can no longer see or touch. Perhaps we simply talk to them or talk about them. We can write a letter to them and read it to our sponsor or other trusted members. We might honor them through a charitable donation or some other acknowledgment. There are even those for whom we simply write their names and put them in a "God Box." The "God Box" contains things we symbolically turn over to a Higher Power. There might come a time when we choose to ceremonially burn the papers from the "God Box" as part of making amends through prayer.

If the person died when we were children, we might have carried long-simmering grudges or an unwarranted load of guilt. We may even have imagined we were somehow to blame. Resentments that started at a young age often became intertwined into our lives as adults. These are particularly hard to release. We work Steps Four through Eight again before trying to make these amends. If there is a feeling of guilt, we can make amends to ourselves.

No two people's experience of working Step Nine is the same. However, the majority of members feel a miraculous restoration of relationships and release of shame under the care of their Higher Power. The energy put into making amends is worth the miracle stated in the Ninth Step Promises found in the book Alcoholics Anonymous. Among these promises: we will come to know a new freedom; we will not regret the past, nor do we wish to shut the door on it; we will lose our fear of economic insecurity and realize that God is doing for us what we could not do for ourselves. Working Step Nine allows us to let go and let God.

Once we have completed cleaning house in Step Nine, we find a practice to keep ourselves spiritually fit. We need a daily practice to make sure resentments and harms don't fester into full-blown addiction again. We are ready to explore Step Ten.

Step Ten

"Continued to take personal inventory, and when we were wrong promptly admitted it."

The personal inventory mentioned in this Step can be considered a brief moral inventory similar to Step Four. When we took Step Four, we took a long look at ourselves, possibly for the first time in quite a while. We searched hard, evaluating the good and the bad. Step Ten, however, requires us to look outward, not just inward. We see how we affect others. Staying aware of how our thoughts and actions affect ourselves and others is an integral part of working the program.

This Step calls for us to "promptly" admit when we are wrong. Promptly is not defined for us, but many consider it to mean as soon as we become aware of a wrong. A guideline often used is to take a daily inventory to keep our awareness current and not to let wrongs fester. This process could mean taking stock at the end of each day, reflecting on our thoughts and actions. When had our ego interfered with turning our will and our life over to the care of God as we understood God? In which situations had we acted based on fear or anger?

Step Five clearly says that we admit the wrongs uncovered in the Fourth Step to God, to ourselves, and another human being. The Tenth Step does not give us this specific direction. Who, then, may receive this admission? We need to admit the wrong to ourselves. Without self-awareness, we are unable to proceed to acceptance and then action. But who else might receive this admission? Many of us find it helpful to consult with our sponsor or another sober sexual compulsive. They can give us another perspective. Perhaps we were too hard on ourselves, or we were not wrong at all. They can help us determine if admitting the wrong would cause injury to ourselves or others.

Often the answer comes to us in prayer and meditation. It may come as we "sleep on it" after taking an inventory at night. As we discovered in Step Seven, with clarity comes the need to act, and with practice, the action becomes intuitive. Anchored in Step Nine, "We will intuitively know how to handle situations which used to baffle us," as promised in the book Alcoholics Anonymous. The action might be to make amends. It also may take the form of asking for our Higher Power to remove a character defect. Taking these actions without undue delay keeps our spiritual fitness clear of fear, resentment, and regret.

After working Step Ten for some time, we find ourselves getting in the habit of taking a spot inventory. This habit may be triggered when we find ourselves taken up in a wave of fear or anger. It can be triggered whenever we feel the need to take control, get even, or seize the spotlight. We have enough recovery under our belts to ask ourselves what's going on? Where does our ego feel threatened?

The more we ask our Higher Power for guidance in challenging situations, the more they seem to crop up. And the more they crop up, the more sensitive we become to the slightest effort on our part to try to evade, cover up, or ignore the truth. Rigorous honesty becomes a steadfast companion. Dishonesty, either through omission or commission, becomes less tolerable.

At this point, the Tenth Step fits us like a glove. Feelings that we previously considered "negative" are now simply guideposts to action. Afraid? Angry? Prideful? Jealous? We ask ourselves at these times for God to show us how we can be of service. And when that happens, we can put aside our ego and promptly admit when we are wrong. This newfound freedom from the burdens of our ego will allow us more room to accept a new sense of purpose in our lives. We will be open to finding and developing this as we move into Step Eleven.

Step Eleven

> "Sought through prayer and meditation to improve our conscious contact with God *as we understood God*, praying only for knowledge of God's will for us and the power to carry that out."

Many religions prescribe a form of prayer or meditation. But SCA is not a religious program. It is a spiritual program. We have come to know the value of praying and meditating. It was hard at first for most of us to pray or meditate regularly. However, we discovered their value by trying and found a restored ability to live in the present. Over time, we found it easier to integrate them into our daily lives.

We might start the day with a Step Three prayer or a meditation before going to work. Perhaps we end each day with a prayer of gratitude or add a second meditation. With practice, we learn to speak to our Higher Power throughout the day. Any emotion we have provides us the opportunity to deepen our relationship with God. When we are troubled, we stop and ask for our Higher Power's guidance. When we are grateful, we thank our Higher Power for grace. Most importantly, we take a breath and listen for our Higher Power's response. Talking is the essence of prayer. Listening is the essence of meditation.

Step Eleven suggests we focus our prayers on "only" knowing God's will for us. This guidance helps clear away the laundry list of things we would like or think we deserve in our prayer practice. Accepting this guidance may change the way we pray because we are trying to connect with our Higher Power's will and not our own.

Like many of the Steps, the word "us" is prominent. The program of SCA is a "we" program, not a "me" program. In time, we stop being so self-centered. This Step shifts the focus with this prayer: "God, I pray for knowledge of your will for us and the power to carry that out…"

One thing we notice is that our world expands when we are "on the beam" of recovery. And it narrows when we are not. Before taking the First Step, we suffered from tunnel vision, or even no vision at all, only fantasies and nightmares. Through prayer and meditation, we broaden our connection to the real world. The real world includes everyone. The more we practice connecting with others, the more we improve and expand our conscious contact with God.

Little by little, we gain knowledge of God's will for us. With that knowledge comes power: not "my" power, but real power. It is the power to act in alignment with God's will and the power to carry that out. It strengthens our spirituality and nourishes our recovery.

Once we have successfully connected to a Higher Power on a regular basis, we are ready to practice everything we learned while working the program in our daily lives. Having accomplished all that the program has asked, we are ready to bring what we have learned to others. We are now ready for Step Twelve.

Step Twelve

> "Having had a spiritual awakening as the result of these steps, we tried to carry this message to sexually compulsive people and to practice these principles in all our affairs."

In our addiction, it seemed as if we were sleepwalking, stumbling around with our eyes shut, bumping into others. We went places where we didn't belong, and often, we did considerable damage to ourselves or others. Every once in a while, we would open our eyes and see the wreckage that was our life. The reaction we had before recovery was to blame others for the mess we saw. "Clean it up the way I want, and fast," we told them. And then we shut our eyes tight once more.

One day, we opened our eyes and found ourselves in a room with a bunch of sexual compulsives. "I'm not like them," we told ourselves. But of course, we were. Our denial of reality didn't change the facts.

The journey to reach this Step has been a long one. We have expended a tremendous amount of energy. Our comfort zones have been expanded. Trust and faith are a part of our lives once again. It might have taken months or years before we "got it," but eventually, we learned that the Steps provide a path to our Higher Power's gift of sexual sobriety.

Have we had a "spiritual awakening?" This term likely elicits a different response for each member. Those with religious backgrounds may believe that God causes the awakening. Some will admit their lives are dramatically different and have no explanation of how it happened. Others will consider their "destruction of the ego" to be this awakening, and that they find grace in their humility. Paraphrasing AA's Twelve Steps and Twelve Traditions: the most important meaning of a spiritual awakening is that a person has now become able to do, feel, and believe that which they could not do before on their unaided strength and resources alone.

It has been said that each of the Steps works to deflate the ego. While this is true, it is not the goal. The deflation of the ego allows the spirit to awaken, grow, and thrive. A spiritual awakening is the only result that the Twelve Steps promise. Whatever our belief about a spiritual awakening, the program tells us that it comes about by working the Steps. Sexual sobriety is a gift given to us by our understanding of God because we work the Steps. We want to hold on to this gift. Step Twelve suggests that to keep it, we try to give it away.

What does "try" mean? It is not "trying," as we did before we came into SCA. It is not making a half-hearted effort before giving up, saying, "Well, I tried..." Consider this nugget of wisdom: When praying for something, believe that it already exists. So, when Step Twelve says, "we tried to carry this message," we take the action and let go of the result. We believe we have carried the message, not necessarily that anyone heard it.

So how, exactly, do we take action? The program of SCA does not provide any specific recommendations about what actions constitute "carrying the message." The wisdom of the program, however, suggests that this means being of service to the still suffering sexual compulsive.

The still suffering sexual compulsive exists both inside and outside of the fellowship. There are so many ways to carry the message within the fellowship: greeting newcomers, putting out chairs, speaking and sharing at meetings, doing a reading, sponsoring another member, and writing literature. This is just a short list.

Carrying the message to sexual compulsives outside of the fellowship is a bit riskier. Some of this work can be done anonymously by working on the website, responding to emails, or answering phone calls. The riskier service involves breaking our anonymity in some cases - things like talking to the media, working at an SCA booth for an event, putting our names on leases for meeting spaces. The riskiest service can be doing a Twelfth Step call.

A traditional Twelfth Step call is two sober members of SCA responding with compassion to a sexual compulsive who still suffers. Sometimes this meeting might take place in a hospital or a courthouse. This intervention may bring up thoughts and places we have been before, but this time we see them with sober eyes.

We do not preach. We do not proselytize. We use attraction rather than promotion. We briefly summarize our stories so that the other person knows that we, too, have suffered and that we have found a solution that works for us. But we do not try to fix the sufferer. That is the job of their Higher Power.

We encourage the person to attend a meeting, and we offer to bring them to one. We understand that the potential newcomer probably thinks as we once did, "I'm not like them..." We do not try to knock down that notion. We simply state our case. If we have succeeded, we have planted a seed, which may or may not eventually thrive, in God's time, not ours.

The more we work Step Twelve, the better we get at it. We used to see the world as a place with scarce resources and full of personalities set to clash with us. We now see the world as it is – a place of great abundance with people struggling as we are to live their lives one day at a time.

The world is a place guided by principles under the watchful care of a loving Higher Power. We become more present in our lives and connected to the wisdom within us. We live happy, contented, and useful lives.

Just as our compulsion affected each part of our lives, so too our recovery affects all areas of our lives. As we practice these principles in all our affairs, we discover that recovery has transformed our lives from a set of parts into an integrated whole. We become whole, passionate, recovering human beings, able to accept our mistakes, and transcend them. We increasingly want to be a part of the human race and have a commitment to give back what we have freely received. Our lives go from being centered on compulsive sex to being centered on service. We become increasingly useful instruments of our Higher Power.

May you, too, be happy, joyous, and free.

Chapter 5: Moving Through Withdrawal

WITHDRAWAL. The word brought up hideous images: addicts curled up in a fetal position, writhing in agony, or crying out in pain. We feared withdrawal and desperately tried to avoid it. Like the book, Alcoholics Anonymous says: "We thought we could find an easier, softer way. But we could not." The only way out of withdrawal, we found, is to go through it.

We discovered that the sexual withdrawal process consisted of four stages. First came the physical withdrawal after we abstained from our habitual patterns of behavior. The second was emotional withdrawal, a cleansing process where we became aware of our emotions to be integrated and healed. Third, as we worked the Twelve Steps of Sexual Compulsives Anonymous and used the SCA tools, the power of lust and fantasy slowly began to diminish in the process of mental withdrawal. Finally, we underwent a spiritual transformation as we replaced sexual compulsion as our Higher Power with a loving and forgiving God of our understanding.

Sometimes we cycled through these four withdrawal stages repeatedly, and sometimes they overlapped. The withdrawal process was unique for each of us, and we eventually began to trust that it was happening in our lives. As our sponsors and fellow SCA members shared their experience, strength, and hope with us, we started to identify with our healing process. The outcome of our withdrawal process was the rebirth of our relationship with ourselves, others, and our Higher Power. It was a journey that no one else could make for us.

When we first came to SCA, we were relieved to learn that our goal was not to repress our God-given sexuality. Instead, we learned how to express it in ways that would not make unreasonable demands on our time and energy, place us in legal jeopardy, or endanger our mental, physical or spiritual health. With the help of our sponsors and the fellowship, we began to abstain from destructive sexual activities. To make this abstention (partial or total) more tangible, we created a written Sexual Recovery Plan. Some of us chose a multi-column format for designing our plans.

In the left or first column, we wrote out those behaviors from which we wanted to abstain. Our sponsors and our fellows gently led us to include only the "musts," in other words, prohibitions on those people, places, or things that would surely lead to severe consequences. We called these "bottom-line" behaviors.

We took note of the warning signs or behaviors that could tell us when we were likely to slip into the first column's activities. For instance, if "public sex" appeared in the first column, we became intensely aware that hanging around a specific, named place was a dangerous sign that a potential slip was in the making. We included these "gray area behaviors" in our second or middle column.

In the right or third column, we listed those people, places, and activities we wanted to bring into our lives, to fill the time and mental space we had devoted to acting out. At first, some of us could not think of what to write in that third column. We found that *Easy Does It* was a useful guide for this section of the Sexual Recovery Plan and that leaving it blank at the beginning was perfectly all right. As our recovery progressed, we realized there were dreams we had abandoned when we were preoccupied with our sexual compulsion. We could add these to our third column, such as: seeing a ballet, learning the guitar, or foreign travel.

Upon entering the fellowship, we often developed an interim Sexual Recovery Plan. We wanted to stop - and stop quickly - our most dangerous behaviors and thus enter withdrawal. If we suffered from romantic obsessions, we prayed that we would not call, stalk - in-person or online - or drive by the home or workplace of the target of our obsession. We realized that our Sexual Recovery Plan's first column was a written record of our powerlessness and an essential part of working the First Step. After completing our First Step, we reviewed our Plan in that light and adjusted where necessary, adding to the first column those items we admitted we were powerless over. We found that by admitting our powerlessness and taking the First Step, we opened ourselves up to a Power greater than ourselves and started making progress in our recovery.

Most of us found that we were not willing to undergo withdrawal until we genuinely hit bottom. In the past, we may have been temporarily able to abstain from first-column behavior, though we eventually acted out again. We could not even admit that we had a problem - that we were powerless over sexual compulsion and that our lives had become unmanageable - let alone accept that we ought to abstain from certain behaviors. Yet, at some point, we came to realize that the pain of withdrawal could not exceed the pain we endured by continuing to act out. When did we reach our bottom? When we finally stopped digging!

Some of us could abstain from all acting out behaviors by coming to meetings and working the program, but many of us experienced slips, falls, binges, and restarts. We found that slipping back into our old behavior was part of the transformation process, similar to learning a new language or playing a new instrument. We found real inner strength when we picked ourselves up after a slip and repeatedly got back on the beam. We collected telephone numbers at meetings and stayed in contact with our fellows in the program. We read and reread program literature, took on service positions, or committed to attending 90 meetings in 90 days. We might have remembered the slogan *Meeting Makers Make It*. Maybe we went for long walks in safe places, or even watched terrible television, or played mindless computer games - whatever it took not to act out that particular day.

We committed to going to any lengths to stay on our Sexual Recovery Plan each day, and the next day woke up and made the same commitment not to act out again until that day was complete – one day at a time.

Many of us decided we needed to undergo total abstinence for a while, entirely withdrawing from sexual compulsion and romantic obsession. However, we did not have to make this decision alone, and we were encouraged to reach out for support. We looked for sponsors and program friends to find support as we moved through the withdrawal process. We went to meetings, made program calls, and took advantage of the support of the program. We also found that being of service and supporting others made our process easier to move through.

PHYSICAL WITHDRAWAL

Our experience taught us that our "dis-ease" had a physical component from which to recover. We experienced a "rush" and a "high" when acting out, which we sometimes enhanced with other substances, such as food, sugar, caffeine, alcohol, nicotine, and other drugs. This recognition sometimes led us into other Twelve Step fellowships. Unlike these external substances, we became addicted to the internal emotional states associated with sexual intrigue and release.

We may have experienced various physical symptoms in withdrawal, such as drastic changes in sleep patterns or appetite, sexual dysfunction, aches and pains, and even hallucinations. Some of us endured periods where we felt so sexually charged that we thought we just had to act out. Some of us considered the role that masturbation played in our lives - whether it was a healthy release or merely a delay in the physical withdrawal process.

Physical withdrawal meant sleepless nights for some, seemingly constant drowsiness for others. As part of our recovery, many of us developed more regular sleep patterns that better served our jobs, relationships, and health.

The process of physical withdrawal can shed new light on how we relate to our bodies. Sometimes in our addiction, we had foregone good meals, exercise, or even a decent night's sleep for weeks, months, or years. In recovery, we learned to pay attention to our medical needs. Some of us confronted sexually transmitted diseases or had our first STD tests. If we had resentments about contracting any diseases, we wrote them down when it was time to work Step Four. If we knowingly transmitted a disease, we wrote that down in Step Eight. We took up third column activities like sports, yoga, dance, or other exercises. We committed to turning off all computers, televisions, radios, phones, and lights by a specific time at night to ensure we got enough sleep.

Along with taking better care of our bodies, we started paying better attention to where we *took* our bodies. We learned we could not keep going to the same old bars, parties, or other triggering places (like "wet areas" at the gym) with the hope that we could "handle it..." Conversely, some of us sought a change in our neighborhood or even a different city to stay sober, only to find that our compulsive behavior was just as portable as our bodies and that we took it with us when we tried the "geographic cure." We realized that porn, apps & internet sex could be available regardless of our physical location. So, we took steps to limit our access, ranging from allowing specified times to those mediums, having our devices "locked" by a trusted friend, or even outright deleting accounts associated with our sexual compulsion.

We took a fresh look at our living spaces, which had also suffered from the unmanageability of our lives of sexual compulsion. We had to clean house, literally as well as figuratively. We went shopping for groceries or redecorated as signs of caring for ourselves. We committed ourselves to create a home for our new life in recovery and not for our dis-ease. Those we lived with could see us begin to recognize our commitment to keeping our side of the street clean, figuratively, and literally. We rearranged the furniture or tossed away clothing. We began to let go of clutter.

We took a good look at our careers and finances: we began to make sober decisions. Whenever we felt the urge to obsess over sex, we could turn our attention to our long to-do lists. However, since as sexual compulsives, we could go overboard - even in a "good" direction - we found it best to be mindful of two slogans: *Keep It Simple* and *Easy Does It.* We lived one day at a time, trusting the new routines of our life in recovery. Instead of trying to conquer the world by painting the living room, installing track lights in the den, and re-grouting the tub - all in one day - we decided that filling our empty refrigerators with groceries was a more realistic goal.

We realized that merely showing up to work on time and doing "an honest day's work for an honest day's pay" could be a victory in itself. We avoided the temptation to "compare and despair," setting our accomplishments against those of others. This behavior had served to sabotage our self-esteem and perpetuate our downward spiral of shame. We remembered HALT: not to allow ourselves to become too Hungry, Angry, Lonely, or Tired. We tried to spend time on the third column of our recovery plans, rekindling the hobbies and interests we had lost to sexual compulsion and discovering new ones.

EMOTIONAL WITHDRAWAL

With the physical aspect of withdrawal underway, many of us started feeling a wellspring of emotions previously suppressed by our sexual compulsion. Overcome by sadness, for example, we might have found ourselves breaking down in tears at work for no apparent reason. As withdrawal made it increasingly clear that the "happiness" we found acting out was indeed a fantasy, many of us became overwhelmed with grief. We realized that sexual conquest could not heal our inadequacies (real or perceived) and that using sex to feel validated and complete was a band-aid for a deep wound. We realized that such actions pushed us further away from family, friends, and the possibility of a healthy relationship. We felt a deep-seated loneliness. Many of us felt anxiety or even anger about our acting out and wished we could rewrite our past. This realization caused us more sadness and frustration.

The repressed emotions rushed over us in a series of relentless waves, almost drowning us in the process. As we considered our careers, finances, and relationships, we often felt the despair of time and energy wasted. During this humbling and sometimes painful process, it was easy to fall into the trap of comparing our *insides* to other people's *outsides*, resulting in the feeling of "It's too late, I give up!" These faulty comparisons - the perception that others' successes were eclipsing our own - drove us to want to act out. It took us a while to realize we each have our paths and that focusing on our program was always the priority.

Among our many fears during withdrawal was, "what happens when I'm no longer active in my sexual compulsion?" Facing this fear improved our ability to face the unknown and to see life as a challenging series of adventures and opportunities - a concept once foreign to us. We started to realize that *we are not our compulsion*. Although we fully admitted to *having a compulsion*, we realized that we could heal and become whole as children of a loving God. The bright side of working through these difficult emotions was discovering a sense of joy underneath them. We prayed to our Higher Power for the willingness and ability to feel all of our emotions.

The honesty that came with emotional withdrawal helped us stop playing mind games with ourselves and our Sexual Recovery Plan. We prayed for the willingness to allow fewer gray behaviors in our lives. Many of us found it helpful to keep a recovery journal, to help us gain clarity under challenging circumstances and work through complicated feelings. We attended as many meetings as possible and made calls when we felt overwhelmed or triggered. If we went to a meeting and did not get the opportunity to speak, we chatted with someone after the meeting or socialized with a group, thus avoiding resentment.

When we started to feel serenity, we knew that recovery from sexual compulsion was happening. When we stopped obsessing about sex or romance, we recognized this recovery. We no longer tried to sexualize every aspect of intimacy. Some of us no longer felt the need to manipulate others into meeting our emotional needs. We often adopted pets for companionship, affection, and unconditional love - and maybe learned a new sense of responsibility from these commitments. We could not stay out all night if we had to walk the dog or change the cat's litter box.

When emotional withdrawal felt like a torrential storm, we reminded ourselves: "This too shall pass." We started to recognize that the events of our lives were opportunities to learn a spiritual lesson – to ask our Higher Power what we needed to learn in order to grow.

MENTAL WITHDRAWAL

Many of us found that "euphoric recall" about our old lusts, fantasies, and romantic obsessions took some time, even years in some cases, to drain away. Even as the lust of the mind receded, we found ourselves seeking out music that reminded us of our cruising at bars, bathhouses, or other locations, with the unconscious hope of romanticizing - or rewriting - our acting-out past. We walked past old acting-out places to get a whiff of the old days, just like someone trying to give up smoking. We listened nonstop to songs and dined at restaurants that reminded us of our romantic obsessions. We heard others tell stories about experiences with hookup apps or other online adventures that sounded similar to the experiences we used to have.

We sometimes even left the fellowship to re-enter those acting out places or re-visit those relationships. Some of us thought we found the "relationship cure," that having a partner meant we could skip going to meetings. But we discovered that the past behaviors did not work anymore. Even if we found temporary relief from pain, we knew that whatever our problems were, acting out would never solve them and could only make them worse, not better. The knowledge we gained in SCA had "ruined" our acting out for good.

We found that even as our compulsion subsided, our obsessions lingered or even multiplied. Some of us became newly obsessed with finding a partner and signed up with numerous dating services or answered countless personal ads. We learned that our obsessions and compulsions could lead us straight to a slip.

Others rationalized that it was okay to slip occasionally because, after all, we were doing better than before. This attitude allowed our compulsive behavior to remain a river of misery in the background of our lives. Our sexual compulsion was relentless, feeding like a parasite on our hearts, minds, bodies, and souls. Knowing this, we had a decision to make: do we keep on living with the dull ache of sexual compulsion or grapple with the sharper, shorter pain of withdrawal?

It was not uncommon for some of us to feel an overwhelming sense of boredom that made us feel very restless and anxious. Nothing seemed interesting to us when compared to stimulating thoughts and images of sex and romance. This loss was, however, a great opportunity in disguise. Many of us used this newly released mental energy to go back to school to finish or attain new degrees or to find new hobbies and interests for occupying our minds. Whatever anxiety, depression, or emptiness we felt, we continued to take actions: deep breathing, meditation, and redirecting our mental energies into something constructive. By using the tools of the program, the critical moments would eventually pass, and a new perspective would arise.

As our obsessions, compulsions, and fantasies drained away, we began to identify "stinkin' thinkin'" as it occurred. We labeled our obsessive thoughts and said, "I don't have to follow that downward spiral." When we found someone triggering or alluring, we followed the "three-second rule:" allowing ourselves three seconds to fully appreciate God's creation, then redirecting our thoughts to something else.

Creating a new focus could be as simple as recalling a slogan or reciting the Serenity Prayer, or as comprehensive as plunging into creative pursuits, advanced education, or a new career. We found more time for relationships and other areas of our lives. We began or continued our Step work. As a result, we became more transparent channels of our Higher Power's will. When the obsessions returned and seemed to be overwhelming, we threw ourselves into service, knowing that to keep our sexual sobriety, we give it away.

FROM WITHDRAWAL TO SPIRITUALITY

The withdrawal process helped us understand that we were searching for a Power greater than ourselves on a subconscious level. We thought we found it in sex, romance, or relationships, but deep down, that never rang true. The final withdrawal process was letting go of sexual compulsion as our Higher Power and discovering a spirituality that works.

As we began to work the Twelve Steps, we started to grasp the concept of God as we understood God. This idea was not a God that wanted to control us through lust or fantasy, but a gentle, loving Higher Power whose care could restore us to sanity. We began to notice what we might once have called coincidences. When we found ourselves in a situation that once invariably led to having sex with a stranger, we would find ourselves having the strength to avoid the temptation that had previously eluded us.

We began to trust this Higher Power a little bit at a time. When confronted with the void within, we decided not to act out, just not for today. We trusted that if we did not act on our compulsive urges, this too would pass. This trust lifted a burden from our shoulders, and we were able to find serenity even in the face of uncertainty in the world around us. As things began to improve in our lives, we began to entrust outcomes to our Higher Power and focus on doing the work of recovery. At the same time, we began to understand how our Higher Power was working in our lives. That growing trust became the basis of our Third Step when we turned our will and our lives over to the care of God as we understood God.

Surrendering our will was not easy. How many times did we make demands on our Higher Power? Did we ask for a new or better lover, more money or respect on the job, greater control over the lives of ourselves or others? But working the Third Step led to a paradox: only when we surrendered ourselves to "Let Go and Let God" did we become light enough to appear attractive to others, instead of appearing desperate and needy. We accepted the possibility that if we did not have a life partner, this was not a punishment or deprivation, but "life on life's terms" – what was right for us at the time.

Some of us, perhaps for the first time, discovered prayer and meditation. We discovered the humility of praying "only for knowledge of God's will for us and the power to carry that out." The word "only" in Step Eleven was difficult for some of us since it precluded praying for the perfect lover (let alone a winning lottery ticket, a penthouse, or world fame). Yet, our previous Step work helped us realize that our Higher Power was about love, not fear. If we had a fearful conception of God in the past, we found the program much more difficult, especially when practicing Step Three, so we sought an understanding of God more suitable for us.

As we became free from the bondage of our compulsion, we came to see our sexuality as a creation of God and a gift to us. In turn, this new understanding made it easier for us to ask only for the knowledge of God's will for us and the power to carry that out in this sensitive and sacred part of our lives. Some of us longed to create more space in ourselves and our lives for a Higher Power to fill. Retreats, new commitments to a house of worship, or other spiritual paths helped fill that void within. We realized we were not empty; in fact, we had always been whole. Our character defects were wounds to be healed, not something innate. We understood Steps Six and Seven as acts of devotion that let our Higher Power reveal our true nature to us.

We spent at least a few minutes praying and meditating in the morning and evening, and as often throughout the day as necessary. We looked at our morning spiritual practice as a chance to align ourselves with our Higher Power for the day and our evening spiritual practice as a good time to do a Tenth Step inventory. When were we selfish, fearful, dishonest, or resentful that day? Even within the busiest and noisiest of neighborhoods, we found stillness. As the clutter in our minds, hearts, and bodies cleared, we could listen for our divine intuition and feel the presence of our Higher Power. We trusted in a Power greater than ourselves that loves us and wants us to be happy. We developed patience and trust in our healing process.

We found spiritual renewal through acts of service within SCA and beyond. Working with newcomers took us further down the path of sobriety. By sponsoring others, we articulated thoughts and feelings about life and recovery that we did not realize we knew. We benefited from every act of service we performed, and we prayed for the willingness to serve as our Higher Power would have us do.

At no point could we become complacent. We knew that sexual compulsion is *always* cunning, baffling, and powerful! We realized we were always one slip away from an even lower bottom than our last. Sadly, many of us hit many bottoms - each worse than the last - before we were ready to go through withdrawal.

COMING OUT ON THE OTHER SIDE

As we attended meetings, we continued to benefit from witnessing the recovery of others. We saw them endure great adversity or enjoy great success without acting out. We grew to understand how flimsy our excuses were for acting out in light of their responses to adversity or success. We stopped seeing ourselves as victims; instead, we learned that we could take responsibility in our lives with the help and grace of our Higher Power.

We sought spiritual progress, not perfection, comparing ourselves not to others but to the people we used to be. We stopped pursuing those who were unavailable or who would reject or abuse us. We lost our fear of other people and our fear of our sexuality. We learned to recognize the difference between sex, love, and affection. Our lives gained a new meaning, whether we were in a relationship or out of one. We discovered ourselves, our spirituality, and our connection to our Higher Power.

Because we underwent withdrawal and saw it through to the other side - while rigorously working the Twelve Steps and maintaining sobriety as defined on a Sexual Recovery Plan - we were able to experience increasing serenity and recovery. We finally found peace with God, ourselves, our loved ones, our fellow human beings, and our sexuality.

Chapter 6: The Tools That Help Us Get Better

Meetings are where we share our experience, strength and hope with each other to better understand our common problem and work together towards the solution.

The Telephone is our meeting between meetings. By making contact with others, we begin to break out of the isolation that is so strongly a part of the disease.

Sponsorship is two people with the same problem helping each other to work the program. It can provide a framework for a Sexual Recovery Plan and for doing the Twelve Steps, and can bring emotional support at difficult times.

Literature is our portable program. We use SCA's Conference-approved literature, as well as that of AA and other Twelve Step programs. We may also make use of other appropriate materials.

The Twelve Steps are a suggested program of recovery based on the Twelve Steps of AA.

Prayer and Meditation are a means of establishing conscious contact with a Power greater than ourselves.

A Sexual Recovery Plan is a predetermined way of expressing our sexuality consistent with our values, so that even when confused, we will have a written guideline to help us.

Abstention (partial or total) We get support in SCA by abstaining from people, places, or things that we consider harmful.

Socializing is a way of breaking down our isolation and getting to know other people in a non-sexual context: at fellowship after meetings, in supportive organizations and groups, and the community at large.

Dating is a way of changing the instant gratification habit and getting to know more about ourselves and another person before committing ourselves to any sexual decisions.

The Slogans are simple statements that can be used in crisis situations so that we have some basic guidelines.

Service is a way of helping ourselves by helping others.

Writing provides a way to become honest with ourselves and our Higher Power. By writing in journals, gratitude lists, emails and letters, we can measure our progress, values, motives, and 12 Step work.

Chapter 7: Sponsorship in SCA

"Sponsorship is two people with the same problem helping each other to work the program. It can provide a framework for a Sexual Recovery Plan and for doing the Twelve Steps, and can bring emotional support at difficult times." - *The Tools That Help Us Get Better*

ORIGINS OF SPONSORSHIP

The words "sponsor" and "sponsorship" were not to be found in the First Edition of Alcoholics Anonymous, the basic text of AA, otherwise known as the AA "Big Book."[3] Sponsorship is an aspect of Twelve Step recovery that evolved. In essence, sponsorship is a form of personal guidance or mentorship. Originally, AA members were asked or even assigned to watch over newer, prospective members of the fellowship. There were no special requirements for being what we now call a sponsor, except that the member doing the helping had more experience of sobriety than the newer member. It could be weeks or days more of sobriety than the new prospect. In time, a bond often formed between the two parties, owing to a common desire for recovery. Sponsorship took hold in AA and spread to the other Twelve Step programs that grew out of AA.

UNDERSTANDING SPONSORSHIP AND GETTING OR BECOMING A SPONSOR

In the beginning, both sponsor and sponsee may ask what this

[3] Sexual Compulsives Anonymous derives from the first Twelve Step program, Alcoholics Anonymous.

sponsorship idea is all about. Whether through reading SCA literature or hearing about sponsorship from more experienced members of the fellowship, we begin to construct a concept in our minds. During meetings, some groups ask for a show of hands, those who have a sponsor, and those who are willing to be sponsors.

If we are looking for a sponsor, this is a good time to note who is raising their hands and when. Do we want to choose a sponsor who also has a sponsor? Or is it enough that this person is willing to be a sponsor? The primary attribute of a sponsor is having the experience of recovering - to whatever extent - from sexual compulsion. This person understands what we are going through from personal experience, unlike someone who merely studies sexual compulsion or knows about it only from an intellectual point of view. Many members of Twelve Step programs will say that a sponsor provides a listening ear and objective input and guides the sponsee through the process of working the Twelve Steps.

Just as having a Sexual Recovery Plan is no guarantee of achieving or maintaining sexual sobriety, having a sponsor is no guarantee of getting or staying sexually sober either. We may think of sponsorship as a "practice relationship" for our other relationships. We often value it for being a somewhat formalized relationship in a sometimes-solitary world. As sexual compulsives, we have a strong tendency toward isolation. Sponsorship can be both a bridge and a catalyst to bring us out of isolation. It can help us engage more readily, effectively, and healthily with the larger world - including within the SCA Fellowship. Both sponsor and sponsee come to terms with their readiness, willingness, and ability to engage in the sponsorship relationship.

How do we know when we are ready to be sponsored? It often begins with the First Step of SCA's Twelve Steps: "We admitted we were powerless over sexual compulsion – that our lives had become unmanageable." When we can make this admission, it is easier to accept the help of another. After all, we could not stop acting out our sexual fantasies and behaviors - our sexual compulsion - unaided for very long. Knowing how hopeless a situation can get may not be as effective a motivator as wanting to live a better life. The Tool of *Sponsorship* extends this hope of a better life. It is a more personal mode of carrying the message of recovery from sexual compulsion. The message is simply this: if you want to stop acting out, you can; furthermore, a spiritual life can be happy, joyous, and free.

So, we decide that we are ready to be sponsored. How, then, do we go about getting a sponsor? One member set a goal of asking three people in two weeks a question such as: "Without making a commitment at this time, I was wondering if you are available to sponsor, and how would it be if you sponsored me?" After two weeks, that member had three people from whom to choose. The first time doing this exercise, however, our friend was uncomfortable with the choices. If we have this experience, as our friend did, we merely set another two-week period and ask more potential sponsors the same question. We may just ask one person from the outset. We are sure to find a sponsor.

In any case, we begin the process. We can ask Trusted Servants of meetings to suggest a sponsor for us, and some SCA groups match temporary sponsors to newcomers. Other groups have experienced members who offer their sponsorship. We can listen during meetings for sharing with which we identify, and then ask that member if they are willing to sponsor us. The prospective sponsee is always free to decide on their sponsor without pressure. Still, if there are many false starts, it is relevant to ask the question, "When will I be ready?"

This question of readiness applies to prospective sponsors as well. How many times do we ask an experienced program member to sponsor us before they agree to do so? Sponsorship has a way of providing additional cohesion to a group. We examine for ourselves the consequences to our group of declining to sponsor others. After all, SCA's Fifth Tradition is that "Each group has but one primary purpose – to carry its message to the sexual compulsive who still suffers." Many of us have found that "To keep it, you give it away" - we assist others in their recovery to maintain our sexual sobriety. Then too, the SCA *Statement of Purpose* reminds us that "Our primary purpose is to stay sexually sober and to help others to achieve sexual sobriety." Sponsorship is a way of working the Twelfth Step: "Having had a spiritual awakening as the result of these steps, we tried to carry this message to sexually compulsive people and to practice these principles in all our affairs." Sponsor and sponsee each arrive at their conclusion regarding readiness.

To ask someone to sponsor us may be an incredible leap of faith. We may feel vulnerable. Our history in the area of interpersonal relationships may cause us to hesitate. Many of us are embarrassed about our romantic and sexual behaviors, which have often been selfish, sordid, secretive, furtive, and a source of shame. However, this may be an opportunity to change old patterns and open up to an unfamiliar honesty, starting with our new recovery relationships. Before disclosing too much information, one may ask the other if there are any "deal-breakers." Agreeing on temporary or interim sponsorship may provide the reassurance we need that SCA is indeed a safe place for us to recover from sexual compulsion.

THE ROLE OF A SPONSOR OR SPONSEE

To some, a sponsor is an authority figure - a kind of boss - and we are afraid of entering into yet another power struggle. So, an examination of our motives will be helpful at this time. Perhaps we can look at what sponsorship is *not*, to see its outline more clearly. A sponsor is *not* a potential sex partner, is *not* our Higher Power, is *not* our parent, is *not* our therapist, and is *not* our employer or employee. No one receives payment for being a sponsor. Likewise, a sponsee is *not* a child, is *not* a minion, and is *not* a target for seduction. Both sponsor and sponsee ought to keep these words from the SCA *Closing Statement* in mind: "In the spirit of recovery from sexual compulsion, we suggest that sex between members not be treated lightly. Sex between people new to the fellowship and other members is discouraged."

One group had a "trophy sponsor," a good example of recovery respected by that group. We say "trophy" because to some in this group, having that person as a sponsor seemed to be a way of acquiring their fellows' respect – a kind of status symbol. By the same token, not all sponsors are immune to the pride that sometimes goes with having large numbers of sponsees.

Having many sponsees and not wanting to be overextended, this popular sponsor asked two questions of newcomers who were also prospective sponsees. The sponsor was troubled by saying "no" to a program request and wanted to maximize their usefulness to the members already being sponsored. The first question was: "What brought you to SCA?" If the answer was "The bus," the potential sponsor would attend to other prospects. However, if the answer was more or less an admission of powerlessness over sexual compulsion and unmanageability, the prospective sponsee was asked the second question.

The second question was, "Do you hear what you need to hear at meetings?" This question was an attempt to discover the newcomer's or prospective sponsee's level of open-mindedness. The answer spoke of the potential sponsee's ability to ask for help and the ability to accept help. The answer also informed the sponsor's subsequent interactions with the member. A good guide in these situations may be to ask ourselves whether we can help the prospective sponsee and in what capacity. It is also sensible to consider our other commitments and weigh our ability to spend sufficient time with a new sponsee, especially if we have several others, before agreeing to sponsor someone.

Sponsorship, like many tools of the program, promotes growth. Sponsoring another is not confined to a certain stage of the program or length of time in recovery. By sponsoring others in SCA, we become more responsible and mature in our recovery. We get to see life from the program's perspective and concentrate on sound, recovery behaviors. We get the opportunity to grow into this new life of recovery.

WORKING WITH A SPONSOR OR SPONSEE

When we find someone who agrees to explore sponsorship with

us, we may initially want to meet in a public place. We can think of this encounter as an interview. It is an opportunity for us to get to know each other and see if we are compatible. It helps gauge if there is a sense of trust between the individuals, particularly for the prospective sponsee. We share our stories, exchange contact information, and begin to establish boundaries. We could even have questions prepared ahead of time: Will there be assignments or suggestions? How often do we meet in person? What communication methods are we to use: telephone calls, voice mail; email; letters; text, or other means of contact? Who calls whom, how often, and how soon do we expect to be contacted in return?

Upon answering a call, we can say things like "I have five minutes to talk," or "Can I call you back in half an hour?" or "I cannot talk now." We can disclose times it is acceptable or not acceptable to call. We can say whether it is permissible to leave messages or not and if there are any limitations on the kinds of messages left.

During this "interview," or a discussion of sponsorship, the two may mutually decide to form a sponsorship relationship or determine that further discussion is needed. When asked to become a sponsor, many members tell the potential sponsee that they need time to decide. This process can take the form of prayer and meditation, consulting with one's sponsor, and the like. Some new sponsors will specify a "trial period" of perhaps 30 days when either sponsor or sponsee can terminate the relationship without hard feelings. We do not leave the matter of sponsorship up in the air: we want a clear understanding of whether a sponsorship relationship exists.

Sexual Compulsives Anonymous – A Program of Recovery – 2nd Edition, also known as the SCA "Blue Book," tells us that "The sponsor/sponsee relationship is *not* a marriage. If it doesn't work, we get another sponsor. However, continuity is valuable. A sponsor who knows our story and has an ongoing sense of our situation is helpful." It also emphasizes that "Confidentiality is an essential ingredient of sponsorship. There are many things about our sex lives that we share openly at meetings, but there are often other aspects of ourselves that we have great difficulty revealing. Sharing our sexual secrets is a crucial part of the process of healing. We can only do so when we know that our secrets are safe with trusted confidants. The sharing of sponsors, sponsees, and other SCA friends is equally confidential."

In SCA, individual members define sexual sobriety for themselves. Abstinence is determined by - among other things - not engaging in our bottom-line or acting-out behaviors. Therefore, we are encouraged to share our Sexual Recovery Plan with our sponsor. We don't expect the sponsor to determine the Sexual Recovery Plan's content but provide feedback and suggestions. We are careful to avoid a Sexual Recovery Plan that is too heavily weighted in one direction or the other. A balanced plan is neither too strict to allow us to achieve and maintain abstinence from our bottom-line behaviors nor too lax in keeping us moving in the direction of healthy sexuality. Some sponsors and sponsees will arrive at an agreed framework for establishing and amending the plan structure. SCA recommends that members share their Sexual Recovery Plans with another SCA member, preferably a sponsor, which extends to changes to a plan. There is also SCA literature on the subject of how to write a Sexual Recovery Plan.

IMPORTANT ASPECTS OF SPONSORSHIP

Understanding, acceptance, and patience are essential qualities in sponsorship. We create a safe environment for sharing and expressing ourselves if we avoid getting angry or taking things personally. For example, if the sponsee discloses a slip, the sponsor may share program wisdom, or express their view, desire, or need. This sharing of perspective goes for both the sponsee and the sponsor. As is defined in *The Tools That Help Us Get Better*, sponsorship is a two-way street, and the sponsor is working the program alongside the sponsee. There is a natural tendency for a sponsee to look up to a sponsor. However, it is wise for the sponsee to avoid putting the sponsor on a pedestal or base their sobriety on the sponsor's. Our First Step does not depend on any other person, but rather on ourselves.

Generally, we keep our sponsor up to date and tell them when some significant event has occurred in our life. This practice saves time in getting current when some other crisis may be imminent. We emphasize the importance of encouraging any member who has had a setback in recovery to stay connected to the program. This connection can help prevent a slip from turning into a relapse. A sponsor is generally a focal point and is often the first contact with SCA in challenging times. Contact with a sponsor can, therefore, help us prevent the compulsion from taking hold again. This interaction is part of discovering how to work the program and negotiate life while staying sexually sober.

Ongoing contact between a sponsee and a sponsor can establish a baseline measure of daily life. The sponsor gets to know when the sponsee needs help or is doing just fine. Both parties develop a sense of commitment and accountability, which was unknown to us in our acting out days. This new arrangement fosters active, deliberate recovery, and an end to our isolation. In recovery, and when being sponsored, we find the courage to acknowledge our need for help, ask for help, and accept help. It is important to remember that help may sometimes arrive in forms we do not expect. Regular contact with a sponsor can help us keep the focus on our recovery. To paraphrase a personal story in the AA Big Book, when we spend time on our sexual compulsion, its influence grows; when we spend time on our spiritual recovery, it grows. Where we choose to spend our time is up to us.

SPONSORSHIP AND WORKING THE TWELVE STEPS

Sponsors provide crucial help and guidance when working the Twelve Steps: they can help us determine how to take a Step, when to move forward, and when to linger on a Step. The sponsor and sponsee work out the details between them. However, a sponsor will usually actively encourage a member to progress through the Steps and point to relevant and helpful literature in the process. Some members choose to share their written First Step work and sexual histories with their sponsors or review them verbally. A sponsee will often look to a sponsor for help with forming an understanding of a Higher Power, as is outlined in the Second Step: "Came to believe that a Power greater than ourselves could restore us to sanity." Also, relating to that Higher Power as is outlined in the Third Step: "Made a decision to turn our will and our lives over to the care of God *as we understood God*." Sponsors often assist with suggestions for how to go about taking the personal inventory involved in the Fourth Step: "Made a searching and fearless moral inventory of ourselves."

Our sponsors often, but not always, hear our Fifth Step: "Admitted to God, to ourselves and to another human being the exact nature of our wrongs." We can expect to receive feedback from those who hear our Fifth Step, but caution against elevating anyone to the level of "expert" in how we view them and against the sponsor assuming that status without credentials. After all, we are "two people with the same problem helping each other to work the program." After hearing our Fifth Step, a sponsor can reassure us that we are in the right place in SCA and encourage us to stay in recovery and press on with the Steps. A sponsor can also emphasize that recovery is possible and worthwhile. The self-examination and disclosure involved in the Fourth and Fifth Steps are challenging, and our problems can seem overwhelming. It means a lot to most members to know that they have someone, in their sponsor, prepared to accept and continue working with them, regardless of their past.

At this point, contemplating what we have uncovered in our Fourth and Fifth Steps and facing our Sixth[4] and Seventh[5] Steps, we may ponder action in additional areas. These actions might include working on other aspects of our health or even seeking other means of recovery before proceeding to the next Step. We may revisit aspects of our earlier Step work or get another sponsor, join another Twelve Step program, or get a sponsor in another Twelve Step program: we push ahead with our recovery.

---

[4] Step Six: "Were entirely ready to have God remove all these defects of character."

[5] Step Seven: "Humbly asked God to remove our shortcomings."

While SCA has no opinion on outside issues, even other Twelve Step programs, the individual is free to find their way.

Some SCA members find that they benefit from seeing helping professionals in the field of recovery from sexual compulsion, along with attendance at SCA meetings. Many of us have experienced trauma of one kind or another, including sexual abuse or exploitation in some cases. SCA has no opinion on therapy as such, but the AA Big Book clarifies that one should not shy away from seeking outside help for health problems that help augment the AA program or do what is outside the scope of the AA program. In the exercise; AA Big Book chapter, "The Family Afterward," it says: "We are convinced that a spiritual mode of living is a most powerful health restorative. We, who have recovered from serious drinking, are miracles of mental health… But this does not mean that we disregard human health measures. God has abundantly supplied this world with fine doctors, psychologists, and practitioners of various kinds. Do not hesitate to take your health problems to such persons…" Try to remember that though God has wrought miracles among us, we should never belittle a good doctor or psychiatrist. Their services are often indispensable in treating a newcomer and in following his case afterward." Very few people in SCA will say that theirs is the only way to recover from sexual compulsion, however it is expressed. A sponsor can help us sort through what we discover as we pursue our recovery and find ways to address it. A sponsor can also help us see ourselves more realistically and accept our shortcomings and challenges as we work to bring healthy changes to our lives. Recovery is there for us if we work for it. Recovery is a lifelong pursuit and goal, but it is always attainable, one day at a time.

As sexual compulsives, we tend to avoid taking responsibility for things we have done and the harm we have caused. Conversely, we may sometimes take responsibility or blame ourselves for things done by others, where we bear little or even no responsibility. A sponsor can be invaluable in helping us to complete our Eighth Step[6] list of those we have harmed and in determining amends to be made as part of our Ninth Step[7], including where it may sometimes be best to leave things well alone. A sponsor can help us view our Tenth Step[8] work of continuing to take personal inventory objectively. Many of us will not have paid attention to spiritual practices before coming to SCA. Even if we have, how we go about them in recovery may very well be different. A sponsor can share personal experience and understanding of the prayer and meditation involved in working the Eleventh Step[9]. Sponsors can also impart their knowledge of the various ways of carrying the message of recovery that form part of working the Twelfth Step[10]. In general, a sponsor can relate how others in SCA may have approached their Step work. Knowing its value, a sponsor will often encourage a sponsee to get involved in service, emphasize the importance of service in recovery, and convey their first-hand experience of various kinds of service and outreach. The input and support of a sponsor can make all the difference.

---

[6] Step Eight: "Made a list of all persons we had harmed and became willing to make amends to them all."

[7] Step Nine: "Made direct amends to such people whenever possible, except when to do so would injure them or others."

[8] Step Ten: "Continued to take personal inventory, and when we were wrong promptly admitted it."

[9] Step Eleven: "Sought through prayer and meditation to improve our conscious contact with God *as we understood God*, praying only for knowledge of God's will for us and the power to carry that out."

[10] Step Twelve: Having had a spiritual awakening as the result of these steps, we tried to carry this message to sexually compulsive people and to practice these principles in all our affairs."

SPONSORSHIP IS A TOOL OF THE PROGRAM AND NOT A SOLUTION

We often find in time on the road to recovery that some of our old problems will seem trivial and that our perspective on our other problems will improve. Sometimes, though, when we are at a low point in our recovery and want to hear words of encouragement from our sponsor, we may be disappointed. Making errors and encountering setbacks is part of finding our way. Our sponsors are only human, and fellow sexual compulsives to boot. They cannot solve our problems for us. The Second Step tells us that we "Came to believe that a Power greater than ourselves could restore us to sanity." The Third Step reminds us that we "Made a decision to turn our will and our lives over to the care of God *as we understood God*." The Slogans tell us in general terms to take it "*One Day at a Time*," and that "*This Too Shall Pass*." Though we may have little else, as SCA members, we see that we are not alone in our struggles and that things will change if we follow the example of others who have persevered with their recovery before us. Ultimately, we are each called in recovery to look to our Higher Power for guidance, protection, and care.

Roadblocks, difficulties, and shortcomings in the sponsorship relationship allow the sponsor to learn from the sponsee, and vice versa. Again, we are "two people with the same problem helping each other to work the program." The addictive process of sexual compulsion is continually looking for ways to work its way into our lives. SCA literature speaks of sexual compulsion as being cunning, baffling, powerful, and insidious for good reasons. Rebounding into compulsive behaviors as a result of disappointments or failings in sponsorship (or indeed in our recovery or lives in general) is a trap of which to be aware. No one knows everything, and sponsors can at times be blunt or fall short. However, "sponsor-shopping" until we hear what we want to hear could be a problem too. Staying with one sponsor works fine for most of us, even when a sponsor disagrees with a sponsee. Forthright communication is essential to any relationship's growth and maturity, so long as we do it in an open, honest, respectful, and considerate manner. Some of us have been friendly confidants only to discover the expectations of sponsorship imposed on us without our consent. If either person detects an unhealthy dependency, the problem can be worked out and used as a growth experience. Sometimes, the problem cannot be worked out. If not, we can decide to end a sponsor/sponsee relationship. This transition can also represent a growth experience.

Reintegrating sex into our lives as a healthy element is a delicate matter. A sponsor often introduces and encourages the sponsee to use the tools of the program as part of the process. *The Tools That Help Us Get Better* are resources and can be used to help us open the door for our Higher Power to show up in our lives. *The Tools* are often merely concepts to us initially, and then they become practical mechanisms when we first start using them as part of our resource list. They change with use and refinement into solid assets, upon which we can depend on a daily basis when we need help. However, the sponsor can only guide and support the sponsee in this process. It is up to the sponsee to take the actions necessary to transition from a life driven by the compulsion and run on self-will to one where we practice the program's principles daily, which depends upon a Higher Power for its source of strength.

The problems that bring each of us to SCA are different. Likewise, members sometimes move on for reasons not readily apparent. Sexual compulsion simply proves too strong for some. For others, departure is a clear and deliberate action; they felt the program was not meeting their needs. Sometimes a sponsee can outgrow the sponsor. Others drift away, never to return, once they get a sponsor. Some leave the group when their reason to attend has been satisfied. It could be that they wanted to get their relationship back, get their job back, save money or recuperate. Did they get what they wanted? It is hard to say why individuals leave exactly, since they may often have trouble perceiving their reason for attending meetings in the first place. AA has a saying, which SCA has adopted: "The program is not for those who need it, it is for those who want it." As SCA members, we can only carry the message of recovery from sexual compulsion and be willing to receive it ourselves. We cannot make anyone else recover. Nor can a sponsor, or anyone else, recover for us.

VARIETIES OF SPONSORSHIP

Most of the discussion in this review is concerned with a formal sponsorship arrangement between two members, who might typically attend the same meetings. Sponsorship of this kind evolved in Twelve Step programs over time: there are no requirements to have a sponsor or engage in sponsorship like this. It is important to note that members are free to have a sponsor as they work the program or not: a member can also have more than one sponsor.

For example, some members find that a second sponsor with specific knowledge for certain areas of their lives can help when their main sponsor does not have particular experience. We let both sponsors know if we are working with a second sponsor. Some members engage in distance sponsorship, where sponsor and sponsee do not typically meet in person but communicate by telephone, email, and the like due to being geographically remote. Some members co-sponsor each other, with each individual being the other member's sponsor.

Sponsorship does not necessarily have to come from a designated individual. In many ways, SCA literature can provide a form of sponsorship to help guide a member in their recovery, including this publication. Sponsorship can come from our groups and sharing at meetings. It can also be informal. Sponsorship can happen spontaneously among two or more members over coffee after a meeting. We can receive sponsorship when we call a program helpline. Therefore, we are careful to distinguish between having a particular sponsor in a formal arrangement and the underlying *concept* of receiving sponsorship. Sponsorship is a tool of the SCA Program that most members find enormously helpful. However, a sponsor is optional, and sponsorship is open to a wide variety of arrangements and interpretations.

SPONSORSHIP IS PART OF A SPIRITUAL AWAKENING

The answers to our questions are revealed in time, as we work the Twelve Steps. Getting a sponsor can promote a sense of hope. A sponsee's responsibility is to summon as much honesty, open-mindedness, and willingness as possible. Some say this Honesty, Open-mindedness, and Willingness are part of working the first three Steps and HOW it works. As we move through the Twelve Steps, we improve our relationships with our Higher Power, ourselves, and society. We become willing to sponsor others as part of our Twelfth Step[11], although we are by no means restricted to working all Twelve Steps before we sponsor someone. This spiritual awakening we speak of is, after all, an awakening to the way our Higher Power manifests itself in our daily lives. Sponsorship and helping others awaken to their Higher Power can bring about recovery, growth, and healing that would otherwise not be possible, and thereby change the world.

[11] Step Twelve: Having had a spiritual awakening as the result of these steps, we tried to carry this message to sexually compulsive people and to practice these principles in all our affairs."

Chapter 8: Sexual Recovery Plans

What Is a Sexual Recovery Plan?

A Sexual Recovery Plan (SRP) is a pre-determined way of expressing our sexuality consistent with our values, so that even when confused, we will have a written guideline to help us.

For many of us, the SRP is at the very core of the SCA program - a commitment to recovery and a new design for living. It's both a practical means of getting a good look at our compulsion and a giant step in breaking away from it.

Newcomers tend to fear the SRP as a repressive measure. But SCA exists to free us from the constraints of sexual compulsion. The purpose of the SRP is not to make our sex lives more rigid but to free them from behaviors that cause problems.

The nature of the compulsion is to veil our true sexual desires with fantasy and confusion. An SRP enables us to break through the chaos and decide how we want to handle this sensitive part of our lives. Creating an SRP is a process of "peeling the onion" to examine our compulsion layer by layer. It helps us to identify which sexual activities have harmed us or others and determine actions we can take to change these behaviors. We also recognize our desires and then decide how to realize them. By setting guidelines for our behavior, the plan frees us from making anxiety-provoking choices in the confusion of sexual excitement. It allows us to interact with another person, honestly.

Beginners often stress the prohibitions and start with ideals that prove impossible to realize. We can be gentle with ourselves by not putting too many restrictions on our initial SRP. We may unintentionally create heavy burdens by listing unrealistic expectations in our plan. Living up to such a high bar could cause additional anxieties that may confuse or discourage us from working our recovery. We suggest that our plan be clear and measurable. We want to know whether we are on or off our plan quickly. This awareness helps us to be honest with ourselves and stay connected to our recovery.

Constructing our SRP also invites us to replace old attitudes about sexually compulsive behavior with new activities, people, places, and things in our lives. These are vital elements of our life which we neglected or never sought in our addictive past. Gradually we can add more and more positive sexual activities. For most SCA members, the SRP is continually deepening and evolving.

Some of us can alter our behavior immediately by following an SRP; others wean themselves away from practices they decide are harmful. Often, we decide on a "bottom line" of activities we do not indulge in under any circumstances. But while one purpose of an SRP is to keep us from "negotiating" with our compulsion, some might allow various types of sexual activity within a "gray area." Others may choose a period of complete abstinence in early recovery, or perhaps later if other plan attempts failed.

Many of us learn in sobriety that we are, in fact, afraid of non-compulsive sex. The Sexual Recovery Plan can be a means of reviewing these fears and of permitting ourselves to enjoy our sexuality - perhaps for the first time.

Why a Written Sexual Recovery Plan?

Most members find it useful to put their Sexual Recovery Plans in writing, working up a list of dos and don'ts for future behaviors. Committing our plan to paper helps us clarify our thoughts about sexual compulsions and romantic obsessions. Indeed, some members did not realize what they wanted their sex lives to be until they began writing their SRP.

One way to start is to decide which activities are harmful to us or others or made our lives unmanageable. For some, the starting point of an SRP is some particular activity they want to alter. Others might wish to rethink every aspect of their sexuality.

Having a written plan also prevents us from changing our Sexual Recovery Plan on the spot, such as when a sexual encounter presents itself. Otherwise, our defense mechanism of denial could tempt us to make sudden changes, depending upon the circumstances.

In addition to providing a guideline, making an SRP reminds us that we seek to overcome our initial fear and confusion. Other members' experience, strength, and hope may encourage us to find our path. We may discover that following a Sexual Recovery Plan also helps us make full use of the Twelve Steps and SCA tools.

What About Discussing My Sexual Recovery Plan with Others?

Many of us find this helpful. Throughout our lives, most sexual compulsives felt unable to discuss sex with anyone. We were unable to discuss the things that were causing us the most pain.

We thought of ourselves as unworthy or ineligible to receive the help and guidance available to "normal" people. Sharing our concerns with other members can help break destructive patterns of isolation and self-pity.

It's not advisable to make spontaneous changes in a Sexual Recovery Plan: ideally, we discuss them first with a sponsor or another member. Sharing our SRP gets it out of our heads and makes it tangible. We might discuss our plan with people in the program we have learned to trust. These discussions could be with a sponsor, at a meeting, or over coffee with a group. Our willingness to share with others can provide clarity and give us a more objective outlook.

What If Others Don't Like My Sexual Recovery Plan?

Nobody has the right to approve or disapprove of anybody else's Sexual Recovery Plan. The SCA *Statement of Purpose* explicitly states that members define sexual sobriety for themselves. We learn to become honest with ourselves and others without judging their SRP. Having a non-judgmental attitude helps foster an atmosphere of love and support, which promotes healing and recovery. By discouraging gossip and criticism, we help maintain SCA as a safe environment.

What Will a Sexual Recovery Plan Do for Me?

We can create our Sexual Recovery Plan at any time in our recovery. Some members might do so as soon as they start attending meetings, or perhaps as soon as they find a sponsor. Others may choose to write their plan when they begin to work the Twelve Steps.

In any case, the first two Steps may provide some guidance, regardless of whether we have formally worked them. Reading or hearing them can help guide us. First, "we admitted we were powerless over sexual compulsion – that our lives had become unmanageable." Second, we "came to believe that a Power greater than ourselves could restore us to sanity." An SRP starts with these principles: by admitting our powerlessness and unmanageability and asking for assistance from our Higher Power, we can replace harmful sexuality with a positive and affirming one. As we progress in recovery, we may want to make changes to our plan.

SCA members define sobriety for themselves. *Abstinence, partial or total*, is a tool that members can use to clarify the choices they want to make with their sexuality. The goal is not to eliminate or repress our sexuality but rather to integrate it into our lives as a healthy element. Like the compulsive overeater, we aim to achieve freedom and responsibility while engaging in a fundamentally human process. We can seek our Higher Power's guidance in determining which sexual actions, relationships, environments, and things are appropriate for our lives.

How Do I Write a Sexual Recovery Plan?

Listed below are several suggested formats for writing a Sexual Recovery Plan. Many members find it helpful to change their plan as they gain insight into their sexual compulsion and progress in their spiritual recovery. We might consider such changes after talking to a sponsor or other trusted friend in recovery. Some members may choose to use columns to define their plan. They may wish to set up several categories:

- By asking for our Higher Power's assistance, we look for relief from the actions, people, places, and things that have made our lives unmanageable. We may wish to list these and identify them as "bottom line" behaviors. If we are using columns, we can place these in our 1st column.

- We may list the times and places in which our compulsions most frequently happen, including periods of emotional stress caused by family, work, relationships, etc. We might also note when we are triggered by feelings that make us fantasize about our compulsive behaviors. Such feelings may be driven by our senses or by events. These "gray areas" could be included in a second column.
- In a new column, we can choose to add actions, goals, people, places, and things that may be desirable in our new life in recovery. We try to be realistic by adding items that we are willing to do, are enjoyable, and not something we think we "should" do. Nor do we need to impress others by adding such items. We can measure our sexual sobriety by our first column and our recovery by this column. When we're having difficulty abstaining from our first column behaviors, we can find strength from taking actions in this column.

By following a Sexual Recovery Plan, we move away from harmful behaviors. We find ourselves gaining time and energy that we had been spending on our compulsions. Adhering to our Sexual Recovery Plan provides us with the manageability that frees and enables us to build a new life in recovery and be of *service* to ourselves and others.

Examples of Sexual Recovery Plans

Recovery Plan One

Those people, places, and things I pray to my Higher Power to free me from:

- Hustlers.
- Love addictions and romantic obsessions.
- Compulsive cruising.
- Use of sex as a drug to escape from feelings.

These are the times I am most likely to act out:

- After leaving work until the early hours of the next morning.
- On the weekends.
- When I'm upset about anything.
- When I'm bored.

Those acts, people, places, and things I want to add to my new life of recovery:

- A period of healing and professional, emotional, and spiritual growth.
- An improved ability to keep my attention in the present moment.
- One more day of sobriety on this plan.

<u>Recovery Plan Two</u>

Those people, places, and things I pray to my Higher Power to free me from:

- Compulsive masturbation.
- Sex on the first encounter.
- Sex is the sole activity of the encounter.
- Sex is the primary activity of the encounter.
- Sex is the reason for the encounter.
- Sex outside of a caring relationship.

Those acts, people, places, and things I want to add to my new life of recovery:

For today, healthy sexual behavior for me is part of an ongoing building of intimacy - an expression of an already existing intimacy. I am comfortable including the person with family and friends; I am interested in just necking with them; I am interested in sleeping with him; have already spent time with them with a nonsexual focus; interested in the person as a friend; willing to be a friend only.

Recovery Plan Three

Those people, places, and things I pray to my Higher Power to free me from:	*These are the times I am most likely to act out:*	*Those acts, people, places, and things I want to add to my new life of recovery:*
Anonymous sex. Hustlers. Poppers. Pornography. Obsessive/compulsive thinking.	Late night Before seeing my ex After a conflict with my supervisor After an argument with my partner	Meetings Program calls Prayer Clarity Journaling Exercise Sleep Healthy eating Music Truth Dating

Recovery Plan Four

After three years on a liberal plan, I had a massive one-day slip. Since then, I have had 90 days committed to total abstinence and a two-month relationship. I am now wholly and comfortably abstinent but interested in a committed relationship. My current plan:

- Sex only with someone with whom I have an emotional and social interest and where there is a possibility of mutual commitment.
- No masturbation.
- Try to get to know people who might be interesting.
- Join groups and go to dances where I might meet potential mates.

- Make dates with people on the street, but no instant sex.
- No cruising at the piers, bookstores, tea-rooms - don't even go in rest areas.
- No pornography, apps, or personal ads.
- Pray for God's help every morning and thank Him every night.

Recovery Plan Five

No sex at all. And no alcohol or drugs.

I started in SCA and AA at the same time. I knew that my sexual acting out was related to my drinking and drugging. After nine successful months with this plan, I decided to change it to allow sex under certain conditions and have been in a monogamous relationship for four months.

Recovery Plan Six

After staying sober on a loose Sexual Recovery Plan (I could do anything so long as I didn't do it compulsively), I entered a relationship and have since worked this plan:

- No sex except with my partner.
- No masturbation.

When I discovered that many personality problems were inhibiting me sexually, I added several new things to my plan. Some examples:

- Watch out for expectations and demands that are bound to be disappointing.
- Try to distinguish the desire for affection from the desire for sex.
- Pray for the grace to learn to trust: me, other people, my partner, the relationship, God.

<u>Recovery Plan Seven</u>

Some SCA members find it helpful to make a three-column plan, putting the behaviors they abstain from in the left column for which they count time on their plan. They may place "warning sign" behaviors in the middle column and list positive actions and goals in the right column:

Left Column	Middle Column	Right Column
No online chat rooms No online video galleries No porn websites	Sexting Stalking people on social media Isolating from people to be online	Socializing and being present Three meetings a week Going back to school

Recovery Plan Eight

Another Sexual Recovery Plan format may be a "quadrant approach." We place behaviors to abstain from and count time away from in the upper left box, "gray area behaviors" in the lower-left box, a positive action plan in the upper-right box, and positive goals and visions to work for in the lower-right box:

Things that I pray to my Higher Power to free me from	*Things that I pray to my Higher Power to bring into my life*
Bottom Lines:	**Action Plan**:
GPS-based hook-up apps Anonymous sex Sex without disclosing my status	Work the 12-Steps Find a God concept that works for me Being of service to the program and my fellows
Gray Area:	**Goals and Visions**:
Being on my phone instead of being present with others Posting suggestive pics on social media Only valuing people based on potential sex	Running a marathon Decluttering my place Traveling not being about acting out

Chapter 9: Using the Telephone in SCA

Making Calls

Isolation is a common trait among sexual compulsives, but one way to break out of it is by making program calls to other SCA members. It's one tool that's always within our reach, and it may serve as a lifeline to stay connected between meetings or when we're unable to get to a meeting.

A phone or video call can be a virtual personal connection and can be the next best thing to being there in person. It can be used as a daily check-in tool and is especially helpful during a crisis or when a member needs to hear a calm, friendly voice of support.

Some of us might prefer texts and emails, which can sometimes be more convenient and perhaps less intimidating. To some, texting or emailing seems the more comfortable option than speaking to a live person or leaving a voicemail. Sending messages can also be useful when short on time since they can be brief and to the point. We can send our message and get on with our lives and assume that the intended recipient will eventually read it and soon reply.

It's Not an Ordinary Phone Call

We define a "program call" loosely as making a call to another SCA member to help our recovery. Making such a call can be considered a leap of faith. We may not know how it will turn out, and we may not hear what we expected to hear. But we also open ourselves up to receiving a new perspective on our situation. Another member might impart their experience, strength, and hope so that we will find some benefit. Another person's story may be quite different from ours, but we may share common feelings of anxiety, fear, shame, etc., that may have contributed to our sexually compulsive behavior.

Aside from getting ourselves to a meeting, a program call also may be the best way to "short-circuit" a possible slip. Hearing another program member's voice and remembering that we are not alone often interrupts that feeling that "we just have to act out now!" If anything, it may help us postpone the slip until we can make it to our next meeting.

It may be helpful to ask our Higher Power to be present when we call someone. This action may help guide us, allow us to be rigorously honest, and give us the wisdom to recognize and accept what we hear from another member.

Making program calls requires willingness. We do not try to over-analyze the situation or talk ourselves out of it: we make that call. It can be helpful to ask members for their phone numbers and to call them at least once. We can also encourage others to call us. By doing so, we may soon find that we have added several SCA members to our contact list.

Newcomers might start with a goal of one call a day. That may be all we need. Some members commit to making three program calls a day, some more. There is no "right" number of calls to make. Making those first calls might seem awkward and make us feel uncomfortable. Perhaps making several calls in one day might lessen those feelings. It doesn't matter if we think the calls are successful or not. At first, we're merely trying to learn to make them, not to enjoy them. The action right now is more important than the result.

Developing a Practice

An SCA program call isn't usually a social call. It's a spiritual tool, and we are mindful that the call not become an idle gab or gossip session. It isn't necessarily a means of striking up a friendship, though friendships often result. We don't necessarily call someone, then wait until they call us back before contacting them again. There may be various reasons the other person might not have returned the call, and these may not be relevant for us.

Making SCA calls takes practice. It helps to begin making program calls before we desperately *need* to call someone. Even if we're feeling fine, we can try calling another member to have a casual talk, perhaps to discuss something we heard at a meeting.

Be Thoughtful and Discreet

When making a call, it's good to ask the person if they have time to talk. We try to respect other people's bedtimes. It may be ok to call until 10 p.m., but we might check with them to see if they would be open to receiving late-night or early morning calls. Some people may be willing to accept urgent calls in the middle of the night, but others might set stricter time boundaries. We might also ask them if we can leave a program-related message on their voicemail.

We might not establish a fruitful connection with everyone we call. We may call several members before finding someone with whom we feel comfortable talking. But establishing such connections may turn out to be a valuable resource to help us get through rough times, especially if we're struggling with our sobriety.

It helps to be discreet when calling someone at work. We may learn that the person we're calling has visitors, is in a client meeting, or is out on the street. They might be unable to say, "I can't talk," graciously. If they do say that, we need not take this personally. They might need to devote their attention elsewhere at that moment. It's not a judgment on us.

We discuss beforehand with the person if it's okay to share personal information in our messages. Otherwise, when the person we call doesn't answer, we leave our name and number. We might also leave a longer message, depending upon circumstances. However, many voicemail systems have a timed "cut-off," making it impractical to leave an exceptionally long message. Just mentioning our concerns in the voicemail may provide some relief about an issue that is troubling us. Whatever we need to say, we can assume that the person we called will eventually hear it and may call us back sooner than we expected.

Making Connections

Once we have found someone with whom we're comfortable speaking on the phone, we can try calling them more often. If that member seems to keep their distance call after call, we can always look elsewhere. But we may also find that we have established a reliable connection with some members on our call list. We can then develop the confidence to talk to those members regularly.

One phone practice that many members have used is "book-ending." Book-ending involves a phone check-in with a sponsor or someone else in the program as a means to avoid a possible slip. We make calls before and after a triggering situation. It provides the feeling of bringing along a program friend to avoid facing the triggering experience alone.

Receiving Calls

Just as making an SCA phone call is different from making a regular call, receiving one from another member is also different. It can be as affirming to the person receiving the call as for the one making it. The experience of listening actively teaches us to be available to people in a new way. Learning how to take program calls is another way to help our sobriety.

We may wish to ask our Higher Power to be present and give us guidance in listening to and responding to the caller, just as we had asked before we called others. We can try to be the channel of our Higher Power's wisdom in responding to the caller.

The Art of Listening

Listening takes skill and patience. It's not a passive thing – it's a positive act that can be very loving for someone asking us for help. We may consider what's being said and discover what the caller needs from us. We may then be in a better position to offer our experience, strength, and hope.

We can inform our caller when we don't have much time to talk. We can set this boundary gently but firmly, giving them the option to call someone else. We may recall how it feels to be on the other end of the line. We try to be gentle and supportive, even when we're unable to speak to them at that moment. We have the right to set our boundaries regarding program calls or any calls. We may also recognize that our caller's sobriety could be in jeopardy and that they might be trying to find someone they can talk to *right now*. If the matter is less urgent, we can mutually agree to re-connect and speak at a different time.

If a caller asks for advice, we might refrain from offering specific suggestions and favor speaking about our own experience. We might suggest they read an appropriate piece of SCA literature or recall some of the slogans that many members have found useful to deal with stress, such as *First Things First; Easy Does It; Think the Slip Through; Don't Just Do Something - Sit There*, etc.

Twelfth Step Calls

Those who have taken on an outreach service position might engage in Twelfth Step Calls. An example might be answering a call to the local (or the international) SCA Hotline. Anyone in the world might call that Hotline. Perhaps it is someone who is suffering from sexual compulsion and who doesn't know where to turn. Perhaps it is a therapist or social worker looking for more information. Or maybe it is a graduate student who wants to attend an SCA meeting as part of their fieldwork for a thesis.

By answering that call and speaking to that person, we have established an initial SCA contact point for the caller. It could be the only exposure to SCA that the caller has for a long time, at least until they are ready to take the next step by attending a meeting.

When speaking to such callers, we give a general description of SCA, remembering that no one speaks on behalf of the program itself. We include a brief description of how the program works for us and how to access our meetings. We focus on the basics and our own experiences of joining SCA - we don't claim to have all the answers. We may wish to talk about some of the tools of recovery. But it’s not our job to engage in a free therapy session, even if we happen to be professionally qualified.

Some callers might go into graphic details about their sexual problems. This type of call may be triggering for us as a sexually compulsive person. We have no obligation to listen to more than we can handle out of politeness. It is okay to ask the caller not to use graphic descriptions; what we call "sensational language." We also try to be mindful at all times to respect their anonymity and to protect our own.

Pick up the Phone

The most valuable advice we can give on making program calls is: pick up the phone. Don’t think about it, do it.

Chapter 10: The Tool of Writing

Writing as a Recovery Tool

As we begin to attend meetings and work the SCA program, we learn that writing is a tool we can use to remain sexually sober. We may first use writing in developing our Sexual Recovery Plan. We find that by writing down our plan, we have a guide we can refer to when we are in a difficult place or are confused about what action we can take to remain sexually sober. Later, we learn that writing helps us work the Twelve Steps. It allows us to explore our thoughts and feelings, encourages us to develop a more grateful attitude, and facilitates communication with our Higher Power and other recovering sexual compulsives.

Writing and The Twelve Steps

Many of us use writing as we work the Twelve Steps of SCA. Some use Twelve Step workbooks, while others meet with other SCA members or sponsors in planning how we are going to take each Step. Many Steps will involve writing. Writing our First Step is a concrete way to get honest with ourselves about our powerlessness over our sexual compulsion and how unmanageable our lives had become.

In Step Four, we write our moral inventory, listing our character flaws, and our character assets. Through this process, we begin to see ourselves more realistically. Through this written task, we obtain a clearer picture of ourselves and our past. Our inventory becomes instrumental in completing many of the remaining Steps.

By Step Eight, we are ready to write a list of those persons we had harmed. We do this by starting with our written Fourth Step inventory and adding others' names we may have harmed since we took that inventory. Using this list, we ask our Higher Power for willingness to make amends to each one.

Some of us practice Step Ten by writing an inventory at the end of each day. We review the day by examining our interactions with others and contemplating our actions and motives to see if we acted according to our values and our Sexual Recovery Plan. Some of us also keep a written checklist of the SCA tools and mark how many of them we used that day. We use this tool to discover those instances when we are wrong, admitting it, and promptly taking corrective action.

In Step Eleven, some find it helps to write our meditations and prayers to enhance our conscious contact with God. Writing can be a powerful tool as we work Step Eleven, connecting us with our Higher Power.

Journaling

In our active sexual compulsion, we suppressed our thoughts and feelings by acting out. We medicated ourselves to avoid both negative and positive feelings and to repress painful or other intense thoughts. As we recover from sexual compulsion, we find the courage to face these thoughts and feelings. Some of us have found that writing our thoughts and feelings in a journal helps us clear the fog in our minds. Many of us do this as a daily practice, checking in, and learning to be rigorously honest with ourselves and our Higher Power. Our acting out prevented us from being in touch with our deeper feelings. Writing in a journal, expressing anything and everything that seems important to us, allows us to become more in touch with our thoughts, opinions, and feelings. Some of our feelings may revolve around shame. By writing out these feelings and the reasons behind them, we begin to let go of the shame and move toward putting it behind us.

When we face a difficult situation in our job, in a relationship, or encounter a powerful sexual trigger, journaling can help ground us emotionally. If we obsess about a particular outcome, writing out our feelings helps us turn the obsession over to our Higher Power. Sometimes our feelings and thoughts are in knots, flying in many directions, or trapped whirling in circles in our mind. Focusing ourselves to write about them can help center us and, at times, be the key that helps us discern God's will for us. When we are in a slippery moment, writing in our journal will sometimes ease us out of it. Writing out how we got through our difficulties is far healthier than acting out on them.

There are those of us who find journal writing overwhelming. As we face a blank page in our journal, we are at a loss about how to start. We can remember that writing in a journal is not an academic exercise. No one else will read our notes, so each journal entry's shape and form can be anything we need it to be. We may sometimes want to write down whatever random thoughts and feelings we have, regardless of whether our sentences are complete, connected, or grammatically correct. Some call this stream-of-consciousness writing - a way to tap into our feelings and emotions. Some might try using their non-dominant hand to make journal entries. This technique may help us to record our feelings in a more child-like way. We do not need to edit our writing except to add clarity for ourselves.

Our only standard as we write is to remain rigorously honest with ourselves.

We protect our journal from others who might read it without our permission. We can only be completely honest with ourselves if we ensure that nobody will read our journal except us. We may share parts of our journal with others, but we take care to avoid sharing our most profound feelings with someone who would betray our trust. Our journal is primarily a tool to communicate with ourselves and our Higher Power. We are mindful of where we keep our journal, ensuring it is only accessible to us.

There are times when we might wish to share some of the insights that we have received from our journal writing, even if it's with only one other person, such as our sponsor or a program friend. We don't want to use our journal as another way of isolating ourselves from others, as we did when we were acting out. As we get in touch with our deeper feelings through writing, we can look for ways to express those feelings with those we can trust.

Gratitude List

Many of us tend to focus on all we don't have in our lives, not seeing what we can be grateful for. Our feelings of shame or perfectionism may affect how we view ourselves and our surroundings. Expressions of gratitude can change that perspective. Some of us write a gratitude list daily. We may start with the "obvious" - being thankful for having food on the table and a roof over our heads. We note a kind comment that we received from an acquaintance. As we continue this practice, we begin to experience a change in our attitude. We may begin to see the good things about a job we previously felt negatively about. We may also start to see the positive aspects of a relationship we previously resented. We may find that we are no longer victims of uncontrollable events, but rather a recipient of gifts given through the care of our Higher Power. Our gratitude list helps us to be aware of how abundant our lives are.

Letter Writing and Emails

Many of us find that we can remain connected with other recovering sexually compulsive people by sending emails, texting, or posting on social media. Some might prefer to send letters. Either way, sharing our lives with others by writing keeps us from isolating ourselves, a habit that some of us cultivated while actively pursuing our sexual compulsion. Virtual attendance and online communications can be a precious link to the program for those who can't attend meetings because of distance or other matters. We can develop healthy relationships with other SCA members by using these forms of communication. These connections help us to review where we are in our lives and our program as we try to communicate these things in writing. We often gain new insight into our feelings, thoughts, and situation as we try to express ourselves to others in writing. However, for some of us, *any* use of social media may cause undue risk in staying sexually sober. We may want to be mindful of how we reach out to others through social media, as these communications may be addictive or triggering.

There are times when we need to have our sponsor or someone else review a written message that we are about to send, especially if it involves an emotionally charged issue. This pause helps us minimize the potential of harming others. In these situations, we listen to the feedback that our sponsor and others may give us. It may be healthier not to send the message, but writing helped us understand and process our feelings. In other cases, we rewrite it, removing accusatory language, and admitting our part in a situation.

Summary

Writing is an effective way to work our program. We work on many of the Twelve Steps through writing and find that it provides a way to measure our progress. By journaling to express our thoughts and feelings, we can better understand ourselves, our values, and our motives. We frequently write out a gratitude list to recognize all the good things we have in our lives. Writing is one of the foundations on which we build a sexually sober life in recovery.

Chapter 11: Sobriety and Responsibility

The SCA *Statement of Purpose* states that our goal is sexual sobriety. We don't advocate celibacy, abstinence, or repression of our basic needs for comfort or love. Instead, we try to integrate sexuality into our lives as a healthy element.

We use the term sobriety because of its more profound connotation of clarity of mind. In sobriety, we are making healthy sexual choices. In compulsion and addiction, we are driven and compelled to engage in sexual behaviors that ultimately hurt us or others.

We might loosely define responsible sexuality as making choices that protect ourselves and others while expressing our sexuality. In this usage, responsibility refers to behavior. SCA is not a behavior modification program: it is a spiritual program. We change our behavior due to the freedom we experience on the spiritual path of this program. In working the Twelve Steps and using the program's tools, we achieve sober clarity of mind, which frees us to make choices rather than be bound by our compulsion. In meetings and through working the Steps, we learn that a Power greater than ourselves can restore us to sanity.

In turning our will and our lives over to the care of our Higher Power, we receive the strength and courage to make choices that we were unable to exercise previously. The SCA program focuses our attention on the source of strength, wisdom, and acceptance, which empowers us with the freedom to make choices, rather than on the unhealthy and often dangerous sexual behavior we want to stop.

Taking responsibility depends upon our willingness to change behaviors as we grow spiritually. When we change our behavior, our lives expand, we become more engaged, and our lives continue to change for the better.

In making sober choices, we become sexually responsible. We change our lives and may experience some of the benefits described in SCA's "The Gifts of Recovery," which appears in Chapter 19 of this book.

One definition of sexual sobriety, which respects an individual's obligation to assume responsibility for their life, reads as follows: Sexual sobriety is an individual abiding by their Sexual Recovery Plan. A Sexual Recovery Plan is a written plan, shared with our Higher Power and another member of the SCA program, preferably a sponsor, and is measurable one day at a time.

Chapter 12: Fourteen Ways to Avoid a Slip

A slip can be an annoying, even painful consequence of an SCA member's desire to seek instant gratification compulsively. Our disease is cunning, baffling, and insidious and is always seeking new ways to trick us into submission.

Predispositions to a Slip

There is a "predisposition" to a slip that we can't always recognize, though sometimes it can be sensed by others. It might include being irritable, depressed, unconnected. We slyly work up to this predisposition. When we have a slip, it is almost always because we talk ourselves into it. Therefore, what we want to do is learn to break deep-rooted patterns. Here are some of the times when our defenses may be weak:

- When things go badly;
- When things go well;
- When we visit our families;
- When we come back from visiting our families;
- When we're in a relationship;
- When we're not in a relationship;
- When our Sexual Recovery Plan isn't working for us;
- When we're secretive, are involved in anything abusive (to ourselves or others), are out of touch with our feelings, or are feeling empty;
- When we're Hungry, Angry, Lonely, Tired (HALT).

Danger Signals to Watch For

Sexual compulsion often sneaks up on us and can easily persuade us that we need to act out even when we don't want to. Not all of the following danger signals will apply to every member, but we may all be able to identify with some of them:

- Wanting a cigarette or a drink;
- Compulsively watching TV or movies;
- Compulsively shopping, eating, doing crossword puzzles, etcetera;
- Compulsively viewing internet images that may involve "soft porn" or other triggering images;
- Reading stories glorifying specific sexual activities or fetishes;
- Compulsively staring at people or their profiles on acting-out apps or webcams;
- Cutting off communication and starting to isolate;
- Letting go of the spiritual side of things. Abandoning ourselves, walking out on ourselves; Cutting down on meetings;
- Indulging in negative thinking (*What's the use - everyone's against me*);
- We abandon healthy disciplines: we don't shave or brush our teeth, don't do our exercises, don't make our phone calls, don't clean our homes, buy groceries, or open mail;
- We begin to lie to ourselves and other people. We have a lot of secrets, including irrelevant, unimportant ones. We don't

want to come out of the shadowy world into the real one, so we need to maintain the "unreal" aspect of it in every way we can;

- Looking for escapes from various areas of our lives;
- When we don't feel centered: when our lives turn chaotic and unmanageable.

The Number One Offender

Resentment destroys more sexual compulsives than anything else. Because what better way to "get even" than by acting out? It begins to seem a solution, a weapon, a means of revenge. It's a way to make people see how they've hurt us.

Consciously or unconsciously, we seek out reasons to justify a slip. *Our life is turning sour. Nobody understands us. Nothing is going right.*

We feel lonely and hurt, and we begin wanting to get back at people: the man in the street who bumped into us, our bosses, our lovers, our parents, ourselves. Even God (after all, God is responsible for our feeling so hurt and disappointed, right? Then we want God to be hurt and disappointed, too).

Our anger feels righteous, and we cling to it. Nothing is going to make us give it away. And when we note the beginning symptoms of sexual compulsion, they only make us angrier.

We start blowing up at people. Or else we suppress the anger, imploding instead of exploding. We may appear relatively calm and reasonable on the outside, while inside, we're simmering with pain and resentment.

Instead of finding ways to heal the situations that cause our distress, we feed on our resentment in a continuing downward spiral. We secretly don't want to mollify the anger because it does for our compulsion what lighter fluid does for a campfire. Gradually, all the good things about our life lose meaning for us, opening the way for our sexual compulsion to come raging in, unchallenged.

The Start of the Slip

The process begins to intensify. A mysterious force seems to be taking us over, and we become fascinated by it, slowly letting go of healthy disciplines and slipping into an almost hypnotic state. These are some of the "rituals" we may indulge in that subtly undermine our healthy thinking:

- We begin to masturbate compulsively;
- We go out without underwear;
- We wander around areas where we know we have acted out in the past;
- We miss meetings we planned to attend;
- We avoid SCA contacts;
- The thought of going to a meeting seems threatening: it's the last thing we want to do;
- We begin dwelling on past adventures. We try on our "acting-out" clothes;
- We begin brooding over pornography, apps, or webcams;
- We pore over internet hookup sites or messages;
- We start rationalizing the slip. "I'm getting older." "Married people have sex all the time." "I've had a miserable week;"
- We don't want to make a phone call. We don't want to give

the slip away or have anybody taking it from us;

- We're full of denial. We tell ourselves that we're not sexual compulsives at all: everybody does these things, it's perfectly normal to go out and have a good time;
- Or we have thoughts like, "I'm not like all those other people in SCA; they could never understand me and my needs. It's my private thing, and I have the right to it;"
- SCA begins to seem like the enemy. "They're all so self-righteous." "It may be good for them but not for me." "They're conning themselves."

We tell ourselves we're only going out to have a look. Or that we'll only act out this one time, tonight, go on that app or unlock that laptop this one time, and go back to SCA tomorrow. Somehow, we seem to be on auto-drive. Our attention is distracted to places we didn't mean to go. There's still a chance to pull ourselves out of the slip. But that feels like the last thing we want to do.

How to Get out of a Slip

We become willing to tolerate a frustrated impulse's discomfort - a challenging thing to do. Because not acting out is like developing a new muscle. It feels as though there's something wrong, that we're being brainwashed and making a terrible mistake.

Ironically, many of us sexual compulsives seem on the surface to be easygoing and flexible people. But when it comes to changing our minds about acting out, it would appear no force on earth can stop us. Here are some practical suggestions designed to break through the sexually compulsive urge to act out.

1. **Pick up the phone.** We don't need to assume that people don't want to be bothered: making phone calls is a tool we can use to stay sober. SCA can be a selfish program, and everything we do in it - including making phone calls - is for our sobriety. We can try calling somebody with a lot of sobriety. In times of danger, it's more important than ever to "stick with the winners."
2. **Get to a meeting.** We can drag ourselves to a meeting, even if we don't want to - especially if we don't want to. We don't talk about it, we just go. If it's a virtual meeting, we can pick up the phone and dial in, or put on some clothes and click to join the "room." We can do this even if we feel that we will die if we don't act out. We can always "bring the body" when the mind doesn't want us to get better. We can go to meetings, even when there is something "more important" or more exciting or more fun to do. Doing this may gradually restore our values and priorities.
3. **Take the First Step**. Repeat the words "We admitted we were powerless over sexual compulsion – that our lives had become unmanageable," until the meaning begins to sink in. If we accept that we have no power over our compulsion, we will be able to turn it over - to our Higher Power, to our sponsor, to the program.
4. **Get an interim sponsor.** It doesn't have to be a permanent marriage. Asking for help is a positive action. It's critical when we are struggling.
5. **Read SCA literature.** It's our "meeting between meetings," and doing so can help us find our bearings until we can speak with another member. It also deepens our knowledge of the program and of how to use the tools of recovery.
6. **Review our Sexual Recovery Plan.** Remembering our goals helps us lose the craving to go back to the anguish and confusion we have so often experienced.

7. **Postpone the slip.** We can always put it off until later. In the meantime, we can talk to our sponsor or another member.
8. **Pray.** We can pray for help from our Higher Power as we understand it. The Serenity Prayer can be helpful: "God grant me the serenity to accept the things I cannot change, courage to change the things I can, and wisdom to know the difference." Some of us use it as a mantra in emergencies, saying it repeatedly until the crisis passes.
9. **Break the habit pattern.** We can't get sober in a vacuum. Merely stopping the destructive behavior is just the beginning: we replace it with healthy new activities. Often, we are as compulsive for a time about sobriety as we were about acting out. We might try taking creative actions, including new activities that we have considered adding to our Third Column.
10. **90 meetings in 90 days.** A surefire way to learn the true meaning of "First Things First." Making a meeting every day, no matter what, is a powerful tool to counteract ingrained habits of "giving in" and self-indulgence. These habits can seem to be so much a part of our character that we can forget that they are expressions of our illness.
11. **Deep breathing.** Deep breathing or other healing physical activities may help counter the effects of a panic attack. Affirmations to ourselves - in front of a mirror, or otherwise - may also be calming.
12. **Become willing.** We can be open to the possibility of giving up the slip rather than giving in to it. We may feel that there's no way we can break the power of our self-will. But we can take positive action. Willingness is action. We can try to remember that there is hope, and there is a future.

13. **Think the slip through.** We can ask ourselves if we will indeed get what we think we want by acting out. We can dwell less on the excitement that we associate with it but reflect more about its aftermath's invariable misery.
14. **Acceptance.** We don't need to blame ourselves for wanting a slip. But we don't need to give in to our compulsion.

Many sexual compulsives have a profound fear of making commitments of any kind because the disease in us is so threatened by it. But by going to meetings and working our program, we accept the idea that "I Am Responsible," perhaps initially for small things like getting chairs arranged or put away. Later, we might volunteer to hold a service position. This service position may involve carrying the message to others. And then - slowly, subtly, and usually without knowing how it happened - we discover that we are taking responsibility for our own lives for the first time.

What to Do After a Slip

We can take responsibility for the slip. It isn't the end of the world. The slip may have been the very thing we needed to let go finally. But we accept responsibility for it. The slip didn't happen to somebody else. It wasn't anybody else's fault. We allowed it to happen because we weren't working our program properly. And now we can change that. The first thing to recognize is that the disease wants us to feel guilty and miserable. That way, we have little choice but to continue acting out, to numb the pain of our self-hate. We try to short-circuit the tendency to isolate ourselves from the very people who can help us.

When any of us has a slip, we have it for all of us. And when we recover from the slip, we recover for all of us. One way to work through the agony is to share it and reconnect with the program in as many ways as possible. We try to make that reconnection a more profound commitment than last time. We might call another member and tell them what happened. It might be our sponsor or any program friend we feel comfortable contacting. The worst thing we can do is hold it in and let shame and isolation build up to set us off on another slip, which may escalate into a binge.

Getting to a meeting right away can be helpful. We can talk about the slip, knowing that we share our pain with people who can help us. We can develop trust in the program and the people in it. We've all suffered the pangs of sexual compulsion, or we wouldn't be here. We're not in SCA to judge each other, only to help each other get well.

Every slip has a painful but priceless lesson to teach us. We review our program and our lives to see what we were doing that might have led to the slip. Next, we try to make sure we don't make the same mistake again. We can ask ourselves questions like:

- Do I have a sponsor?
- Am I using them effectively?
- Am I working the Steps?
- Am I connected to the fellowship? Going to meetings, doing service, going out with the group for coffee, or food after meetings?
- Do I call people every day?
- Is my Sexual Recovery Plan too severe, too vague, too flexible?

- Am I moving ahead with my life?
- Am I making any effort to integrate sex into my life as a healthy element?

Compulsive sex is a cleverly wrapped package that, when we open it, always turns out to be full of disillusion and pain. By recognizing the tremendous power of the disease in us, we can surrender to the power of SCA's First Step. And that can be the beginning of more profound sobriety than we ever dreamed possible.

Chapter 13: Avoiding Common Pitfalls on the Road of Recovery

In our experience, recovery is not a destination but a journey of self-discovery. Our sexual compulsion continues to be cunning, baffling, and powerful, even as we walk this road of recovery. Though we may have joined Sexual Compulsives Anonymous with tremendous enthusiasm and began to enjoy sexual sobriety, most of us encountered certain pitfalls along the way.

Below we describe some of the frequent diversions that can cause us to veer off the path of recovery. We have grouped them according to when they are most likely to occur, but we may run into any of them at any time in recovery. We also offer suggested courses of action to take when they arise.

Keep in mind that SCA is a spiritual program, offering a spiritual solution to the problem of sexual compulsion. We do not speak of being "cured" of sexual compulsion. The book, Alcoholics Anonymous, 4th Edition tells us, "What we really have is a daily reprieve contingent on the maintenance of our spiritual condition" (Page 85).

Taking any of these actions alone may not be enough to keep us sober, but many sexual compulsives have found them to be helpful. Our willingness to take suggested courses of action shows that we want recovery and demonstrates our openness to allowing our Higher Power to help us. Many recovering sexual compulsives can confirm that in difficult times, "God is doing for us what we could not do for ourselves" (Alcoholics Anonymous, Page 84).

It's a good idea for a driver on the road to be prepared by taking driver training courses and ensuring there is a spare tire in the trunk. By being forewarned, you can recognize hazards when they arise and be prepared to face them. The same goes for using the Twelve Steps of SCA and developing a relationship with a Higher Power.

Common Pitfalls for Newcomers

Compare and Despair: We can sometimes have trouble identifying with people in the rooms. We can get distracted by perceived differences. We may have thoughts like, "They're so much older (or younger) than me," "Their sexuality or acting out is different than mine," "Their Sexual Recovery Plans are too strict."

Actions we can take: We remember helpful slogans like *Principles Before Personalities* and *Take What You Like and Leave the Rest*. We try to attend at least six meetings before deciding whether a meeting or even the SCA Fellowship overall is for us. If our area has many meetings, we try to attend several different ones. We might also attend phone or online meetings. Attending other meetings enables us to meet various members and hear different members' histories and experiences in recovery. We look for the similarities, rather than differences – to identify with the feelings, not the facts, of what we hear. Over time, we come to recognize that all SCA members identify with the powerlessness and unmanageability of compulsive sexual behaviors, whatever their individual stories may be.

Terminal Uniqueness: We may take the attitude that no one else understands us or that our experiences are unique. Members who fall into this trap tend to close their minds (and often their ears) to any evidence that other SCA members have problems much like theirs.

Actions we can take: One of the most effective ways of dispelling terminal uniqueness is reading SCA and other Twelve Step program literature. They contain descriptions of people's attitudes, thought processes, compulsive behaviors, and compelling personal stories of people in recovery from all walks of life. Reading recovery literature can open the eyes of even the sexual compulsive who is determined to use their "terminal uniqueness" to reject the SCA program. We also encourage listening to others' shares at meetings. We keep sharing as much of our own stories at meetings as we are willing. Many of us have felt terminally unique at least to some degree – until the day that we heard someone else tell "our" story and recognized that we do indeed have things in common with other SCA members.

Cliquishness and Exclusion: Expressions of openness and inclusion foster unity within the fellowship and help us become more accepting of others and ourselves. However, we can sometimes lose sight of this principle and seek to stay within our comfort zone by excluding others. For example, we might only go out for fellowship with members we know. Many who seek recovery in SCA rooms feel separate and isolated from the rest of the group. We may feel invisible or observe others who are "part of the gang" receiving all the attention without including us. Sometimes we do not see our identities reflected in those around us and may feel the group is not welcoming us. If we are a regular group member, we may feel more comfortable staying close to those we already know. Some of us tend to include only newcomers we find physically attractive. It may feel awkward approaching unfamiliar people or those that we perceive as "different." These perceptions of alienation and cliquishness reduce the unity and cohesion within the group and the fellowship and are detrimental to individual recovery.

Actions we can take: We can remember how it felt for us when we were new to SCA and make a conscious effort to reach out to newcomers and people we don't know. Making connections with diverse members can expand our awareness of recovery issues we may never have previously considered. Our welcome will never be perfect, but neither is our recovery: if we want to make progress, it is beneficial to reach out to others who share our disease. Reaching out requires effort since we often take comfort in being part of a group to which we already belong. Introducing ourselves and extending a friendly greeting can mitigate the isolation many may feel. If group fellowship is happening, it benefits everyone's recovery to invite those who may seem different or "not part of" to come along. Once we break down the initial barriers that separate us, we find that what we have in common enhances our recovery as sexual compulsives.

Fear of Losing Friends and Changing Our Lifestyle: Our patterns of acting out put us in contact with people who may share our sexual compulsion – both those with whom we have acted out and those with whom we've shared euphoric recall of our sexual encounters. Such people might not share our desire for a new way of life and may not understand or support our efforts to stop having compulsive sex. Also, specific neighborhoods, business establishments, apps, websites, publications, and types of parties often beckon us to return to old behaviors. Some of us found that particular articles of clothing or other objects could trigger obsessive fantasies. If we do not take action, we may find ourselves running back to these people, places, and things, and our old ways of behaving.

Actions we can take: We try to accept that being around certain people, places, and things that trigger us can jeopardize our sobriety, and we choose to avoid them. We seek the company of people in recovery – not just at fellowship after meetings, but between meetings, too. We invite other members to participate in sober activities, such as seeing films, concerts, and shows. We plan visits to museums, go to restaurants (even if it's just for coffee or dessert), or host (or help others host) a game or movie night. In doing so, we may come to agree with the simple wisdom of SCA members who say, "If you want to avoid a slip, you avoid slippery places."

Having Sex with Another Member of the fellowship: There's a good reason for this wording in our *Closing statement*: "We suggest that sex between members not be treated lightly. Sex between people new to the fellowship and other members is discouraged." We may find ourselves attracted to people at SCA meetings. This attraction is natural, but what do we do with those feelings? Having sex with another SCA member can derail our program by distracting us from our primary purpose: to stop having compulsive sex and help others achieve sexual sobriety. Having sex with other SCA members can create awkwardness when we see the other person in the rooms and can foster gossip and uncomfortable feelings for either (or both) of us.

Actions we can take: For the sake of our recovery, we may want to avoid contact with SCA members to whom we're strongly attracted. In some instances, we may find that by starting a conversation with the person we're attracted to, we break the mystique we created around that person, and our obsession diminishes. We seek our sponsors' input as to whether it would be better to avoid these people or cautiously engage with them to humanize rather than idolize them. We might seek guidance from a fellow recovering sexual compulsive who has experience and objectivity in making this choice.

Common Pitfalls Further Down the Road of Recovery

Illusion That Recovery Is Making Things Worse: As we continue the process of SCA recovery, sometimes our lives may initially seem to be getting worse, not better. Even if we are abstaining from sexually compulsive behaviors, other addictive behaviors may sprout up in their place. We can expect such sudden cravings to appear. It can feel uncomfortable when we let go of old thoughts and behaviors before establishing new, healthier ones. This period is a critical time in our recovery process. Before recovery, we could often escape unpleasant and unfamiliar feelings by numbing out with compulsive sex. When we abstain from addictive behaviors, we may begin to experience painful symptoms of withdrawal.

Actions we can take: We can practice keeping our perspective. We can remember the slogan: *This Too Shall Pass*. The SCA pamphlet titled *Moving Through Withdrawal* reminds us that others have gone through what we're experiencing and have come out the other side better for it. Also, we share at meetings about how we are feeling and what we are experiencing. We reach out to other members and ask for help and support. We may be surprised at the support we get by showing our vulnerability. During times like this, we may find that we forge friendships with other recovering sexual compulsives who will become close friends in recovery. We realize that a healing process is taking place, causing discomfort, and may not be progressing according to our preferred timetable.

Frustration at Slow Progress: As sexual compulsives, we are accustomed to instant gratification. Accordingly, we tend to seek a "quick fix" to our problems. We hear about *The Promises* as described in the book Alcoholics Anonymous, and when we don't see them materializing right away, we may become discouraged and return to compulsive sex. We then remember that *The Promises* appear in the context of working the Ninth Step, although many of us have found some of them begin to come true for us even before we have fully completed this Step.

Actions we can take: First, we remind ourselves that our recovery follows our Higher Power's schedule, not our own. We work the Twelve Steps and use *The Tools That Help Us Get Better*, then let go of the outcome. We compare how we used to spend our time versus how we spend it now. We recall the negative consequences we suffered when acting out and ask ourselves if we are experiencing them at the moment or if we are free of them. We consider whether we had any hope for changing our life patterns before joining SCA. Writing the answers to some of these questions can provide us with a fresh perspective. Often, we are the last ones to notice our improvement. We can also find encouragement from reading SCA's *The Gifts of Recovery*.

Believing We're "Fixed:" Sometimes, in recovery, our outer circumstances change for the better. We may get the job we've always wanted, go back to school, or get involved in a new relationship. The job, school, or relationship then starts to take up the time we previously devoted to attending meetings and working on our program. Our new significant other can become our new Higher Power. We may forget that SCA recovery is what made it possible to have a stable job or relationship. We may even conclude that our lives' positive developments are evidence that we are "cured" and no longer need to work the SCA program. We have seen many members stop attending SCA meetings at this point. For members who make this choice, everything may seem stable for a while. However, when problems arise under these new circumstances, they may be genuinely surprised to find themselves returning to their old acting out behaviors.

Actions we can take: We may want to keep this slogan in mind: *Once an addict, always an addict*. That may seem like a harsh verdict, but it is the bitter experience of many people who have turned to Twelve Step programs and found relief from their compulsive behavior, one day at a time. It's not an admission of hopelessness. On the contrary, it reminds us that there is a process in the first Three Steps which we keep in mind – admitting our powerlessness, believing in a Power greater than ourselves, and turning our will and our lives over. We were honest with ourselves about our compulsion; we became open to a Higher Power in our lives and willing to let go of our need to be the only one in charge. Our lives may have gotten better by working the SCA program, but that doesn't mean that we don't need it anymore. Besides, we consider this thought: If our lives got better by working the program, doesn't it make sense that they would keep getting better if we keep working it? Another slogan we remember is *First Things First*. A truism is, "When you put your recovery first, everything that comes second becomes first-class." Working our SCA program empowers us to make better choices and promotes serenity to accept "life on life's terms" when things don't go the way we had planned or hoped.

Feeling Entitled to a Reward: After a period of sexual sobriety, we may feel entitled to *reward* ourselves with compulsive sex. In recovery, it's vital to realize that the negative consequences of acting out are more significant than any short-term pleasure we may derive from these behaviors. Instead, choosing sober behavior gives us the long-term satisfaction we sought (but never found) by acting out.

Actions we can take: We review our Sexual Recovery Plans with our sponsors, paying particular attention to the list of positive things we want to do instead of acting out. Are the rewards listed things that we can get excited about doing, or are they merely a *should* list? Suppose we are used to the adrenaline rush of compulsive sex. In that case, we are unlikely to get very enthusiastic about rewards limited to things like eating more vegetables, losing weight, and cleaning our homes. We ask ourselves what we would be excited about doing. We try listing some items that are within easy reach and commit to doing them. But we also include some longer-term goal items, such as earning or saving money for a vacation, beautifying our home, or starting a garden. We imagine things we have always wanted to do but could never get around to doing because we were spending so much time or money (or both) on compulsive sex, and we add those to our list of rewards.

The "Geographic Cure:" Some of us decided to move to a new locale. We felt that our problems were *caused* by the people and situations around us, and the idea of starting a fresh new life in another city appealed to us. Unfortunately, those of us who have tried this approach soon found that our problems were within us, and we brought them with us no matter where we went. If we haven't made recovery our priority, the stress of moving can quickly lead us to compulsive sex in our new location. If SCA has meetings in our new area, we may choose not to attend them right away; we're too busy with the details of moving, and decide that we'll start going to meetings when things "settle down…" Of course, there are always virtual or phone meetings and these would likely be accessible no matter where we move to - if we choose to attend them! The idea of meeting a new group of SCA members or seeing familiar faces from our former locale in a virtual meeting might seem too much to digest while we adjust to our new environment. If we use these justifications to avoid meetings in our new location, it won't be long before we're finding new acting out places and partners. Ironically, our sexual compulsion often found it easier to acclimate to a new area than our recovering selves did!

Actions we can take: We resist the urge to relocate if that urge is driven by a desire to escape problems, rather than by sober reasons, like family obligations, a new job or business opportunity, or a healthy relationship. If we find ourselves wanting to run away from our present circumstances, we talk about it in meetings. We may be surprised how many members will relate and share what happened when they tried to move away and leave their addiction behind. If we've already moved, we may consult the SCA website to find nearby meetings. If no meetings are available in our new location, we might consider starting a new meeting. Reliance on our Higher Power can help us bloom where we are – and wherever we go!

Half Measures: We may be going through the motions – not attending meetings for weeks at a time, calling our sponsor only sporadically, or avoiding working the Steps. We treat the program as something useful but optional, failing to commit to recovery. We may ease off our "rigorous honesty" and begin telling half-truths – or refrain from sharing at meetings at all because the truth is not pretty, and we don't want to lie or look bad. Rationalization starts to set in. Or, we may take a legalistic approach, looking for a *loophole* in our Sexual Recovery Plan that would allow us to act out without it technically being a slip. The result? At best, our progress in the program slows (or stops altogether); at worst, we return to acting-out behaviors. Working a program half-heartedly (and getting little recovery as a result) can cause us to conclude, erroneously, that the program doesn't work for us.

Actions we can take: The book Alcoholics Anonymous, 4th Edition tells us, "Half measures availed us nothing" (page 59). We remember the fundamental slogan of Twelve Step recovery, *It Works If You Work It*. We ask ourselves, "Am I really working a program of recovery, or just dabbling in it?" We can prepare a daily program checklist, including prayer, attending meetings, making outreach calls, reading program literature, journaling, or Step writing. These tools can be an effective way to see, daily, whether we are truly "going to any lengths" for recovery, and if not, where we need to ramp up our efforts.

Complacency: At some point, we may become comfortable in our recovery and decide to "coast" by cutting back on working the Twelve Steps or reducing our use of tools such as meetings, using the phone, and service work. We may decide that attending a meeting that gets us home at 9 p.m. is too late – conveniently forgetting that we often stayed up past dawn while acting out. We may tell ourselves that we're "taking care of ourselves" by going home early and skipping a meeting – then end up online to look for compulsive sex "just for a little while."

Actions we can take: We take care of ourselves by working the SCA program and connecting with our Higher Power and other recovering sexual compulsives. In our experience, recovery is either on an upward spiral or a downward spiral. We remember that each seemingly minor decision we make can bring us closer to sexual sobriety or closer to a slip. Some of us say that the letters in the word "slip" stand for "Sobriety Losing Its Priority." Our recovery can get a boost when we attend meetings regularly, use *The Tools That Help Us Get Better*, and work the Twelve Steps with the same honesty, openness, and willingness we had as a newcomer. If we fill our days with those activities, rather than with compulsive sex, we feel better.

Putting Personalities Before Principles: The Twelfth Tradition reminds us to place "Principles Before Personalities." Unfortunately, it is easy to do the contrary and develop resentments toward people in SCA (or the program as a whole). We might look at a program phone list and say, "I'm not going to call this person; they're not taking the program seriously enough!" In the next breath, we can look at another name and think, "They're taking it way too seriously." One by one, we eliminate SCA members from our recovery circle until there is no one left to call. It's easy to become discouraged by seeing others in SCA having slips and sometimes relapses. We might decide that we don't like the format (the day, time, or location) of a meeting and use that as an excuse not to go. We can eliminate each meeting one by one until none are left that suit our capricious standards. We're still secretly drawn to acting out. We want to blame a slip or relapse on other people in the fellowship or on meetings that we have decided don't meet our own arbitrary needs.

Actions we can take: We recognize that any attitude we hold that gets in the way of attending meetings, interacting with fellow sufferers, reaching out to our Higher Power, using *The Tools*, or working the Steps endangers our sexual sobriety. Instead of finding fault with others, we recognize how their character defects may closely resemble our own. When we find ourselves criticizing some aspect of a meeting, we ask ourselves, "How important is it?" We can decide that our recovery is the most important thing, not whether we like every member of the program or whether a particular meeting suits our preferences.

Perfectionism: Before recovery, we might have thought that perfectionism was a character asset rather than a character defect. In early recovery, we often demanded too much of ourselves, too fast. Was our Sexual Recovery Plan too restrictive? Did we honestly want to stop doing the things that we defined as a slip? Or were we merely conforming to someone else's expectations, trying to impress our sponsor, therapist, or partner? We began to see that the problem was not our striving for success, but instead using our perfectionism as a way to sabotage ourselves. We are not saints. Our goal is spiritual progress, not spiritual perfection. Often, we find that "the perfect is the enemy of the good."

Actions we can take: We try to recognize how perfectionism can appear. Do we criticize others for not living up to our standards? If so, we aren't surprised when they pull away from us, leaving us feeling angry and lonely. Do we set impossibly high goals for ourselves, then stop trying when we fail to achieve them – or use this failure as permission to have a slip? Some of us tape this message to our bathroom mirror and read it aloud to ourselves every morning: "I am a good person. I am very good at being a person – I make mistakes."

Common Pitfalls for "Long-Timers"

Two Steps Forward, One Step Back: People with a long time in the program sometimes feel they should be further along, considering the amount of time they have been in recovery. It's easy to "compare and despair," comparing our insides to someone else's outsides. "Long-Timers" can be reluctant to share their day-to-day struggles in recovery for fear of "setting a bad example" for their sponsees and newcomers.

Actions we can take: We remember that recovery does not usually progress in a neat, linear fashion. We can expect frustrations and setbacks. However, over time, our lives improve as we continue to embrace recovery as a way of life. We remember to be gentle and kind to ourselves. If we do slip, we can be grateful for lessons learned that will help ourselves and others. We read the section in this book titled "Fourteen Ways to Avoid a Slip" and try some of the ideas it describes. Also, we remember that when Long Timers share their frustrations and struggles with other members, it doesn't set a bad example. On the contrary, it shows that no matter how long a member has been in SCA, life's challenges do not disappear. It's an opportunity for us to share with other members how we applied the spiritual solutions of the Twelve Steps and *The Tools That Help Us Get Better* to address life on life's terms.

Burnout: SCA members with longtime recovery can "burn out" by taking on too many service commitments or working with more sponsees than they can handle. They may begin to feel unappreciated or resent other members who are doing little or no service work. Spending hours talking with sponsees on the telephone or doing face-to-face Step work, carrying out service commitments at regular meetings, plus attendance at Intergroup or ISO business meetings can leave these Long-Timers feeling they need a break. Sometimes, rather than cutting back their service work to a more reasonable level, they make a complete break with the fellowship.

Actions we can take: We keep in mind the slogan, *Easy Does It*. We make a list of how we participate in SCA, both for our recovery and service, and review it with our sponsors. In doing so, we may realize that we have clung to specific service commitments to "make sure that they are done right," rather than allowing for the Twelve Step tradition of rotation of leadership. We may also realize that we did not share with our program friends or did not emphasize to our sponsees the value of the *Tool of Service* to strengthen their program. For SCA to survive and thrive, it cannot rely on only a few people who are willing to do service. A meeting in danger of closing due to a lack of people willing to do service may be just the wake-up call other members need to realize the importance of SCA service.

Conclusion

The First Step tells us we are powerless over sexual compulsion, but that doesn't mean we are helpless. We have found we can recover by taking specific actions to keep our feet on the road of recovery. We can think of each of the pitfalls as an obstacle to our recovery remaining from our compulsion.

Each of the above suggestions is a way to practice the Third Step – turning our will and our lives over to the care of God as we understand God. We may find it hard to choose which of these suggestions to follow. We can take time to pray and meditate about this. We can also talk it over with other recovering sexual compulsives, especially our sponsor. A common characteristic of these pitfalls is the tendency to try recovering alone. SCA is a "we" program, not a "me" program. Recovery is a shared experience. We gain strength from our fellows and give support in return.

Chapter 14: What About Masturbation?

Masturbation and Recovery

Masturbation may encompass many different experiences and as many different attitudes and opinions among SCA members. SCA neither endorses nor opposes masturbation. Members are encouraged to define their boundaries around masturbation: what works and what doesn't work for them.

Many of us began to masturbate during our childhood or teen years and may have continued to do so as adults, whether or not we were also engaging in other sexual behaviors. As the First Characteristic says: "As adolescents, we used fantasy and compulsive masturbation to avoid feelings and continued this tendency into our adult lives with compulsive sex."

We may have used masturbation as a substitute for sex with another person, or perhaps as a way to build up expectations ahead of other sexual behaviors. Some of us engaged in masturbation as an end in itself and found it difficult to set or maintain limits that would keep us from self-harm. Masturbation may have felt compulsive: we wanted that momentary *high* to last. We may have masturbated, again and again, trying to reach and maintain that feeling. By doing so, we could momentarily escape from less pleasant emotions, such as anxiety, fears, anger, and resentments.

When Is the Right Time to Address Masturbation Issues?

Those of us who have compulsive masturbation issues might consider including this on their "bottom line" or "First Column":

we would like to stop this compulsive activity. Masturbation, whether compulsive or otherwise, may often be associated with porn, webcams, phone sex, or other mediums for fantasies. Many of the characteristics of compulsive masturbation are common to compulsive behaviors involving porn, apps, the internet, etc. Those traits are listed and discussed in Chapter 17 of this book.

Taking Inventory

We may not be sure how masturbation fits into our sex lives. It may be a useful tool for some; for others, it may have become an unmanageable activity we are powerless to control. We can make an inventory of our masturbation behavior, which may provide some clarity. We might share our findings and discuss our masturbation history with our sponsor or another member as a basis to develop our Sexual Recovery Plan.

- How often do I masturbate?
- Is my masturbation habitual? Do I always masturbate at consistent times, in the same manner, and are my fantasies always the same? If so, how is this satisfying? And how is this unsatisfying?
- Do I sometimes or always feel compelled to masturbate?
- Can I easily abstain from masturbation?
- Do I ever abstain?
- Do I feel shame about masturbating or the fantasies used while masturbating?
- Am I focusing on masturbation to avoid dating and relationships?
- Do I generally masturbate to avoid feelings?
- Do I masturbate to avoid "worse acting out?"
- Do I masturbate to turn off my sexuality?

- Do I masturbate when I don't want to?
- Do I masturbate before acting out?
- Do I need accessories to masturbate (pornography, webcams, phones, sex toys, lubricants, etc.), and if so, what do they signify?
- When I have fantasies during masturbation, how do they relate to my current Sexual Recovery Plan? Are these fantasies risky for me, or am I comfortable knowing they are just fantasy?
- Have I ever injured or pained myself during masturbation?
- What do I feel before masturbation, and is there a pattern?
- What do I feel during masturbation, and is there a pattern?
- What do I feel after masturbation, and is there a pattern?
- Is my masturbation loving to me?
- Is my masturbation isolating?
- Does masturbation make my life in any way(s) unmanageable?
- Do I find any positives in masturbation?
- Do I use masturbation as a tool for my recovery?
- How does masturbation impact my relationships? My dating?
- How does masturbation impact my spirituality? My self-esteem?

This self-examination may help us to see both the positive and the negative aspects of our masturbation activities. We may then find it easier to discern what is healthy and harmful for us.

Shared Experience from Meetings

We attend SCA meetings to share our experience, strength and hope with other members. Others may talk about their masturbation experiences during their shares, and we may learn how they deal with these issues in their recovery. We may also speak of our own experiences, including difficulties we might be having with our masturbation behavior. We do this mindfully, avoiding provocative language that might "trigger" other members. Nevertheless, we remember that we are free to talk about anything we wish regarding our sexual compulsion during our shares.

Acting Out Is Not Loving

Many SCA members may discover apparent differences between "acting out" and loving sexual behavior. Some members might be unaware of their problems with masturbation; others might not have problems with masturbation. SCA encourages members to be guided in their recovery process by the principles of honesty, openness, and willingness.

Into Action

Having taken inventory of our masturbation behaviors and having shared about it with other members and with our sponsor, we can decide how masturbation fits into our Sexual Recovery Plan. We use this plan to list the behaviors that we consider harmful, including some or all of our masturbation activities. But we may also list those behaviors that we find affirming or healthy, and these may include masturbation in various forms. We might set certain limits or boundaries over frequency, duration, types of fantasies, and tools used, as well as listing appropriate places or other conditions for engaging in masturbation.

Constructing a plan that includes masturbation can involve trial and error. Our initial attempt might cause us to form too strict a plan - one that might set us up for repeated failures and frustration. Working with a sponsor or other trusted member may help us avoid making a too rigid or too flexible plan. We might also ask them for feedback before we make any decisions to change our plan.

Masturbation as Expression

Masturbation, for some, is a useful self-loving expression, an exploration of one's safe and sober sexual identity; an opportunity to feel the difference between object sex and personalized loving.

Some make a "date with themselves" to masturbate; some feel spontaneity is better for them. Some find masturbating without any fantasies a very different and self-loving experience. Some learn more about their sexuality and themselves from contemplating the implications of their fantasies.

We may redefine masturbation for ourselves, changing the focus from orgasm to sensuality, sometimes purposefully abstaining from orgasm. Some might romance themselves with music, candles, bubble baths, or other sensually pleasing external elements.

Some SCA members find masturbation works as a tool to relieve their desire to engage in bottom-line behavior(s). For some, masturbating includes beneficial elements of self-care and self-protection.

Living Our Plan

Over time, we may discover how masturbation fits in the context of our recovery. The differing emotions we experience during masturbation may help us determine the difference between "acting out" and self-love. Our Sexual Recovery Plan may have established new boundaries or limits for masturbation activity. As our recovery progresses, we can change our Sexual Recovery Plans. We can learn how to trust our Higher Power to help, sometimes sooner, sometimes later, to discover both a livable plan and lasting serenity.

Chapter 15: The Tool of Abstinence

SCA's *The Tools That Help Us Get Better* includes Abstention (partial or total). Our literature says: "We get support in SCA by abstaining from people, places or things that we consider harmful."

Abstention from certain sexually compulsive behaviors is a choice and a matter of discernment. Most of us entered SCA looking to break a cycle of sexual compulsivity, in whatever forms it took. We may have tried to break that cycle many times while trying to "control" our lives. Sure, abstaining from those behaviors sounds straightforward enough, but how do we achieve it? Telling ourselves, "I just won't do that anymore" seldom worked for long, and often many of us reverted to engaging in those harmful behaviors with even more intensity than we had done previously.

Unlike recovery from drugs and alcohol, when total abstinence from addictive substances is a measure of sobriety, completely removing sex from our lives is not an objective in SCA. Instead, it is to abstain from compulsive sexual behaviors that make our lives unmanageable so that we can integrate sex into our lives as a healthy element. We develop our definition of healthy sexuality over time, with the help of our Higher Power, our sponsor, our fellows, the Twelve Steps, and other tools of the program.

Our experience has shown that setting strict rules and regulations, or even "punishing" ourselves, doesn't remove our compulsions. We may stop engaging in our acting out behaviors for a while, but that period may be fraught with anxieties and painful withdrawal symptoms. By creating a Sexual Recovery Plan, in partnership with our sponsor, we define for ourselves the specific "...people, places, or things that we consider harmful." Discernment is useful when taking this inventory. We may find that total abstention from certain behaviors is possible or that partial abstention is more practical and preferable.

However imperfectly, we try to adhere to our plan, knowing that we can make adjustments as we move through our recovery. We can use the various tools of the program, such as attending meetings, socializing, working the Steps, making calls, reading literature, journaling, doing service, using slogans, etc., as a way to enhance spirituality, build self-esteem, and to find support within our community.

We often use the words "celibacy" and "abstention" interchangeably in casual conversation, but they typically don't mean the same thing. Celibacy is generally associated with a commitment not to have sex, either temporarily or permanently. Someone might make this decision based on a religious vow or a personal pledge. There may also be a medical or other reason why a person may practice celibacy. Our program does not consider celibacy a recovery tool in SCA, though some sexual compulsives may feel it best suits their needs.

Through Abstention, we may experience spiritual growth that frees us from the desire to engage in behaviors that could harm us or others. Instead, we can embrace activities we find healthy and affirming. We may find that practicing Abstention - total or partial - is a choice we can make, not a punishment to be endured.

Chapter 16: Recovery from Sexual Anorexia in SCA

Sexual anorexia is not the same thing as abstinence or celibacy. It is a compulsion to avoid sex and intimacy. Many sexual anorexics have found that by using the Steps and tools of SCA, they can be relieved of this compulsive avoidance of sex.

Sexual anorexia may be challenging to recognize in ourselves at first. When reviewing SCA's *Twenty Questions* to determine if we are sexually compulsive, we may only answer "yes" to a few. Still, when we read *The Characteristics Most of Us Seem to Have in Common*, we often identify with those relating to fantasy and obsession. We often relate to the feelings expressed by SCA members who share about their acting-out behaviors, even though we might not be engaging in any such activity.

We can be sexually anorexic with other people yet compulsively masturbate, lost in a cycle of obsession and fantasy. We may be entirely sex-avoidant. Instead of "acting out," many people who identify as sexually anorexic find themselves "acting in." It is not uncommon for sexual anorexics to feel deep shame about not having sex when we compare ourselves to our more sexually active friends in and out of fellowship.

Some of us have found ourselves to be sexually anorexic even when we have a partner - unable to be sexually and emotionally intimate with them. This inability to connect can be what drives us to act out in the first place. It is not that we recoil from sex itself. We may want to be fully sexual with someone, but creating an emotional connection seems impossible.

Sexual anorexia may develop from various causes, often originating from traumas as far back as childhood. Physical, emotional, or sexual abuse; incest; or neglect may have happened during our early years. Some of us may carry the weight from those traumas throughout our lives. Others may have repressed them or even forgotten them, only to have them re-appear in our consciousness as we began working on our recovery.

Our family of origin might have been an uncomfortable or even dangerous place for us. We may have been brought up in a strict religious family environment that often shamed us and forced us to repress our sexuality. Relatives, teachers, or religious leaders may have taught us that sex was dirty, low, or shameful and that the only acceptable form of sex was between husband and wife for procreation. We may have also experienced various types of body shaming that made us believe that nobody would want to have sex with us. Some of the shame we acquired from early teachings may have stayed with us. These may have been heightened by humiliations and embarrassments that we associated with our first sexual experiences.

As we grew older, we began to have sexual feelings. Some of us began engaging in sexually compulsive behavior, sensing that we were rebelling against the teachings that had shamed us in the past. Our desire to overcome inhibitions or leftover "critical inner voices" scolding us about sex might have made us even more determined to seek validation through sex. Some of us might have found that our initial sexual experiences reinforced those early lessons that sex is "bad," and we shied away from it.

Those who had suffered trauma may have felt repelled or even revolted by sex. The lack of any affirming sexual experiences added to these feelings. We may have hesitated to form relationships, even non-sexual ones. The struggle to escape intense feelings of shame, guilt, or terror might have driven us to distance ourselves from others.

Conversely, those of us who had been actively engaging in compulsive sex might have found ourselves “shutting down” our sex lives in early recovery. We tried to escape the cycle of behaviors we found damaging to us and others. At first, we may have felt a sense of relief that we had at least temporarily stopped acting out. But this relief might have soon faded, and a sense of emptiness eventually took over.

We may have found it relatively easy to stay on our Sexual Recovery Plan but may have struggled to define and seek healthy sexuality for ourselves. We knew that we didn’t want to revert to our previous sexual behaviors but may have had the feeling that seeking healthy sex just wasn’t worthwhile. We had let go of the sense of excitement that we associated with our earlier sexual behaviors, but stopping them left a void.

We may have had an unconscious desire to punish ourselves for previous excesses. If we couldn’t have sex the way we used to have it in our compulsion, then we shouldn’t have any sex at all. Perhaps we told ourselves that we had no idea how to have healthy sex - it was just a phrase we heard in the rooms of SCA. Other people seemed to have healthy sex; we thought we didn’t deserve it.

Some of us had intimacy issues that made us reluctant to seek or maintain relationships. Honest communication with partners often became increasingly challenging; we began to hold onto our secrets. These strains turned into resentments and feelings of low self-esteem that made us want to avoid sex in the relationship. If we no longer were having sex with our partners, we could seek it elsewhere. But by doing so, we might be straying into gray areas or even into our bottom-line behaviors. As a result of these choices, we may have become sexually avoidant. Avoiding sex might have been a temporary solution, but it soon developed into a long-term lifestyle that made us dissatisfied. Whatever the circumstances, we might have seen avoiding sex as a way of harm reduction. Still, we didn't necessarily accept this way of life as our only path to sexual sobriety.

SCA recovery offers the opportunity to have a spiritual awakening by working the Steps and using other SCA tools that allow us to break through the fears that have held us back from healthy sexual, social, and emotional intimacy with other people. In recovery, we affirm that our Higher Power wants us to heal from these traumas and integrate sex and intimacy into our life as a healthy element.

Chapter 17: Pornography, Apps, and Internet Addiction

Part 1: Do I have a Problem?

Today's digital technology has opened new avenues for sexually compulsive behaviors. It's now faster and easier than ever to watch porn, create webcast fantasies, use apps or the internet for hookups, engage in sexting or intriguing, and allow our search for sex and sexual "acting-out[12]" places to take over a more significant portion of our lives. The nature of this medium allows many of us to create and live in a virtual reality, in which immediate gratification is not only possible but also feels mandated. We expect this medium to fulfill our addictive desires instantly.

Cybersex offers virtually limitless possibilities to satisfy our sexual yearnings. It has become much easier to create or act out fantasies without any personal contact. Porn has always been an enabler of fantasies: its present, easy availability makes it even more attractive for casual and extensive use. Apps provide an easy way to search for "hookups" through a medium that allows us to create a new or idealized persona, often distorting the search for sex into a shadowy world of make-believe and mind games. Webcams, chat rooms, and other internet sex sites offer a blend of people, porn, and apps, enabling us to act out pornographic fantasies that others can view – or view others behaving in similar ways.

[12] "Acting out" refers to compulsive sexual behavior used to avoid feelings: instead of feeling them, i.e., "we act them out."

The widespread availability of these channels and their semi-anonymous nature can powerfully boost our addictive behavior in a way that can feel unmanageable. What could be easier than to watch online porn, repeatedly clicking from image to image, from video to video, voraciously seeking that "perfect" scene that we crave? This constant search tends to encourage perfectionistic behavior; we continually hunt for what exactly matches our urges and desires at the moment. We can find ourselves captivated by the images, which leads to isolation and a desire to escape reality.

It is equally valid for hookup apps, where we may find ourselves continually checking to see if a new face, a new response, or suggestion appears like magic on our screens. We may find that we can't bear to let go of an image or an idea that we might persuade this or that person to have sex with us. The desperate quality of our need makes us so eager for validation that another person's rejection, perhaps in "blocking" our connection, seems not only frustrating but also a personal judgment against us. Webcams feature addictive possibilities: the availability of pornographic images and storylines give us the illusion of control, like that of the apps.

Technology spins the cycle of seeking and rejection faster and faster. We can feel swept up by a whirlwind of fleeting pornographic images mixed with a swirl of faces, body parts, and enticing messages from apps and webcams. The "high" accompanying a sudden rise of expectations contrasts sharply with the depressing "low" of anger, shame, or lost self-esteem that follows an online rejection or lack of response. Even though this swirl of emotions now takes place behind the "screen" of digital anonymity, the sharp mood swings tend to become addictive in themselves, on top of our underlying desire for sexual satisfaction and validation. Our need to "numb out" within cyberspace's seemingly protective walls can impede us from becoming aware of our compulsive behaviors. We find ourselves in a trap of our own making, repeating the now-familiar pattern, a cycle of stress and anxiety.

A helpful way of understanding self-discovery and achieving meaningful change in a spiritual program of recovery is to see it as a process beginning with **Awareness**, passing on to **Acceptance**, finally leading to **Action.**

Awareness is when we step back and objectively view our relationship with porn, apps, or the internet. We can see how it takes up so much of our time and energy and how our lives seem out of control. **Acceptance** is an acknowledgment of the reality of the situation. We admit we are powerless over our use of porn, apps, or the internet and that our lives have become unmanageable. Emerging from the fog of denial, we discover the tools of Sexual Compulsives Anonymous (SCA), which allow us to decide what we will do about our problems. **Action** is when we take the steps necessary to make lasting change and to pursue healthy sexuality, as we define it for ourselves.

SCA can help each of us address the compulsive use of pornography, like other sexual behaviors, on an individual level. SCA has no opinion on outside issues (Tradition Ten[13]) and,

---

[13] Tradition Ten: "SCA has no opinion on outside issues; hence the SCA name ought never be drawn into public controversy."

therefore, neither endorses nor opposes pornography, dating apps, webcams, or any internet vehicles for sex. Instead, SCA encourages members to define what sexual behaviors are acceptable or unacceptable for themselves. One of the critical tenets of SCA is that we are not here to repress our sexuality. The SCA program helps us express it in ways that will not make unreasonable demands on our time and energy, place us in legal jeopardy, or endanger our mental, physical or spiritual health. But we first examine our situations to gain a greater awareness of what our difficulties are.

Part 2: Awareness of Unmanageability

Eventually, we begin to see how these online activities affect our lives. The list below identifies some of the thoughts and feelings reported by members engaging in porn, apps, and internet-related behaviors:

- "I knew I shouldn't be watching porn at work, but I just couldn't resist."
- "After I posted pictures of myself online, I worried that my boss or other people I know might see them."
- "I got set up and robbed by a guy I hooked up with on the apps."
- "Chills ran down my spine when my computer froze up with the message that my computer is infected and that I must contact (some department that could be a law enforcement agency)."
- "This guy I chatted with on an app invited me to hookup, and I traveled miles out of my way to a

sleazy motel, only to find out that he was ghosting me."

- "I would masturbate while glued to my computer. I would often be on the computer for over two hours, and therefore got only a few hours of sleep on those days when I had to work back-to-back shifts."

Many members joined SCA seeking recovery after long-standing periods of unmanageability with porn. It might have begun early in life: while exact figures are hard to come by, some studies suggest that the average age of digital porn exposure could be as young as 8-years-old. With many younger children having access to smartphones, they may be exposed to pornography, whether they are seeking it or not. What might have started as a pre-adolescent fascination with the images often became associated with the power of suggestion and fantasy. Pornography - through print publications, films, videos, downloads, etc. - became part of our masturbation rituals that continued into our adult life, as the First Characteristic[14] reminds us. The use of porn added to our sense of isolation and fear of intimacy. These conditions often led to sexual anorexia: the avoidance of sex with another person.

Some of us who came into the program because of our powerlessness over sexual compulsion, or romantic obsession, may have turned to pornography as a means of harm reduction, i.e., less risky self-gratification. At first, pornography may have seemed safer because it kept us away from more high-risk forms of compulsive sex. However, we soon came to realize that we

[14] "As adolescents, we used fantasy and compulsive masturbation to avoid feelings, and continued this tendency into our adult lives with compulsive sex." *The Characteristics* - Sexual Compulsives Anonymous: A Program of Recovery © SCAISO 1995

were merely swapping one addiction for another. It eventually became apparent to us that we were powerless over pornography in much the same way as we were powerless over sex and romantic obsession. Many of us began to see the internet as a powerful enabler for porn and sexual/romantic instant gratification. It was itself a significant catalyst for our sexual compulsion, perhaps becoming an addiction in and of itself. It became apparent to us that change was necessary.

We may have chosen to replace searching for anonymous sex by trying online dating sites and phone apps searching for intimacy. But our fears of intimacy made the use of these sites frustrating, and we found ourselves drifting toward seeking more immediate sex-focused connections. Once this desire took over, we neglected our search for intimacy: we had no time or patience to learn how to socialize with new people; we just wanted the sex.

The apps allowed us to contact likely sex partners without having to be physically present - or even having to leave our homes. These features became a powerful magnet, which made us spend more and more time hunting for hookups. Some of us ended up checking the apps multiple times an hour, both night and day. We became compulsive about repeatedly using them and addicted to the cycle of validation or disappointment they brought us. We discovered that online app usage was very similar to porn addiction and other forms of compulsive sexual behaviors. We ultimately turned to them as a means of seeking relief from painful feelings.

How can we determine if pornography, apps, or internet use have become a problem for us? We can review our sexual history as part of our First Step[15]. This process will help us more clearly identify whether our porn, apps, or internet use have made our lives unmanageable. Below are some useful questions we can ask ourselves to help see our situation more clearly. In these questions, we found that the word pornography can be interchangeable with "hookup websites or apps," depending on our circumstances:

- How much time do I spend looking at pornography, looking for sex on the apps or the internet each day, each week?
- Am I powerless over my use of these platforms to search for sex? Am I unable to stop by willpower alone?
- Is my behavior unmanageable? Does it interfere with other areas of my life, such as work, relationships, or self-care? For example, do I find myself glued to my computer for so many hours that I forget to eat?
- Have I become more isolated by viewing pornography? Has my app or internet use made me feel safer with a virtual connection than with real people?
- Do I turn to these activities to avoid facing up to the challenges of daily life? Does the search for sex through apps/internet or porn use enable me to "numb out?"
- Do I use pornography to avoid facing difficult tasks or feelings? Do I view it as a reward for an accomplishment?

---

[15] Step One: "We admitted we were powerless over sexual compulsion – that our lives had become unmanageable." - Sexual Compulsives Anonymous: A Program of Recovery © SCAISO 1995

- Do I look at pornography, apps, or internet sex sites at inappropriate times, such as while at work or when I should be going to sleep?
- Do I look at pornography, log onto the internet, or go on the apps when I am on the telephone or when I am among others in a social setting? If so, does this behavior keep me from being present in the conversation or social interaction?
- Do I idealize and endow the images I see with powerful symbolism, which inevitably becomes a poor substitute for the intimacy that I might otherwise find by being with a real person?
- Do I use pornography as a means of "not acting out?"
- Do I masturbate with pornography as a substitute for expressing healthy sexual behaviors?
- Do I view pornography, go on the internet, or use apps merely to kill time?
- When I have fantasies during masturbation, do I focus on the fallacy of the "perfect" partner whose physical attributes are outside the norm? Are these fantasy behaviors risky for me?

In examining our histories and behaviors honestly, we can usually identify with specific characteristics many porn addicts seem to have in common:

- Pornographic images create fantasies of pleasure far beyond what we can realistically construct in our lives. These fantasies create unrealistic expectations, set us up for disappointment, and damage our ability to connect with others, who can never compete with our fantasies.

- Because most pornography glorifies youth, many find that our sexual appetite is trained to desire younger bodies, distorting our view of desirable partners.
- We find euphoric recall in looking at pornography. We tend to remember past experiences positively while overlooking the negative consequences associated with those events.
- We objectify strangers, fixating on and fetishizing body parts.
- Because pornography pays homage to the perfect body, we may develop insecurity about our bodies. We may feel embarrassed, ashamed, or anxious about what we perceive as flaws in our appearance: consequently, we avoid face-to-face social situations.
- We discover that pornography often celebrates anonymous sex, making it seem reasonable, admirable, and aspirational.
- The vast trove of pornographic images can also provide displays of other forms of sex that have been outside our previous experience, making these behaviors seem exciting and desirable.
- By posting images of ourselves on websites and apps, we seek to be objectified by others and often see ourselves as mere sex objects. This desire for attention often degrades the respect and dignity we wish to have for ourselves.
- We seek oblivion in fantasy, lose ourselves in looking at pornography or hunt for sex online.
- We use pornography to escape from uncomfortable feelings such as anxiety, fear, anger, resentment, guilt, etc.

- We become emotionally detached from our partner during sex because we are not fully present but lost in our fantasies. This pattern reinforces a disconnect we feel between sex and intimacy.
- We are readily able to climax with pornography or a stranger but have trouble getting aroused with a regular partner. Even when aroused, we have trouble climaxing.
- While we repeatedly try to stop or reduce the amount of time spent looking at pornography, we cannot do so.
- Many of us suffer from feelings of low self-esteem and turn to apps and webcam rooms as a soothing mechanism, seeking the validation we cannot seem to find elsewhere. However, we find that these activities eventually take a toll on our physical, emotional, and spiritual well-being.
- After repeated and intense use of apps, pornography, and the internet, we find that our lives have become smaller. With the ever-present fear of rejection, lost time, and isolation, these “rewards” often turn into punishments.
- We find that watching pornography or engaging in digital sexual intrigue with others can easily lead to other forms of compulsive behavior. Most of us realize that these “virtual” sex encounters undermine our capacity for real connections with others.
- We isolate ourselves, generate digital intrigue, and engage in anonymous sex when what we want is to create a connection, develop romantic feelings, and build an intimate relationship with another human being.

Experiences with Porn and Online Sexual Activities: Testimonials

•

"In my teens, I pursued pornography despite being underage. I found a source that offered to sell me pornographic magazines. It became a part of my everyday life, always scraping money together for my next fix. There was also a sense of shame – I had never had secrets from my family and friends. The two feelings became blended: excitement followed by shame and fear: feeling shame increased the need for more excitement to override the negative impact of these feelings, if only for a short time.

To reconcile these entirely separate worlds, I learned to compartmentalize my life. I became an expert liar, always quick with a falsified explanation for the missing time spent pursuing porn."

•

"I have different types of porn needs that relate to my stress levels. I might be happy just to look at pictures of bodies when I'm relaxed. But if I'm stressed out, I usually go to BDSM porn sites. I open one site and scan it, and then I quickly chase links to other sites that might offer me a more intense high. I keep opening more and more pages in my web browser, going back and forth, and trying to get more and more specialized to find the exact scene that I think I need.

I'm aware that this is destructive behavior, but that awareness recedes further into the back of my mind as I get more and more engrossed. After an hour, or maybe several hours, I finally have an orgasm, even though I never did find that perfect scene. Afterward, I have feelings of shame and worries over the potential harm I've done to myself and my relationship. My porn fantasies create a loss of intimacy with my partner that I notice and worry about whenever we have sex..."

•

"When I was twelve, I discovered my adult brother had a collection of hardcore porn stashed away. I would spend hours looking at pictures and reading about the fantasies, and I assumed that these magazines represented typical sexuality. The pornography numbed my loneliness and helped me cope with the dysfunction in my family. I came to believe that if I were "good at sex," everyone would want to love me.

At thirteen, I began to have sex with others, but I was very passive. I didn't know what I wanted sexually, and I didn't feel like I was participating in the sex I was having. I realized that all my sexual fantasies were of other people, driven by porn."

•

"A few times a week from high school until my mid 20's, I would go home and wait until everyone was asleep to log on and meet strangers from around the world who would masturbate with me. I would log on to various webcam sites for hours, showing strangers my genitals/nude body. It was exhilarating and comforting that I wasn't the only one up at 5 a.m. feeling the need to masturbate. It didn't matter to me who was looking at me. I let any man with a camera look at my nude body. I would be logged on for 5 hours and not even notice that the sun had come up."

•

[A humorous parody of real experiences using apps, compiled by SCA members]

"The apps aren't for everyone. Use of the apps may cause the following symptoms: carpal tunnel, lack of interest in sex, lack of interest in actually talking with a live human being, full-body shame, feelings of inadequacy, syphilis, chlamydia, gonorrhea, Herpes I through IV, Hepatitis A through C, molluscum contagiosum, the condition known as 'not good enough,' anhedonia, phantom taps, insomnia, loss of friends, unmanageability, complete loss of time, instantaneous phone battery depletion. Trust your instincts. You are totally in control. Don't reach out. Just let go and log on.

Oh, and you should give us some money too. That way, we can find even more ghosts and flakes for you. And you shouldn't just stop at one day on the apps, just for you, we're offering a trial program for $3.99 per day that renews at $99 bucks a month. You're so distracted you'll probably forget to cancel, and your life is a bit too unmanageable for you to track your finances. We're counting on that.

Take a minute to turn on notifications too. It's easier for us to totally f*** up your life that way. Who needs a solid night's sleep? And nothing good ever comes from showing up on time and paying attention at work all day. Your friends and family will respond very positively to your complete distraction during dinners and other social gatherings.

Remember those times when you used to just sit and think? Well, that's not gonna happen. Say goodbye to the next five years of your life. Don't forget to share your location, give us access to your photos, contacts, your camera, and text messages. Don't compartmentalize us! Integrate us into your life as an unhealthy element."

●

"From the moment I installed the app on my phone, I felt that it had almost become part of me. I found myself checking it again and again, desperately seeking the validation of being desired by someone, anyone. Day or night, I would feel a thrill surge through me if I heard the "ping" that signaled someone had reached out to me. If I tried to contact some hot guy and he didn't respond right away, I felt crushed, utterly bereft of that feeling that I so craved from having some stranger wanting to have sex with me. If someone did respond, what a high: a rush of fantasy and expectation would wash over me as I responded, hoping and praying that he would continue the dialogue. And of course, there was the sense of deprivation and outrage if he didn't respond again, or worse, blocked me.

I spent hours intriguing with people on that app. We would exchange words, then pictures of selected body parts, each leading the other to want to have sex immediately. I felt so desperate for a connection that I would even engage in drawn-out and meaningless text exchanges, still hoping that I could persuade them to agree to a specific hookup. They would often become ghosts; either they would suddenly block me or stop responding. Sometimes they would agree to meet somewhere: perhaps at their home or a hotel. Several times, I would show up, knock on the door, but would get no response. I had gone to great lengths to see them at a place of their choice, only to find that they had ghosted me. I would try to take out my frustration and fury by getting back on the app to look for another hookup, or if I were feeling vengeful, would take out my frustrations by ghosting someone trying to connect with me."

•

"I was attending SCA meetings, and I felt as if I was finally getting control of my life. All was good, or at least I thought it was. Although "acting out" was no longer something I did often, "acting-in," using my PC and the internet became a very convenient way to pass the time. It started as a very controllable activity. I was aware of what time, energy, and money I was spending and would pull back when I felt I spent too much. I was always convincing myself I was in control and that my use of porn and online sex chats helped me stay away from my old acting out places. Perhaps it was. But really, I had transferred my old addictive behavior to another one.

I began using online sex chat and porn more and more. Although there were many free sites, for some reason, I was more triggered and satisfied by sites where I had to pay. The monthly fees and per-minute charges began to add up. I stopped paying attention, and my credit card balances began to rise. Before long, I was in for a big and very unpleasant surprise.

One afternoon I was deep in my isolation routine, and I logged onto a sex chat site. I was flirting with a model and agreed to his invitation to an online sex show. At this point, I pulled out my credit card to pay for some minutes. As I pressed the button saying "Purchase," my card was declined. I realized that I had exceeded my credit limit and that the bank refused to provide any more. I immediately tried two other cards that I had, but the site rejected both of them. I went into a panic, but then I realized I had ordered a new credit card a few months back and had never used it. I wanted to get that card but had forgotten where I put it. I tore my apartment apart looking for the card. I had no control over my actions. I had to find that card. After looking in every drawer and desk in my apartment, I found it. I went back to the website and tried to purchase the needed time. I then noticed a white activation sticker on the card, which meant I had to call the bank before using it. I don't know how, but this break in my acting out routine brought me back to reality and made me aware of what I was doing. I looked around at my ransacked apartment and realized that although my behavior had changed from acting out to acting in, I was no better off. My addiction was still a big problem."

Part 3: If This Behavior Is a Problem, What Can I Do?

When we finally accept that looking at pornography, using webcams, or searching the apps has become unmanageable for us, we can accept that it is time to work with others to consider modifying our Sexual Recovery Plan. We can't recover from addiction by only abstaining from our "drug of choice" or "white-knuckling it." Even if we try that method, we might find ourselves repeatedly failing, thus adding to our low self-esteem and the sense that we cannot change our behaviors.

But we begin to recover by accepting the possibility that we can create new ways of living. Acceptance gives us a willingness to break the cycle that had become routine to us. We want to be entirely ready (though not necessarily overjoyed or enthusiastic) to change our habits.

It isn't easy. So many of our daily rituals had focused on pornography or the use of apps and the internet. We might feel very uneasy or even scared at the notion of quitting "cold turkey." To some, it's as if we are turning our backs on our best friend; that we are about to cut ourselves off from activities that brought great comfort to us, even if they were unmanageable.

Perhaps porn, apps, webcams, and the internet can be part of our healthy sexuality, as we individually define it. There is no "right" way for us to follow. Some look to combine sex, love, affection and experience intimacy through a relationship. Whichever way we choose to proceed, our primary goal is to replace our compulsive behavior with a healthier way of expressing our sexuality. We want to embrace the changes that will allow us to accomplish this.

Action

By turning to SCA's *The Tools that Help Us Get Better*, we begin to learn how to help ourselves. Just telling ourselves "Not to do it anymore" never worked in the past, nor would we expect it to work now.

Recalling that 12-Step recovery is a spiritual process, we consider making changes that can lead to recognizable shifts in our behaviors. We work toward a willingness to accept a shift in our way of thinking: a different outlook, a sense that we aren't alone, that help is available.

The Twelve Steps are the backbone of SCA. They outline a simple program of action that results in recovery from the agony of our sexual compulsion. All other tools of recovery act in support of "working the Steps." A sexually sober sponsor who has experience working the Steps guides the newcomer through this program of change and growth. While the other tools provide support for behavior modification, we can receive the grace of a "spiritual awakening" that transforms us from within through working the Twelve Steps. This awakening provides the basis for a fundamental change in our attitudes, behaviors, and interactions with others. Anyone seeking a more lasting solution to these symptoms of "dis-ease" will ultimately find it by painstakingly working the Steps.

Whatever choices we make that seem right for us, we also try to use the program's various tools. Each of these may help free us from our compulsive behaviors. We begin to use some of these tools, however tentatively, certainly imperfectly, with the idea of achieving "progress, not perfection." That slogan, along with many other SCA slogans, can help keep us heading in the right direction.

Meetings, either in person, via telephone, or online, are where we share our experience, strength, and hope with each other to better understand our common problem and work together toward the solution. The support of fellow members helps us to stop acting out and to start sorting out our confusion about sex.

As we listen to others share, we see more clearly how sexual compulsion affects our lives.

Using the **telephone** to contact other members is a way for us to break out of the isolation that is so much a part of our compulsive behavior. It can also be a lifeline to us when we might be in crisis and are unable to get to a meeting. If we are in the habit of turning to pornography, the internet, or apps for emotional relief, we might consider calling a fellow to talk about our feelings instead. "Book-ending" can also be an effective tool. If we feel compelled to view porn, other internet sites, or go on the apps, we can call our sponsor or other program friends – both before and after we engage in any of our bottom-line or risky behaviors. Taking this action can give us a dose of reality that may help to counteract the compulsion.

Developing a working relationship with our **sponsor** can be another vital tool of recovery. We can learn to ask for insight and guidance: this can help us step out of our isolation. In the past, many of us had compartmentalized our lives. Certain people knew specific things about us, but no one person knew us fully. There can be tremendous personal growth from trusting at least one person with all the details of our sexual histories. The development of such a trust is also a way to safely practice intimacy in our lives.

Literature is our portable program. We may use SCA Conference-approved literature in and outside of meetings and other 12-Step programs or other appropriate literature. Reading about the kind of experiences we are having can bring us insight into our patterns and change them.

Carefully working **the Twelve Steps** with a sponsor, perhaps in a Step-writing group, allows us to share the details of our sexual histories in a safe environment. Talking with the other group members helps us understand that we are not alone in our struggles with pornography. In working with our sponsor or a Step-writing group, we can develop connections with other members by honestly revealing ourselves and our compulsive behavior to the group. The relief and positive feedback we receive can reinforce the value of intimacy. Working on our Step-writing in the company of fellow sexual compulsives grounds us more firmly in our recovery. It reinforces that what we cannot do alone, we can do with the help of others.

Prayer and Meditation are a means of establishing conscious contact with a Power greater than ourselves. Re-reading the Second and Third Steps[16] and discussing these with our sponsor or other members provides us with some clarity and encourages us to develop our prayer and meditation practices, including *our* concept of a "Higher Power."

A sponsor can also encourage and assist us in making and living our **Sexual Recovery Plan**. SCA's *Statement of Purpose* says: "Members are encouraged to develop their own Sexual Recovery Plan and to define sexual sobriety for themselves." Constructing our plan involves many choices. Working with another SCA member may help us decide what might work for us now and avoid being too strict or lax with our intentions. The Sexual Recovery Plan sometimes includes three columns:

---

[16] Step Two: "Came to believe that a Power greater than ourselves could restore us to sanity" – Step Three: "Made a decision to turn our will and our lives over to the care of God *as we understood God.*"

The first column (abstinence column) lists "bottom-line" behaviors corresponding to relapse from which we may ask our Higher Power to free us.

The second column (high-risk, or "gray area") includes behaviors, emotional states, ritualized activities, and situations that might make us vulnerable to relapse.

The third column (recovery column) includes positive behaviors that support our well-being and encourage us to expand our lives.

Many use other formats, focusing on different recovery areas, according to what works best for them.

Abstinence—partial or total: For some of us, a temporary measure of "harm reduction" might seem advisable. With the encouragement of our sponsor and others, we might establish limits on access to porn sites, use of the apps, or the internet. Or perhaps we might ask a sponsor or program friend to *deny* our access by disabling or locking one or more of our devices and giving these (along with the passwords) to a trusted person.

Socializing is a way of breaking down our isolation and getting to know people in a non-sexual context. By affirming that we are part of a community, we don't have to cope with our compulsive behaviors alone. Socializing with people in general, whether by going to fellowship with members, joining other supportive organizations and groups, or re-establishing ties with friends we had lost touch with while acting out, can also help us break the isolation. It lets us be a friend first; to practice having different kinds of relationships.

Dating is a way of changing the instant gratification habit and getting to know more about ourselves and another person before committing ourselves to any sexual decisions. Dating is a valuable tool of the program and learning how to meet people we would like to date *soberly* can be one of the most complicated but rewarding challenges of our recovery.

Using the slogans can help us keep our attitudes in check. These simple phrases or acronyms are easy to remember and may help interrupt negative thoughts and emotions that can lead to relapse, such as "stinkin' thinking." If we find that we are spending time in our gray areas and are edging toward engaging in first column (bottom line) behaviors, the slogans can help remind us to stay in the moment and not spiral into negativity and denial.

Service is a tool that involves us doing for others, getting out of our heads, rather than living in the self-centric world focused on isolating digital behaviors. We practice asking ourselves what we can bring *to* the situation rather than what we can get *from* it. Various forms of service, whether chairing a meeting, serving as a "spiritual timekeeper," group treasurer or any other type of service, help us connect with others. We begin to feel at home in a meeting. Continuing to be of service can transform us as we maintain our existing connections and develop new ones. In helping others, we become nourished ourselves. We come to identify with the slogan: *To Keep it, We Give It Away*.

Writing provides a way to become honest with ourselves and our Higher Power. By writing in journals, gratitude lists, letters, and emails, we can measure our progress, values, motives, and 12 Step work. It helps us recognize patterns in our daily lives.

By paying more attention to how we got through our lives than what happened, we have a window into our thought processes.

Epilogue: Life in Recovery

As we utilize these and other tools that help us get better, we also learn how important it is to identify and avoid high-risk situations. Sometimes we are not aware of these until we are in the middle of them, so we might wish to list those situations we consider to be triggering or otherwise harmful in the second column of our Sexual Recovery Plan. We may also periodically revisit our plan in its entirety to adjust or change some of those activities or triggers as our recovery progresses.

Some of us may decide to change our focus on using the internet, finding other healthier areas for us. Others may find that *any* use of the internet can become compulsive for them and that they need to strictly limit their screen time, especially at certain times of the day and night. Some members find that watching TV, reading print books and magazines, spending time with friends and fellows relieves, at least temporarily, the compulsion to engage in digital acting out.

If we want to feel higher self-esteem, we engage in esteemable actions. Receiving validation from these actions may be more satisfying than a shallower, briefer form of validation on the internet. These actions can include doing service in the SCA fellowship or volunteering in other capacities with other organizations.

Adopting and practicing these tools to help manage our compulsive behavior steadily leads us to a more sober life. As we learn to modify our behaviors and choose the next best actions, we will carry out our daily lives with more serenity. The progress that we see creates positive momentum for us to move forward.

The first few weeks and months of decreasing our use of pornography, the internet, or apps may be difficult. Many of us face various symptoms of withdrawal - physical, emotional, mental, and spiritual. Some may experience unwelcome changes in sleep patterns, appetite, and sexual function. We may also feel sadness and grief, often with resentment, which could cause us to seek comfort by losing ourselves in our old cybersex behaviors. Others might experience euphoric recall, which may tempt us to want to relive our bottom line acting out, looking again to comfort ourselves with those familiar behaviors. The SCA pamphlet *Moving Through Withdrawal* (which is included as Chapter 5 of this book) describes these processes in detail and suggests practical ways to counter them in our recovery.

The early stages of recovery can be quite trying and frustrating at times. There are often slips back into our compulsive use of the internet, porn, and apps. However, we have found that many who are willing to continue to come back to meetings after these episodes finally find serenity and reprieve from the compulsion. Included below are some personal anecdotes from members who have struggled with these behaviors:

— "An important part of my recovery is to identify what I like sexually and include myself in my sexual fantasies. I still have trouble expressing it to my partner, but I can now recognize when I'm playing a role rather than being intimate."

— "I eventually came to realize that I was just looking at pixels on a computer, while isolated, alone, and disconnected from the world. Viewing porn several hours a day did absolutely nothing for my life, hurting my relationship. I had been comparing a real-live person - my partner - with any one of a thousand bodies projected on the screen. I no longer wanted to do this."

— "In a triggering situation, I found myself drawn back into feeling I needed a hookup - any hookup - badly. I arranged with someone to come to my room. About 10 minutes before my hookup was due to arrive, I began shivering violently from chills. It was to the point where my teeth were chattering. Even though I was by myself, I felt embarrassed and scared. The last thing in the world I wanted at that moment was sex: I canceled the hookup. I was surprised to feel a sense of relief that none of my efforts had led to a sexual encounter. I felt as if I had awakened from a bad dream. I didn't want to have sex that way; I checked in with my sponsor, then went for a long walk, relishing the feeling that I didn't need to seek validation through that app at that moment. I deleted it and felt relieved."

— "As I started to attend more meetings and focus on my recovery, I made friends in the program, socialized more, and started doing service. It took time for me to find myself again and years to pay down my debt, but with the help of the fellowship, meetings, and others in the program, I was able to restore a sense of order into my life, relieving me of my unmanageability. Without the program, I felt lost. But being a part of SCA and working my recovery, I found the strength and courage to face my addiction and reclaim my life."

Many of us learn how to experience intimacy once we begin to recover from our bottom-line porn, internet, or apps compulsions. Using *The Tools* of the program, we develop practices to help us resist old behaviors in ways that work for us - always progress, not perfection. We find that we no longer fall back into those behaviors; these changes shift our perspective toward self-awareness and self-acceptance. Acceptance can be a huge relief: we no longer use our compulsion to numb our feelings or lose ourselves in hours of endless isolation. We have learned how to benefit from the experiences of others through meetings and fellowship. Whereas our life in our ongoing digital compulsion was small and narrow, we find that our lives become broad in recovery and include aspects we could never have imagined.

Chapter 18: Secret Shame

SCA sponsored a three-part seminar on shame in the spring and summer of 1990, attended almost entirely by gay and lesbian members. The notes taken at these sessions were edited and revised by members of an SCA literature committee. This chapter is the result.

As sexual compulsives, we live almost continually with shame but often are hardly aware of it. We can act out repeatedly on this secret, pervasive shame while never even knowing it's there.

Our secret shame manifests in many ways:

- When we feel shy because we feel like we don't deserve something we desperately want
- When we fear we can't compete
- When we look for perfection in others or ourselves
- When we're inordinately upset by criticism
- When our bodies and their functions disgust us
- When we obsess about body parts
- When we hold on to memories of being abused, ridiculed, or humiliated
- When we need others to reassure us
- When we feel invisible or wish we were
- When we abandon ourselves – physically, mentally, or spiritually
- When we want to run away

It can come as a shock to discover that the general malaise so familiar to us – the "hole in the soul" we sometimes believe we were born with is shame. For the sexually compulsive person, shame may be a compulsion in itself: something one hates but cannot resist.

For many of us, feelings of shame seem ingrained. We may have carried shame about sex from our childhood and have grown accustomed to it. Shame has become familiar to us, and we found we were often drawn to reenacting painful situations, somehow attracted by their familiarity, even while repelled by the emotions.

Shame is how we perceive ourselves and how we perceive the world. Shame is what drives us to act out and increase our deprivation. The sexually compulsive person uses shame as a defense mechanism that keeps them paralyzed. We subject ourselves to the idea that someone may think that we are *less than* or otherwise inferior. Shame becomes an expression of perfectionism, which leads to an avoidance of situations where others may criticize or devalue us. For many, shame has become pervasive, overshadowing our thoughts and actions.

We distinguish shame from guilt. Many of us are willing to talk, sometimes obsessively, about guilt. But guilt is not shame. We can define guilt as this feeling: I've done something bad. Shame can be defined this way: I am something bad. Guilt says, "I made a mistake." Shame says, "I am a mistake." Unlike guilt, which is a cognitive thought, shame resides deep in the body and, when chronic in childhood, creates a freeze response defending us from intense pain.

It's possible to learn from guilt, but shame only drives us ever deeper into self-hatred. As long as we're unaware of it, shame serves to heighten the sense of confusion in which we always seem to be floundering. Something feels fundamentally wrong: we don't seem fully alive the way we perceive other people. Yet, we shy away from facing the truth. The inadequacy we have always suspected in ourselves might prove to be real. *What if it turns out we're even worse than we'd feared? What if we can't do anything about it?*

A Family Disease

Shame tends to run in families. Many of us seem to stumble through life, burdened with our parents' shame as well as our own. Sunk in depths of self-absorption and self-hatred that our parents may have inherited; they were often incapable of realizing we were people in our own right. We seemed mere extensions of them, existing chiefly to validate their lives. Though often enthralled by the idea of parenthood, they were somehow unwilling or unable to do the work. The facade they presented to the world seemed more important than any meaningful family life they might create. Particularly for parents who inherited shame, the essential thing was that shame remains hidden: never to be confronted in any way. Our parents may have been too attentive to us or not attentive enough. Sometimes they treated us like "showcase objects," meant to inspire the world's admiration for them. In their self-centeredness or narcissism, we carried their shame, becoming invisible, never properly developing our sense of self.

Such parents might have considered us exceedingly important, yet somehow a disappointment. Often, they formed their concept of our identity only in reaction to their feelings, or lack of feelings, about us. Even as we strained to remain loyal to them, we knew there could never be any bonding with our parents, only bondage. They expected us to show compassion for their unhappiness: ours didn't count. Often, they abused us as their parents abused them. They may have abused themselves, allowing their true selves to die and creating an example for us that was all too easy to follow.

Our parents' distortions and hang-ups about sex affected us deeply, often without our realizing it. Many of the physical dreads and obsessions we experience have nothing to do with our desires and needs but are driven by shame. We have a profound desire to be validated, wanted, and loved because we continuously monitor ourselves in comparison to others. Sex in adulthood becomes a paltry stand-in for the love and attention we didn't get as children.

Incest may occur in families where members continually disregard boundaries. The most extreme form of ignored boundaries is actual sexual relations between adults and children, but many forms of abuse function as covert or emotional incest. For instance, a parent who turns to a child for solace, a secret confidante or partner, indulges in emotional incest. Such a weight of intimacy and responsibility is beyond any child's capacity to understand or deal with, hard as they may try. In effect, it robs the child of childhood, and victims of this kind of abuse often pay a great price in later life. Growing up with an uncertain sense of boundaries or limitations, we may learn that the real world's standards don't apply to us. It can also teach us that in some baffling, terrifying way, we do not exist.

Thus, unable to function as examples for healthy lives, our parents were role models for unhappy, compulsive ones. They taught us early the importance of secrecy and silence, hiding what we feared we might be, and pretending to be something we were not. Our very sense of self is erased from existence, leaving us alone and lonely.

Growing Up Ashamed

As children, we wanted to be liked by everyone. No one must perceive how loathsome we believed ourselves to be; no one must ever know what we were feeling. Compared to our unhappy selves, almost everyone else seemed better off, and we feared we could never make friends spontaneously, the way other people could. We had to work for it and work overtime. We considered ourselves unworthy of any affection we got; nevertheless, real or imagined deprivations made us feel entitled to special consideration.

For some of us, religious services seemed to reinforce our unique needs. Our early religious training often held an uncanny fascination for us and deepened our prudish disdain for physical reality. This hunger for the supernatural helped shape our adolescent lives, and especially our spiritual lives. Instead of seeking spiritual connection within ourselves, we turned to movies, operas, television, or sports. Such realms of fantasy were intoxicating for many of us. They presented us with images of the ideal that our shame-infected everyday existence could never match.

Making ourselves into models of good behavior – or bad behavior, if that worked better – we learned how to get what we wanted at any cost. We sought ways to outwit and outperform, and the need to be "as good as" soon became the need to be "better than." But no matter how often we excelled, we always secretly felt it wasn't good enough, that we'd failed again.

To our other miseries, we added envy: yearning for what others had, even their identities. We placed people in categories. Most seemed drab and beneath consideration. A select few were "perfect" – beautiful, brilliant, happy, ideal – and these we obsessed about, seeing ourselves as even more inadequate by comparison.

For many of us, our bodies were a source of continuing anxiety. We regarded our normal bodily functions as embarrassing and degrading and strove to detach from them. Sometimes even our natural gifts seemed shameful: having intelligence or talent made us different and to us, different meant inferior. Distaste for our bodies turned to disgust with ourselves. We envied those we desired – idealizing them simply because they seemed unlike us. Partners were magic mirrors, revealing whatever we longed or dreaded to see. We wanted to become the people we were attracted to or absorb them into us, dimming our real selves. Often, especially while acting out sexually, we felt invisible.

In our fantasy, we often sought to emulate images of them that may or not have been real. In some cases, this longing manifested in shameful behaviors, like wearing articles of their clothing that we obtained by deceit. This use of deceit increased the "rush" we experienced in acting out our shame. Often, the "rush" felt better than the deadness within us, enticing us to act out repeatedly. We eroticized the experience of engaging in behaviors we felt were illicit, taboo, and shameful since they affirmed our sense of ourselves as people with no value. If we were going to be dirty anyway, we felt we might as well wallow in it.

Building walls within walls, we imprisoned ourselves in a kind of perpetual childhood to prevent harsh reality from interfering with our secret inner life. And then, when sex came into the picture, it attached itself to the processes of envy, fantasy, secrecy, and self-hatred already in operation.

Acting Out Our Shame

Looking back, many of us believe that compulsive behavior in various forms was with us from an early age. It seemed almost inevitable that sex would be an addiction. We were alarmed by our awakening sexuality's strange power and its capacity to make us lose control. It brought on a jumble of anxiety-provoking sensations: fear, excitement, fascination, and a new depth of emotional need. Then, when we began to realize we were sexually "different" from the way we perceived other people to be, it seemed further proof of our wretchedness and inadequacy.

Convinced that our sexuality must be an evil thing, some of us attempted to control our natural drives. We tried to divorce ourselves from our sexual nature and often equated being sexual with being bad. We lost the ability to imagine sex as healthy and life-enhancing. If it didn't feel shameful, it didn't feel sexual. With our lives split in two, we became locked in a compulsive cycle of either denying our sexual side or recklessly abandoning ourselves to it. We hated and feared what was happening to us, yet the numbing rush of adrenaline each time we gave in was irresistible. When we first gravitated to the dismal world of compulsive sex, most of us felt simultaneously excited and sickened. We found ourselves sneaking back again and again. It was as if we had at last found a place where all our inner loathing could come into play so that in some way, we were finally "at home." We seemed to be playing out some inner drama, compelled to repeat the same old story repeatedly, hoping each time for a better ending.

We often felt afraid when we found someone attractive and felt threatened when anyone found us attractive. If we didn't feel continually validated by the other person, we felt rejected. It seemed we had found a "lose-lose" situation: being desired temporarily masked the shame we still felt; rejection affirmed our low opinion of ourselves, activating the shame cycle all over again.

We shielded ourselves from the reality of what we were doing so that even during our most sordid episodes, we inwardly felt untouched. However, underneath our increasing hunger for sex, our anxiety intensified. We used certain people, acts, or places as fetishes to ward off this anxiety. Sex itself became a kind of fetish.

Our sexuality could be a means to express anger at others and ourselves. Soon the giving or getting of abuse, whether physical or emotional, provided a significant element of our shame-based identity. We regarded humiliation, others' or ours, with a contradictory sense of superiority and contempt. Many of us used pornography to dampen the shame from unexpressed feelings of anxiety, fear, anger, and resentment. Pornographic images created euphoria and fantasies of pleasure far beyond what we could realistically construct in our lives. We associated those images with real people, who seemed to enjoy a world of erotic activities that we somehow failed to achieve. Our experiences with porn produced a conflict between our fantasy world and the reality of our daily lives. Comparing ourselves to the idealized bodies and situations in porn might have caused us to question our self-worth, diminishing our already low self-esteem.

The shame that had at first seemed unbearable eventually became buried so deep as to be unnoticeable. Any notion of who we were grew cloudier, and we seemed to be watching our lives from a distance. It was as if our lives were happening to someone else. Isolated though we were, we became more and more needful of others. When we didn't have an audience, we hardly seemed to exist.

It grew steadily more difficult, outside of sex, to express our shame-driven rage, and we kept trying to "package" ourselves to give the illusion that we were the nicest, the most accommodating, the best. Forever comparing and competing, we craved success to hide the growing emptiness inside. And yet, we feared success, often pushing it away. Invisible observers seemed always to be evaluating us, and we felt unable even to approach the perfection they demanded.

Venturing deeper into our double lives, many of us became more rigid and puritanical even as our standards sank. We scorned anyone who reminded us of ourselves or did the same things we did. Whether openly or surreptitiously, homophobia flourished within many of us. Our powerlessness over life and death frightened us, and we tried to stand apart from the day-by-day cycles of existence. We regarded growth and the aging process as a constant threat.

The more our compulsion damaged us, the more we required perfection in others, alternating sleazy episodes with giddy romantic extravaganzas in relationships that had little chance of survival in the shallowness of our real lives. It wasn't an authentic partner we were seeking. We needed a role model, savior, symbol, pornographic fantasy – someone to worship or be worshiped by – a passport to a new identity, to obliterate the one we could not bear – or felt deep inside that we never had.

The Healing Process

Accustomed to lives of confusion, chaos, and vagueness, where obsessions could multiply unchecked, most sexual compulsives are fearful of simplicity. Initially, we might be wary of the healing process in SCA. The threat of our defenses coming down, facing a pool of pain, prevalent in all of us, was incomprehensible to some, terrifying to others.

SCA is not psychotherapy, nor a "get well quick" self-improvement scheme. It is a spiritual program that gradually loosens the compulsion's grip with the help of a power greater than ourselves. This word spiritual, conjuring up images of ritual, authority, and forays into the absolute, tends to dismay many of us at first. Yet if we look objectively at our compulsion, we find that what we were so desperately seeking was not degradation but an experience of wholeness, fulfillment, joy – in fact, a spiritual experience.

Some come into the program thinking of themselves as deeply religious, while others have an ongoing resentment at religion that seems to fuel their addiction. There were, for many of us, elements of ritual in our compulsive behaviors. Our episodes of abandonment and loss of self felt religious. Others seemed to need to inflict shame and humiliation on themselves so that they could then seek absolution. Indeed, our romantic obsessions had all the trappings of idolatry. In retrospect, our escapades seem an effort to attain spiritual results without paying any requisite spiritual price.

The experience of being driven by a lower power is, for most sexual compulsives, all too familiar. Yet, the idea of a Higher Power guiding their lives makes many newcomers uncomfortable. Often, our most vivid and immediate early experience of a Higher Power at work is at meetings. How often have we witnessed a transformation in ourselves and others due to merely showing up at meetings? Such a simple change is the kind of Power greater than ourselves that can help reshape our lives.

SCA does not require us to "believe" anything. It's more often the case that as we recover, we stop believing something – believing that by applying pressure and will power, we can somehow pull our lives together on our own. In sobriety, some of us decide to give an earlier religious discipline a fresh try; others take a whole new approach to the subject. But while most SCA members gain a deep respect for the wisdom of the world's faiths, most of us are content to settle for sanity rather than sanctity.

With the help of the program and our Higher Power, we take an honest look at ourselves. Shame is a devastating defense that has obscured some of the defects we most need to resolve. The more we risk dismantling our defenses and exposing our defects, the more they lose their negative power. When recovery begins, we are amazed to uncover new levels of emotion. Slowly we learn to recognize, trust, and express genuine feelings. When we put emotion into motion, depression begins to lift. To receive loving attention is a mirroring process that rapidly begins to heal shame. To bestow loving attention does, too. Hugging somebody else means getting a hug in return. But unconditional affection can be a frightening thing, and sharing our deeper feelings always seems dangerous. At first, we're ashamed to share our feelings with other SCA members, but when we do, the shame gradually lifts. Eventually, we see *The Gifts of Recovery* start to come true.

We're troubled by the enormous investment we seem to be giving up. Coming to terms with shame can mean abandoning the identity we brought with us to SCA and admitting we built much of our lives, dreams, and personalities upon a false foundation. *What will happen if it's pulled away? Who will I be without my false self? Why should I trust this process?*

The more we participate in SCA, the faster we heal. But for most of us, sexual sobriety is unfamiliar territory. We're not used to believing we can make our lives work, but we learn to replace the old demeaning voices in our heads with new messages of approval and self-assurance. Little by little, through fellowship and self-compassion, we stop trying to reform the frightened child inside us and learn to love them instead. But our true identities can take some getting used to as we begin exploring them.

Slips in SCA can make every particle of shame come rushing back, sometimes worse than before. We recognize that a slip is a harsh but priceless lesson our addiction is teaching us about our humanity. As we grow in the program, we give up any illusions about attaining perfection, including "perfect sobriety." Success in SCA means learning to live contentedly with our imperfections and our sexual identity, not transcending it – much as many of us would like to.

We begin to accept that our sexuality is no more an excuse for self-pity than for self-blame. We renounce any sense of gay "exceptionality" and come to terms with homophobia – our own and other people's – and the damage it's done to us. We accept that we're human beings like everybody else, with the same rights, privileges, and responsibilities.

The spiritual awakening we experience in SCA has no set time frame. Other members often see the healing process working in us before we notice it ourselves. We might even be the last to realize how much the program is doing for us. We're aware of the progress others are making but are so used to thinking of ourselves as failures that many of us go on despairing about never getting well, even as we're getting well.

The work we do on our character defects may subtly change these defects into assets. For example, our anger may turn into power, fear into courage, recklessness into healthy risk-taking, shame into self-esteem, etc. As we release perfectionism, we may discover that the same intensity and passion with which we once surrendered to shame is now encouraging us in sobriety to create for ourselves ever richer, more rewarding lives.

Forgiving the Past

One of our most challenging tasks in sobriety is making peace with our original caregivers. An abusive or neglectful childhood can leave ongoing resentments that blight every chance at happiness. We try telling ourselves that our parents were also damaged or "they did the best they could," but it doesn't always work. Some of us remain unable to accept the ways our role models hurt us: it's still too painful and incomprehensible. We go on perceiving them from the vantage point of vulnerable children as if, in some way, our caregivers were still in charge of our lives – even of our recovery! And so, we stay angry, as if being angry enough, for long enough will somehow remake our childhoods. But staying angry keeps us in a relationship with our family of origin in a dysfunctional way, eating up vital energy that we could be putting to practical use in our current relationships or work. It's best to remember that one definition of forgiveness is giving up hope of ever having a better childhood. The process of grief and loss that accompanies this shift can bring forth another round of pain that, eventually, liberates us to move forward in our lives.

Many SCA members manage to improve their family interactions, with or without the families' cooperation, and some even enjoy genuinely making peace with them. Others try valiantly, only to be frustrated, newly embittered, and ashamed. In their enthusiasm for the new life they find in SCA, other members make a sudden dramatic decision to "come out" to their families. Still others choose to stop seeing them. Some of us deal with resentments over parents who don't wish to speak with us or are no longer alive. It's best to work out these situations as lovingly as possible, making no impossible demands of parents or ourselves. A deeply affectionate relationship with our families may no longer be possible or even desirable. Perhaps the time has come to look elsewhere for this kind of intimacy. When we literally or figuratively leave our family of origin, we can move toward creating the family of our choosing. This shift is an adult developmental task that's part of becoming a whole, integrated person. In any case, we strive to be honest, fair, and loving with this challenging part of our recovery, and then we turn it over to our Higher Power. The critical relationship now is not with our parents, but with our Higher Power and ourselves.

The Next Step

We learn the truth of our stories by telling them. First, we discover our needs and feelings; then, we seek ways to express them. In trying to shape a happy and healthy sex life for ourselves, we have many choices to consider. Abstinence is a discipline that appeals to some members. Accepting it as a kind of vocation, if only for a time, they feel it enriches their lives. Most members, though, prefer to reach out sexually to others, and here too, sobriety offers many options. For some of us, a committed relationship seems the most desirable goal. We had always fled from any possibility for a genuine partnership with another human being, despite all our romantic obsessing. Either we ended it before it had a chance to grow or suffocated it with expectations no relationship could ever meet. Other members prefer to remain single but strive to embrace their sexuality by expressing it in a way that is loving to themselves and others.

Trying to grow up sexually presents particular challenges for people recovering in SCA. We were in the habit of only envisioning sex with partners who were in some way unavailable or unreal: in many ways, we were unavailable and unreal. Still tending to perceive sex as something bad, we confronted a dilemma with any partner we respected. "Normal" sexual experience seemed too commonplace to satisfy us; at the same time, we feared any intense sexual arousal would drag us back to the shame-inducing world of compulsive sex. We realized that, in a relationship or out, we had never been our authentic sexual self. With the help of our Higher Power, we began to experiment with authentic sexual expression, gradually learning to truly surrender ourselves instead of acting out our customary charade of self-abandon. If we veered toward a dangerous path, the program (and our sponsors) soon made us aware of it. Sobriety enabled us to learn from our mistakes instead of endlessly repeating them. Whatever path we chose to take toward a more rewarding sexual and emotional life, many of us felt as if we were starting over from adolescence to rebuild our lives. For the first time, we began to learn how to grow despite our doubts and fears, rather than manipulating ourselves and others.

After negating ourselves for so long, it's not easy to reverse the process. It often feels that we're making a dreadful mistake, and the rage and fear that boils up can be terrifying. We were never able to deal with such emotions before, but now we have the SCA fellowship to support us and help us face any situation that comes our way. Slowly we bring the techniques of recovery into our daily lives. We learn to treat ourselves as patiently and as compassionately as we would a child, affirming our values even when we're not always sure we have them. We begin to establish boundaries, and that helps us accept both our limitations and our real potential. We realize that we're never going to have all the answers for ourselves or anybody else. And we decide we may just as well accept ourselves one day at a time – for the complex, lovable people we are.

Chapter 19: The Gifts of Recovery

When we each work the Sexual Compulsives Anonymous program to the best of our ability and find a Higher Power on which we can depend for recovery and healing, our collective experience has shown us that we can expect the following results:

When confronted with the void within, we will be able to decide not to act out, at least not today. We will realize that we are not our addiction, and find we can stop obsessing about sex and romance, or avoiding them compulsively. We will let go of sexual compulsion as our Higher Power, and discover in our own way a faith that works. We will grasp the concept of God as we understand God.

We will find it progressively easier to stay on our Sexual Recovery Plan and discover that sexual sobriety is more rewarding than compulsive sex. We will stop pursuing those who are unavailable, or who would reject or abuse us.

We will lose our fear of other people and our fear of our own sexuality. We will learn to recognize the difference between sex, love, and affection. We will discover ourselves, our spirituality, and our connection to our Higher Power.

We will find it easier to entrust outcomes to our Higher Power, and at the same time, we will begin to gain an understanding of God's work in our lives. We will allow our Higher Power to be our guide in relationships, even if this means no relationship for now. We will surrender to the possibility that if we do not have a life partner, this is not a punishment or deprivation, but God's will letting us know what is right for us at this time.

We will experience a rebirth of our relationship with our Higher Power, ourselves, and, then with others. We will become relaxed enough to be attractive to others instead of coming across as desperate and needy. We will rekindle hobbies and interests we had lost to addiction, and discover new ones. We will trust in a Power greater than ourselves that loves us and wants us to be happy.

We will develop patience and trust for our healing process, and continue to benefit from witnessing others recover. We will stop seeing ourselves as victims; instead, we will learn that we can take responsibility in our lives with the help and grace of our Higher Power. We will realize we are not empty; in fact, we have always been whole. Our character defects are wounds to be healed, not something innate.

We will discover prayer and meditation, and find spiritual renewal through doing acts of service within SCA and beyond. We will seek spiritual progress, not perfection, comparing ourselves not to others, but to the people we used to be.

Our lives will gain new meaning, whether we are in a relationship or out of one.

Our lives will become manageable, and we will experience increasing serenity and recovery. We will finally find peace with God, ourselves, our loved ones, our fellow human beings, and our sexuality.

Chapter 20: What Happens at SCA Meetings

Meetings are an essential tool in recovery from sexual compulsion. They are a focal point of the program, where we learn about recovery from our fellow members and often build long-lasting friendships. They help us break down the isolation in which sexual compulsion thrives. Meetings give us the strength to stop having compulsive sex one day at a time and to reshape our lives in realistic ways. The support of fellow members helps us stop acting out and start sorting out our confusion about sex. As meetings heal us, we begin to see how sexual compulsion affects all areas of our lives.

Meeting Format

While SCA meetings may follow various formats, the original 12-Step Program, Alcoholics Anonymous, provides the core elements. Some meetings focus on specific topics, such as developing spirituality and may include a short meditation. Some might have a reading and sharing about one of the Twelve Steps or another piece of literature. Others may focus on porn and web apps or may choose a theme, such as intimacy or creativity. There are also Beginners' meetings, which tend to be more general in format, with specific time allotted for newcomers to share. Of course, newcomers are welcome to attend and share at all SCA meetings. Conversely, many SCA veterans also attend Beginners' meetings.

SCA welcomes anyone who has a desire to stop having compulsive sex. Most meetings are "closed," which means attendance is limited only to those who identify as or think they might be sexually compulsive. Other meetings are "open," welcoming anyone interested in understanding sexual compulsion/addiction, such as friends, partners, guests, therapists, etc.

Meetings are typically between 60 and 90 minutes long. Most begin with a reading of SCA's *Statement of Purpose*, SCA's Twelve Steps, and a reading from SCA-approved literature. Often a member speaks for 15-20 minutes, called a "qualification" or "long share." In a general way, the speaker may disclose their personal experience of sexual compulsion, how they came to SCA, and how they are working on their recovery. Not all meetings have a "qualification" - it depends on the meeting format, as agreed upon by the group. Not all meetings may be in-person. Some may be by telephone, videoconference, or online.

The speaker or leader of the meeting may also introduce a topic or theme: one of the Twelve Steps, *The Tools That Help Us Get Better, The Characteristics Most of Us Seem to Have in Common*, or another subject related to recovery. After the speaker finishes, the meeting is open for shares from the attendees. There is a voluntary collection that pays for literature and rent of the meeting space. This collection may take place immediately following the qualification or may take place midway through the meeting. Some meetings incorporate a five-minute social break.

Everyone is welcome to "share" in the discussion, but no one *must* do so. By listening, we identify with others and start to see our behavior more clearly. We realize that we are not alone in our pain and confusion. As we start sharing, we experience the benefits of being open about our sexuality, and by being honest, we help others. We ask members to respect the anonymity and confidentiality of every person we meet and everything we hear at meetings. We usually close our meetings with a short prayer, such as the Serenity Prayer.

A Process of Progress

In SCA meetings, we develop a new sense of identity, feelings of belonging, and increased clarity about our problems. We begin to have hope for our recovery. But meetings can also make us uncomfortable. We may discover some painful facts about ourselves. We learn how isolated our secrets have made us. We may soon realize that sexual compulsion has permeated our work life, emotional development, family and social relationships, and spiritual endeavors. As we attend more meetings, others' experiences may help us become more comfortable with our sexuality and find ways to express it appropriately. We learn how to build new lives based on reality rather than fantasies, and we begin to rely on meetings as one of many tools helping to establish and maintain sexual sobriety.

Frequency and fellowship

Many find that the support we receive at meetings is a critical factor in breaking compulsive sexual habits. Members who have trouble staying sexually sober can find help by going to more meetings. When we consider how much time most of us spent pursuing compulsive sex, it's not unreasonable to devote some time every day to pursuing recovery.

Attending meetings also helps us make new friends. In the fellowship of meetings, we come to know each other by sharing our laughter and tears and learning how to relate to people in new and healthy ways. We often continue the fellowship by going out for coffee or a meal afterward. Socializing breaks down the sense of loneliness and isolation in which our addiction thrives.

Meetings and fellowship lead us to use our program's other tools, such as getting a sponsor, developing a Sexual Recovery Plan, using the telephone, texting, emailing, journaling, prayer, meditation, doing service work, etc., and working the Twelve Steps.

SCA is a recovery program for all sexual orientations and gender identities. Our Third Tradition states: "the only requirement for SCA membership is a desire to stop having compulsive sex." Some of us stop acting out right away. Others find that by attending meetings and working the program, they can gradually recover from sexual compulsion - one day at a time.

We keep coming back because we believe that there is a power at meetings greater than our sexual compulsion, which offers us sanity, serenity, and sexual sobriety.

Chapter 21: Q&A – Questions and Answers for Newcomers

1. Q: What is SCA?

A: Sexual Compulsives Anonymous is a spiritual program of recovery from the problem of sexual compulsion or addiction based upon the Twelve Steps of Alcoholics Anonymous. Members of the SCA program work toward achieving sexual sobriety and recovery by attending SCA meetings, reading literature about sexual compulsion and recovery, talking to other SCA members, writing, prayer, and working the Steps, among other actions suggested by the program.

2. Q: If SCA is a spiritual program, do I have to belong to a church or believe in God to be in SCA?

A: SCA's recovery program is spiritual rather than religious, and we believe there's a difference. SCA does not affiliate with any religious denomination. No member of SCA is required to be a member of *any* religion, to believe in God, or not to believe in God. Members have come into the program as atheists, agnostics, and practicing members of many denominations. Some members find that their beliefs change as they work the program; others continue to hold fast to their beliefs. SCA sets no requirements for such things. We only recommend that there be no discussion of specific religious beliefs at meetings.

3. Q: How do I handle this "Higher Power" business if I'm an atheist or agnostic?

A: In SCA, we each define for ourselves what the concept of a "Higher Power" means to us. Many of us use our SCA group as a Higher Power. Some people discover that they do have a spiritual connection through working the program. Whatever works is appropriate. There may be other members with shared beliefs who can provide some guidance.

4. Q: If I have compulsive and addictive sexual problems, how do I know I'll be safe in a room full of sex addicts?

A: While members are encouraged to help newcomers feel safe as they begin to deal with their sexual compulsion, there is no guarantee that someone in the program won't make sexual overtures. By and large, each of us is here for our recovery, not to find addictive sexual encounters. We're here to get a handle on responsible sexuality, not to make our sexuality even more compulsive and addictive. If something like that does happen, please feel free to say "No."

5. Q: When I see a person to whom I'm attracted - and this could happen at a meeting - I'm afraid I'll forget where I am and come on strong. Any advice on that?

A: We're all human. We just happen to be human and sexually compulsive as well. If this happens at a meeting, we encourage sharing our feelings with trusted members or a sponsor. Many members find that sharing it with their groups, without identifying the person involved, is also helpful.

6. Q: Are meetings a place to meet people?

A: Yes, meetings are places to meet supportive people who share their problems and desire to stop compulsive sexual behavior. Meetings are not for connecting with partners to "act out" our sexual compulsion. Such activity is discouraged. Occasionally it does occur, but most people come to meetings to deal with their compulsion, not fuel it. Many sexual compulsives are attractive and sexually stimulating people. It is natural to be turned on sexually or "triggered" by such people. We have learned that these feelings tend to lose their power over us when shared openly, honestly, and appropriately with others.

7. Q: What is compulsive sex?

A: Compulsive sex takes many forms. It is sexual behavior that we feel is out of control. Part of the problem is our delusion that we have power over such behavior. It might be that we can't stop checking out the apps, internet porn, webcams, and hookup sites or phone sex lines. Perhaps we can't avoid parks, restrooms, bathhouses, bookstores, or sex parties, no matter how hard we try. We may spend rent and food money on prostitutes, pornography, and sex toys. Maybe we can't keep our eyes and our attention off certain body parts of others. Excessive, repeated, or painful masturbation may be a problem for us. We may end up having sex with just about anyone, no matter how dangerous, unattractive, abusive, or unhealthy, just because we feel we need to have sex. We feel we can't stop ourselves. Sexual compulsion could be an inability to stop saying things that have a sexual connotation, make suggestions and innuendos to others, or persistently misuse sexual humor. It may take a variety of other forms as well. It may even be an obsession with avoiding anything sexual. The variations are endless.

8. Q: How do I know SCA is for me?

A: Attending meetings can help determine if SCA is a good fit for us. We suggest attending six different meetings before deciding if SCA is the right place to pursue recovery. We recommend looking over the list of *The Characteristics That Most of us Seem to Have in Common* and the self-test *Twenty Questions.* If there is identification with a number of those characteristics or traits, then working the SCA program may help. It may feel uncomfortable with a particular group even after a few meetings. If so, and if there are others in the area, try other meetings or even meetings of other 12-Step sexual recovery fellowships. If there is a desire to stop having compulsive sex, a program that works will surface.

9. Q: What is a Sexual Recovery Plan, and do I have to stick to a list of SCA "rules" in making one up?

A: A Sexual Recovery Plan is a *personal* listing of sexually-related behaviors that we believe to be unhealthy, self-destructive, dangerous, obsessive, degrading, or simply unwise. This list may include things that fuel our addiction or trigger us and make us want to act out our compulsion. It is a list of our bottom-line compulsive behaviors that we wish to abstain from one day at a time. These are the things we are ready and willing to give up and which we attempt to turn over to our Higher Power.

On the other side, we balance the list by those things we want to reward ourselves with and add to our lives in recovery. These rewards are an essential aspect of the plan. They may consist of personal, professional, and spiritual goals that we sacrificed through acting out our compulsive patterns. They may be as specific or as general as desired. Many members, especially newcomers, find this side of the recovery plan incredibly difficult because they are accustomed to thinking of themselves as unworthy and undeserving of rewards, but the rewards are necessary. They are the things that make staying in recovery worthwhile.

The plan may be unwritten or written. However, the program suggests that we prepare a written Sexual Recovery Plan. A written plan is more precise, more concrete, easier to remember, and helps us measure our sobriety. There are no rules to follow in developing a plan. The best question to ask is, "What works best for me?" Our SCA: A Program of Recovery book has some examples of plans. A group or sponsor may have some suggestions. It's up to each of us to set our boundaries of responsible sexuality that are comfortable for us. If the first plan doesn't work, there's nothing wrong with changing it. We expect revisions as members grow in recovery.

10. Q: What is a "slip?"

A: In the SCA Program, a "slip" is a violation of one's Sexual Recovery Plan: that is, engaging in an act defined as an unhealthy, compulsive problem, a behavior no longer serving a healthier life. Engaging in such activity is a slip.

11. Q: What does "counting days" mean?

A: It simply means keeping track of the time we've been abstinent from our bottom-line behaviors and being sexually sober according to *our* Sexual Recovery Plan. Some members consider their time very important and are proud of even a relatively short time in sobriety. Being abstinent for even a single day may seem like a miracle at first. Others may have difficulty in avoiding acting out, and counting days might be too intimidating. Counting days is only a tool some people find useful in staying sober. If it works, use it. If not, concentrate more on the rewards of recovery on the other side of the plan. We don't count days as a way to beat ourselves up for acting out.

12. Q: Can I go to meetings even though I may still be acting out?

A: Acting out is probably the best reason to continue going to meetings. In the meetings, find a sponsor or another trusted member. Talk with other members about acting out and the feelings behind it, both before and after the slip. The next time the desire to act out arises, call someone in the program right away and share these feelings, rather than waiting for a meeting. Talking about our problem with loving, supportive people is one of the most valuable things we can do for ourselves in the program. Acknowledging the shame and reducing its impact interrupts the addictive cycle and keeps us on the road of recovery.

13. Q: How many meetings do I have to attend?

A: As with everything else in SCA, the number of meetings to attend is a personal choice. We do not require that anyone attend a specific number of meetings. Eventually, we learn that the SCA program works not for those who *need* it, but for those who *want* it. We do not pressure members to feel they have to go to meetings. They go because they know it is one of the best ways to deal with sexual compulsion. Many members feel that not wanting to go to a meeting is the best reason to go, and they often share that they feel better because they resisted the temptation not to go. Going to meetings is an essential tool in working the program and taking care of ourselves. It's as simple as the ending statement at most meetings: "Keep coming back; it works when you work it!"

14. Q: Must I speak during sharing or at any other time during a meeting?

A: There are no requirements to speak or to participate in any SCA meeting. We suggest that members speak only during the time allotted for general sharing; that there be no crosstalk or criticism of one another, and that they raise their hands and wait to be recognized by the meeting leader. We ask that everyone stick to SCA issues since that's why we're here. Most SCA members find that sharing at meetings on SCA-related problems or issues helps them in recovery. Some meeting formats suggest that the appropriate time to get questions answered is after the meeting. Directing questions to individuals during the sharing portion of the meeting tends to encourage crosstalk.

15. Q: Are newcomers identified at meetings?

A: At some point in most meetings, we invite newcomers to state their first names. We do this not to embarrass newcomers but to allow other longer-term members to welcome them, introduce themselves, answer questions, and be supportive. SCA members understand that newcomers are often uncertain of themselves at their first meeting. They may not even feel comfortable with giving their names. We've heard things like, "I don't want to tell my name, and I don't even know why I'm here." We have no problem with that.

16. Q: What am I required to do at a meeting?

A: Nothing at all. If things get uncomfortable, anyone is free to leave at any time. We hope that moving through any discomfort is possible, but if not, we understand. We've all been there. The hardest part is getting through the door the first time. Most of us feel very much at home after that.

17. Q: In addition to going to meetings, what else can I do to help myself?

A: If the meeting has a phone list, pick one up and take it home. Another option is to ask other SCA members for their phone numbers. As suggested in *The Tools That Help Us Get Better*, the telephone is our meeting away from meetings. It may be challenging to make those first few calls, but it helps others when we make them. Also, get a Sponsor as soon as possible. We may ask a member with whom we identify. If that person doesn't feel comfortable with it, ask another. It needn't be a permanent arrangement. It helps to talk openly with someone who has similar problems and understands. We don't, however, expect any sponsor to "fix" us. Recovery is the responsibility of each individual. Being there to listen and give support is all another person can do. Pick up SCA literature available at the meetings. Most of our literature is also available in e-book form, and some may be on our website. Program literature will always be there, even when we can't contact someone on the phone or attend a meeting. We prepare a Sexual Recovery Plan, even a basic one at first, to get us started on a commitment to recovery. Setting some responsible boundaries is a vital first step.

18. Q: I'm scared I'll act out again. What should I do?

A: When the urges start, make a call, get to a meeting, read literature, do something nurturing, or do all of the above. We've all had these problems, and we know from experience - painful experience at times - that it's more difficult to handle them alone. It's OK to want help. Help and support are available: we have only to ask. When we learn to use that support, as uncomfortable as it may be and as resistant as we may be at first, we find the strength to start on the road of recovery.

19. Q: Will other members judge me if I have a slip?

A: This program is not about judging people or putting them down: it's about support. We feel it is vital to share the slip, no matter how horrendous, with someone else as soon as possible - on the phone, privately, or at a meeting. If we try to handle it alone, the shame and guilt, and sense of worthlessness may build up quickly, possibly leading to another slip. Don't forget: we've all been there. We're not alone.

20. Q: I'm ashamed of myself and of the things I'm doing or have done in acting out. I'm afraid if I talk about all this stuff to members, I'll be laughed at or kicked out. Will I?

A: No! We all know that talking about our troubles and stories lifts the shame and guilt and helps us be honest with ourselves. We try to break the cycle of shame, low self-esteem, and acting out to heal from our compulsive behaviors. The support and love of our groups is a significant and effective way to break it.

21. Q: Can I speak frankly about sexual experiences at meetings?

A: Yes, members are encouraged to be open and honest in sharing their sexual experiences. Rigorous honesty is an integral part of the program. We always remember that we are in a room full of other people trying to recover from *their* sexual compulsion. Therefore, talking about specific acting-out places is highly discouraged. Learning about new acting-out locations can be very destructive to our recovery. General types of acting out places may be mentioned (bars, the baths, the park, the apps, online bookstores, sex clubs, etc.) without identifying the specific name or location. Graphic descriptions of our acting-out behavior can trigger some members and be destructive to another's recovery. Acting out behaviors can be discussed in a general way without using specific, graphic, or sensational language. One may speak of voyeurism, fetishism, masturbation, anonymous sexual experiences, porn use, phone sex, etc., without explicitly describing the act. The critical thing is to talk about what we felt when we acted out, get our shame out in the open, and get rid of it. Sometimes there's a fine line about how detailed our sharing can be. Members may provide some helpful feedback after a meeting if the sharing has been too explicit.

22. Q: What is a "Qualification" (a pitch, story, long-share)?

A: When we do a "qualification" (pitch, story, or long-share), we may speak for 15 or 20 minutes regarding our experience, strength, and hope on our personal history of sexual compulsion. We might explain how we came to SCA and talk about how our recovery is going and what it means to us.

23. Q: Does my sexual orientation or gender identity make any difference in SCA?

A: Although a group of gay men founded SCA, it is a recovery program for all sexual orientations and gender identities. Our Third Tradition states, "The only requirement for SCA membership is a desire to stop having compulsive sex."

24. Q: I'm HIV positive. Will that make any difference with the members?

A: No. Some of our members are HIV positive or have other sexually transmitted infections, and they find the same support and love as any other member.

25. Q: How do I know others won't blab my name or spread my story around the group?

A: Confidentiality is of utmost importance in our program, as with all 12-Step programs. Each of us has a reason to be in a meeting; each of us would suffer if we failed to maintain confidentiality. Gossip and judgment of others are very damaging to both individual and collective recovery and are actively discouraged.

26. Q: I hurt inside, and sometimes I hurt so much I can't help breaking down. Will I be judged for this?

A: Expressing our hurt and pain is an integral part of recovery, and many of our members experience it in varying degrees. Fellow members support those who can share their tears and anguish with others.

27. Q: Do I have to give up sex entirely?

A: SCA is a sex-positive program of recovery. We are not here to repress our God-given sexuality but to learn how to express it in ways that will not make unreasonable demands on our time and energy, place us in legal jeopardy, or endanger our mental, physical or spiritual health. Some members use SCA's *Tool of Abstention (partial or total)* for some time in their recovery but abstention is a tool and not our goal.

28. Q: Do I have to stop masturbation?

A: In general, no. If masturbation fuels more serious acting out behaviors or becomes obsessive to the point where it interferes with our health, we may wish to abstain for a while. Others may view masturbation as a means of harm reduction. Masturbation may be a healthy outlet while dealing with more severe aspects of sexual compulsion. It's a subject that can be brought up at meetings and discussed openly to get input from other members.

29. Q: I hear the word "sobriety" used in the program. What does it mean?

A: We use the term "sobriety" to describe adherence to our Sexual Recovery Plan. Members are encouraged to develop their Sexual Recovery Plan and to define sexual sobriety for themselves. A Sexual Recovery Plan is a written plan, shared with our Higher Power and another member of the SCA program, preferably a sponsor, and is measurable one day at a time.

30. Q: If SCA members define their sobriety and boundaries, couldn't that end up being self-deceiving?

A: Yes, it could. But we've found that usually, it doesn't. As sexual compulsives, each of us has behaviors that we can no longer practice *and* remain healthy and responsible. These vary considerably from member to member. There may be, and usually are, other behaviors that we'd like to be free from eventually, but which we allow ourselves for now since they aren't so damaging to us and may act as a safety valve. At the same time, we work on our more serious problems. What is dangerous for one person could very well be harmless for others. If we allow ourselves behaviors that really are bottom-line, we'll soon realize that for ourselves. Rigorous honesty is an integral part of the program. Through sharing honestly with others, we learn to recognize if what we're doing is self-deceiving.

31. Q: Will I get cured of my sexual compulsion by participating in SCA?

A: Most of us accept as reality that we may always have the urge to be sexually compulsive: but it gets easier not to follow through on the urges. We may never be "cured," but we're not discouraged by that. Through participation in and working the program, we reach a point where we can express our sexuality in healthy and responsible ways. We've found it does work - when we work it.

32. Q: How long do I need to work the program?

A: In SCA, we learn we can work on our recovery more effectively when we focus on today, rather than on regrets about the past or worries for the future. We work our program one day at a time, knowing that just as our compulsion has no time limit, there is no limit to the growth we can attain.

33. Q: Is there a time limit for me to get through all the Twelve Steps?

A: Members work the program in their own way and at their own pace. A sponsor can guide this process. There are many ways to work the Steps. The point is to do them in such a way that they produce some benefit. There is no schedule and no time limit involved.

34. Q: I have to show the Judge that I've been going to meetings. What's the best way to do this?

A: Many courts provide their forms. If not, some groups have forms available. The meeting Secretary or other group officer will be happy to sign these forms at each meeting. Please check with the local SCA Intergroup for more information.

35. Q: How long are the meetings?

A: Most SCA meetings last for an hour to an hour and a half. There is usually time, either before or after meetings, where members may talk informally. We call this fellowship. As part of their format, many meetings announce fellowship at a nearby restaurant where members may discuss issues in an informal and relaxed setting or they just socialize.

36. Q: Are there different kinds of meetings?

A: Each meeting varies a little in its format. Many have speakers (qualifications or long shares), and most have a period set aside for individual sharing. Some devote some time at each meeting or once a month to studying a Step or a Tradition. Some meetings are open to all, and others are closed - that is, limited only to those who identify as SCA members or think they might have a problem with sexual compulsion. A few meetings specialize in recovery topics. It all depends on the group and the group conscience of the members.

37. Q: How much does SCA cost? Do I have to contribute?

A: There are no dues or fees for SCA membership; we are self-supporting through our own contributions. Each group relies on donations to pay its rent and other expenses, but no one is excluded or turned away because of their inability to contribute.

38. Q: Is literature available about my problem?

A: Meetings generally have SCA literature available, either free or at cost. Our website provides some of it free of charge. Other SCA literature is available in e-book or print format at a nominal cost.

39. Q: I'm a long way from the nearest SCA meeting, so it's hard for me to get to one. Any suggestions?

A: SCA has both phone and online meetings. Some of our meetings may take place using videoconferencing platforms. These meetings are generally accessible for anyone with a phone or internet service. Please check https://sca-recovery.org for more meeting information. Another alternative is to start a new SCA group. SCA can supply formats and other meeting information to help out. It only takes two people to have a meeting. When one's life or sanity is at stake, meetings can make all the difference in the world. There is a slogan, *Meeting Makers Make It*.

40. Q: Who is in charge of the meeting? Of SCA?

A: SCA is governed by the Twelve Traditions, as adapted from Alcoholics Anonymous. The Second Tradition of SCA states: "For our group purpose there is but one authority - a loving God as may be expressed in our group conscience. Our leaders are but trusted servants; they do not govern." Each group elects volunteers to serve for a specific period. Someone usually volunteers or is asked by the Secretary to facilitate the meeting. Everything affecting a group is put to the group conscience (i.e., voted on) during a meeting or at a business meeting after the regular meeting. Intergroups are service boards formed by meetings in a particular area to address common issues. In 1990, the meetings and intergroups approved the formation of the SCA International Service Organization (ISO) to work on world-wide projects such as formulating Conference-approved literature, SCA general policy, and related matters.

Chapter 22: How to Start an SCA Meeting

(Service Manual)

It only takes two people to have an SCA meeting, but starting one with three has advantages. We have designed these basic guidelines and questions to assist in starting a Sexual Compulsives Anonymous meeting.

Literature donations are available (upon request from the ISO) after consideration by the Inreach Committee: contact them using the email address inreach@sca-recovery.org. Purchasing literature for the new meeting online using the "Literature Store" on our website is also an option (https://sca-recovery.org/literature/).

If there is interest in starting an SCA meeting in an area where there are no SCA meetings and people would like to know if others are also interested, please use the "Contact Us" link on http://www.sca-recovery.org. In your message, please give your first name, your city or town, and an email address or phone number for others in the area to make contact.

A Quick Guide to This Material

1. Design a format for the type of meeting the group wants and write it down, including a name for the meeting.
2. Get any necessary literature.
3. Find a location, a day, and a time.
4. Make arrangements to reserve the space on a month-to-month basis: this may require a deposit or a signature.
5. Register your location, day, and time with the fellowship at large by sending the details to startscameeting@sca-recovery.org. Check local resources for announcing when and where the new meeting will take place.

6. Elect a Chair, Treasurer, Literature Person, and Intergroup Rep (if there is a local Intergroup; see the section below).
7. Register the meeting officers with the people who manage the facility hosting the meeting to pay the rent if needed.
8. A meeting might accumulate a treasury beyond a prudent reserve. In this case, consider a donation to the local Intergroup or the ISO. The section "What Are the Duties of the Treasurer?" describes this process later in this guide.
9. Keep Intergroup and any other relevant people apprised of any changes in the meeting (i.e., location, time, name, officers, etc.) Notify the ISO by emailing inreach@sca-recovery.org.

What is an Intergroup, and How Does It Work?

Intergroup is a service board directly responsible to the meetings it represents. Intergroup meets regularly and discusses concerns of individual meetings and matters of common interest. Also, Intergroup updates the local meeting directory; returns calls received on any SCA voicemail; maintains the website, which lists meeting times and places. It sometimes produces literature for Intergroup-approved distribution at the local level and possible submission to the SCA's International Service Organization (ISO) for approval at the international level. It provides suggested guidelines for meetings and plans for SCA special events. Intergroup is also involved in community outreach through its 12-Step committee and may order literature from the ISO for local distribution.

In addition to meeting-elected Intergroup reps, any individual SCA member is welcome to attend Intergroup meetings, make or second motions, and participate in the discussions. However, only elected reps vote.

It is important to note that Intergroup is NOT a ruling or governing body for the SCA fellowship; as stated in Tradition 2:

"...Our leaders are but trusted servants; they do not govern."

How Can I Create a Meeting to Suit My Needs?

This is probably the most important question in starting a meeting. After all, a core group is putting the meeting together. If it works for this group, chances are, in the long run, it's going to work for a lot of other people as well. Here are some ideas to incorporate. Ultimately, the meeting's format will be decided by group conscience, under our Second Tradition.

- Pitch Meeting - A meeting where the person who just shared picks someone else with their hand raised who is interested in sharing, and so on.
- Round Robin - A meeting where everyone sits in a circle with each person getting an opportunity to share (if time permits).
- Women's/Men's - These have the specific needs of either women or men in mind. However, under our Third Tradition, any SCA member may attend any meeting,
- Feedback - A meeting where each person who shares may ask for constructive, non-shaming feedback from people in the meeting. Feedback is optional. Feedback can simply mean identifying with the speaker, sharing words of encouragement, or relaying program slogans or tools that have helped. Feedback is not "cross-talk." (Cross-talk is when one person, unsolicited, responds to

another person's share by giving advice or criticism. Therefore, cross-talk is discouraged).

- Open/Closed - An open meeting is open to anyone uncertain whether they are an addict, as well as health professionals and - unless stipulated - the general public. In contrast, a closed meeting is open only to people who are, or think they might be, sexually compulsive.
- Step Meeting - A meeting that focuses on the 12 Steps of SCA. The Steps are available in the SCA Four-fold or the SCA Recovery Book. These meetings may choose one specific Step (e.g., a First Step meeting) or advance through the Steps each at each meeting. Generally, Step meetings involve reading a Step aloud in the group (perhaps from 'SCA's "12 Steps & 12 Traditions" or from Hope & Recovery) and then having shares on that particular Step. Pass around the book and let each person read a paragraph.
- Qualification - This generally means that the Chair of the meeting asks an SCA member to speak (or qualify) at the meeting. This person usually shares part of their life's story related to their addiction, including their experience, strength, and hope in recovery. A typical qualification lasts approximately 15-20 minutes. After the qualification, the speaker usually picks people with their hands raised to share, or they may decide to make it a pitch meeting and allow each sharer to pick the next person to share.
- Writing Workshop - This type of meeting involves members reading literature as a guide to help write down feelings or past experiences and then sharing what they have written. A period of 20-30 minutes provides members time to write (e.g., Fourth Step or Personal

Inventory Workshop). 12 Step workbooks can provide materials and questionnaires for this type of workshop.

- Topic Meeting - The people at the meeting suggest topics that they would like to talk about, and then everyone votes upon which topics are of more interest to those in the group. Often, members choose more than one topic. There may be a qualification (see above) where the speaker chooses the topic. The topic might be "letting go," "keeping it simple," "rigorous honesty," "testing the addict," etc.

These are just some of the ideas to incorporate. Some meetings have time limits on shares, and some meetings don't. There is a large variety of styles to include. There are topic meetings, Higher Power meetings, and some that focus on the Steps - decide which meeting would be best for you. Once a format is established for the meeting, get it down on paper. This document will aid in the stability and success of the meeting. The document can always change as the meeting progresses, but having an outline will help keep things clear. The meeting will grow and eventually take on a shape all its own. The material that follows includes sample meeting formats.

It is essential to give the meeting a name or a title. This name establishes the general boundaries for the meeting and gives people an idea of whether the meeting is appropriate. Some examples of titles are "Gay Men & Lesbian Round Robin," "Women Only Pitch Meeting," "4th Step Workshop," "Dating Workshop," "Incest Survivors," "Beginner's Meeting," etc.

What Is the General Format for a Meeting?

The format for each meeting may vary. Here are some examples:

Example #1 (Beginner's Meeting)

- The Chair welcomes everyone to the meeting and reads the *Statement of Purpose*. The Chair starts by asking those beginners present to introduce themselves by their first names only. After beginners introduce themselves, people in the group generally say, "Welcome." Pass around the 12 Steps. Each person introduces themself by first name only and then reads one of the Steps.
- The Chair introduces the speaker/qualifier (if any).
- The qualifier tells their story of "experience, strength and hope" (usually lasts 15-20 minutes), after which people applaud.
- The qualifier then opens the floor to pick people with their hands raised to share. The Chair announces (if it's a large meeting), "Since this is a large meeting, please try to keep your shares between 3-5 minutes so we may get in as many shares as possible. Also, please refrain from using any graphic language or naming any specific people or acting out places, either physical or cyber. Is there anyone here for the first time who would like to share first?"
- Somewhere halfway into the meeting (but not during someone's share), the treasurer announces the 7th Tradition Break.
- After the break, we'll have a 5-minute social break. (This break can be a time to greet and welcome newcomers).
- After the break, people go back to their seats, and the shares continue.
- The Chair announces 5-10 minutes before closing the meeting that the next person picked be the last share.
- After the last share, the chair asks for a volunteer to read *The Gifts of Recovery.*

- The Chair then reads the SCA's Closing *Statement*.
- Everyone joins hands in a circle and recites the Serenity Prayer, and the meeting ends.

Example #2 (Feedback Round Robin)

- The Chair welcomes everyone to the meeting and reads the *Statement of Purpose*. The Chair asks everyone to introduce themselves one at a time and do a "brief check-in with a few words of how you are feeling physically, emotionally, and spiritually."
- After the check-in, the Chair asks if someone would like to do the reading. (The material chosen for this meeting can be a daily meditation from Answers in the Heart – from the Hazelden meditation series.) After the reading, the Chair announces that each person will be allowed 3 minutes for feedback after their share if they so choose. The Chair reads: "Feedback is optional. Feedback is open to anyone in the group; however, we encourage people new to the fellowship to refrain from giving feedback and to use this time for listening. Feedback is not criticism. Feedback can simply mean identifying with the speaker, sharing words of encouragement, or relaying program slogans or tools that have helped you. Please try to keep your feedback brief, non-repetitive, and to the point."
- The Chair then asks for someone to time the shares. Each share is allotted an agreed-upon amount of time, with a one-minute warning. After the first person shares, they are allowed 3 minutes of feedback from those with their hands raised.
- The shares move in a clockwise direction around the circle until everyone has had the opportunity to share.

- Somewhere in the middle of the meeting (but not during a person's share), the treasurer announces the 7th Tradition break. (There is no social break during this particular meeting.)
- After everyone has had an opportunity to share, the Chair reads the *Closing Statement*.
- Next, everyone forms a circle with their arms around each other and recites the Serenity Prayer. The meeting ends.

Example #3 (Fourth Step Workshop)

- Chair welcomes people to the meeting and reads the *Statement of Purpose*.
- The Chair then passes around the chosen book with a commentary on the Steps (SCA's 12 & 12, <u>Hope and Recovery</u> or other), and each person introduces themselves by first name only and then reads a paragraph from the chapter on Step 4.
- Then the Chair announces that "we will take the next 20 minutes and write our Fourth Step using the questionnaire provided." (An appropriate questionnaire can be found online).
- After the 20 minutes, each person goes around the room in a round-robin fashion and reads what they have written. (If people arrive late and have not written anything, they usually wait until those who have written share first.)
- Somewhere in the middle - a Treasurer's break.
- After everyone has shared, the Chair reads the *Closing Statement*.
- People join hands for the "Serenity Prayer," and the meeting ends.

Example #4 (Higher Power Workshop)

- The Chair welcomes everyone and reads *Statement of Purpose*.
- Each person introduces themselves by their first name only and optionally identifies as a sexual compulsive, romance, lust, relationship addict, etc.
- The Chair asks for 5-15 minutes of silence for meditation.
- The Chair announces when the period of silence has ended and opens the floor for shares. The Chair picks the first person to share, and then it becomes a pitch meeting.
- Somewhere in the middle - a Treasurer's Break.
- Before the end of the meeting, the Chair announces, "I'm sorry, but that's all the time we have. If you didn't get to share, please try to find someone after the meeting." They then read the *Closing Statement*.
- All who wish to join hands for the Serenity Prayer and the meeting ends.

Example #5 (Typical Regional Meeting)

- Each meeting generally has a chairperson, a treasurer, and a literature person.
- The chairperson opens the meeting with the *Statement of Purpose*.
- The chairperson passes around the yellow Four-fold and asks each person to introduce themselves by their first name only and optionally identifies themselves in some way as a sexual compulsive, or romance, lust, relationship addict, etc., usually reading a characteristic, a Step or a Tradition from the literature.

- The chairperson usually follows a written script that describes the meeting format. The Chair might suggest that members identify with the speaker's feelings, rather than focusing on factual differences. The Chair may also recommend that members avoid provocative language in their shares. They may also indicate how long the "qualification" or speaker's share will be and that afterward, there will be shorter shares from members. This process is informal, but the chairperson generally conforms to the agreed-upon script.
- The Chair introduces the speaker, usually someone they have arranged to speak some time before. The speaker speaks for fifteen to twenty minutes, talking about their experience while acting out, how they came into the program, and how their recovery is proceeding. Sometimes the speaker introduces a topic, or a topic will develop from the speaker's qualification.
- At some point - either after the qualification or about halfway through the meeting - the treasurer announces that it is time for a 7th Tradition break and will pass around a bag to collect donations to cover rent, as well as possible Intergroup and International Service Organization donations. At this time, the meeting recognizes people counting days, those visiting or celebrating anniversaries of sobriety or time in the program. There is usually applause. Announcements are made and at most meetings, and there may be a five-minute break for socializing.
- After the qualification, members raise their hands and get called on to share. Sometimes we have a "pitch" meeting where the person called on picks the next person to share. In these shorter shares, usually ranging from two to five minutes, the member shares how they

identify with the speaker and about current issues in their life.

- At the end of the meeting, we thank the speaker with applause, read the *Closing Statement*, and join hands to say the Serenity Prayer together.

Example #6 (Another Regional Meeting Script)

Introduction:

Leader: Good evening. Welcome to Sexual Compulsives Anonymous. My name is ____________. I am sexually compulsive and your leader for this evening's meeting.

If this is your first time with us, you may not be sure what SCA is all about, what a sexual compulsive is, or if you may belong here. We assure you that we all had the same questions at our first meeting. We encourage you to stay, make friends, and find out if this is for you. At this meeting, we have readings of helpful literature, a speaker, and personal experiences dealing with this compulsion. Feel free to join in during the sharing portion. Take a copy of the literature with you. Most importantly, know that you are in a safe space to express yourself about anything you wish regarding compulsive sex. You will develop your understanding of the term as we continue. We are glad that you're here! Would all who care to join me in the Serenity Prayer?

Group: (Recites Serenity Prayer)

Leader: I have identified myself as sexually compulsive. If you wish to introduce yourself by your first name only, please raise your hand.

(Reads the SCA *Statement of Purpose*)

This meeting is for people whose lives have been deeply affected by their compulsive sexual behavior. Others are welcome to attend but are asked not to participate. Members of other

Anonymous Twelve Step Programs are also welcome, but we ask them to confine their sharing to SCA issues.

Starting with my left, we will now go around the room, identifying ourselves by our first names.

Group: (Individuals introduce themselves. Each introduction is followed by a "Hi, ____________.)

Leader: I have asked ____________ to read *The Characteristics Most of Us Seem to Have in Common.*

Reader: (Reads the Characteristics)

Leader: The SCA Program adapted the Twelve Suggested Steps of Alcoholics Anonymous. Like AA, SCA is an anonymous fellowship. Everything that is said here, in the group meeting, and member to member, must be held in confidence. In this way can we feel free to say what is in our minds and hearts, for this is how we help one another in SCA. I have asked _________ to read the Twelve Steps.

Reader: (Reads the Twelve Steps of SCA)

Introduction of Speaker:

Leader: The speaker tonight is __________. Who will speak for 15 or 20 minutes, emphasizing "How it was, what happened, and how it is now with recovery in the program."

Speaker: (Describes their experience, strength, and hope in recovery for approximately twenty minutes.)

Introduction of Newcomers, Announcements, Seventh Tradition

Leader: Are there any newcomers in their first 30 days of meetings? We ask you to please raise your hand and introduce yourselves by your first name. We do this not to embarrass you but to welcome you to SCA.

Newcomers: Hi, my name is __________.

Leader: We welcome all of you. We introduce newcomers so that we may all greet them during the break.

We will now observe the Seventh Tradition, which states that each group is self-supporting through its voluntary contributions. A portion of the amount collected goes to pay for the use of this room. The remainder is used for photocopying, literature, refreshments, etc. The secretary, ____________, will ask for announcements and then we will break for ten minutes.

Break (10 Minutes)

Leader: I have asked ___________ to read the Twelve Traditions.

Reader: (Reads the Twelve Traditions)

Leader: I have asked ____________ to read (leader chooses *Four Obstacles to Success* or *The Tools That Help Us Get Better*).

Reader: (Reads one)

Leader: We now come to the sharing portion of the meeting. Members are encouraged to share breakdowns and breakthroughs and how you used the SCA program to stay on your Sexual Recovery Plan, or if you acted out, how you handled it. If you are new to SCA, you may feel like sharing how you heard of the program and why you are here. Please try to keep your share to three minutes so that all who need to may share, and do not mention specific acting-out places.

Group: (Sharing until five minutes before the conclusion of the meeting).

Leader: The opinions expressed here tonight were strictly those of the individuals who gave them. Take what you like and leave the rest. The things that you heard here were spoken in confidence and are considered confidential. A few particular words to those who haven't been with us long. Whatever your problems, there are those among us who've had them, too. If you try to keep an open mind, you will find the help you need. Anyone who can handle what comes up at six consecutive meetings without retreating into denial has begun the process of recovery. Our living situations are bound to improve as we apply SCA ideas and principles. Without such spiritual help, living with the effects of sexual compulsion is too much for most of us.

We are not perfect. The welcome we give you may not show the love and warmth we have in our hearts for you. After a while, you will discover that, though you may not like all of us, you will love us in an extraordinary way - the same way we already love you. If you identified with anyone you heard here tonight, please consider talking to them after the meeting. In the spirit of recovery from sexual compulsion, we suggest that sex between members not be treated lightly. Sex between people new to the fellowship and other members is discouraged. Talk to each other, reason things out with someone else. Let there be no gossip or criticism of one another. Instead, let the understanding, love, and peace of the program grow in you one day at a time.

I have asked ___________ to read (leader chooses *Just for Today* or *The Gifts of Recovery*).

Reader: (Reads one)

Leader: After a moment of silence for the sexual compulsives who still suffer, would all of you please join me in the Serenity Prayer?

What Most Meetings Have in Common

Most meetings open with the SCA *Statement of Purpose* (found on the front of the Four-fold) and close with the *Closing Statement* and the Serenity Prayer. Here is a list of things that most meetings include in their format.

<u>Treasurer's Break</u>: According to our Seventh Tradition, "Every SCA group ought to be fully self-supporting, declining outside contributions." Therefore, a Treasurer's break is generally taken somewhere during the meeting. Although we are self-supporting

through our contributions, we are all encouraged, but not required, to give. During the Treasurer's Break, it is customary to ask if there are any SCA-related announcements.

The following is an example of how a Treasurer's announcement would start the break:

"It's time to take a Treasurer's break. SCA is self-supporting through its own contributions. We have no dues or fees for membership. However, we do have expenses. We ask that each person give what they can to help cover the rent of this room. If you can't give anything, don't worry. The important thing is just to keep coming back. Are there any SCA-related announcements?"

Pass around a basket, can, or paper bag to collect the money. Also, at this time, the Literature Person can announce that they have SCA literature available if anyone would like some.

After the announcements, ask if anyone would like to share their day counts or anniversaries (either on their Sexual Recovery Plans or time in SCA - usually, members applaud each other after these announcements). Also, the group may wish to have a five-minute break so that people can socialize. Several meetings forego day counts and extended breaks so they can get in as many shares as possible. The core group decides what is best.

<u>Opening/Closing</u>: The opening (*Statement of Purpose*) and closing statements define the meeting as part of the SCA Fellowship. These two statements establish the basic principles and rules of SCA membership. The SCA Recovery Book or the SCA Four-fold contain these statements.

<u>Serenity Prayer</u>: Customarily, the group closes by saying the Serenity Prayer. No one is required to participate.

<u>Reading the Steps</u>: After the opening statement, groups often read the Twelve Steps of SCA, *The Characteristics*, or *The Tools* of SCA. The reading of other literature depends on the group conscience. Each person ordinarily introduces themself by their

first name only. Meetings may combine these; a person states their name, reads from the literature, and passes it on to the next person.

What Is the General Time Frame of a Meeting?

Meetings generally last anywhere from 1 to 1-1/2 hours. Make it any length that suits the group's needs (for example, one hour at lunchtime).

What Kind of Literature Do I Want for the Meeting?

Choose literature that would be appropriate for the structure of the meeting. The literature chosen will probably set the mood for the meeting. There are many pieces of literature that may be helpful.

Members of SCA wrote these pieces that have been pre-approved for use at meetings. SCA's International Service Organization (ISO) publishes this literature: (See our Literature area for placing orders and prices).

- SCA: A Program of Recovery (the "Blue Book")
- *Secret Shame* (also part of the "Blue Book")
- *Q&A: A Guide to Newcomers*
- *Sponsorship in SCA*
- *Moving Through Withdrawal*
- *For the Newcomer*
- The SCA Four-Fold

Alternative 12-Step Literature

These are not pre-approved by the members of SCA. However, many members have found them helpful and inspiring, and they are therefore listed here for possible use by the group.

- Hope & Recovery
- Hazelden meditation books
- Alcoholics Anonymous (the AA "Big Book")
- AA's 12 Steps & 12 Traditions
- Other 12-Step workbooks and books on recovery from sex addiction.

At meetings, the SCA Four-fold is generally distributed free of charge. Feel free to use the Four-fold until the meeting's treasury has grown in size, and the meeting can afford to purchase copies of the Blue Book, *Secret Shame*, and *Q&A*. Or, front the money and receive reimbursement once the meeting treasury is large enough. Once people in the meeting purchase these materials, the money goes to the treasurer to be kept in the meeting treasury.

To order literature online, visit:

https://sca-recovery.org/literature

To order literature by mail, print and complete an Order Form and mail it with a check for the total to:

Literature Orders
SCA International Service Organization
PO. Box 1585, Old Chelsea Station
New York, NY 10011

Order forms are available at:

https://sca-recovery.org/SCALiteratureOrderform.pdf

Does Literature Need to Be Pre-Approved?

No. However, SCA does offer and recommend pre-approved literature if there is uncertainty about what literature would be appropriate for the meeting.

Will the ISO or Intergroup Provide Literature for the Meeting at the Outset?

No. The ISO and Intergroup do not supply the money for literature purchases. However, donations of literature (e.g., a "Starter Kit" are available by request) through the Inreach Chair at inreach@sca-recovery.org.

To use a book or some more expensive material at the meeting that the meeting cannot yet afford to purchase:

- front the money and seek reimbursement directly from people in the meeting;
- wait until the meeting treasury has grown and then use that money to purchase the books; or
- suggest that members go out and buy a copy.

How Do I Find a Location for the Meeting?

Find a location that is convenient for the core group. Remember, this small group is starting the meeting. It may take time for the meeting to grow in size, and therefore, may take time before the duties as Chair can rotate more easily.

Generally, social centers, churches, synagogues, and some schools make the best locations for meetings. The people who run them are usually pleased to help out. Choose a safe environment where people's anonymity and sobriety are not compromised. As our Twelfth Tradition reminds us, "Anonymity is the spiritual foundation of all our traditions, ever reminding us to place principles before personalities."

Some places require a nominal rent for space (depending on the location). The meeting collection generally covers this rent. If they ask rent for the room, make sure they understand that it may take a little while before there is enough money coming in regularly for the rent since the meeting is just starting. (Perhaps the meeting space will reduce the rent for a short period, e.g., four weeks.) Also, explain that meeting sizes vary, and some weeks will have fewer people than others. Getting this said out in the front establishes a responsible relationship with the meeting's venue.

What Are the Alternatives to an In-Person Meeting?

Technology has enabled meetings online, by telephone conference call, or videoconferencing software. The same guidelines for in-person meetings apply to online meetings, as do SCA's Twelve Traditions. If the meeting uses a written script, the host (with help from others) prepares instructions for participating in the meeting and the text of the leader's script. One option available is to virtually conduct the meeting using videoconferencing software. Offering a virtual meeting enables anyone who has access to a device or telephone to attend the meeting. Several SCA intergroups rent virtual platform space for such meetings, as does SCA's ISO. The meeting may eventually migrate to a physical meeting space.

Whom Do I Tell About the Meeting?

Once a day, time, and location are established for the meeting, register it and its officers with SCA Intergroup (or the ISO). Please include a name for the meeting. Pick a name that best describes the overall context of the meeting. It is desirable to find several other members or newcomers to attend during the first few months to help the meeting get established.

What if Nobody Comes to the Meeting?

Be patient. Meetings can take anywhere from a few weeks to a couple of months before they start to catch on, sometimes even longer. Don't be discouraged. However, to speed up the process, have the meeting announced at other SCA meetings or hang flyers at appropriate locations. An example of an inappropriate place for a flyer is a telephone pole or shopping center. In smaller communities, contact therapists, hospitals, clinics, or possibly post information at other 12-Step fellowship meetings such as AA, AL-ANON, OA, NA, etc. Some publications have lists of community activities, including 12-Step meetings. Since anonymity/confidentiality is the foundation of our program, please preserve anonymity in letting people know about the new meeting.

Who Holds the Offices of the Meeting?

The founder of a new meeting usually becomes the Chair of the meeting right from the start. This service is vital for two reasons: (1) they know best how the meeting runs, and (2) the people who are allowing the group to use the space will feel more comfortable if they see a familiar face every week, at least at the beginning.

Not all cities hold the same offices for their meetings; however, the group may decide to establish some of the other offices: Treasurer, Literature Person, and Intergroup Representative. The founder may start out being all of these, but don't worry: once the meeting takes off, people interested in doing service will fill those positions.

If possible, register the names of the officers of the meeting, with the Intergroup Secretary (if there is a local Intergroup). Then, after the meeting is well on its way, it is customary to hold elections every 3-6 months to relieve the people currently holding the office of their duties. This process is known as "doing service." Service is one of the tools that help us get better - it's "a way of helping ourselves by helping others." Don't be afraid to ask for help. One person may have started the meeting, but that doesn't mean that they have to carry the meeting for the rest of their life.

What Are the Duties of the Chair or Secretary?

They generally run the meeting from start to finish. The treasurer will announce when the Treasurer's Break is, but other than that, follow the established format. If it's a qualification meeting, the Chair is responsible for finding speakers. They are responsible for seeing that the meeting starts and ends on time and that all furniture, lights, etc., are restored to how they were at the start.

What Are the Duties of the Treasurer?

The Treasurer is responsible for collecting and keeping track of the meeting donations. This money gets distributed in several ways: (1) paying the meeting's rent; (2) covering any additional expenses, e.g., literature purchases; and (3) making a donation to the Intergroup or the ISO as means allow; or (4) for other purposes relevant to the meeting. When keeping track of the treasury, it is beneficial to maintain a "prudent reserve" of funds if donations fail to meet rent expenses. A rule of thumb is that a prudent reserve might be enough funds to cover the weekly rent for four (4) weeks. It is essential to keep a ledger for the meeting, maintaining accurate records of the meeting's donations and a running balance after expenses.

An example of a meeting ledger follows:

Ledger for Monday, 7.00 p.m. beginner's meeting

Prudent Reserve = $80.00

Beginning Balance	Meeting Date	Amount Collected	Expenses	Expense Type	Closing Balance
$112.00	7/25	$28.00	($20.00) ($15.00)	Rent Literature Purchase	$105.00
$105.00	8/1	$22.00	($20.00)	Rent	$107.00
$107.00	8/8	$12.00	($20.00)	Rent	$99.00
$99.00					

It is beneficial to the group to make a regular Treasurer's report (perhaps monthly) that summarizes donations, expenses, current balance, and a prudent reserve. If there is a surplus, groups may choose to donate to their local Intergroup (if there is one) or the International Service Organization (ISO) of SCA. The ISO relies on the contributions of members, groups, and Intergroups to fulfill its purpose of furthering the recovery of those who suffer from sexual compulsion.

To contribute to the ISO, go to the web address below:

https://sca-recovery.org/donate

Rather than donate online, groups may make out a check or money order to "SCA" and mail it to the Intergroup Treasurer in the area (if there is one). Don't forget to indicate the location and time of the meeting on the check or money order. If the area has not yet developed an Intergroup, please donate to the ISO Treasurer at the following address:

SCA/ISO Treasurer
P.O. Box 1585, Old Chelsea Station
New York, NY 10011

What Are the Duties of the Literature Person?

The literature person is responsible for seeing that the meeting has Four-folds and other SCA literature. If the meeting has purchased additional literature, such as 12-Step, meditation, or other books, they are responsible for those as well. During the Treasurer's Break, the Literature person will have a chance to announce that literature is available if anyone is interested. They may obtain literature through the Intergroup, or if the area does not have one, it is available directly from the ISO online:

https://sca-recovery.org/literature

To order literature by mail, print and complete an Order Form found on our website and mail it with a check for the total to:

Literature Orders
SCA International Service Organization
PO. Box 1585, Old Chelsea Station
New York, NY 10011

Order forms are available at:

https://sca-recovery.org/SCALiteratureOrderform.pdf

What Are the Duties of the Intergroup Representative?

If there is an Intergroup in the area, the meeting will benefit by electing an Intergroup Representative. In that case, it is the responsibility of the elected representative to go to the regularly scheduled Intergroup meetings. Intergroup Reps have the privilege to vote on issues relating to SCA in the area. Upon attending the Intergroup meeting, it is their responsibility to report back to the members of the weekly SCA meeting with any pertinent information relating to SCA activities, events, etc., as well as any minutes from the last meeting.

The Twelve Traditions of SCA form the framework for all SCA meetings and our community. Our First Tradition states, "Personal recovery depends upon SCA unity." The founding members are fostering a significant part of that unity by starting a meeting in the local community. We encourage the group to read the Twelve Traditions as a means of laying the roots of a meeting and personal recovery in healthy soil.

Starting a new meeting, particularly where there previously were none, is a constructive and encouraging step toward everyone's recovery. It is also strengthening the well-being of our program and its outreach services. So, when someone calls us and asks, "Is there a meeting in my area?" we can proudly say, "YES!" - all because of these efforts. Thank you.

Chapter 23: Four Obstacles to Success

The SCA Traditions affirm that all SCA meetings be constructive, helpful, loving, and understanding. In striving toward these ideals, we avoid matters that can distract us from our goals, causing discord.

1. Discussion of Religion

SCA is not allied with any sect or denomination; it is a spiritual program based on no form of religion. Everyone is welcome, no matter what their affiliation or none. Let us not defeat our purpose by entering into discussions concerning specific religious beliefs.

2. Gossip

We meet to help ourselves and others to learn and to use the SCA approach to achieve freedom from our sexual compulsion. In such mutual support, we discourage gossip. We do not discuss other members; our commitment to anonymity assures that our meetings are safe for those in pain. Careless repeating of matters heard in meetings can destroy the very foundation of our work together. Let us be ever vigilant in resisting the temptation to criticize others, judge others, or make comparisons.

3. Dominance

Our leaders are chosen not to govern but to serve. No member of SCA should direct, assume authority, or give unsolicited advice. Our program focuses on suggestions, sharing of experience and personal insight, and rotation of leadership. Everyone makes progress in their way and pace. Any attempt to manage or direct is likely to have disastrous consequences for group harmony.

4. Sensational Language

In the First Step of the program, we admitted our powerlessness over sexual compulsion. In SCA, we seek to recover the power to choose times and places to express our sexuality responsibly. Therefore, using sexually explicit expressions or graphic language can impair our recovery. We also avoid identifying specific locations or online platforms where persons can "act out." Such identification may defeat the efforts of others seeking freedom from sexual compulsion.

Chapter 24: The Twelve Traditions of Sexual Compulsives Anonymous (SCA)

THE TWELVE TRADITIONS OF SCA[17]

1. Our common welfare should come first; personal recovery depends upon SCA unity.
2. For our group purpose there is but one authority — a loving God as may be expressed in our group conscience. Our leaders are but trusted servants; they do not govern.
3. The only requirement for SCA membership is a desire to stop having compulsive sex.
4. Each group should be autonomous, except in matters affecting other groups or SCA as a whole.
5. Each group has but one primary purpose — to carry its message to the sexual compulsive who still suffers.
6. An SCA group ought never endorse, finance or lend the SCA name to any outside enterprise, lest problems of money, property and prestige divert us from our primary purpose.
7. Every SCA group ought to be fully self-supporting, declining outside contributions.
8. Sexual Compulsives Anonymous should remain forever nonprofessional, but our service centers may employ special workers.
9. SCA, as such, ought never be organized; but we may create service boards or committees directly responsible to those they serve.
10. SCA has no opinion on outside issues; hence the SCA name ought never be drawn into public controversy.
11. Our public relations policy is based on attraction rather than promotion; we need always maintain personal anonymity at the level of press, radio, television and films.
12. Anonymity is the spiritual foundation of all our traditions, ever reminding us to place principles before personalities.

---

[17] The Twelve Steps and Twelve Traditions are reprinted and adapted with permission of Alcoholics Anonymous World Services, Inc. Permission to reprint and adapt does not mean that Alcoholics Anonymous is in any way affiliated with this program. AA is a program of recovery from alcoholism. The use of the Twelve Steps and Twelve Traditions in connection with other programs which are patterned after AA, but address other problems, does not imply otherwise.

Commentaries on the Twelve Traditions of SCA

Sexual Compulsives Anonymous derives from the first Twelve Step program, Alcoholics Anonymous. During its first decade, Alcoholics Anonymous accumulated substantial experience which indicated that certain group attitudes and principles were particularly valuable in ensuring the survival and welfare of the AA Fellowship. In 1946, the Fellowship's international journal, the *AA Grapevine*, committed these principles to writing and they became the Twelve Traditions of Alcoholics Anonymous. The AA Fellowship adopted them as a whole at the first AA International Convention in 1950.

Sexual Compulsives Anonymous has adapted and adopted the Twelve Traditions for use within the SCA Fellowship. Like AA, we have found that just as the Twelve Steps permit our individual recovery, so too do the Twelve Traditions make possible our collective recovery. By following the Twelve Traditions, our members, groups and service bodies will continue to maintain our common welfare and allow SCA to thrive in its primary purpose – of carrying the message of recovery to the sexual compulsive who still suffers. The following commentaries illustrate the Twelve Traditions as we apply them in SCA, reflecting the experience and specific circumstances of Sexual Compulsives Anonymous.

Tradition One

"Our common welfare should come first; personal recovery depends upon SCA unity."

In our active compulsion and unrecovered state, we were self-centered. For the majority of sexual compulsives, it was all about "me." Most of us come into Sexual Compulsives Anonymous obsessed with ourselves, and the unmanageability of our own lives. On joining SCA, we soon realize that our recovery from sexual compulsion depends on our membership in the fellowship and the survival of the group. Our experience shows that it is essential that SCA meetings be places where members feel accepted and free to share their experiences with sexual compulsion honestly and openly, without fear of being shamed or judged. We achieve SCA unity at a primary level by making the meeting rooms safe places for sharing, and through the love and support that members give one another in their collective journey toward recovery. This unity depends on the tolerance of others' differences: differences in background, gender, sexual orientation, and gender identity; differences in approaches to working the Twelve Steps; differences in individual Sexual Recovery Plans, and differences in the types of compulsive sexual behavior that brought us to SCA.

Members say that SCA is a "we" program. This concept emphasizes that recovery in SCA is a collective undertaking. The various formats of our meetings reinforce this concept. We approve the meeting formats themselves as a group, by group conscience. We take turns in leading the meeting, and in reading the literature aloud. We share our experience, strength, and hope with each other, relating together how we are working our program of recovery and overcoming the compulsion. Some meetings may limit the amount of time each person can speak so that as many members as possible may have the opportunity to share. Some meetings deliberately set aside specific times for newcomers to share, or use other means to ensure that sharing is open to all.

Some members may struggle longer than others with letting go of their compulsive behaviors and embracing recovery. Whatever the condition of each member's recovery, SCA unity provides each group with a powerful strength for the individual to rely on. Even if an individual is having difficulty recovering, the group as a whole remains strong. The group collectively demonstrates a higher level of recovery and draws its members toward growth. The fellowship as a whole engages in this process through its literature and service structures. Only together are we strong enough to overcome the physical, mental, emotional, and spiritual afflictions of our disease.

Our experience has been that we cannot recover in isolation: that we cannot overcome sexual compulsion on our own. We have found that we need the support and collective experience of other sexual compulsives to recover. We rely on mutual support for our personal recovery. Therefore, the continued existence of SCA groups is essential. Unity is fostered and maintained throughout the network of SCA groups worldwide. A fundamental source of unity in the SCA Fellowship is adherence to the Twelve Traditions of SCA.

Tradition Two

> "For our group purpose there is but one authority – a loving God as may be expressed in our group conscience. Our leaders are but trusted servants; they do not govern."

In SCA, we recognize that the ultimate guidance for the group comes from a loving God, as may be expressed through the group conscience. We form a group conscience by careful discussion, with decisions formed by a majority vote. Members make decisions with the best interests of the group at heart. The group strives for consensus where possible. The leaders chosen to serve the group are not authorities, but trusted servants. They come and go with each new election or rotation. They are entrusted by the group to take care of tasks and carry out the group conscience.

We take a group conscience when deciding anything from practical matters for individual meetings to fellowship-wide matters at the International Service Organization's (ISO) annual conference. For example, at the meeting level, the group conscience would elect a new group Treasurer, or decide whether or not to time individual sharing at a meeting. At the ISO level, the group conscience would decide whether or not to approve a proposed new piece of literature for the fellowship.

The principle includes all members present having a voice and a vote in a group conscience decision. Regardless of whether a member is relatively new or has many years of experience, it is also an indication that we understand that no one person has it all figured out on any given issue or a monopoly on wisdom. It may also be detrimental for groups and service bodies to become dependent on a small number of individuals who take service positions over and over again. The dominance of a meeting, intergroup, or other service structure by any individual or group can soon lead to a loss of group harmony and unity[18], as it will exclude some individuals and their experiences. Rotation of leadership chosen by group conscience has been of proven benefit to the welfare of a group.

Many of us at one time or another may have had the fear that if we did not somehow "take control" of a cherished meeting or service body, it would become unsafe or ineffective. The desire to protect our recovery - which in many cases is vital to our survival - may lead some of us to be tempted to try to mandate what we consider to be the "right" way to run an individual meeting or service board. Listening to others and being open-minded promotes spiritual growth in the individual and the group, and is a way of gaining access to a Higher Power. In trusting that the spiritual process of forming a group conscience will bring about a better decision or solution to a problem than we as individuals could arrive at alone, we forego seeking to impose our will on others.

---

[18] *Four Obstacles to Success*, SCA - A Program of Recovery © SCAISO

Tradition Three

"The only requirement for SCA membership is a desire to stop having compulsive sex."

SCA is a 12-Step fellowship, inclusive of all sexual orientations, open to anyone with a desire to recover from sexual compulsion[19]. The fellowship does not discriminate. Individual members and groups cannot determine whether another person's desire to stop having compulsive sex is sincere or not. We do not require that anyone identify themselves by a particular label, or by any label at all. The group does not decide whether or not someone is to remain a member of SCA. As long as an individual has a desire to recover from sexual compulsion, they are welcome in SCA.

For some newcomers, merely attending meetings consistently seems like a Herculean effort. Others have a "revolving door" experience of coming in and out of the fellowship until they are finally willing to admit in earnest that they have a desire to stop having compulsive sex. They find that involvement in SCA is an essential part of achieving that aim. Still others have deep-seated shame issues, and even if they accept that they need to attend SCA, they have difficulty believing they belong anywhere, let alone in a group of people in recovery who are healing and even thriving in their lives. A member may "visit" SCA for a while before deciding to attend regularly, or may attend and instantly feel they have found a new spiritual home with like-minded people. All are welcome.

---

[19] "Sexual Compulsives Anonymous is a twelve-step fellowship inclusive of all sexual orientations, open to anyone with a desire to recover from sexual compulsion." SCA Self-Identification Statement © SCAISO

The Third Tradition states that the only requirement to be a member of SCA is a desire to stop having compulsive sex. In our collective experience, this includes not only impulsive and harmful sexual behaviors, but also problems such as romantic obsession, addiction to people, love, or relationships, addiction to sexual or romantic fantasy, and the constant search for intimacy. SCA is open to everyone with a desire to recover from sexual compulsion in any of its manifold forms of expression[20], including the use of technology to avoid intimacy and the compulsive avoidance of sex, also known as sexual anorexia.

Sexual Compulsives Anonymous also accepts the Third Traditions of some other sexual recovery programs as being equal to its own. Therefore, members of SAA[21] and SLAA[22] may attend SCA meetings under the Third Traditions of their programs, equally with SCA members.

We are not the arbiters of anyone else's sex conduct. As individuals, we may feel we do not want people with certain types of sexual compulsion in our meetings, but we do not attempt to exclude or change SCA to exclude such individuals. We have often found that the very people around whom we felt uncomfortable, or whose presence we feared would harm SCA or our recovery, turned out instead to be people who helped us. It is not only the acceptance of others but also self-acceptance that is a principle at work here because welcoming others, regardless of differences, is an indication that we have come some way toward accepting ourselves.

---

[20] Affirming resolution passed by SCAISO April 26, 2015

[21] Sex Addicts Anonymous

[22] Sex and Love Addicts Anonymous

Some service positions within SCA may suggest lengths of time on a Sexual Recovery Plan or a specified prior length of membership in SCA as a recommendation. However, no one can lose their membership in SCA for having a slip on their Sexual Recovery Plan, or for failing to work a "perfect" program, were such a thing even possible.

In the same way that the requirement for SCA membership is minimal, the requirements for forming an SCA group are minimal. Any two or more sexual compulsives gathered together for sexual sobriety may call themselves an SCA group, provided that, as a group, they have no other affiliation, and meet together to work the SCA Program of Recovery.[23]

---

[23] The SCA Program is described in SCA - A Program of Recovery and other conference-approved SCA literature.

Tradition Four

"Each group should be autonomous, except in matters affecting other groups or SCA as a whole."

An SCA group is any group that meets regularly, at a specified place and time, for the purpose of recovery from sexual compulsion, provided that it adopts the Twelve Steps and follows the Twelve Traditions of Sexual Compulsives Anonymous. Any two or more groups can form an SCA intergroup. An SCA intergroup can so designate itself provided that it agrees to adopt the Twelve Steps and follow the Twelve Traditions of Sexual Compulsives Anonymous. Likewise, the International Service Organization of SCA is organized solely to further the recovery of those who suffer from sexual compulsion, and endorses SCA's Twelve Step recovery program, adheres to its Twelve Traditions, and aims only to serve as the Trusted Servant of the SCA Fellowship. These fundamental qualifications provide the framework for the abundantly varied approach to recovery from sexual compulsion that we find within the SCA Fellowship, where groups have complete autonomy, except in matters affecting other groups or SCA as a whole.

There is a principle of freedom at work in this Tradition, but one that balances against group willfulness. Autonomy means that each group is self-governing. Each group follows the Twelve Traditions but has latitude to adapt them to its particular circumstances. The positive aspect of this Tradition is that SCA employs a variety of group formats, and reads different literature at various meetings, all determined by group conscience. Some people may find some group formats or approaches appealing, but not others. This freedom and variety may allow SCA to reach a larger number of still-suffering sexual compulsives than it otherwise would.

In addition to its own situation, a group considers how its actions could affect other groups or SCA as a whole. For instance, one group's bad relationship with a landlord may negatively affect the chances that *other* SCA groups could secure a meeting place at that location. Likewise, SCA groups maintain friendly relations with one another. One of the best ways to do this is for groups to form an intergroup to work together on projects, and for that intergroup to join SCA's International Service Organization to work together on matters affecting the fellowship as a whole.

In a fearful attempt to guard our recovery, as members of one group, we might have wanted to try to control the other groups in our area so that their meetings ran in a certain way. Such action is not in keeping with the principles of the Fourth Tradition, or the spirit of individual responsibility fostered by recovery. What the Fourth Tradition tells us is that the way for our fellowship to remain vital, secure, and effective is if we trust each group to take care of itself. Unless what is happening at one group is directly affecting another group or the fellowship as a whole, we stand back and let the members of that group determine what works for them, and let them respond to whatever problems arise. These are the lessons of this Tradition: letting go of control, getting out of the way of others' recovery, and trusting the program and its spiritual principles.

Just like individuals, groups and service bodies are also allowed to change their minds. They do this by taking another group conscience. If they reach a different conclusion, they can then take a different course of action than was previously decided.

Over time, as individual members, we feel less need to control the business of a group or service body. This change happens because we learn that if a particular group conscience does not work out favorably, a group or service body can always change direction. In this way, we learn to trust that everyone is learning and growing spiritually from the unfolding of events.

Tradition Five

"Each group has but one primary purpose – to carry its message to the sexual compulsive who still suffers."

The first four Traditions give us a sense of place and belonging in the world and within our fellowship. Together with related experience, the Fifth Tradition tells us that our hard-won independence, interdependence, and sense of ourselves will continue to be ours if we share our well-being with those within and beyond the fellowship. We pass on to others what we have so freely received ourselves. We maintain the cohesion and effectiveness of our groups by focusing on our message of recovery.

What is our message, and how do we carry it? In attending meetings and working the SCA Program, we become familiar with its message of recovery: that by acknowledging our powerlessness and living by a set of spiritual principles, we can be free of sexually compulsive behavior. Our recovery offers hope that others can find relief from the chaos of addiction as we have. Our collective experience holds out the prospect of peace and serenity. Once we have a grasp on sobriety, and once we have dismantled the compartmentalization that governed our lives before finding recovery, we are encouraged to let others know of our newfound freedom and the way we have attained it. We carry the message of recovery, both as individuals and as members of a group, by sharing the results of working the Twelve Steps and using *The Tools That Help Us Get Better*, and working with other members of Sexual Compulsives Anonymous. This outreach maintains our sobriety and helps others to find the same freedom, thereby fulfilling the group's primary purpose. Our group purpose, as suggested by Tradition Five, is to help others to recover from sexual compulsion.

By listening to one another in meetings, sharing our struggles with recovery at meetings (which can sometimes be difficult), and welcoming newcomers at meetings, individuals as part of the group are practicing the Fifth Tradition. Continuing to tell our stories, continuing to remind ourselves and others where we have been and how far we have come, keeps us recovering, and helps others.

Who is "the sexual compulsive who still suffers"? Traditionally, we mean the newcomer in the room or those who are not aware that there is recovery from sexual compulsion. The Fifth Tradition asks us always to keep these individuals in mind as we go about our life as a group. We would also be dishonest if we did not admit that we all remain, to some degree, "sexual compulsives who still suffer." As the book Alcoholics Anonymous tells us, "What we really have is a daily reprieve, contingent on the maintenance of our spiritual condition."[24] No one achieves perfection, and all need support. The group tries to carry its message to all who suffer from sexual compulsion, whether they are present at a meeting, in the local community, or elsewhere.

Groups collectively carry the message of recovery by doing such things as holding regular recovery meetings, putting on service meetings, taking meetings to hospitals and institutions, and maintaining and providing meeting lists. They fulfill their primary purpose by providing a framework for sponsorship; obtaining, distributing, and selling SCA literature; hosting and

---

[24] Alcoholics Anonymous – 4th Edition – "Into Action," page 85.

supporting service board and committee activities; performing outreach to therapists, institutions, and the public at large; and responding to inquiries about the SCA Program. Groups also carry the message by publicizing the fellowship in printed form and via the internet, arranging Twelfth Step calls for interested individuals, putting on Step Study groups, and hosting social events, workshops, and spiritual retreats for members. They also do so by corresponding and communicating with loners and prisoners and supporting those in treatment centers, rehabilitation facilities, hospitals, and nursing homes. Indirectly, the groups carry the message by demonstrating the principles of recovery in their everyday dealings with their landlords, local businesses, and suppliers. These third parties may inform others of the SCA Fellowship's work and be a source of positive comments and referrals.

Technology has enabled Twelve Step programs to carry the message of recovery to people in distant places in ways their founders could not have imagined. Not only do we have face-to-face meetings, but telephone and online meetings as well. Sponsorship can take place by telephone, email, internet conferencing, and other electronic means. Recovery literature and information can be shared electronically worldwide at the touch of a button. Websites can reach untold numbers of people who may need to hear the SCA message of recovery, learn of the hope it provides, and find the solution it offers.

The larger message of SCA is that there is recovery from sexual compulsion and that it is a spiritual solution. Individual members of SCA may have their interpretations of the Steps, Traditions, and other literature. How then do we carry a group message? It has been SCA's experience that so long as we keep the focus on our primary purpose, open and honest sharing allows our underlying spiritual message to be carried by the group, despite individual interpretations of the program.

This Tradition is primarily concerned with carrying the message of recovery from sexual compulsion to those who still suffer. It is, therefore, comparable to Twelfth Step[25] work for an individual; it is relevant to consider discussion at SCA meetings of issues that are related to other aspects of compulsive illness, or that may seem unrelated to sexual compulsion. Many of us are cross-addicted or have concurrent disorders. Some of us may, at times, also need to share about other problems that may be affecting our sexual sobriety or well-being. However, we do well always to remember that our primary purpose in SCA is to stay sexually sober and to help others to achieve sexual sobriety. Accordingly, some groups have suggested sharing guidelines, reminding members of our primary purpose, while others specifically permit sharing on cross-addiction or similar topics. Some groups have cross-talk guidelines encouraging members to share for themselves and not comment on what others have said during their sharing. These and other group guidelines ensure that SCA meetings are safe and healing places for all who wish to recover from sexual compulsion.

All SCA meetings intend to be constructive, helpful, loving, and understanding. In striving toward those ideals, we avoid matters that can distract us from our goals, and that can cause

[25] Step Twelve: "Having had a spiritual awakening as the result of these steps, we tried to carry this message to sexually compulsive people and to practice these principles in all our affairs."

dissension[26]. These can include discussion of religion and politics, gossip among members, member dominance, and the gratuitous use of triggering or sensational language. Focusing on our primary purpose keeps a group from getting distracted, and helps provide the maximum possibility for recovery from sexual compulsion to all in attendance. Having new members to sponsor and work with helps those of us who have been in the program for any length of time to keep the program fresh and vital for ourselves.

---

[26] *Four Obstacles to Success*, SCA - A Program of Recovery © SCAISO

Tradition Six

"An SCA group ought never endorse, finance or lend the SCA name to any outside enterprise, lest problems of money, property and prestige divert us from our primary purpose."

If an SCA group affiliates with related facilities, we would mix our message of recovery with that enterprise's ideology or mission. This mixing could create conflict and dissension among the membership, divert time and energy away from helping the newcomer, and distract us from our primary purpose of carrying the message of our spiritual solution to other sexual compulsives.

An SCA group's use of routine commercial services, such as banking or printing services, does not constitute an endorsement of a service or a particular vendor, and SCA may use such services to assist its work in carrying its message.

It is often difficult to determine where cooperation with outside enterprises ends, and endorsement begins. This distinction is probably best determined on a case-by-case basis through the group conscience. For instance, many SCA intergroups invite outside speakers to events. If handled correctly, this can be a humble admission that we do not have all the answers to the problem of sexual compulsion and that we remain open, as a fellowship, to listening to new ideas.

The Traditions offer several guidelines for cooperation with outside enterprises. We take care to state explicitly to the enterprise and the intended audience that such cooperation does not constitute an endorsement. Other suggestions are to monitor publicity around the cooperation and to ensure that we enter into no permanent relationships with outside entities.

SCA also has a long history of cooperation with other Twelve Step fellowships that carry the message of recovery to the sexual compulsive who still suffers. For example, SCA intergroups may cooperate with other fellowships' intergroups in producing shared meeting lists, thus carrying the SCA message of hope even further. As part of the same spiritual family, SCA also cooperates as may be appropriate with other Twelve Step fellowships that address areas other than sexual recovery.

Groups need to review their cooperation with outside enterprises regularly. We might ask the following questions: has the outside enterprise changed its focus or methods since we began cooperating with it? Has it gotten into controversies, which might damage SCA's reputation? Has the enterprise publicly misrepresented its relationship to SCA? Has cooperation been beneficial to our fellowship?

We are also on the lookout to ensure that our motives do not revolve around "money, property and prestige." Acting on such motives, grounded in fear and pride, is not conducive in the long run to the spiritual recovery of SCA members. In all our actions, we are careful not to act when motivated by fear and pride, making sure that all our decisions are conducive to the spiritual recovery of SCA members.

Tradition Seven

"Every SCA group ought to be fully self-supporting, declining outside contributions."

The Seventh Tradition is about responsibility. Primarily, it is about financial responsibility. Part of addiction is an unwillingness to accept responsibility for one's actions, to accept that there is a cause-and-effect relationship between acting out sexually and a multitude of negative consequences. It is as if, as active addicts, we wanted to live in a fantasy world: one in which the principle of reality does not apply. Recovery, by contrast, requires us as individuals and as members of the group to engage with reality. As part of taking responsibility for ourselves and our lives, Tradition Seven asks us, as individuals and as groups, to explore how we support ourselves, including our relationship to money.

Moreover, it asks us to take responsibility for our financial independence. This responsibility involves the practical need to pay the rent and other expenses for the group. Here we realize that the spirituality talked about in the program is not a fantasy world in which we merely wish for a desired outcome, but that it involves planning, determined action and monetary support on our part.

At some point in every SCA meeting, whether in person or via electronic means, there will be an announcement or indication that we have a Seventh Tradition. We use this time to call for contributions from members. When the basket, hat, envelope, bag, or collection box comes around, or a contribution link or notice is displayed, members can contribute toward the group's expenses. These can include not only group rent and refreshments, but also literature expenses, the funding of telephone lines, websites, social and recovery events, and paying contributions on to service bodies. Many group and service body websites will also have online contribution features. As members, the cost of our compulsion has often been great, including in monetary terms, and the financial cost of our Twelve Step recovery, by comparison, is minimal.

Tradition Seven also involves supporting SCA's service bodies, which perform the work of the fellowship beyond the levels of the individual and the group. When an SCA service body such as a local intergroup, a convention committee, or the ISO needs funding or groups consider contributions to them, we make the distinction that these are not self-supporting groups within themselves. They are service bodies consisting of trusted servants, funded by and directly accountable to those they serve. Service bodies may accept direct contributions from SCA members. Still, they will ideally establish an annual cap on individual donations and a maximum amount for one-time bequests in wills, to encourage broad support and avoid undue influence.

Sexual Compulsives Anonymous has a history of groups, intergroups, or the ISO supporting newly-formed meetings and service committees. This support is a way of carrying the message. Such meetings or committees - if they are to be healthy - duly progress to supporting themselves. Self-support, at a minimum, means paying rent and covering other group expenses out of group funds.

Part of being self-supporting includes being good stewards of the funds in our possession; therefore, we ought to take care when electing a Treasurer, or serving as Treasurer of a group, meeting, or service body. Our servants are trusted, but it is prudent for SCA groups at all levels to establish simple checks and balances to ensure that we account for program funds and property.

The simplest interpretation of this Tradition is that groups cannot rely on any entity or individuals outside of SCA for monetary support. Contributions from outside the SCA Fellowship - of any size, but especially large ones - could entangle Sexual Compulsives Anonymous with other organizations that ask something in return for their money. By following this Tradition and being self-funding, as in all matters, SCA stays with its primary purpose – it does not have to be distracted by serving the goals of other organizations or being subject to their influence.

Tradition Seven points us to the idea that “self-supporting” can also refer to our service needs and the responsibility of filling service positions. SCA depends on service by individuals at all levels: personal, meeting, group, intergroup, and the ISO. If SCA is to thrive, members ought to step up to provide this support. Beyond service positions, support can be given to the group in other ways, for example, even by setting up chairs before a meeting. Attending meetings, honest sharing, and assisting other members in their recovery are also important forms of individual support for the group.

Regardless of these considerations, membership in SCA never depends on the amount of money a member can give to the group. If members are not in a position to make a financial contribution, we remind them that their presence at meetings is what matters. There are no dues or fees for membership; the only requirement for SCA membership is a desire to stop having compulsive sex.

Tradition Eight

"Sexual Compulsives Anonymous should remain forever nonprofessional, but our service centers may employ special workers."

The SCA *Statement of Purpose* sets out that "Sexual Compulsives Anonymous is a fellowship of people who share their experience, strength and hope with each other, that they may solve their common problem and help others to recover from sexual compulsion." We are a spiritual recovery program, not a commercial enterprise or business. As such, our members are not professionals, but individuals with the same problem helping each other to work the SCA Program voluntarily. We carry the message of a spiritual awakening and a spiritual solution to each other, and others like us, free of charge, based on our experiences within SCA, and Twelve Step recovery.

Tradition Eight tells us that there is no monetary compensation for SCA's sponsorship and rotating positions in SCA's service structures or professional positions. Such positions do not require special education or highly specialized skills. Anyone who meets the requirements set by group conscience can hold these positions. Holding temporary offices does not elevate individuals to a special "professional" class within SCA.

Sponsorship is a tool of the program, and it is not a professional relationship. We do not charge someone to sponsor them, nor do we pay someone to be our sponsor.

Sexual Compulsives Anonymous, although relying on volunteers for much of its service work, can employ special workers. It can do this when particular knowledge or skills are required, or when no volunteers exist to do work that is not covered by the rotating service structure. For instance, a group might pay a lawyer to look into insurance issues; an intergroup might employ an answering service, or the ISO might hire a computer consultant or a translator. If we ask members to perform special jobs in SCA, it is permitted to pay them as we would non-members.

Some members of SCA come from or have gone into professional fields. These fields draw on knowledge from sources outside our program. To maintain clear boundaries, it is probably best for such individuals, especially in the areas of therapy, medicine, and the law, if they wish to give professional advice to SCA members, to do so only within the confines of a professional consultation.

SCA depends upon the rotation of the volunteer service of its members to carry its message. When one's term of service is complete, we make every effort to train the person following in the position. Service positions may evolve, but we seek to ensure that transitions are as seamless as feasible. In this way, we minimize any disruption to SCA in carrying its message to the sexual compulsive who still suffers.

Tradition Nine

"SCA, as such, ought never be organized; but we may create service boards or committees directly responsible to those they serve."

SCA is not organized in the sense of a top-down structure. Instead, we create only necessary service structures, and they do not give directions to members of SCA. Service boards and committees exist to serve SCA, not to govern it. Intergroups are voluntary associations of local SCA meetings that work together on common projects. Each intergroup is directly responsible to the groups that it serves. Representatives from the groups guide intergroups, not the other way around. Likewise, any service committees formed by an intergroup are directly responsible to that intergroup.

In time, after SCA had grown to include meetings in several locations, the need arose for an umbrella service board to coordinate between the SCA groups and intergroups and be responsible for such things as maintaining a uniform, fellowship-wide body of approved literature. In response, the fellowship created SCA's International Service Organization. The International Service Organization (ISO) of SCA is a service body intended to further the recovery of those who suffer from sexual compulsion and aims to serve as the Trusted Servant of the SCA Fellowship. The ISO is directly responsible to the intergroups and groups that belong to and support it.

SCA members serving in intergroups and the ISO are "trusted servants." This consideration means they are trusted to make decisions without continually consulting the groups. Like the groups, intergroups and the ISO use their group conscience process in making decisions. The ultimate authority in SCA lies in a loving God, as may be expressed in our group conscience. Groups use this authority prudently and with restraint.

Tradition Ten

"SCA has no opinion on outside issues; hence the SCA name ought never be drawn into public controversy."

No part of the SCA service structure may make public statements other than to describe our program of recovery. We restrict ourselves to simple statements outlining the basics of SCA. We are especially careful, as a fellowship, not to express opinions on politics, social reform, laws regarding sexual offenses, religion, medicine, or specific therapeutic approaches. To express such opinions would inevitably bring us into public controversies that would divide our membership, divert us from our primary purpose, and perhaps alienate those seeking recovery from sexual compulsion.

Individual members are free to hold their own opinions on such matters and to participate in public issues as they wish. They are careful, though, not to involve SCA in any way. When members choose to share about such matters in meetings, we have only one suggestion. We suggest that they ask themselves what their motives are. If it is for a motive other than furthering their recovery, or if they are unsure of their motives, it may be best to talk with other members privately.

Tradition Eleven

> "Our public relations policy is based on attraction rather than promotion; we need always maintain personal anonymity at the level of press, radio, television and films."

Under all circumstances, we maintain our anonymity at the level of the mass media. New types of media are now available since the publication of this Tradition, and more may yet arise. It has become necessary to define the term "mass media" in the most general sense. One definition is any form of communication that reaches a large and indeterminate group of people. At this level, we maintain personal anonymity. This mandate exists mainly because each member does not represent SCA as a whole. Our actions do not represent the whole message of the program. Otherwise, this may affect the ability of SCA to carry its message. We also maintain anonymity to keep our humility - that is, we see ourselves as equal to other members of SCA, neither better nor worse.

In Sexual Compulsives Anonymous, we maintain "personal anonymity," not "program anonymity." We reach out to the general public and to specific organizations to ensure that people know about our program of recovery. If the mass media approaches us for information, we provide it. We can even publish advertisements in places appropriate for Twelve Step programs. When we do this, our message is descriptive and educational. We do not make overblown claims or use celebrity endorsements. We trust that some people will find SCA attractive and contact us, or seek out a meeting.

Tradition Twelve

"Anonymity is the spiritual foundation of all our traditions, ever reminding us to place principles before personalities."

Tradition Twelve is the "spiritual foundation of all our traditions" perhaps because, like other spiritual principles, it takes practice to uphold. Moreover, what we have come to practice in recovery is humility. This is humility in the sense of seeing ourselves as we truly are. We can do this because we have, through the Twelve Steps, worked in partnership with a Higher Power to uncover a self that is distinct from our character defects. Once we have worked the Steps, we are able to view others and ourselves with proper perspective, and compassion. We become "right-sized," recognizing an unhealthy ego for the spiritual trap it is.

What we want to try to avoid is acting out on our character defects in meetings and with the fellowship. Frequently, our deep-seated shame is the root cause of our acting out. This shame can lead to either perfectionism, grandiosity, or overdependence on others. Many of us also have a ferocious appetite for attention or a powerful drive for recognition or status. All of these character defects can produce conflict within the groups. None of us are completely free from our character defects, so the potential for conflict is always present. This Tradition is a gentle reminder of this fact and a suggestion that we become aware of the principles behind the Traditions so that we act counter to our defects as they may manifest themselves in the group. We want to avoid letting our personalities get in the way of the principles of recovery that we and others need for our survival.

In a spiritual sense, anonymity means that the whole program is even greater than the sum of its parts. The significance of this for SCA is its guarantee of survival for groups, and the fellowship as an entity. It reminds us that no one individual, and no one group, is more critical than SCA as a whole.

Anonymity means we generally do not identify ourselves as members of SCA by name publicly to people outside of the fellowship. This practice certainly needs to be categorical at the level of mass media, but most often, members will keep their anonymity in public in general. Within the fellowship, there is no need to maintain personal anonymity, but if a member wishes to do so, we respect their choice. If we encounter public figures at meetings, we are especially careful to preserve their anonymity.

In doing service for a group or service board, individual members necessarily deal with the everyday world, and will sometimes likely need to disclose their identity and provide their full names on behalf of the group. We may have to disclose our membership in SCA in situations such as when making arrangements to rent space to hold a meeting, dealing with financial institutions, or doing specific outreach work to carry the SCA message. These actions are in keeping with Traditions Eleven and Twelve: maintaining anonymity here is a question of personal comfort for the individual member.

The same applies to the certification of attendance at SCA meetings for court-ordered attendees. It is a group conscience decision for a particular group whether or not to accommodate such requests from members, and each group or an individual member is free to decide whether or not to sign certificates of attendance, thereby disclosing their identity.

Regardless of what we choose to do with our anonymity, we do not identify who we see in meetings, or those we know to attend SCA meetings, to people outside of the fellowship. This respect of anonymity keeps the program safe for members and prospective members to attend.

Anonymity also protects us from gossip and criticism. Mutual respect is fundamental to our shared recovery. The SCA *Closing Statement* reminds us that what is said by individuals at a particular meeting should be treated as confidential. This admonition maintains the integrity and safety of intimate self-disclosure.

Anonymity is the mechanism that maximizes our focus and minimizes issues of "money, property or prestige" and anything else which would endanger "our primary purpose." Sometimes we are selective about who and what we listen to, and tend to judge the rest. However, following the Twelfth Tradition as the very foundation of our fellowship's existence ensures the continuation of that existence. The benefit reaped from this is a deepening sense of humility, inevitable when we truly view each other as equal in recovery.

Speakers at SCA meetings sometimes ask the group to listen to the message rather than focus on the messenger. Others ask that the group identify with the feelings rather than the facts, or that they "take what they need and leave the rest." These examples of anonymity help to foster an atmosphere of openness, mutual support, and community. Members can both share freely and identify with what is shared.

Indeed, anonymity is a powerful vehicle of transformation that allows the members of a group to experience healing through the collective consciousness. Some of us have harbored intense rage, fear, and sadness in our compulsion, and the opportunity finally to express and release these feelings in a meeting is the relief of a lifetime. Through the anonymity offered at meetings, we find a refuge where we are neither judged nor shamed.

"Principles before personalities" allows members to strongly disagree at a business meeting, and support each other in recovery afterward. When we value the principles of the program above all else, SCA thrives. We preserve "our common welfare" and help the fellowship to grow. We have come around full circle to our First Tradition: "Our common welfare should come first; personal recovery depends upon SCA unity."

Chapter 25: Service in SCA

Service is a way of helping maintain our sexual sobriety by helping others. Service can take many forms, but one thing we continually hear in the rooms is, "Service keeps us sober…"

Being of service at a meeting, as a sponsor, working on Intergroup projects, taking phone calls from other members, and attending meetings are all forms of service that promote our recovery and assist the continuation of SCA as a whole. Service is a commitment to ourselves, to our fellowship, and our fellow sexual compulsives.

One of the most visible forms of service is chairing a meeting. In taking on such a role, we commit to our recovery - willing to do what it takes to stay sexually sober. Some meetings require a certain length of sobriety on a formal Sexual Recovery Plan to chair or serve in positions requiring financial obligations. Other meetings don't have such requirements. Whatever the case, service work helps us shift the focus off ourselves and onto others. We can arrange for speakers, set up chairs, collect and keep track of money, or provide literature at meetings. Doing service at a meeting leads to our regular attendance at those meetings. We get to know the people who attend that meeting, and they get to know us. We can learn how to break out of our painful isolation and realize that we belong in the fellowship. We may begin to experience the love and support SCA offers.

Another way to engage in service and learn more about the program is to participate in SCA business meetings, intergroup meetings, the International Service Organization, and specialized committees for literature development, convention planning, and retreat planning. These groups contribute to forming policies and practices and influence SCA's future direction.

Starting a new meeting is a valuable service. It can be challenging because to find a meeting space, we speak about SCA to people who may have no concept of sexual compulsion or 12-Step programs. Searching for a location can be hard work. It can also be a humbling experience. By doing so, we provide a real service for innumerable people who may attend meetings in that room, now and in the future.

The sponsor/sponsee relationship is another important form of service. They help each other work the program and solve their common problem, sharing perspective, strength, and hope. Sponsees often help sponsors recall the pain and anguish of acting out and the strengths and rewards of recovery. When we sponsor others, we commit ourselves to be there for them, and as a result, we feel more firmly involved in the process of recovery. We can also serve as interim or temporary sponsors, giving people new to the fellowship immediate access to a sponsor's experience, strength, and hope.

Some members, especially newcomers, may not feel "ready" to chair a meeting or become a sponsor. Perhaps they don't have much time on their plan or are reluctant to take on a long service commitment. Some might think, they're "not good enough" to raise their hand to volunteer, or they might say to themselves, *"I don't want to do all this service business; I just want to stop acting out!"* Many of us have felt that way about doing service from time-to-time, but we have also found that service is a tool directly linked to our recovery. We can all be of service by coming to meetings and not acting out, but further participation in the fellowship can significantly change how we feel about ourselves. We come to realize that we have something to contribute. Our self-esteem may increase, and we may find it easier to stay on our Sexual Recovery Plan.

Here are some simple ways we can all contribute to the fellowship and boost our self-esteem:

- Chat with newcomers
- Invite members for fellowship after meetings
- Contact someone we haven't seen for a while or who may be going through a rough time
- Share our phone numbers
- Return phone calls, emails, and text messages
- Set up chairs for a meeting and put them away
- Make an effort to connect with people at the meeting who seem isolated and separate from the group
- Find acceptance and empathy in meetings when things crop up that may irritate us, such as occasional emotional outbursts, overly long shares, or inappropriate language
- Share at meetings.

Service rescues us from isolation. While we were acting out, and when we first arrived in SCA rooms, many felt isolated and desperate. It was often difficult to imagine how we could successfully relate to others in a non-sexual way. As we attended more meetings, we began to sense that we might belong there. We began to find it easier to overcome early anxiety about being at meetings, raising our hand, or even staying until the end of a meeting. We discovered that small acts of service made us feel at home and connected with others.

Continuing service transforms us. Our needy lives become thoughtful and generous through nourishing exchanges. We come to know that we all have something to give and that the more we give, the more we receive!

Doing SCA Outreach Work

The purpose of outreach is to spread the word about SCA. There are several ways to engage in outreach. We can inform local therapists, clergy, lawyers, elected officials, and health professionals that SCA is a 12-Step fellowship open to all who think they may have a problem with sexual compulsion. We can mail primary SCA literature, such as our Four-fold brochure and *For the Newcomer*, to these professionals or notify them through letters, emails, or social media postings of our presence in their area. We can make phone calls to professionals we know or ask other members for referrals. Other forms of outreach include setting up a booth at a therapists' convention or a Pride parade, attaching a flyer to a bulletin board in a location used by other 12-Step programs, or placing literature near a bar or acting-out place.

Another form of outreach, which is somewhat uncommon in the SCA program, is making a Twelfth Step call. Based on practices developed in Alcoholics Anonymous, a traditional Twelfth Step call is for two sober SCA members to meet with a sexual compulsive who still suffers. We recommend that no one goes on a Twelfth Step call alone. Having another SCA member with us helps protect us from the temptation of acting out. This meeting might take place in a hospital or a courthouse.

We do not preach or proselytize during a Twelfth Step call. As in all outreach interactions, we use attraction rather than promotion. We briefly summarize our stories so that the other person knows that we, too, have suffered from sexual compulsion and that we have found a solution that works for us. But we do not try to *fix* the sufferer. That is the job of their Higher Power.

We encourage the person to attend a meeting, and we may offer to bring them to one. We understand that the potential newcomer might resist this for any number of reasons. But we make our offer and let Higher Power take it from there. We state our case. If we have succeeded, we have planted a seed, which may or may not eventually take root and thrive - in Higher Power's time, not ours.

Another form of outreach is to prisoners. We try to let prisoners know that SCA is a resource used during their incarceration and after their release. While we can't necessarily visit prisoners to engage in Twelfth Step calls, we can respond to their needs through letters and send them SCA literature. We know that some prisoners have attended or even started SCA meetings. We try to remain in contact with these members and help them as much as possible, perhaps arranging for an interim sponsor. We may also help newly-released prisoners by engaging in a type of Twelfth Step call, agreeing to accompany the ex-prisoner to an SCA meeting.

Outreach work includes being available to answer phone calls, emails, and letters from anyone who contacts us with questions or has a problem with sexual compulsion and doesn't know where to turn. Outreach work can be very intense, perhaps even tense, but it's usually enriching. We realize that it's not about us, but about the entire fellowship and being a resource for the sexual compulsive who still suffers. By making outreach calls and speaking to or writing to people who contact us with questions, we are doing an excellent service for others and ourselves.

Chapter 26: What are Intergroups and the ISO?

SCA's Ninth Tradition says, "SCA, as such, ought never be organized; but we may create service boards or committees directly responsible to those they serve." Intergroups and the ISO are two such service boards within our fellowship.

Intergroup is a service organization whose members represent the SCA meetings of a particular region. There is also an intergroup for the SCA phone/online meetings. The purpose of the intergroup is to conduct business on behalf of the meetings it serves. Intergroup may enable shared resources, such as maintaining a local website, storing and distributing literature or sobriety chips, organizing and promoting conferences, retreats, and other special events. Intergroup also engages in community outreach by contacting and maintaining connections with health professionals and making itself available as a resource for the sexual compulsive who still suffers. As in all business affairs involving SCA, intergroups adhere to the Twelve Traditions. By doing so, an intergroup helps to promote SCA unity.

SCA's Fourth Tradition states: "Each group should be autonomous, except in matters affecting other groups or SCA as a whole." This principle is an essential guide for the business of each meeting and intergroup. Intergroup is a service body, not a governing one. Each SCA group decides what format it follows, the literature it reads, when and where it meets, etc., and is also responsible for any financial obligations it may incur, such as space rental. Each SCA meeting may elect a member to represent that meeting at its local intergroup. In adhering to the Fourth Tradition, an intergroup may make decisions that affect *"other groups,"* meaning the group of meetings in its region. The same spiritual process makes decisions at the intergroup level as those made by individual meetings. SCA's Second Tradition says: "For our group purpose there is but one authority—a loving God as may be expressed in our group conscience. Our leaders are but trusted servants; they do not govern."

An Intergroup generally meets regularly, often once a month. It makes decisions on matters common to its group of meetings, but it cannot make decisions that pertain to an individual meeting. Some intergroups may have applied for and received non-profit status, either as an Association or as a non-profit 501(c)(3) corporation (these options may be different outside the U.S.). In addition to its various fiduciary, outreach, and inreach matters, an intergroup may choose to send one or more delegates to any ISO conferences.

Most intergroups have officers, such as the Chair, Secretary, and Treasurer. These positions are generally filled by election for one-year terms. The intergroup may also have other standing or ad-hoc committees, such as literature distribution, outreach, special events, etc. Any SCA member may attend an intergroup meeting. Some intergroups only allow one representative per meeting to vote.

A typical agenda for an Intergroup meeting may include:

Statement of Purpose
Reading of the Twelve Traditions
Introductions of meeting reps, committee chairs, etc.
Approval of Agenda
Approval of Minutes from the previous meeting
Treasurer's Report
Committee Reports
Old Business
New Business

ISO

The purpose of SCA's International Service Organization (ISO) is to further the recovery of those who suffer from sexual compulsion and encourage SCA unity. It does this through various outreach and inreach initiatives. One of the ISO's primary functions is to develop, approve, publish, and distribute SCA literature. It also maintains the www.sca-recovery.org website, including an international meeting list and updates on worldwide SCA events and initiatives. The ISO also reaches out to families and friends, institutions, the courts and prisons, the media, and health professionals. SCA's ISO is a non-profit 501(c)(3) corporation, whose officers are elected to serve two-year terms. The ISO is a service body, not a governing one. Its members consist of representatives (delegates) from all SCA meetings and intergroups. The ISO adheres to SCA's Twelve Traditions, particularly the Second (regarding Group Conscience) and the Fourth (regarding the autonomy of meetings).

The ISO holds at least one business conference per year. The conference venue generally rotates among different regions, and one or more local intergroups may host it. Some conferences may take place remotely. The ISO business conferences include reports from various intergroups/meetings and from the standing committees: Fiduciary, Outreach, and Inreach. The ISO considers all submitted draft literature for possible approval as SCA Conference-approved literature, and it may vote on motions related to various projects, policies, and proposed by-law changes. The ISO also holds quarterly conference calls, whose purpose is to update the membership on current projects and issues facing the fellowship as a whole. These quarterly calls are held remotely (platforms/phone). Any SCA member may attend any ISO conference, but voting is limited only to elected ISO delegates, representing one or more meetings. Each SCA meeting is entitled to one vote at ISO Conferences. ISO's Executive Committee consists of the elected ISO officers: ISO Chair, Fiduciary Chair, Inreach Chair, Outreach Chair, Director-at-Large, and the Outside (non-SCA-member) Director. The Executive Committee may act on behalf of the ISO between conferences, but all their actions are submitted to and ratified by ISO members at the next conference.

Chapter 27: Closing Statement

The opinions expressed here today are strictly those of the individuals who gave them. The things you have heard here are given and spoken in confidence and should be treated as confidential. If you try to absorb what you have heard, you are bound to gain a better understanding of the way to handle your problems.

In the spirit of recovery from sexual compulsion, we suggest that sex between members not be treated lightly. Sex between people new to the fellowship and other members is discouraged. Talk to each other, reason things out with someone else, let there be no gossip or criticism of one another, but only love, understanding and companionship.

Serenity Prayer

God, grant me the serenity

To accept the things I cannot change,

Courage to change the things I can,

And wisdom to know the difference.

Chapter 28: Origins of SCA

In New York

Bill L.'s Story

Looking back to September of 1977 when I went to my first AA meeting, little did I know that I was putting down one drug just to pick up another: compulsive sex. Actually, most of my adult life from the age of nineteen had been devoted to the pursuit of sex, searching for sex, having sex, feeling ashamed afterwards but starting the whole cycle over and over again. I would also romanticize these events in the hope that one of them would develop into a relationship. Of course, it never did. However, the pain, despair and shame did lead me to start to search for help. As soon as I started to go to AA meetings, I stopped drinking and I remember how frightened I felt. "Who are these people, can I trust them?" I thought. I found some sort of escape and solace in the darkness of the bathhouses. It makes me sad now to think that the darkness was what I felt I deserved. In all honesty I have to admit at first it was a way of discovering my sexuality and a big boost to my ego to discover that so many other men were interested in me. That didn't last long and soon I started to live with a lot of despair. Talking about this area of my life in AA was uncomfortable even though I did it anyway. I even remember talking to Frank H about what was going on. Little did I know that a few years later Frank H would reappear in my life, in such a profound way.

During this time, I started a number of things. It seemed that even though I talked about my acting out to my sponsor and just about anyone else who would listen, I just couldn't stop acting out. I felt so out of control. Sometime during 1977, I started going to consciousness-raising groups. No one had heard about AIDS and the sexual revolution was in full bloom. For the next two years I was in three of these groups and they did help. I was able to start to feel better about myself and to accept myself as a gay male. Two other things happened at this time which I did not then realize how significant they would be in my recovery. I started to use my creativity again and stopped using amyl nitrate. Getting completely sober and honest with myself really woke me up. At that time, I stopped bringing strangers home and/or going to their apartment. At first, I managed to stop this behavior only for several weeks but then the periods grew longer. This was a difficult time because I was trying to control the disease.

In 1981, I went to my first DA meeting. Even though I thought I was making progress, I continued to act out and even started to go back to bathhouses on a regular basis. I remember one incident very vividly. I was lying on a bed in one of the little rooms and as I glanced at my outstretched arm, I realized that there was no difference between me and a heroin addict waiting for his next hit. I closed the door, got down on my knees, and prayed for help. I certainly didn't have much hope, but the next evening I went to a DA meeting. I shared about my frustration, despair and helplessness about my not being able to stop acting out sexually. A few months earlier I had brought the idea of starting a program of self-help for sex addicts to my therapist. He told me that a program for sexual sobriety would never work because everyone needs sex. Fortunately, I stopped seeing him a week later.

John the founder of DA approached me after I had shared and just held me. He shared with me that it sounded to him like I was in a place like the one he was in when he started DA. My first thought was how could I start a program? But when Collin, Jim J, Thomas T, Nochem, and a few others said that they would support me, I did just that.

On a Sunday evening in 1981, the first meeting focusing on acting out sexually met in my apartment. I felt so scared and also so excited. What would this actually be about? Who would come? For the next few months, the group met every Sunday at my apartment. In the beginning the people were mainly from DA: Collin, Saul M, Jim S, Thomas T and a few others, including women. We didn't have any structure and certainly we had no literature. At that time, I had not read anything about sexual addiction. After a few months I received a letter from someone who had been in one of those consciousness-raising groups I had attended a few years earlier. He enclosed the names of three programs: SLAA in Boston, SA in Simi Valley, and another whose name I can't remember now. I wrote to all three and received information from SLAA and SA and presented the information to the group at the next meeting.

I was beginning to get some recovery and didn't act out nearly as much. Also, I was beginning to have hope again. We liked what we read in the SA literature, even though we didn't like the tone of what was said about homosexuality. Some of the other people in the group felt the same. When the founder of SA, Roy K, met with us, we brought this to his attention and he said "No problem" and that it could be taken care of. We took a vote and became SA New York. I felt so good. I felt I was walking on air for I had hope again.

We continued to meet and, in a few months, new literature arrived. It directly put down homosexuality and personally I felt I had been betrayed. The more I learnt about the principles and the underlying beliefs of SA, the more I began to feel that SA came from a place of feeling guilt about one's sexuality. With all the work I had done on myself I was determined not to feel guilty about having sex. SA was based on the idea that you couldn't have sex unless you were in a committed relationship. It was based in the fundamentalist religion I had been taught as a child. I decided that this was not for me and that it would not be being true to myself. I said that I couldn't be part of SA and suggested that the meeting find another meeting place. They found a place at St Jean's on Lexington Avenue. The meetings had at this point been taking place in my pottery-filled apartment for six months. With no meetings to attend, needless to say, in a short time I was back to my old acting out behavior.

When the phone rang in May of 1982, I was surprised to hear Tom L at the other end. Even though I knew him from AA he had never called me before. He told me that he was interested in attending one of the meetings he heard were meeting in my apartment. I explained all that had happened and added that I was desperate for a meeting myself. I arranged to meet Tom at an SA meeting. Somehow, I had got the information wrong and when Tom and I arrived we found no SA meeting. I must say that I was relieved and at the same time felt that I needed a meeting. It was such a beautiful spring day that Tom L. and I decided to walk to Central Park and there talked for a few hours. I felt so uplifted. Later Tom L. came back to my apartment and I gave him the SA literature that I had. We decided that we would try to find a meeting place, since I wasn't comfortable using my apartment at that time.

A few weeks passed and on the morning after one of my binges I got down on my knees and prayed to God for help. That afternoon I was walking up Seventh Avenue and I heard a voice call to me from across the street. It was Tom L. I was overjoyed to see him and embraced him. He told me that Richard from AA was allowing a sexual recovery meeting to take place in his apartment. It had just started and the second meeting would take place next Monday. He asked me if I would speak. Would I ever!

I couldn't wait for Monday evening to arrive. Little did I know that I would see Frank H there. I remembered our talks a few years before in AA. It made me feel good inside. Saul was there and a few other people from OA. We met in Richard's apartment for six months before we started to meet in other people's apartments. We used the SA literature with parts I didn't like crossed out. I put everything I had, all my energies, into not acting out. While some of my behavior seemed to have stopped, I just couldn't seem to stop going to bathhouses. With just one meeting a week I started to call people up on the phone for help and support.

There were times when I felt I would die if I didn't have sex. What really helped was being able to go to my studio and work with clay. It was a very painful time for me, but having my creativity was a spiritual and healing outlet. A few of us kept showing up week after week to meetings. We began to get stronger. I don't know if at the time any one of us knew what was going on. In time we became Sexual Compulsives Anonymous. Frank H found a meeting place at Washington Square Community Church. It was a wonderful learning time for me. For the first time I started to try different approaches to deal with my sexual compulsion. I stopped cruising on the streets and soaking in those seductive images. I tried dating without the goal of ending up in bed. SCA helped me to stop viewing people (as well as myself) as sexual objects. I started to be not so seductive. My friendships with people changed for the better.

SA asked us not to use its name on our literature. Soon afterwards the first SCA Literature Committee was formed. The Literature Committee meetings were very unstructured, but we continued to meet. Richard, Bruce, Saul, Nochem, Bob M and I (I hope I haven't left anyone out) started writing out the Characteristics. Bob took notes on our discussions and formalized the first piece of SCA literature: The Characteristics. Even after sixteen years, when I read them, I am still amazed at how true they are. I now know that God was guiding us during these Literature Committee meetings, as well as in starting Sexual Compulsives Anonymous.

Frank H.'s Story

After I'd been sober in Alcoholics Anonymous for a few years I began to be able to see the addictive nature of my sexual activity. I wanted to stop but I couldn't. I tried all combinations of sexual activities in the hope that one or another combination would "work," and that I'd be freed of the compulsion.

I talked to a couple of other AA members who shared my problem. One of these friends was Tom. We shared with one another our successes and failures. Once Tom suggested that I pray while going to and being in acting out places. This seemed to help me to accept myself as someone who couldn't stop running from one sexual episode to another. There was a part of myself that was good and virginal and another part that felt like a turd. Praying helped to let these two parts of myself come together a little bit.

About a year before the first meeting of our program, I had a sort of spiritual awakening in a bathhouse in Amsterdam. I wasn't getting what I wanted in the orgy room. But instead of going on to look for sex elsewhere, I was able, somehow, to go back to my hotel.

On returning to New York, with the support of Tom, AA and my therapist, I was able to stay on what we now call a sexual recovery plan. At this point I thought it would be great if we could have Twelve Step meetings to support recovery from the craving for sex. I tried to find a meeting place in churches, a meeting house and other institutions, but had no success. I finally became discouraged and stopped looking.

In June 1982, my friend Tom called to say that Richard, another AA friend of ours, was interested in a sexual recovery meeting and that he was willing to donate his apartment for the meeting, at least for a start. On June 22, we had our first meeting. Tom, who was scheduled to speak, didn't appear at first. So, I became the first speaker. I don't remember what I said, but I suppose I must have talked about my long history of going to tea-rooms, bathhouses, trucks and other acting out places. Then I must have said a little about my year of uncertain and shaky sobriety. Tom showed up somewhere during the qualification. There couldn't have been more than four or five people present at the meeting.

At the third or fourth meeting, Bill L. spoke. We'd known Bill since he first came into AA. I think it was at this meeting that I learned that Bill had started the first Sexaholics Anonymous group in New York, based on the principles established by Roy, the founder of SA on the West Coast. After meeting at Bill's apartment for several months, the group had moved to St. Jean's Church. Bill felt the SA literature was overtly anti-gay and decided he didn't want to participate anymore.

At that time, we also called ourselves Sexaholics Anonymous, not because we considered ourselves a part of that program, but simply from lack of imagination. We had already clearly differentiated ourselves from SA in our determination that each member would define his own recovery plan for himself. It was my feeling that each person came to the program with something that they wanted to change about their sexual behavior and that they would start their sexual recovery plan with that. In addition, the membership for at least the first six to eight months was exclusively gay men. The literature we had from the original SA seemed very homophobic to us. We were out to create a program that would support the self-esteem of gay people, not put it into question.

Almost from the beginning we had members from Al-Anon and from OA. Some of the early members included George, Saul and Bob McC. Not too long thereafter, Bob R., Robert N., Nochem and Barbara McC began to appear. Most of these members are still with us, though some no longer attend meetings.

In the fall of '82, there was to be an eclipse of the moon. A friend told me I shouldn't watch it on my roof because it would be too dangerous. I concluded that I would have to watch from the park where I'd acted out most consistently before I got sexually sober. The night of the eclipse was the beginning of a two-month slip for me. I just couldn't stop. I visited temples in Bangkok and prayed for sobriety; for the lifting of the compulsion. Then I went, powerless, directly to the octagonal tea-room right outside the temple.

When I returned to meetings in New York (still only one a week at that time), I feared they'd throw me out. Here I was, a founding member back "out there" again. But no. They said keep coming back. They understood. It still makes my eyes teary to remember that I was wanted; I belonged. With great difficulty, I got sober again. It was like swimming against the current, but the fellowship sustained me.

About this time, we started talking about getting a meeting place in a public space. We had stopped meeting in Richard's and the meeting moved from place to place, making it difficult for new members to find us. We met for a while at Bill L.'s, and for a while at the Gay Synagogue. I finally agreed to look for a space again. Bob O'C. suggested that another program met at the Washington Square Community Church in Greenwich Village, and that they might be willing to give us space. I called. I talked as best I could about who we were and what we were trying to do. None of us had a lot of sobriety at this point and I found it hard to talk about sexual compulsion. It felt very much like I, a sex maniac, was asking for a place in the church. I didn't see how I, or we, could be accepted. But we got the place and began to meet in a long, narrow room looking out onto the street. I still feel so grateful to that church where we still meet on Monday nights.

It was also at the Washington Square Community Church that our first literature committee was formed, and put together the Characteristics which have become such a keynote for us.

We were approached by SA in California and asked to change our name, since we were infringing on their copyright by calling ourselves SA and being a different program. We had a long business meeting at which I maintained that I wanted to continue to call myself a sexaholic and to have the group called Sexaholics Anonymous. I liked the name and felt defiant. But group conscience ruled after much debate that we would be called Sexual Compulsives Anonymous.

The next landmark was when Paul F. decided that he was going to start another meeting. The new meeting was to be for gay men only with no smoking and no eating. Paul wanted a meeting where he would feel safe sharing, and a woman and a smoker had started coming to meetings. Neither the smoker nor the woman are still with us, but the meeting continues on. It is interesting to note that without any conscious decision, except at the beginning of that Tuesday meeting, all of our meetings have been non-smoking.

Bob R., who like many of us was finding Sundays a difficult day, located a space for a meeting on Sunday evenings at the Lesbian and Gay Community Center on 13th Street in the Village. The Center was to accommodate most of our new meetings for several years.

In Los Angeles

H.B.'s Story

In the Los Angeles, California, area in the late 1970s a small group of men - all of whom had been arrested for engaging in sexual behaviors in the parks and other public places - banded into a self-help group to support each other in trying to stop these actions which they could not stop by themselves. In 1979 Peter took over as leader of the group and the focus moved to confrontational reality therapy. This direct confrontational approach continued for several years. Slowly others began to hear about the group and the courts began to refer those arrested to attend meetings just like drinking offenders were sent to AA meetings. But more important was that a few individuals showed up with some Twelve Step experience and the tone of the meetings began to change.

Michael M. came back from a visit to New York City where he attended SCA meetings. He brought back SCA literature, including the original version of the common characteristics. This became a strong cohesive agent, to know that there were others out there with the same problems, and that the Twelve Steps could be worked on sexual compulsion as well as on alcoholism and drug addiction. The seeds had been sown for the program to grow.

The original focus of SCA in LA was primarily on stopping illegal sexual behavior, and later also "unsafe" sexual activity. With the arrival of the Twelve Steps, the Common Characteristics, and the other SCA literature from New York, the focus broadened to address recovery from sexually compulsive behavior as described in the characteristics. With this new focus and a nonthreatening spiritual base, the group started putting new meetings together. As attendance grew, the first Saturday afternoon meeting moved from the little room at the back of the Gay and Lesbian Community Services Center into the large upstairs meeting room. Also, a Tuesday evening sharing meeting was formed, and a Friday evening round robin meeting was begun.

During this initial swell of new information and people, Peter encountered a major stumbling block; he could not deal with the Higher Power issue and chose to resign. This was a sad time, for his dedication had helped the group to stay together for many years.

Nevertheless, the introduction of the Twelve Steps and the new focus opened the group up to faster growth and a wider circle of people interested in getting sexual sobriety and recovery, rather than just those wanting to avoid arrest. In November 1985 the first Sunday evening meeting was started in Plummer Park by several members including Michael M. and Anthony. Also, Joe, who had been working SCA in New York, moved out to LA and was able to share the experience of hope and recovery that he had gotten from the New York meetings.

About this time, I tried getting sexually sober and just couldn't get any time together. My interim sponsor suggested I go to a meeting a night and talk. Well, even with going to all four SCA meetings and the one Saturday meeting of another sexual recovery program on the other side of town, I still had nights that I needed meetings. Therein began a daily search for rooms that would have our group, and for three people who would commit to supporting the new meeting for its first three months. A few outlying meetings had been tried but never lasted long enough to develop a true base of support. During this year the word really began to get out; people started coming, staying and getting some time together. Some of them went off to Orange County and Long Beach and started meetings there as well. It took another three years for Jim K. to get the first San Diego meeting going on a regular basis with the help of George M. As of this writing Southern California has had a very active Intergroup with lots of special workshops and retreats for the membership. It has also been of service in developing and coordinating literature, and contacting the courts and therapy community.

Chapter 29: Personal Stories of Recovery

Story #1 – *Never Give Up*

I remember when Bill Clinton was being impeached and people could not figure out why he would do such a stupid thing as to have sex with an intern and ruin everything he had worked for. It was then that I first heard the words "sex addict." At the time I was in a relationship with a man who I thought was the love of my life. When we first got together, we decided to be monogamous and I was completely in love. Then one day at the gym I had sex with a stranger in the steam room. It was at that point that I started hanging out in the wet area of the gym, and it was not long after that I was introduced to chat rooms online. This new thing called the internet kicked my sexual compulsion into high speed. My boyfriend and I had a little apartment, and I began hooking up with guys when he would go to work despite the high risk. Afterwards, I would feel such shame and guilt, and I swore I would never do it again. One day I went to the neighborhood bookstore and I was intriguing with a cute guy, and as I walked past him, I saw a sign with the words I had heard used about Bill Clinton, "Sex Addiction." And in that section, there was a book called "Don't Call It Love" by Dr. Patrick Carnes. I bought the book and secretly read it on my way to work. As I read the stories, I knew I was a sex addict.

My addiction was out of control. I could not stop cheating. I created a huge fight with my boyfriend and broke up with him. I was heartbroken, but I knew of no other way because I did not want to hurt him. With him out of the picture, I started going to the bathhouse and hiring massage therapists. I would go to the gym on my lunch break to have sex in the steam room. One acting out partner was a doctor and I told him that I was a sex addict. He said he had a friend who worked with sex addicts and gave me his number. I saw this addiction therapist for a few months, and he did confirm that he thought I was a sex addict. He advised me not to go to SCA because "they just hook up there." He also helped me identify that I had been sexualized as early as fourth grade by a neighborhood friend who had been molested by an older cousin. It was good to know these things about my addiction, but the behavior did not stop. The therapist asked me not to masturbate for a week, and I thought I was going to die. Even with a therapist who specialized in sex addiction, I could not stop.

It was around that time that I decided to move to another city. It was a fresh start, and I swore that I was going to change and I would never act out again. It is not lost on me that my massage therapist helped me drive halfway across the country to my new home. The first week after I arrived was amazing. I did not act out and I had no desire to. I had relief from acting out for the first time in years. I was staying at a friend's apartment. After I finally got the internet hooked up to my computer, the acting out resumed with a vengeance. I was bringing strangers into my friend's apartment and having unprotected sex with them in his bed.

I got my own apartment, a car and a job, so the acting out opportunities increased. I had changed cities for my writing career, but each time I would sit down to write, I would get drawn into the chat rooms, looking for my next hookup. My acting out had become a time killer.

My friend convinced me to join hundreds of bicyclists riding to fight AIDS. I began raising funds for the ride while the whole time I was having unprotected sex with prostitutes and massage therapists. I was living a double life. I pretended to be such an upstanding person by raising funds for AIDS-related causes and I was having unprotected sex. I could not stop. There was no PREP at that time. I was in constant fear that I would contract HIV, and I still could not stop. I would get tested every few months and pray to God, "If it comes back negative, I won't do it again." The test would come back negative, and I would celebrate by having unprotected sex with a stranger, and the cycle continued.

On my 36th birthday, the same age as Marilyn Monroe when she died, I was doing the AIDS Ride and I was riding that morning with a friend. I had already hooked up with several guys on the ride and it was only day 3. I could not take it anymore and I broke down sobbing, telling my friend the whole story. He told me his husband went to a group called SCA and it might be good for me to talk to him. His husband and I rode together the rest of the afternoon and he introduced me to SCA. A few weeks later I went to my first meeting, and when I heard the 14 Characteristics read aloud, I knew I was home.

My first few months in program were great. I created a sexual recovery plan: "No unprotected sex. No paid sex." It was so clear. And in the first few months it seemed to work. I wanted this so much I would do anything. I even went to an SCA retreat.

The night before the retreat I went out drinking and hooked up with a guy I met at a bar. He went into my bathroom and did crystal meth. He came into my bedroom and started simulating sex, but I was not involved, it was all in his imagination. It was like seeing a blind mole dig into the dark earth. I was so lost. When I got to the retreat, I broke down and told my story to the group. Again, I had a reprieve. That is where I met my first sponsor. I was in the honeymoon phase of recovery. I started doing the Steps with my sponsor. At some point I didn't call him when he wanted me to, and I missed a meeting we had scheduled, and he fired me. I had never been fired from anything in my life! I thought he was supposed to call me. How could he do this? Didn't he know how hard this was for me?

Later that year, I went to an SCA convention, and at a workshop I heard a man speak. He had the kind of recovery and life that I wanted, and I got the courage to ask him to be my sponsor. I told him I was nervous and afraid he might fire me. He told me that he was not getting paid to sponsor me and therefore he could not fire me. The first thing he asked me to do was call him for 30 days. I missed a few days and he would ask why. Then he asked me to remove my computer from my home for 30 days. How could I? I needed it for work! Reluctantly, I did. I got my first little bit of sobriety. I got 30 days on my plan. But then around day 31, when the computer returned, I acted out. My sponsor had me install a device that blocked pornography and inappropriate websites. That stopped the hookups from the internet, but I started going to bars instead. My sponsor then told me that I might have a drinking problem. I could not believe he would say that. After all, I could stop for long periods of time and not even desire a drink! He asked me, "When you drink, does your life become unmanageable?" Well, I did always seem to act out sexually when I drank, and my life did become unmanageable. I was a sex addict and an alcoholic. It was as if I had been asleep in a bad dream and my sponsor woke me up.

I got about two years of sobriety at that time. I had a boyfriend and I did not cheat on him. Then we broke up. The problem was, I did not know what healthy sex was when I was single. When I was in a relationship it was simple, no sex outside my relationship. But what was healthy "single" sex like for me? Then I had to create my new "single" sexual recovery plan: "No paid sex. No unprotected sex. And I have to go on a coffee date with the person to get to know them a bit." Sounded simple, but I could not stop losing my time. When I had a partner, I was more motivated because I did not want to hurt him. But when I was alone, I didn't see how I was hurting myself. And I really didn't care. At that time, I allowed sensual massage on my plan as a part of having "single" sex.

I started drinking again because I still was not totally convinced I was an alcoholic. I mean several years went by and I never really had the craving to drink, not like I did for sex, so therefore I could not possibly be an alcoholic. It was in this period that I met the love of my life. We quickly became exclusive and within a few months moved in together. I changed my plan to, "No sex outside my relationship." And it worked for a few months. Then I started getting sensual massages. I would hire a bad boy, tell him to be good and then try to seduce him. Cut to five years later. We had a work Christmas party at our house. I had been drinking and a new employee decided to stay later than the rest. My partner went to bed and the employee tried to seduce me. We engaged for a brief moment and then I told him I didn't want this, that it felt wrong. At that point he said he wanted $30,000 or he would sue me. He was blackmailing me. I immediately called my sponsor and he told me exactly what to do; he got me a lawyer and had me file a police report. He had me go to 30 meetings in 30 days. I stopped drinking again and I had another 2 years of sobriety.

Then life happened and my mother died of cancer. While I was taking care of her, I had the gift of sobriety, but a year after she died, I started drinking again. The sensual massage started again, and for the first time I had a blackout from drinking while I was getting a massage. It was my bottom. I now have no doubt that I am an alcoholic and a sex addict. When I stop drinking, I stop acting out. As I write this, I have 455 days of sobriety. I cannot drink. I cannot get a massage. I cannot have sex outside of my relationship. I cannot look at porn. That is what I have to do to stay sober.

I also have to replace that acting out behavior with positive new behaviors. I now have 4 sponsees and we have a Step study at my house every other Tuesday. I have a ritual every morning before I start my day: I meditate, do yoga stretches, read program literature and literature that helps me with my private religious practice, and I journal. If I do not meditate, I don't have a great day. I have been the secretary of several meetings, worked on several convention committees and directed several of the SCA shows. I have served on several committees for the retreats. I have also started writing screenplays as a part of my sexual recovery plan. I have to attend a minimum of one meeting a week. If I dabble in my gray area, I have to attend a meeting within 24 hours.

I don't know why it works, but I know that if I do the combination of things mentioned above and make outreach calls, it seems to work. I also know I am willing to do anything necessary to maintain my sobriety. The most important thing I have learned is never give up. Never give up. No matter how many times I have fallen, I go back to a meeting and I share my story. It is progress not perfection, and it is one day at a time.

Story #2 – *My Crisis of Faith*

There weren't enough beds for all of us that night. I had to sleep on a mattress placed on the floor between the other beds. One of the others was snoring loud enough to make the room shake. Screams were coming from nearby rooms. Even though there wasn't much silence it was the first time in the last 36 hours I was able to think about everything that had happened to land me in jail.

The days leading up to my arrest weren't much different from any other. I had not been working for a few months, so I had a lot of time on my hands. Most of my day would be spent in front of the computer trolling for a connection with someone. The dream of finding a soul mate had long since been discarded as an impossibility. All that was left for me was the chase to fulfill sexual fetishes and fantasies.

My sexual fetishes and fantasies mostly revolved around haircutting and body shaving. The fantasies had been carefully cultivated for 25 years and had become extremely elaborate. It was these fantasies that drove me on a daily basis to get online and search for actors to play the parts in my scripted fantasies. One common characteristic some of us in recovery have developed for those suffering from fetish and fantasy addiction is "We began to see others only as objects of our fantasies, ignoring anyone who was unable or unwilling to participate in our fetish." This is what my life had become.

The computer keyboard became an instrument of my acting out. I mastered that instrument and played it with the skill of a concert pianist. I would be connected to 3 or 4 different chat services at a time, entering 4 chat rooms in each and managing instant messaging conversations with a dozen people at once. None of this seemed insane; it was simply what I had to do to get what I thought I needed.

The attraction to younger guys had always been there for me, even when I was one of those younger guys. I didn't exclusively seek out those under 18, but I was definitely putting myself in situations where it was possible and prevalent. Ten years of hearing stories about how sexual those under 18 were created a false sense of reality for me. I began to believe that it would be all right to have sex with someone under 18. It seemed like it was commonplace. However, I still had an internal struggle over this. I knew it wasn't in alignment with my values.

A few days before my arrest I had really worked myself into a sexual frenzy. The person who I had made plans to hook up with (he said he was older than 18) had blown me off. It was rare for me to find someone interested in indulging my fetish, so I was really pissed. I didn't want to masturbate for fear of releasing the sexual energy before some payoff might occur. I turned my attentions back online, determined that I would get what I wanted.

Ding! My computer alerted me to someone having logged on who was in my list of friends. I immediately opened up an instant message window to him and began chatting. We exchanged pleasantries. He did not remember who I was. I reminded him that we had chatted in the past. We exchanged pictures of us both in clothes. He seemed to recall me now. I asked him what he was doing and if he might be interested in meeting. He thought it would be cool to meet but he couldn't for a few days. He also reminded me he was only 15 years old. I tried to put that thought out of my mind. I asked him if he would indulge me in my fetish. He said yes, he would and he also wanted to have sex. I ignored the voices reminding me of my values and agreed to hook up in a few days.

My mind was racing and my heart was pounding. I was really nervous about the prospect of having sex with someone underage, but it did not matter because I was going to be able to fulfill my fantasy. The next few days were spent frantically looking for someone online who would take this 15-year-old's place. I needed to find someone who was legal. My desperate attempts yielded no other prospects.

The day and time came for us to meet and I was left with a choice. I could break the law and go against my values, or I could act out and fulfill my fantasies. The choice, of course, had already been made; I was powerless to turn away from my sexual desires. I showed up and I was arrested.

The next few days involved experiences I had never had before and certainly never want to repeat. I was so naive about the legal system. I honestly thought I would be going home after I confessed. I was put in a holding cell the first night where I was given a bologna sandwich and tried to sleep on a bare stainless-steel bunk. Guys in the other cells were yelling most of the night. The next morning around 5:00 a.m. all of us were rounded up and shackled together and transported to the county courthouse.

The one phone call I had made was to a friend. I didn't want anyone in my family to know what happened. I was sure I could handle this all myself. The judge set my bond at $75,000. This meant that I needed to come up with $7,500 to get out of jail. My friend was not able to come up with that kind of money. The public defender asked me if I wanted my friend to call my parents. I was still determined to deal with this in my own way, so I said no.

The next 8 hours were spent being processed into the county jail. The cells were packed. There might have been 100 men in a 12' x 12' space. I felt as if I were being cooked, it was so hot in this claustrophobic space. The thought of using the communal toilet was completely out of the question. Drug deals were being conducted openly. Guards were spreading the word that I was a pedophile. Other inmates would ask me if I was the one. I denied it every time. Although I never showed it, I was scared shitless.

In the midst of all this chaos my Higher Power was looking out for me.

The first chance I had to make a phone call from the county jail was the morning after I was processed in. We were allowed to use a pay phone only. The only type of call you could make was a collect call. I dialed my sister. She picked up and a recording announced that this was a collect call from the county jail and to beware that this might be a scam. She hung up. I dialed her again. She hung up. I dialed her again, desperate for her to figure out something was up. She hung up. I was almost in tears at this point.

I tried one last time. This time she accepted the charges and she could hear me. I could barely keep my composure as I sobbed and explained to her what happened. I begged her to not tell Mom or Dad. She assured me she would take care of things and get me out of jail.

Hours went by and I received no word about someone posting my bond. I had no idea what was going on in the outside world. I was unaware that my sister had to call one of our brothers to come up with the cash to get me out of jail. I became concerned that I would have to spend another night in jail. When the opportunity came, I went to the pay phone to call my parents. The same series of messages and hang ups occurred. I finally spoke to my mother and I sobbed uncontrollably as explained where I was and what I had done. She had not spoken to my sister or my brothers. Like many mothers, she had already had the sense that something was up with me before I even spoke to her. She told me she would call my sister and make sure bail was going to be posted.

A few more hours passed and then the word finally came. My bail had been posted. I was going home. It took about 6 hours for me to be processed out of the county jail. In one of the final holding cells there was a young man who recognized me from the day before when I was being processed in. He looked me up and down. The sentence he uttered next has never left me, "Someone must have been watching over you." He could see that I had no cuts or bruises. Pedophiles are treated as the lowest of the low in jail and are often targets of violence. I had made it through the ordeal physically unharmed. I was certain he was right. I have come to understand my Higher Power was watching over me even in my darkest moment.

It was 11:00 o'clock at night before I stepped outside the gates of the county jail and onto the street as a free man. No one I knew was in sight. I then saw my sister waving a block away. I started with a walk and then broke into a run toward her. Seeing and hugging her felt comforting and reassuring. Her husband was also there along with my nephew who was a few months old. My sister gave me a gift that night beyond bailing me out of jail. She handed me my sleeping nephew to hold in my arms despite what I had just done. To this day I feel more bonded to this nephew than any of my other wonderful nieces and nephews. He helped show me everything would be all right.

A month passed before I found my way to my first meeting of Sexual Compulsives Anonymous (SCA). I have no recollection if I said one word during that first meeting. If I did it was likely spoken between the crying and tears which were typical in my first few months of program.

My first sponsor was likely in that meeting, but again I couldn't tell you for sure. He taught me about acceptance and showed me that the program could work. He didn't do this through his words, but through his actions. He had stayed sober from bottom line behaviors for 8 or 9 years when I met him. He showed up religiously at 4 meetings a week. He took my calls. He brought meetings to my house when I had a curfew during probation. He always greeted the newcomer. He spoke at nearly every meeting. He was rigorously honest. This man, a stranger to me at first, gave of himself without expectation. I am so grateful for the gifts he gave me. He is a part of my program today even if he is no longer my sponsor.

Determining my bottom line (part of a sexual recovery plan) was a painful process. I could set aside the prospect of anonymous sex without too much difficulty; after all, I rarely found the kind of sex I wanted anyways. Cutting out pornography was doable but certainly not desirable. However, giving up online chat seemed impossible. How would I meet people? What about all those friends I would leave behind? I was convinced it was impossible to live without the chat despite the unmanageability it had just brought into my life.

It took a few more months of trolling online and coming to meetings for me to see that it had to go. No one I met online was truly a friend. None of the people I thought I connected with online could give me a hug or an encouraging word. I was not sure how long I could hold out, but I turned it over to my Higher Power and learned what the power of faith was about.

My Higher Power has shown me, one day at a time, that it is possible to live without these compulsive activities in my life. All I needed to get started was a sliver of faith that my life could be different. I stopped the online chatting, pornography, and anonymous sex for 6 years. It was truly a gift from my Higher Power.

After about 6 years into my program the world I knew ceased to exist. It was a period in my life where everything was turned upside down. I was confronted with more consequences from my criminal past when background checks became commonplace in the world of white-collar work. I lost several job offers as a result of background checks, and my career and self-esteem took what felt like fatal blows. The memories of being a victim of childhood sexual abuse could no longer be repressed. A potential love interest turned into a romantic obsession. This obsession powered a crippling depression and brought tons of internalized homophobia to the surface.

This period of darkness almost swallowed me. I was brought to the edge of suicide. What prevented me from going over that edge? It was the sliver of faith that my life could be different I had heard so much about in program. I never stopped going to meetings. I continued to reach out and accept the help of professionals, family, friends, and program members. I consider this part of my life as a "crisis of faith." I had lost all hope and stopped believing in a Higher Power. It was the people in my life and the principles of the program that carried me through to the other side of this "crisis of faith." The last 7 years have been about rebuilding my life and finding ways to continue to keep faith alive in my life. I don't know a better way of doing this then continuing to work my program of recovery.

Today the challenge I face is figuring out how to bring a healthy sexuality into my life. I am finding it important for me to listen to my values and bring my Higher Power into the process. As a gay man I have found it hard to rid myself of the internalized homophobia and the stereotypes of the gay subculture. Defining my sexuality based on external influences hasn't brought me happiness. I don't believe that sex is bad, even sex that includes fetish, fantasies and pornography. What is bad is when I use sex to harm. With this idea in mind, I redefined my bottom lines to be simply "To do no harm to myself or others."

My first 6 years in program were filled with a lot of "Thou shall nots." I needed rigid rules to learn a different way of living. It served me for a time, but it was obvious after my "crisis of faith" that a new way of living was needed to grow further. I have been able to recapture the possibility of having a soul mate some day in my life. It hasn't happened yet, but all things are possible in God's world.

Story #3 – *The Willingness to Stick Around*

It was in the year 1981 when Bill L. began SCA meetings in his New York apartment. Bill had attended SA meetings in the past; but he didn't get what he needed there, so he decided to start a gay-friendly sex addicts meeting in his apartment. Bill's apartment was small, and full of pottery. There were four of us all in one room. I remember sitting on a piece of pottery at the very first meeting, and I didn't know what it was. All I knew was that it was hard and I was sitting on it.

The first few meetings were very interesting. We had a phone network - what we called a phone tree - to decide where we would meet from week to week. We didn't have a static space, we had a fluid space, so meetings were held from one apartment to another. We were the first people out there. I felt very blessed and wondered if there ever would be other survivors of sexual addiction?

I originally started with the Debtors Anonymous (DA) program, which is a very disciplined fellowship. That's where I met Bill, who became my sponsor and twelve stepped me into joining SCA. At first, I was upset and offended since I was also in Overeater's Anonymous (OA), which was also disciplined with its Food Plan. I was totally out of control, spending money on hustlers, going to back rooms and bathhouses, and not getting any sleep, so I decided to give SCA a shot. After going to SCA and being able to write my own Sexual Recovery Plan I joined seven more programs.

There's really no merit on my part in my still being in SCA. My karma is loyalty and stick-to-it-ism. I've done that with all my programs. I have loyalty to organizations. I just realized that is my merit.

The first few SCA meetings we were like war stories of how we couldn't stop acting out. No one had a day count. One member actually described what they were going to do physically with someone after the meeting. Then someone with sobriety in another program said "First Step! We don't do that!" The rest of us in SCA were in a complete fog on how to work this program. The literature that was available to us was either homophobic or simply from another 12-Step program with the name of their addiction blacked out with a marker. There wasn't any SCA literature; the program literature had not coalesced. We were like one of those stars that had not coalesced - amorphous and not yet formed. New SCA meetings began from that first one, then grew into five, then to ten a week. New literature started to be written almost every day.

There was a point where we were desperate for funds. We had to pay the rent and if there were only ten people in the fellowship, where could we get the money? Recovery was still possible, by the Grace of God. That was the great insight we had, and we were willing to stick around to see it happen. Then there were the ones who died. During this time, we lost a lot of people to AIDS. Back then it was thought that it was a gay men's disease. With time we saw that this disease does not discriminate.

I've attended meetings for all these years, often because I had nowhere else to turn. I've realized that recovery was possible through the humility of knowing there was no solution to my addiction without the belief in a Higher Power. That was one insight I learned, and I was willing to stick around to see it happen - and it all started from sitting awkwardly in Bill's apartment at that first meeting.

Story #4 – *Moving Past the Past*

I come from a large family and I am the youngest of six children. My family decided to have a family reunion after 20 years of living basically separate lives. The reunion and my one-year AA anniversary were the same weekend. I was scared to death to go, but somehow knew that I really needed to. Since I couldn't remember at least 95% of my childhood, I had always assumed it had been pretty "normal."

At this family reunion my three sisters, two brothers and I ended up confronting our father about the overt sexual abuse he had done to us. Separated as we had been, those memories were easier to drink, sex, work, spend, shop, gamble or achieve away; but once we all came together for the first time in twenty years, resentments about the way he treated us started to shoot forth like an oil well. Confronting our father probably wasn't an item on my sister's list of "Things to do together." I came back to New York devastated, but sober.

When I was first getting sober in AA, I had all these ideas like, "I'll stop having unprotected anal intercourse with complete strangers. "I really thought it wasn't possible to keep having that type of sex without drugs and alcohol. But by the time of the reunion, I had participated in unsafe sex numerous times, I was addicted to porn, and I was dating people who worked in the sex industry.

I had decided that "sex" fell under my sixth step and it would be taken care of by AA. For six months, I white-knuckled it. No sex with another person. Then, one night, I had sex with a stranger who was staying next door. We had intrigued through the living room window. I was devastated. I knew once again that I was powerless over "something." All my life I had had a love/hate relationship with sex; I loved it while doing it, but afterwards I felt enormous guilt and shame. I had been raised a Catholic, so all my life I remember hearing that homosexuals were very bad people who would go to Hell.

My mother was Hispanic and had the belief that sex was a woman's obligation and should only be enjoyed by the man. For her, this meant that if she enjoyed sex she was "bad" and "dirty". I'm quite certain today that both of my parents were themselves sex addicts. My father had been asking me from the age of eleven if I had gotten "laid" yet. It felt like he was waiting to throw me a party if I did, or on a darker note, to make sure "the sins of my father" hadn't turned me "queer."

On New Years of 1993 I went to my first SCA meeting, held in a church basement. I read the Four-fold and said to myself, "I belong here." I got my sponsor at that meeting and he was my sponsor for many years. We've been through a lot together and I love him in a very special way, as I'm sure he loves me. My favorite slogan from him is "lighten up girl!" When I came to SCA, I was working four jobs, going to meetings, dance class and working out. I refused to go therapy; I was taught that only sick and weak people "air their dirty laundry." A month after my first meeting, it all fell apart, my back gave out and I was an emotionless zombie. I went to a therapist and chiropractor on the same day for the first time in my life. That day marked the beginning of my re-parenting and self-nurturing, two extremely foreign concepts to me. That day, I bought myself a really nice gift for being a brave, good boy.

I've gone to meetings ever since. I've sponsored people, I've done service at meetings, been on conference committees, conference shows, and been a member of Intergroup. My therapist specializes in incest and I've worked on that issue diligently for 6 years. I have gone to two retreats for male survivors, facilitated an incest meeting, participated in two conference workshops on incest, and have participated in a free group therapy offered by a local hospital. I also attend an incest and child sexual abuse meeting.

I enjoy sex now! I've kicked my parents, siblings, society, and the priests out of my bedroom and invited God in. In the past, I always felt like I was perpetrating or being perpetrated when I had sex. Now, it's just having sex with another consenting adult. Sometimes it's within dating or a committed relationship and sometimes it's with someone I don't know very well. But most importantly it is my "choice" and I have a healthier sexual life as a result. I still have times that are difficult. (I will always be a sex addict.) Now, I have tools that help me get through those difficult times: meetings, telephone, service, sponsor, sponsees, fellowship, the Steps, and most of all "God."

I've had complicated plans (I'm a perfectionist) and I've had really loose plans (I'm an addict). Right now, it's just three simple things to abstain from. Simplicity is key! It's really working. I'm dating, I'm exploring areas of my sexuality that I had always had too much shame to look at. It's fun, scary, hard, but it's living and it's my life now. As long as I am true to mine own self, I can't go wrong. I'm learning to worry less. I love the slogan "why worry if you pray, why pray if you worry." Another favorite is "The doors of enlightenment are pillared by confusion and paradox." Wow!! I'll say.

I have no contact with my parents. That really works for me. I don't feel I, in any way, owe them an amends. What they did to me: I discovered in therapy that the medical, educational and sexually-based rituals performed on me by my mother were "not what mommies do to their little boys" and were wrong. The effects almost drove me to destroy myself. They stole something from me that can never be replaced, and even though it may have been taken from them too, that is no excuse. If anything, it should have been the reason to protect me.

I am building relationships with my siblings and their families. I am also working on my non-sexual and sexual relationships. One of the relationships that I'm most proud of, is the loving relationship I'm having with me and God, which really are the same. This is all due to 12-Step recovery.

I thank God for Bill W., AA, SCA and all the fellowships that are bringing people back home. My life has never been better and as I stay in program, work the Steps, and help others, my life keeps unfolding like the blossom of a desert cactus. I love you all and thank you for my sobriety.

Story #5 – *A Moment of Grace*

When I hit bottom, I was at the pit of despair in my life. OCD had taken over my brain, and I was homeless. I was a failure as an artist – the career I had hoped for. I was working at temp jobs I hated and severely under-earning in the process.

I was spending my nights at a bar, drinking and sometimes having sex in the bar to numb my despair. I was filled with utterly paralyzing romantic obsessions with geographically unavailable people, and I was addicted to fantasies no real person could ever make come true. I would go out at night and dare myself to see how unsafe my sexual behavior could be. What little money I had was spent at bathhouses and adult video arcades - all to cover up crushing pain, resentment, bitterness, envy, and tons of toxic shame.

At that point I had a spiritual experience - a moment of grace. I was in my car with all my belongings. I had nowhere to go, hadn't eaten or showered for 36 hours, and had 13 cents to my name (not enough to even make a phone call). I was too ashamed to call any of my friends and explain my situation. I didn't have enough gas in my car to drive the 330 miles to my parents' house and beg them to take me in. Even then, I still thought my most important need was for a boyfriend/lover. Sitting there in my car, someone came up and propositioned me. After we had sex, I never felt more disgusting in my life. I sat in my car, thinking that I had to either die or change. The pain of acting out had surpassed my fear of the pain of not acting out. I took a moment to pray. In the quiet, it was as if God said, "Are you done now? Can we finally start?" At that moment my pager went off - a call from a close friend. How I kept up payments to a pager when I couldn't get it together to pay rent, I don't know. Having only 13 cents, not enough for a phone call, I called my friend "collect…" She was an angel by taking me in so that I wouldn't be on the street.

My friend called the community mental health clinic and got me an appointment with a social worker, thanks to someone else's last-minute cancellation. This was followed by another mysterious cancellation, which allowed me to see a county psychiatrist. The county even picked up some of my medication costs. I resumed temp work, and within a month I was living in a beautiful house in Santa Monica. I joined a 12- Step study group and began the process of Step work. I will always be grateful to the other five members of this group and the people who attended my home meeting there.

I had been in sexual recovery, including SCA, for over three years when this moment of grace took place. But it wasn't until that moment in my car - just before my pager beeped - that I finally became willing to change. After that moment a process of recovery surely began because I had willingness and took action.

I had several slips, at 30 days, then 60 days, then 30 days again. Each slip was demoralizing, filling me with fear that I would end up back with all my possessions in my car or in a shopping cart. I also knew the pain of repeatedly going through withdrawal every time I slipped, and I really didn't want to subject myself to going through it again. Once I stopped acting out, there was definitely a period of withdrawal: physical, mental, emotional, spiritual. I didn't want to put myself through that anymore. I said to myself: "Now that I am back on my plan, why don't I do whatever it takes to stay here – Steps, tools, service, whatever it takes."

I have learned many things over the years, some of which I would like to share:

— I get a daily reprieve from the compulsion to act out based on my spiritual connection that day. Some days I get more of a reprieve than others. Did I start my day in prayer? Or did I turn on the news and start cursing the government of the day?

— There is no substitute for Step work. I can write a thousand plans, but it is only by doing Step work that the obsession and compulsion are lifted.

— The behavior stops, and then the compulsion stops and gradually the obsession lifts. It is not the other way around. We cannot think ourselves into recovery. As someone with a severe case of OCD, I firmly believe and can testify to this.

— The Traditions are as important as the Steps and should be read at every meeting. It lets the newcomer know how the group functions. It also shows how the Traditions contribute to our individual recovery.

— No matter what the problem, acting out is not the solution. If I have a problem, and then I act out because of my feelings, I have more severe problems coming, in a down-spiraling pattern.

— Nothing justifies a slip. My sponsor testified as to how he processed his parents' sickness and passing without acting out, despite some very deep feelings.

— I have one of those mental and emotional disorders spoken of in the Big Book of AA ("Obsessive-Compulsive Disorder to the "nth degree..."). However, I have stayed on my plan thanks to my willingness and capacity to be honest with God, myself, and appropriately with others.

— This is a program of principles, not personalities. However, it is a program of people and my Higher Power often works through people. The people in my life, whether I am fond of them or not, are there by Divine appointment.

— Isolation is a recovery killer. Also, I need to remember to also call people when things are going well.

— My early recovery did not provide me with a boyfriend/lover. If I had known that at the beginning of that period, I might not have bothered. However, I am being restored to sanity. Should God's grace bring me together with an appropriate partner, I believe I will have the sanity enough to show up for it. I may not have found the love of my life, but at least I am no longer looking in all the wrong places.

— Being sober and on my plan doesn't insulate me from life's difficulties and obstacles. However, recovery allows me to approach them with sanity.

— Feelings are temporary: they pass - all of them.

— Sex is holy: the desire to sexually express love and have fun with another man is holy. The choice to use protection is primarily that of sanity. However, I do not need to condemn myself for the desire, for that is natural, and the way God created gay sex.

— Sexual pleasure is 90% in my mind. Safer sex can not only be hot, but in my recovery, it can be hot enough.

— The journey from Steps 2 and 3 to 11-from when I made a decision to turn my will and my life over to the care of a power greater than myself that can restore me to sanity to the point of praying ONLY for the knowledge of God's will for me and the power to carry it out - is accomplished by Steps 4 - 10. I found Steps 6 and 7 very helpful in working Step 11.

— If I don't like the concept of God I was taught, there are countless other ways to think of and know a Higher Power. I am allowed and now have a Higher Power that loves me and approves of my sexuality and wants me to feel good about myself.
— Keep coming back, even on the days I don't want to. Recovery is often like exercise. It works even when I don't particularly like it.

I can still feel great fear about issues such as money, and I can feel shame about what my life hasn't become. I can also worry that it is way too late for my creativity to become unblocked and for me to succeed in life. Of course, these thoughts are preposterous.

Nevertheless, these feelings seem real and can cause knots in my stomach. But I realize that these were the exact same feelings I didn't know how to cope with, and thought would destroy me, back in 1997. But the obsession over those feelings and the compulsion to act out has been lifted for today.

I don't see finding a boyfriend/lover as my most important need today. I am no longer avoiding the deep, core issues I need to face. I have seen a million program miracles and will no doubt see a million more, in all of my programs. I guess I was destined to relive these feelings and fears. Only this time, I won't act out. I will respond as sanely as possible. I will keep praying for the knowledge of God's (Love's) will and the power to carry it out. I will continue to ask for God's (Love's) will to be done, and for God (Love) to remove my character defects so that I may be of service to others. Today my needs are met. I won't worry about tomorrow until tomorrow. I know that I will be taken care of.

I know that if God can work miracles for me at my lowest, why would it be so hard for God to help me through this while in recovery? A logical thought. A sane thought. My journey continues. If I can stay on my plan for all these years, then it is possible for anyone. I am not terminally unique.

Story #6 – *Screaming without a Voice*

I am a recovering sex addict, but I'm no SCA prodigy. I've learned from my many mistakes, and have been blessed by having been offered this program and saying yes to it. I'm deeply grateful for every day of sexual abstinence that has been given to me by God's grace and for learning from the experience of countless sex addicts I've known since I came into recovery. I will always be a sex addict. My acting out is just a symptom. What I get is a daily reprieve based on the maintenance of my spiritual condition.

I know that no psychologist, pastor, policeman or anyone else could have helped me with my sex addiction. It took one sex addict sharing with me how he got help through working the Steps and using the principles of the program that taught me how not to act out one day at a time.

Right up to the afternoon of September 24, 1984, when I was arrested in a public area for trying to pick up a police officer, I thought nothing could possibly happen to me. "I am the best little boy in the world," I thought. "There will never be consequences. I'll never get caught. I'm too good, too smart. Nothing will happen to me." I lived in the illusion of denial.

My acting out started in childhood. I was abused by a neighbor when I was around 5 and he was about 12. It changed me. My father drank and raged. My mother tried to hold the house together and had her own emotional problems. There was a lot of chaos and drama between them. Sexual touch became a way for me to relate to my peers. Every year I would say to myself, "When I get a little older, I will stop this."

How did I feel? There was little sense of nurturing, trust or comfort in my home. There was little accountability. I rarely felt any affection or love from my father and I was mostly afraid of him. I longed for connection and didn't know a healthy way to get it. As a young boy I was plagued with feelings of insecurity, inadequacy, rejection, abandonment and fear. In acting out, I was screaming when I could not voice my pain.

My acting out took a giant leap when I got my driver's license at 16 and was able to drive to the public acting out places I had heard about. How did I feel? I was obsessed. I would feel a trance-like "aura" come over me. I had to have it, and I felt very little fear. I felt a great sense of anticipation leading up to acting out, then afterward felt remorse, fear, anguish and self-hatred. My acting out was anonymous sex with men in public places. This addictive cycle became ingrained in me.

Addiction served me by repressing what I would not allow myself to feel. Addiction kept me from any authentic feeling. This compulsion to avoid my emptiness became a familiar state of mind, and it drove me to act out. I knew once this state started, there was no turning back. I rarely thought about why. I just did it.

I did have some spirituality in those days. At 16 years old I went to see *Brother Sun, Sister Moon*, a movie about St. Francis of Assisi. I was struck with a feeling of love and inner peace that I had never known. I loved St. Francis, and especially related to his struggles with his father and his longing to experience the love of God. I yearned to be free of the all-consuming guilt and shame. St. Francis has been with me now for over 40 years, never far from my mind and heart, transforming me at a subconscious level. Reading and memorizing the St. Francis Prayer was a significant spiritual experience that offered hope. A seed was planted, but went dormant until I got into recovery.

In college in the '70s I led a double life. I lived in a fraternity house by day, and by night had anonymous sexual encounters. It became a daily obsession. I would wake up and tell myself that I was not going to act out, and then find myself cruising for sex a short time later. I was filled with anxiety and had no insight into why I did the things I did. I started drinking compulsively and took prescription drugs for anxiety. A counselor was very concerned about my drinking, but I ignored it. Life was a struggle, but I managed to continue in school.

It wasn't until much later in my recovery that I understood that the compulsion to act out was a convoluted human survival instinct for affection. Unconsciously I felt I had to act out in order to survive - that if I didn't get my fix I would die. The acting out was tied to my human instincts for survival and my desperate need to avoid authentic feelings.

I did a graduate Internship in the summer of 1979 in Santa Barbara, CA. I felt dead inside. I learned how to "act as if" I was a real human being, but everything I did was with the addiction in mind - always searching for the next fix, the next trick. Southern California was beautiful. I lived near the beach and the acting out areas. There I did cocaine for the first time. But there was nobody home, nobody inside. Acting out was the only thing that made me feel alive. When I wasn't working, I was acting out.

I moved back to St. Louis in 1980. I spent countless hours in acting out places, hating it, feeling empty when I left, vowing never to go back. I couldn't get any clarity or vision for my life, and I felt horrible about myself.

Compulsive cruising became driven by resentment, feeling victimized and cheated by life. I would rehearse the resentments, mostly about my parents, over and over, all about what they didn't do, what I didn't get. How I felt cheated.

In 1981 I was diagnosed with chronic, aggressive Hepatitis B. That was a game changer, because it was life threatening. I was told not to drink. It scared me and I felt powerless. I thought I would die from it.

A year later, friends came back from Key West with stories about a strange disease affecting gay men. It scared them, but I remember saying it was probably no big deal. 1983 brought more news about HIV. I was scared. I had already had several venereal diseases by then. Gay men started talking about taking care of their health. While I knew that my acting out was like playing Russian Roulette, I couldn't stop.

Next came a dream move to Munich, Germany for a geographic cure. I was determined to get out of the vicious sex/drug cycle. But within 48 hours of my arrival, I had found the acting out places and the patterns just started repeating themselves. I lived within walking distance of a huge acting out area and it became a daily and nightly obsession. I lived in the fog of active sex addiction and my drinking escalated.

I had no insight or awareness into why I was doing what I was doing. It was a cycle where the pressure built, cruising started, obsession kicked in, I scored the fix, burned out, and felt the remorse, and the pressure built again. Over and over: same show, different actors. Same outcome: empty, dead, and filled with guilt and shame. I knew something was terribly wrong. I knew I was wasting my life and vaguely sensed it couldn't go on. But the justification to act out always kicked in. I desperately wanted to find that special someone and thought, "How else am I going to meet someone to date?" When I met someone acting out who wanted to get to know me, I felt either claustrophobic and had to get away, or became overly attached and scared him off. I feared I would become like the older men I saw at the acting out haunts - haggard with longing, empty eyes, having lived lives of regret and despair. That's what I believed I was sentenced to. My life was hopeless.

I came home from Germany in 1984, and three months later I was arrested for sexual misconduct. I started a year-long decline toward my bottom, and came to know incomprehensible demoralization on a daily basis. I was put on probation and knew that if I got caught again, I would go to jail. Still, I could not stop acting out. Neither the fear of going to jail nor the possibility of contracting AIDS could stop me. At age 27, all I wanted was to stop acting out - the same wish I had had since childhood. One part of me wanted to survive, to have a life, a career, a partner. But the other part, the addict, always got his way.

I attended my first 12-Step meeting in November 1985, and had a spiritual awakening. A weight was lifted off my shoulders when I heard that my behavior wasn't all my fault - that I suffered from a disease and that there was a solution. Eventually I got up the courage to ask someone if they'd ever heard of a 12-Step program for promiscuity, and I found a sexual recovery program.

I learned in meetings that emotional growth stops when the compulsion starts. Where was I emotionally? I was a scared child who ran from challenges and intimacy because he didn't know how to deal with them in a healthy way.

I got a sponsor and began to heal. However, after six months of white-knuckling abstinence, I decided I had had enough. I was miserable and made the decision to act out. Watching myself go through the same old rituals was an out-of-body experience. I went to act out, and started talking to someone. The first thing he said was that he had just gotten into AA. I told him I had just gotten into sexual recovery and he said, "Well, what are you doing here?" I told him I shouldn't be there and he said, "Well, let's get out of here." We left. I didn't act out that night. This was God doing for me what I couldn't do for myself.

Still, I was in a very bad place. I stayed on the couch wrapped in a blanket and just shook. I was scared to death. I called a treatment center and met with a therapist the next day. I poured out my story to him and he said, "Although it seems like you're at the lowest point in your life, I think you're actually at the highest point you've ever been, because you've finally gotten to a safe enough place where you're ready to deal with your unconscious wounds. You're ready to recover."

SCA has given me the power to face my pain and has taught me how to live authentically - out of the sex addict fog. My connection with fellow addicts gives me the language of authentic communication. I have started to discover and nurture my True Self.

At 27, I was lost to the vicious cycle of the sex addict fog. At 37, I was sober, going to meetings, growing, doing therapy, dating, struggling with my job, and frequently angry about something. At 47 I was sober, going to meetings, still growing up, still angry, and still dealing with depression and anxiety. Now at 62 I'm getting a taste of emotional sobriety and I am grateful for most things, most days.

In the past I used my body to blot out painful messages and feelings. Today I know that my body is the vehicle to healing, and that every time I don't act out, I'm stronger. I have gone back and worked through the repressed anger, sadness, frustration, and disappointments I avoided by acting out, in order to heal those old wounds.

It is more important to me now than ever to stay connected to my Higher Power, my recovery community and to the deepest part of me. Practicing the 11th Step through a daily meditation practice keeps me open to the gifts of the program. Any time that I am on the beam, close to my heart, grateful, generous, loving, kind, compassionate, helpful, thoughtful, forgiving, productive, or open, it's the spirit of the program and all the good people I've known and loved working through me.

Thank you.

Story #7 – *Teaching and Staying Teachable*

I didn't have the worst childhood, but I certainly had the longest. At least that's how it felt.

I grew up in the 1960s, in a small town in Southern California. I loved playing with my sister's dolls and wearing my mother's high heels. I hated sports, fire engines and everything else boys were expected to like. In other words, I was a big sissy and because of that, I was teased at school, in the neighborhood and at home. Now they call it bullying. Back then they just called it the 60s. I dreaded going to school each day because I knew what to anticipate - a lot of name-calling, no friends and an overall feeling of not being safe.

When I was about 13, I discovered masturbation. It happened quite accidentally and really freaked me out since I had never had "the talk" with my father. Once I got over thinking that I had permanently damaged myself, I was on my way. It wasn't just the physical sensation that I loved. When I would think about doing it, while I was doing it, and for a while afterward, my world turned gray, soft and fuzzy, and I was able to forget about the name-calling and all the loneliness I felt.

And so, my sexual compulsiveness began. I'm sure most boys at that age enjoy this newly discovered pleasure, but my relationship to masturbation felt compulsive from the start. I remember trying to control it by giving it up for Lent, putting restrictions on the number of times I did it per day, confessing to the parish priest and telling God I would never do it again. But the soothing effects it produced and its ability to change the way I was feeling made it impossible to stick to any of these restrictions.

In high school I discovered alcohol and sex with boys. The combination was more than intoxicating. I knew I was gay my whole life, I just didn't know where the rest of the gays were hanging out. But when I found them, I was off and running. I snuck into gay bars at 16 with a fake ID, drinking and having sex with guys twice my age. What I liked even more than the physical sensation of sex was the feeling of being desired. I had the desire to be desired. When I got drunk and had sex with strangers, I felt I had some value. That was the feeling I craved. It seemed that all of my life up to that point, all I wanted was to feel loved.

Nothing much changed for the next 12 years, and at the age of 28, I found myself still living with my parents, drunk most days and spending most nights at the Baths.

I decided to leave home and move to West Hollywood. Within 6 months, I was in my first AA meeting. My life changed. I got sober from drugs and alcohol by working the 12 Steps, and I was given a second chance. Unfortunately, this was the 80s, and suddenly a lot of my friends started dying of AIDS. The feelings I had as a child came back. I felt alone, scared and very unsafe. So, I returned to what I now know is my first addiction, sexual compulsiveness. It felt like the right medication at the time.

Soon I was out in the sex clubs every night hooking up with strangers, chatting on the phone lines, watching pornography and cruising the parks, just looking for some relief. With nine years of sobriety from drugs and alcohol, I was putting myself in some very dangerous places. Finally, it became clear to me that if I didn't change, I would relapse and eventually drink or do drugs again. I knew that if I did, I would die, get arrested or wind up in a mental institution. I was that clear about my AA sobriety.

Then, in 1995, what some would call a coincidence but I call a God-shot happened, and I wound up in my first SCA meeting. I came in with a bad attitude. I didn't want to be treated like a newcomer, since I had nine years of experience in AA, but because I was made to feel welcome and because I was so desperate to get a handle on my behavior, I was teachable.

The first thing I did was to get a sponsor and start working the 12 Steps with the same dedication I did when I first joined AA. I now understand that my sexual sobriety is as important as my chemical sobriety.

Next, I made a sexual recovery plan. Looking back, I see that it was unrealistic, and not really based on my history, but it was a place to start. Because my first SRP was so strict, I wound up being completely celibate for the first year, including from masturbation. In the second year, at the urging of my sponsor, I incorporated masturbation as a way to reintroduce sexuality back into my life. In my third year of sobriety, I started to date and have sexual experiences again. This led to two relationships over the years, and for someone who had never dated, that was quite an accomplishment.

What I do to stay sober today, first and foremost, is to have a sponsor and be a sponsor. I need to always remain a teacher and a student. I must always remain teachable and willing to share all the knowledge I have gained. That duality keeps me right-sized. Leading others through the 12 Steps has kept me sober through many challenging days.

I try to be of service in and out of the program. It helps me to remember to put the chairs away "out there" and never let my program get so big in the rooms that it won't fit out the door.

I have a relationship with God that involves daily prayer and meditation. Being in SCA has led me down many different spiritual roads and I hope I never stop searching.

I understand that doing the footwork is important. If I'm praying for potatoes, I had better have a hoe in my hand.

I have a sexual recovery plan, which has certainly changed over the years. I have been in relationships and I have been single. I didn't get a computer until I was sober five years, and that came with a set of new challenges, as did my smart phone. My SRP now reflects my history and my current situation. I have never changed my sexual recovery plan without discussing it with my sponsor and God. On the left side I list the things I want to stay away from or put boundaries around. On the right side I list the things I want to add to my life. I measure my sobriety by the left side, but I measure my recovery by the right side.

What I've really learned in SCA is that recovery is not a race, but a ride. I have learned to enjoy the scenery.

It's impossible to fully express the love I have for the program of SCA. Sobriety has given me everything that acting out promised me.

Story #8 – *Self-esteem Through Service*

I have low self-esteem, and barely any boundaries. I crave connection, but I have a fear of intimacy. I am healing from a sense of being somehow terribly defective, and that acquiring these defects was my own fault. I used to think I couldn't justify the air I breathed.

From the middle of elementary school onward, I spent large swaths of time masturbating. I used to have to follow up on every possible sexual opportunity, regardless of my personal feelings of attraction, or the appropriateness of making a sexual connection with that person.

I now recognize these as outgrowths of dysfunctional parenting, bullying by peers, codependency, chronic stress during essential developmental stages of my childhood and young adulthood, a genetic predisposition for mental illness, and - last but not least - sexual compulsion.

SCA happened to be the first fellowship that I had heard of for sexual recovery. The information came from the local LGBT center, which made me feel more comfortable. Even the name, Sexual Compulsives Anonymous, sounded like me, because it had the word 'sexual' - and sexual was who I was. But the consequences of my sexual acting out were too drastic to ignore, and I begin sexual recovery in my mid-twenties.

Who I am now in recovery is a middle-aged woman, trying to live each day fully by showing up and staying in the moment. I use all the tools of the SCA program such as a sponsor, a written sex plan, and meditating. Service has helped my recovery, by boosting my self-esteem when I accomplish service tasks, and by connecting me in appropriate way with other members of our program. I have several sponsees, which connects me to the miracle of how this program inspires positive growth. My life automatically has more meaning when I do service.

I pray every day to my Higher Power. I have found that the term God or Higher Power is a "spiritual placeholder," and what's most beneficial is our attitude and effort in turning our lives and our will over to God's care - regardless of the details of how we envision our Higher Power. There is room for all who want the SCA program.

Story #9 – *Learning to Trust Myself*

I was born just over fifty years ago into a farming family in rural England, the youngest of three children. My mother could be both kind and strict and was sometimes accused of over-protecting me as I was "clingy." In fact, I would cling to my mother rather than be exposed to verbal and sometimes physically violent outbursts by my emotionally distant father. The family belonged to a rigid branch of Christianity whose teachings left me with a feeling that there was something wrong about my body, my emotions, my sexuality, even my very being, a syndrome that I would later name as toxic shame.

I was exposed to adult sexuality as early as three years old with several experiences of sexual abuse, a confusing experience as I was both frightened and stimulated at the same time. On top of this was a physical condition that gave me excruciating pain until the cause was discovered and rectified by an operation when I was seven. Both of these experiences were denied by adults around me. This caused me to deny the emotions associated with these experiences and some confusion about what was actually real. I started to use fantasy to get me through painful experiences and emotions, much of which was sexual in nature. By the age of six I was having extreme fantasies that involved both males and females, and I was also preoccupied with trying to see the genitals of other children. I have strong memories of masturbating behind window curtains while watching builders working on a new house opposite my home.

To present a complete picture, adults in my family could be kind and loving, and I was happy in certain ways with some good friends, lovely holidays, and seemingly endless summers playing in the fields and woods near my home. The happier aspects of my childhood came to an end quite abruptly, however, when two good friends moved away, leaving me lonely and the target of bullies at school. Although the physical and verbal bullying was sometimes homophobic in nature, the motivation for singling me out seemed to be more about my relatively small size and strength, as homophobic insults were directed at just about everybody. There were days when I would go to school and not talk to anyone else, since I was too shy and frightened to approach others.

When I was thirteen my father died of a long-term illness, leaving me with grief, anger, guilt, but some relief. The bullying stopped at this point, perhaps because people felt sorry for me. As we were not an emotionally literate or expressive family, I was not encouraged to name and talk about my emotions. This led to yet more confusion about what was going on inside me. Meanwhile, my masturbation and fantasy life was in full swing. I was obsessed with every aspect and variation of sex that I could find out about on TV and in the porn magazines that I had started to use. My attraction to the male body was becoming strong, and at the age of fourteen I had my first sexual encounter with three adult men in a public toilet in another town. Although I felt guilty and scared by this, I returned later that evening for more sex, starting a cruising habit that lasted into my late twenties. I gained a huge self-esteem boost from this experience, so instead of feeling like a shunned loner, I felt I was being strongly desired by others. This made me feel proud and superior to other boys at school who I suspected were just pretending to have had sex.

For the next five years I continued to seek out older men in toilets, sometimes wasting hours to no avail. I had a few girlfriends too, but nobody knew or suspected that I was mainly sexually attracted to men. Some days I would be very busy sexually, having intercourse with a girlfriend, just half an hour before or after having had sex with men. I had no moral problem with this, as I thought I wasn't really "cheating" on my girlfriend, as there were no other women involved and HIV had not yet shown up in Britain.

My academic goals had gone down the drain by the time I moved to a town with a large gay population, and my primary sense of confidence came from being sexually desired and active. I view this period of my life with a mixture of both positive and negative feelings, as it was a relief to be in an environment where I could be "out" and express myself more freely. I came out as bisexual to friends in my hometown, gaining the confidence to do this from being out in my new city. There were mostly positive reactions, excluding one from a close "friend" who decided to react in a physically violent way that still shocks me. The lid came off sexually around this time, and I spent the majority of my time in bars, toilets, saunas, and cruising areas having as much sex as I possibly could. I contracted sexually transmitted diseases on several occasions but managed to avoid HIV. I would sometimes have a boyfriend that I attempted to remain faithful to, but this would normally last about a week at the most. I also had an affair with a married woman and became obsessed with men who were unavailable or couldn't meet my emotional needs. In fact, I had no idea what my emotional needs were.

At twenty-three I came to a rock bottom with a codependent relationship and the use of cannabis that enhanced my capacity to live in fantasy. I made a half-hearted suicide attempt, which was the only way I felt I could show others how desperately unhappy I was. It was soon after that I began a relationship with a man who was in AA. He introduced me to emotionally honest people who didn't need to be drunk or high in order to enjoy themselves, and I changed my drinking and drugging habits accordingly. I gained employment that was the beginning of a new career. Cruising and frequent sex outside my supposedly monogamous relationship continued. However, when my behavior was discovered, our relationship became abusive on both sides. We would fight and have make-up sex just minutes later. I attempted to engage my partner in threesomes to feed my hunger for sex and novelty, but that resulted in more fights. When the relationship ended, I went on what I told myself was a final binge before I intended to go to a sexual recovery fellowship I had heard about from a friend.

SCA was not available in the city I lived in, so I started to work the program in another "S" fellowship. I found a sponsor but felt misunderstood by him. Although gay himself, he appeared to have attitudes to sexuality that were from an earlier age and rooted in religious rigidity. I was confused about the relationship of my addiction to what I had come to recognize and name as childhood and teenage sexually abusive experiences. It is only after years in the program, along with therapy, reading, and agonizing that I have found some helpful answers to the questions that plagued me.

When meetings became available, I began attending SCA in London and later in Canada. I found the program to be the key to questions that had flooded my mind with confusion during recovery. Was my homosexual attraction in itself an addiction? Was my apparent sexual orientation simply a reenactment of my early abuse? Was I really heterosexual but simply choosing men as they were easier to "score" with? Was my labelling of myself as bisexual an attempt to make myself more socially acceptable in a heterosexual mainstream?

I am grateful to SCA members who have listened and who were non-judgmentally affirming my decision to change my bottom line when I needed to find sobriety a true sexual expression. A major realization was that my mind was definitely clearer when I abstained from certain sexual behaviors that put me at risk or numbed my mind with hours of porn. SCA helped me be honest with my bisexual self. I could share more and feel relaxed among LGBT people in a way I couldn't in other fellowships. This led to a relationship with a man that lasted fifteen years; and because it was emotionally honest, supportive, and sexually faithful, it raised my self-esteem enormously.

Although this long-term relationship was satisfactory to me in many ways, I continued to have slips with other men and porn. I have found the middle column of the Sexual Recovery Plan very helpful in being able to experiment with new behaviors in recovery. The question of how to have an open relationship within sobriety has been a tough one, much depended on the circumstances surrounding it. Internet porn and cruising bars were definitely addictive and problematic to me emotionally. The open relationship finished when I realized I wanted to have sexual and emotional intimacy together, in the same person.

For the past three years I have been in a sexually monogamous, fun, and emotionally intimate relationship with a man with whom I share love, a house, and many interests. This may not be the pinnacle of what sexual recovery should be for everyone, but it is the one I find myself in now and it's very fulfilling. I'm now comfortable in the eyes of my Higher Power. The understanding of my Higher Power has been arrived at through direct experience, learning to trust my body, intuition, and emotions that I negated to the point of utter confusion before recovery. The wise words and fellowship of other SCA members has helped me through the dilemmas of my recovery and has been a direct experience of spiritual power in action.

Story #10 – *The Empty Promises of Pornography*

Nine years ago, I recognized that I was powerless over my sexual addiction. My life was isolated, secretive, and promiscuous, and my conversations were too often filled with suggestive and provocative language. Consequently, I joined Sexual Compulsives Anonymous (SCA), and my goals have been to stop my sexual compulsion and learn to combine sex with intimacy.

Sharing my thoughts and feelings with people in SCA has served as a useful practice for me to create intimate relationships in my life. One main component of my learning process has been working with my Step-writing group. I feel a deep camaraderie with other members because I can truly be myself with them. Their courageous actions have inspired me to make better choices for myself, and working with them has rooted me more firmly in my recovery. I have begun to clear up the gray areas that were surrounding my plan.

Developing a close relationship with my sponsor has been another significant tool for recovery. I have learned to ask for his insight and guidance. Asking for help from others does not come naturally to me, but I find that it helps me to step out of my isolation. In the past, my life had been too compartmentalized. Certain people knew specific things about me, but no one person knew me fully. I now see the importance of having at least one person who knows everything about my life.

One major issue that has kept me from developing intimate relationships in the past is that I have often been emotionally volatile. My family had more than its share of tragedies, and the pressure of dealing with these problems pushed my father to become hostile. He was relentless in his verbal and physical abuse. The windows of the house were often closed so that the neighbors could not hear the noise. While I could go on about this, suffice it to say that I did not have a happy childhood.

Looking back on my life, I can see that I inherited my father's rage. I have always been impatient with other people. I have a habit of lashing out at innocent cashiers, blameless waiters, and the unfortunate person walking slowly in front of me. I have heard others in SCA meetings say that they, too, shared this characteristic of explosive behavior.

As I work through the Twelve Steps, I have become aware that my sex addiction has intensified my explosive behavior. The hyperactive, unending search for sex made me irritable, cantankerous, and dismissive of others. Although I have had several long-term relationships in my life, all of them were dysfunctional and disloyal. I have always been promiscuous. I trained my brain, early on, to become aroused by the novelty of anonymous sex. I had no problem climaxing with a stranger, but when I was with a boyfriend, I had trouble even getting aroused. If I could get aroused, I was not able to climax. I needed the stimulation of something new and different, which created the great schism between sex and intimacy in my life.

Once I stepped into SCA, I curtailed my promiscuity dramatically. The result was that I increased my use of video chat rooms, and porn websites. At first, I thought these mechanisms were a healthy means of harm reduction because the sites kept me away from promiscuous sex. However, I soon came to realize that I was merely swapping one addiction for another, and my newfound interest in pornography was actually ratcheting up my volatile behavior even further.

Pornography had intensified my desire for sexual novelty. It glorified youth, and created unrealistic expectations for sexual pleasure. Watching the rapid fire of images on the Internet programmed my brain waves to become frenetic and my emotions to become erratic. Each time I looked at porn I got a hit of dopamine. The more dopamine I got, the more I craved. This meant I needed to look at an increasing number of images to find novelty and become aroused. The amount of time that I spent looking at pornography was out of control. I decided that I needed to redefine my sexual sobriety. I had heard other people in the SCA meetings talk about stepping away from pornography. I noticed and appreciated their positive results and sought their guidance.

I was amazed to find that pornography addiction is so prevalent. Knowing that such a vast number of men suffer from the same addiction woke me up to how serious this disease is. I learned that I am not alone, and that I cannot fix it alone. I realized that having a meaningful relationship would require me to step away from masturbation, video chat rooms, and pornography. In order to change my situation, I had to replace these old, unwanted behaviors with new sober behaviors. I turned to my list of chosen activities that I wanted to bring back into my life: cooking, reading and socializing with the people I had pushed away. Additionally, through the Serenity Prayer, I began to find the "courage to change the things that I can" through doing service. Taking these estimable actions helped me to build my self-esteem. Each day, I challenged myself to reach a new level of recovery.

The first four weeks of stepping away from pornography were extraordinarily difficult, but profound. My brain suffered a steep decline in endorphin and dopamine levels, and my body experienced a rise in stress and anxiety. The sexual tension was almost unbearable. However, stepping away from pornography quickly propelled my recovery into fast-forward. During this period, I also went through a great deal of introspection and documented my thoughts in a journal. My first realization was that I had been single for ten years. I was astonished! I believe that I had been single for so long because the criteria I had been using to find a boyfriend were too strict. The dating websites had prompted me to set my benchmark too high, and I took their questionnaires too seriously. I was not willing to deviate from my standards that I had set.

One Saturday morning, while fretting about being single, I said a prayer that I use often in program: "Dear God, help me shift my perception of this situation." A sudden shift occurred, and I made a conscious decision to ease up on the criteria that I had been using to search for a boyfriend: he did not have to be a particular height, weight, age, or even HIV status. While my rationale had made sense to me in the past, I chose to drop these rigid standards from my online dating profiles.

Magically, the phone rang that same day, and I was asked out on a date. This person that called had perused me for several years. But even though we had a strong mutual attraction I had always said no because we were sero-discordant - I am HIV+ and he is HIV-. So, this time I said yes to a date, instead of no. I saw him through a new filter. I rediscovered courtship and generated romance in my life. When we made love, I was completely present; for the first time in my life, I was not fantasizing about being with someone else. This was a miracle! I changed the paradigm and integrated sex with intimacy. I take the relationship one day at a time. Each day, I step up to the plate and do my best, and the experience has been transcendent, surpassing any intimacy I have ever known.

In my sober life today, I have the tools to actually manage my disease of addiction. I have learned to modify my behavior and choose the next-best action that will enable me to carry out my daily life efficiently. The progress that I see building has created the positive momentum for me to move forward.

I see that I alone cannot restore myself to sanity. Everything I have expressed here has come from conversations with my sponsor and my Step-writing group, as well as in SCA meetings. Being intimate with people in recovery has been a great practice for me to create intimacy with the man I am now dating. Although I have noted many dramatic changes in my behavior, please know that I am not speaking in absolute terms. My progress comes from a shift in my perception. My recovery is about progress, not perfection.

Story #11 – *Breaking the Shame Cycle*

At 9 am, on New Year's Eve of 1986, I asked the two hustlers to clean up and leave my apartment. I was finally exhausted from the combination of six hustlers and seven drugs I had been using in the last 24 hours of acting out. I had spent $1,000 on this binge; the same amount I had spent on each of the two preceding nights.

Alone, on the floor, I sat listening to people going to work in the "real world" just outside my windows. I had never felt more degraded, empty, unworthy of existence.

At that moment, I realized that one hustler was too many and a hundred not enough; that my disease was a thirst that couldn't be quenched – an itch that I could never scratch – and that my bottom was bottomless. I was ready to stop.

I had used sex for twenty-eight years to escape from painful feelings – for the most part a titanic sense of low self-worth, fear, and shame of being gay. From age thirteen to twenty-one, I engaged in compulsive masturbation. I came out as a gay man in the late '60's, after college. The message from my gay peers was that lots of anonymous sex was OK because that affirmed our gay identity. At first, this helped to make it feel like acceptable behavior to me.

I started my own business under the crushing weight of feelings of low self-esteem and incompetence. I turned to alcohol and to more and more compulsive sex for relief. In fact, I became cross-addicted to both alcohol and sex. I rarely used one without the other. The alcohol acted as a disinhibitor for sexual behaviors I would never have engaged in it without its influence. And once I had "done it," I repeated it. And so, the next twenty years were a descending spiral of acting out behavior.

Though I preferred meeting people in bars and bringing them home, I also acted out in parks, baths, theaters, bookstores, and at rest stops. My estimated body count is certainly over 3,000.

Early on, my reasons for acting out became lost in the behavior itself, since acting out took on a life of its own and became self-perpetuating. I often couldn't identify what I was feeling before having compulsive sex, though afterwards, I felt remorse, guilt, and shame, which often led to alcohol and more compulsive sex to expunge the feelings.

Once, after an uncomfortable, alcohol-fueled dinner with a friend, during which I couldn't get in touch with my feelings of anger, I tried to pick up a car full of straight young men. They took me to a deserted marsh near the local airport. I was held at gunpoint, bludgeoned and almost gang-raped when I broke free, running through the marsh with blood pouring into my eyes. After getting stitches at a hospital, I compulsively masturbated all night and, soon after that, went out looking for a similar situation. That was fourteen years before I found SCA.

I was involved in serial relationships, often to retreat or rest from my compulsive behavior, remaining monogamous for brief periods, then permitting myself to have sex outside the relationship. Almost all ended badly. Filled with self-loathing and near suicide, I dove into my last relationship pledging monogamy, convinced that the relationship would save me. I was faithful for nearly two years, but, as it always had, alcohol pushed me over the edge one night while alone on a vacation. Once I started again, I couldn't stop.

I became involved with hustlers, feeling that what I did with them was play-acting out old high school fantasies of the sort that I wouldn't do with my partner. Because I didn't extend any affection to them, I thought I could protect my relationship. I quickly saw that I was out of control.

The first week, I tried to stop by setting monetary limits. Initially, I allowed myself a $1,500 ceiling – the cost of a vacation. At $3,000, I set a $5,000 "for life" ceiling. At $9,000, I was looking for a new therapist. At $15,000 and eight months into my spree, I tried hypnosis and cognitive therapy. At $25,000, I actually gave up alcohol, but substituted Antabuse and Xanax, a powerful tranquilizer to which I became addicted.

I continued to buy hustlers, spending many thousands more. My therapist prescribed a combination of drugs which, when taken, would cause me to pass out in about forty minutes. He thought I could use them as a chemical restraint when I had the urge to hook up with a hustler. Often, after twenty minutes, I was in a taxi on the way to my hustler service where I would purchase cocaine to counter the effect of the sedatives and be able to act out. When I wasn't drinking, I used cocaine, grass, Xanax, and poppers to abandon myself to compulsive sex.

I kept all this hidden from my partner for fear of losing him. Maintaining this double life was one of the most painful aspects of the disease for me. Sometimes, I would lie about having an evening freelance job. I'd check into a seedy hotel and go off to score a series of hustlers. I would always carry my own soap so that my partner wouldn't detect the scent of cheap hotel soap.

I became suicidal and was hospitalized for a month in 1986. This experience was the beginning of my recovery. It was there that I first sensed that a power greater than myself could restore me to sanity. Upon discharge, it was suggested that I find a group like AA for sex addicts. Two weeks later, I found SCA.

After my first meeting on June 17, 1986, I deeply sensed that I had found something that would finally work. I stayed sober for a week. I slipped. Contrary to what I felt I deserved, I was not asked to leave, but rather, supported and given guidance. I got a sponsor and devised a recovery plan which stated that I would not have sex outside of my committed relationship. Alcohol and drugs were not addressed.

I stayed sexually sober for four and a half months while trying to control or limit my drinking. It was hard work! Finally, one night during a very stressful period, I had a little alcohol to relax.

Suddenly, I felt myself losing the willingness to stay on my plan. I was with my partner that night, but all I could think about was acting out. The desire to stay sober didn't return in the morning, but I did make a phone call at 7 am, and was having breakfast with a program friend at 7:15. I met with two other program friends during the day and by the evening SCA meeting my willingness had returned.

I vowed not to drink anything for at least a week. One week later, I picked up a drink, lost my willingness again, did not make a phone call, and went out on a month and a half binge. My sponsor took me to an AA meeting. I started to go to those rooms daily, but when I acted out, I drank. When I drank, I acted out. My acting out was worse than it had ever been. As they say, my disease had been doing push-ups in the hall while I sat in the meeting rooms. I finally bottomed out on that New Year's Eve.

That night, the champagne that I had counted on to relieve my guilt and shame only depressed me. By Grace, I was finally able to admit that if I continued to drink and drug, I could never stay sexually sober. I stopped acting out and took my last drink on that same day.

The withdrawal from compulsive sex – the feeling of always being on the edge of slipping – took almost two and a half years to abate. With each choice of sitting with a feeling, instead of avoiding it, I get stronger. The more time that passes since my last slip, the safer I feel. I ask for daily strength and guidance from my Higher Power and continue to work on myself using the Steps as a guide. If I don't continuously work the program, I believe I'll slip again. I go to meetings daily (either SCA or AA), and I give away what I've been given through a lot of service.

A prayer, a phone call, a meeting, and service are the powerful tools that keep me sober.

Today, my life is filled with promise. Continued sobriety and working the program has helped to raise my self-esteem. The relationship with my partner is flourishing. I'm happier than I've ever been and I believe that if I stay on this path, I'll continue to experience the happiness which I believe is God's will for me.

* * * * * *

Follow-up

This story was originally written to celebrate my fourth sober anniversary in SCA and a version of it was printed in an early issue of The Scanner.

Decades have passed, and I'm still on my plan – the core of which continues to be: no sex with others outside of my committed partnership and working an AA Program. My relationship with a Higher Power has deepened and my relationship with my partner of well over three decades continues to thrive. I regularly attend meetings in both programs and still work with my SCA sponsees. As a result of all my efforts I enjoy a wonderful and fulfilling life!

Story #12 – *I'm More than My Mistakes*

My first sexual experience took place during a sleepover when I was six. An older boy initiated sexual touch with me and I did the same in return. At that age, I didn't know anything about sex, except that what I had done was bad and that I couldn't tell anyone because I'd get in trouble. This incident, along with growing up in a household where such topics were never discussed, helped build a mindset that sex was bad. When I was ten, an older friend across the street found his father's adult movie collection. He invited us over to watch - this was my introduction to pornography. I remember the rush of excitement and nervousness about what we were doing. The secrecy of how we engaged in watching it helped reinforce the idea that sex is bad. In addition, learning how to masturbate during this time added to my sense of "badness."

Throughout my high school years, I liked girls but never felt attractive enough to try to date. I'm not sure where these feelings of being undesirable to females came from, but it reinforced my already low self-esteem. This negative view of myself carried on into college. Being a somewhat skinny kid with glasses, I didn't like myself very much. Despite this, I found something I was good at as a cadet in a military training program. I achieved success and recognition for my reliability and discipline. I was selected to serve as the lead cadet for my senior class, a tremendous honor. In fact, during our military ball that year, as was traditional, some of the underclassmen did a skit in "honor" of the seniors. I was the subject of the main skit. The highlight was the portrayal of me being identified in the likeness (glasses and all) of a popular nerdy TV character of the time.

Though I was somewhat flattered - imitation is the sincerest form of flattery, right? I ultimately took this as confirmation of how unattractive I was, which solidified my doubt at ever being able to date a woman, let alone ever having the opportunity to be sexual with one. That being the case, the viewing of pornography continued and at one point I remember literally thinking to myself: “I can’t wait until I’m out of college, on my own and making money, so I can buy as much of this stuff as I want.” Once I graduated college, that’s exactly what I did.

After college, I entered the military and went to my first duty location. Soon after my arrival, I found a local adult store and began a binge-purge cycle of buying and viewing videos, feeling guilty and throwing them away, and eventually doing it again...and again...and again. Eventually, that wasn’t enough and my addiction expanded into phone sex. This opened a whole new level of addiction and isolation for me. The manufactured feeling of being wanted by these women was enough for me. They were always there when I wanted them and never rejected me. Since I felt I’d never be desired or accepted by a real woman, they basically became my girlfriends.

Fitness was an important part of military life and I began working out (and got contact lenses). Within a few months, I was at a gas station and a woman pulled up alongside me and asked me if I had a girlfriend. Wow! That was some feeling! It was the first time a woman had expressed that kind of interest in me. This started a life of nightclubs and partying in pursuit of sexual encounters. Despite this attention, I still used porn and phone sex. My rationale, thinking I had things under control, was simply that I would stop once I got married. After all, I'd be so grateful for finally having someone. This was the first personal line in the sand that I eventually crossed; not surprisingly, it wasn't the last.

I met my first wife during one of the nightclub outings (even though I had told myself I'd never meet my wife in a club). She wasn't very financially independent and she also had three kids. We had a very sexual relationship, but it didn't stop me from crossing another line I had in my mind – that I'd never cheat on anyone I was dating. I cheated multiple times while we were dating, in addition to the continued use of porn and phone sex. I liked being labeled as a great guy for pursuing a relationship with a lady with kids, but eventually I had to face the reality that I didn't want to be part of a ready-made family. Ultimately when I decided to end the relationship, I couldn't even muster the courage to tell her it was because of the kids. Instead, within a 10-minute span, I went from breaking up with her to asking her to marry me. Yes, this is very comical in retrospect. As my sponsor put it, there is about 10 years of therapy in that 10-minute span. Not surprisingly, this marriage didn't last a year.

I started dating my second wife before the first divorce was final. She was a very spiritual woman and inspired my own spiritual curiosity and growth. However, I continued using porn and phone sex during our dating and eventual marriage. To my credit, I did share my addiction with her after we were married. In a fit of tears, I confessed my problem to her and made yet another personal commitment to stop. But within a short time, I was back at it with the addictive behaviors. When she discovered my actions, she gave me an ultimatum: either get help and stop acting out or the marriage is over. In response to that, I attempted a very devious plan to show her I was "being clean." Since my primary method of acting out was buying adult movies through our cable system, I edited our account so we would no longer receive a cable bill in the mail. Of course, she discovered my deception and the marriage was over.

The ending of marriage #2 put me at a crossroads. Part of me thought, "what difference does it make now whether I act out or not? I'm going to be by myself forever anyway, so who cares?" Fortunately, my spiritual awareness made me know that I didn't want to fall deeper into addiction. To get help, I began seeing a therapist and joined an addiction recovery group at my church. I had some success staying sober and feeling better about myself. Eventually, I was inspired to give back and help other guys find freedom from similar problems. I became a volunteer leader in my church and started a small support group for men struggling with porn. Yet, despite my newfound sense of purpose, the lure of the addiction soon had me back to acting out in secret.

Around the same time, I began dating the woman who became my third wife. She worked on the staff at our church and was a very strong woman and spiritual leader. We were admired as the model Christian couple. I was well known throughout the church for my sexual purity, and even shared my testimony of freedom in front of the church. With the praise and affirmation heaped upon me, I concluded the stakes were way too high for me to reveal that I'd fallen back into addictive behavior. Besides, I figured I could fix myself on my own. However, instead of fixing myself, things spiraled out of control. My acting out escalated to the point where I was spending hundreds of dollars each month on phone sex. My life had become unmanageable. Further evidence of this is that I began making sexual advances to some women at church, as well as to strangers. When I made an advance on my sister-in-law, I had hit bottom.

It was at this point, after some continued effort to deceive myself into thinking I didn't have a serious problem, that I turned to 12-Step recovery. Upon entering my first SCA meeting, what struck me most was the warm, welcoming way I was greeted. As the Characteristics were read, I was amazed at how they spoke to me personally. Specifically, when I heard "even when we got the love of another person, we were unable to stop lusting after others." I realized that despite my self-esteem issues, three women had chosen to love me. Yet my thirst for porn and phone sex had never ceased. As folks shared in that first meeting, I realized I was not alone in my life-long struggle with these compulsive behaviors. These were quality, caring people who were living their lives and recovering from this addiction. For the first time, I had hope that things could change for me too. The biggest aspect of this hope was how these people spoke about themselves; I could tell that recovery had helped them feel better about themselves. I had come to define myself by my addiction, and didn't like myself, so this was so important for me. What I saw in these people helped me realize there is so much more to me than just my mistakes; I'm more than an addict.

I've been a grateful member of SCA for over 5 years. Fellowship and service have been the foundation of my recovery. I often share that how program members treat me is a reflection of how God treats me. The unconditional acceptance and encouragement have helped me love myself and I'm so grateful.

This gratitude has inspired me to serve the program through sponsoring other members and chairing meetings, where I focus on my belief that we are each valuable and worthy of the better way of life this program has to offer.

Story #13 – *The Power of Choice*

End of May of 2017, I sat in an abandoned parking lot, lost in more ways than one. Texting with my ex- boyfriend after failing to locate the church of what was supposed to be my first sexual recovery meeting, I realized I was at a crossroads in my life. I was head over heels in love with a recently released felon who was in the middle of a meth binge, I didn't want to be anymore, and I didn't know how to walk away. I was terrified of losing my life and the relationships that meant the world to me. I finally knew I needed help.

Things hadn't always seemed so grim. As a kid, on the outside looking in, I appeared to have a typical cookie cutter life. I grew up in a middle-class home in the suburbs with two parents, a parochial school education, and a younger sibling. I made good grades, played CYC sports, and lived a fairly sheltered life. On the inside, both parents suffered from mental illness, but I was none the wiser. Beyond a general feeling of not fitting in, my life seemed normal enough. I was Daddy's favorite. Mom and I were never close. Looking back now, the overwhelming feeling of never being good enough was always with me.

As I grew, I remember checking out quite a bit. I was an imaginative and creative kid, and easily lost in fantasy for hours. When I lost my dad at age 12, my seemingly normal life drastically changed. Any love, guidance, or security I had known was gone. I went into survival mode, and at this point, my coping mechanisms surfaced. Around this time, I had my first boyfriend, and I felt the ego trip and validation that came from the relationship. Someone smart, popular, and cool looked my way. But I came second to his school, work, hobbies, and friendships, and our phone calls were never enough for me. He was all I could think about some days, but because I wasn't his priority, I broke things off. I pined for him for a good 2 years after ending things.

I continued to date, and during a camping trip when I was 15, my boyfriend date raped me. This was how I lost my virginity. Prior to that, I had physical boundaries in place. After this happened, all bets were off. The first time I "acted out" I was 16 years old. It was with a stranger I had just met. I was drinking heavily, and before I knew it, I was engaging in everything imaginable with this person, and it was very sexually gratifying. I felt validated, powerful, in control. I would never see that person again.

I got pregnant at 17, by my first love, a lost kid trying to kick a heroin habit. He wanted nothing to do with raising a child, so we broke up and I was left during one of the lowest points in my life. But even during this low point, after giving birth to my daughter, that I realized I was meant to be her mom. It was a gut feeling stronger than any other I had known before, so I decided to raise her. I threw myself into being the mom she deserved, and started taking care of myself. For a good five years I left my vices behind. I met a man when I was 19, and after a year and a half of dating, we were married. He was hard working, studious, and had a bright future ahead of him. I was working full time, attending school in the evenings, and on the outside things couldn't look more perfect. On the inside, though, our relationship was a vacant wasteland. We co-existed but never talked. We were both void of any intimacy.

So, after much thought and fantasizing over other men, I decided my relationship and husband were to blame for the lack of intimacy I was experiencing, and left. Shortly after, I began my downward spiral. My drinking increased substantially. I had random encounters with men. Then, in an attempt to stop my sexual acting out, I would pick a lost soul with which to enter a serious, long-term relationship. It would work for a short time, until I got bored and started fantasizing outside the relationship. When I was in a relationship, I put my and my daughter's needs on hold. I did anything and everything I could to help save my partner, trying to mold them into the person I saw them becoming. The relationship would always end, and I would be left emptier and more desperate each time.

Finally, in 2011, after my third failed relationship and completely alienating everyone I cared about, I entered into counseling for codependency. I only did it to appease my loved ones. I didn't feel I had a problem, but I went. For two and a half years I worked through my family of origin issues and started learning what a boundary was. I didn't date during that time, not because I didn't want to, but because no one wanted to date me. I was simply too unstable emotionally.

After that, I dated a functional alcoholic. I ended things a year and a half later when I realized he could never be there for me emotionally and the relationship was devoid of intimacy. I vowed to give myself six weeks of being alone before dating again. But during that time, I slept with four people and contracted HSV-1. Right after this, I made the decision to date one of these people, a friend struggling with heroin addiction. He was staying in a half-way house, newly out of prison, and after hanging out with me for a few months, he decided he was serious about quitting the drug lifestyle and professed his love for me. For all of the wrong reasons, I committed to the relationship. He went back to prison three weeks later, and eventually he relapsed.

With him away, I was finally completing my engineering degree, repairing my finances, steadily paying rent, repairing my relationships, and working on myself. I knew If I didn't walk away, that relationship would cost me all of it - my job, my daughter, my best friend, my family, my health, everything. So, I broke things off, but I wasn't capable of doing so alone. I started online sexual recovery meetings. I attended online meetings five times a week, and strung together some sobriety for a few months. Then, after my attendance slipped for three weeks during finals time at school, I relapsed with an ex-boyfriend. When my ex-boyfriend was released from prison, he called and I went running. At this point I decided I had to start attending face-to-face meetings and find a sponsor. I was willing to work the Steps and do anything and everything I had to, to get myself out of this situation.

I came to my crossroads and dove headfirst into SCA and another sexual recovery program. I came in just trying to get away from a dysfunctional relationship, build healthy sexual boundaries, and date in a normal way. What I found in the rooms was so much more. The first thing to come was my relationship with my Higher Power. I went from being as disconnected spiritually as one can be, to praying every day. It was all I knew to do to help get myself through the withdrawals.

Second to come was my relationship with myself and with my sobriety community. I began to learn what intimacy really is. The impenetrable walls of lies and isolation I had spent years building began to crumble, as I had a safe haven to come to each week where I was loved and accepted for exactly who I was. The compartmentalization from my life began to lift. I began to sit with myself, and feel my feelings, no matter what they were and how hard they were to feel. I began to piece together what self-care looked like for me, what I wanted and needed given what life threw at me each day. I remembered who I was and reflected that to others without a façade or fear of their disapproval. I learned how and what it means to be there for others without my own selfish motives. I learned that being of service equals getting outside of my head, and doing so deepened my sobriety and sense of belonging.

Through that process I found choice. A choice I always had, but never knew the tools to exercise. For as long as I can remember, I was a victim of life, reacting to whatever self-induced drama came my way. Today, I breathe, I pray, I reach out to my sponsor and program sisters. Some situations I choose to react to, and others I decide don't need my reaction. Whatever the situation may be, I always choose not to act out. I never have to do that again.

Story #14 – *Finding Something Better*

I had been sober from drugs and alcohol for a couple of years when I realized I was stuck. Although my life was changing for the better, I was still unable to grow in areas where I felt the greatest amount of despair. My relationships at that point in my recovery were limited and fragile at best usually with people I had met at the baths, parks or bookstores while acting out. They were the same people, just in different places.

My best friend kept suggesting to me that my relationship issues had something to do with how and where I was spending the greatest amount of my time. I was unable to hear him and resented his suggestions. I felt that my issues certainly could not involve addictive behaviors, since I was already recovering from drugs and alcohol. I had always judged this friend, because it seemed he had recovered from everything through a different Twelve Step program. I didn't want to be that neurotic about relationships.

That year my employment situation also changed. I received a promotion and relocated to a new city. Although I was scared, I believed that I was sober in AA. I had all I needed to make this transition in my life. Yet my move opened up a new world of addiction and a very dark world at that. Suddenly my acting out escalated to different places, activities and behaviors than those I had experienced in the past. What was particularly upsetting to me was that even though I was attending AA meetings, I was still unable to connect with people or make new friends. My life continued to feel empty and seemed to be getting worse.

I remember when the shift finally occurred in my life. I was at the baths and had just finished acting out in a particularly disgusting manner. Suddenly I realized that there had to be another way to relate to people other than the process I had just completed. No big revelation just a clear understanding that there had to be something else out there. I wasn't sure what it could possibly be, but I was sure that the way I was trying to connect to others no longer worked.

The next day I reluctantly wandered into my first SCA meeting. Ironically, the chair of the meeting was someone I recalled acting out with many years prior. This alone piqued my curiosity enough to stay through the whole meeting. Somehow, I kept coming back.

At times, my sexual recovery has been very difficult and painful. I can remember feeling once that if I didn't act out, I would die. In fact, I once considered suicide as an alternative to the pain I was experiencing. But God's grace and the support of other recovering sex addicts has helped me through that pain and continues to provide me with support time and time again.

Once I decided to ask someone to be my sponsor, wrote out a bottom line, and made a commitment to my home group to attend meetings, I began to experience the relationships I had always hoped for in my life. There were often challenges in these new friendships. Frequently I confused my emotional needs with my physical needs. However, by using my sex plan and by discussing my feelings with these individuals and other recovering sex addicts, my relationships grew into healthy friendships.

Today I have been sober and abstinent for two years and nine months. I am in the first monogamous relationship of my life, and we are planning a commitment ceremony. Relationships and friendships continue to be my constant challenges as well as my opportunities for growth. Yet I am very grateful that I am available for these challenges and that I am present to experience my own growth.

There is no doubt in my mind that while Alcoholics Anonymous saved my life, Sexual Compulsives Anonymous helped and continues to help me live my life in relationships one day at a time.

Story #15 – *You're a Fine Person and It'll be Alright*

I am an exhibitionist, which I believe is a result of getting positive reinforcement for exposing my body. I became sexually compulsive the moment I unsuccessfully attempted to stop exposing myself to strangers and masturbating in front of them. Now that I have time away from acting out my exhibitionism, I see that I need not be judgmental about my sexual compulsion: I was conditioned to respond to stimuli, as much as any animal in a lab experiment.

The first clear example of my exhibitionism took place while driving to college classes a long time ago. I noticed that the vehicle next to mine was pacing me. The driver was making sexual overtures, but he seemed content merely to watch me as we drove side by side. I had never engaged in sex with a man, and was nervous. But I was confident that I was not going to have sexual contact with him. My participation was limited to moving my arm to permit a clearer view of my genital area. I kept my clothes on, kept driving, and there was no physical contact. Because I was in my car, I felt safe, like I could break off the activity at any time, and yet, I missed my exit.

I was flushed with excitement. When I finally got to school, I got out of my car and looked around to see if anyone was looking at me strangely. No one was. I realized that other drivers probably had no idea of what had happened, and I had easy deniability of any homosexual exhibitionism. I enjoyed what happened but was also worried by it.

Another crucial incident occurred about five years later, when I was in my car and soaking wet from being caught in a downpour.

I drove home partially disrobed. By then I had come out of the closet as homosexual, and was living with a lover. I was somewhat shy about putting myself in a position to be seen by other drivers while in a state of undress. But I did so deliberately, and tried to use as much subtlety as I could manage while doing it. Soon I got a response, and even though I wanted to pursue it I did not. I was afraid of being attacked, in a traffic accident, caught by the police, or having sex with a stranger. And besides, I had already gotten what I wanted the moment he let me know he wanted to have sex with me.

This was the start of a rapid descent into a life of exhibitionism. Within weeks I lost all subtlety. I no longer had anything resembling an excuse for exposing myself, but found ways to do it and to maintain deniability of intent if confronted. I learned to turn the tables, making it seem like anyone who felt strongly enough to confront me was overreacting. Exposing myself, especially to truck drivers, was something I could do and no one stopped me. I gained excitement from the powerful negative responses I received. Other drivers waved knives at me, veered into my lane, or pulled in front of me and slammed on their brakes. I felt powerful, but in seven years of what I have come to call my "career" as an exhibitionist, direct sexual contact with the object of my obsession occurred only once.

I masturbated while another driver watched, and another time I watched someone masturbate to climax. Watching the other driver was a strange experience, like I was seeing myself in someone else's body and vehicle. It compelled me to examine my own behavior.

In the later stages of my addiction, when I desperately tried to stop exposing myself, it was like someone else was operating my body when I was triggered. I had no power to stop and even though I screamed at myself inside, I did it anyway.

I could no longer sustain the lies I made up about my behavior. My exhibitionism became the rotted centerpiece of a life I describe as vulgar and poverty stricken. I believe I quit the highest paying job I ever had as a result of my sexual compulsion. I enjoyed the job, but it was only a matter of time before I would have had sex with one or more of the workers I supervised, and we all knew it. I made up an excuse when I left, but looking back I see no other reason to have quit.

I did not mind rush hour traffic unless I had a passenger, because then I couldn't expose myself. I even sought out traffic jams. I timed my drive to work so I would be stuck in the back-up traffic resulting from a regularly scheduled, slow-moving train. I could almost take my pick of drivers to whom I would expose myself. The first thing I would do upon arrival at work was to check my watch and fuel gauge to see how long I had driven in that trance-like state.

One time, after a day of drinking with my lover, we got in a fight and broke up. I went to a bar and found a potential sex partner. On our way to his home, my exhibitionism attracted the attention of the police. That led to my arrest, but all they could prove was that I was drunk, so they sent me to some Alcoholics Anonymous meetings. I continued going, because I recognized my alcoholism, but mostly I went to avoid being arrested again.

Though I hit bottom in my alcoholism, my exhibitionism continued to worsen. I later endured some of my most painful moments without the anesthetic of alcohol or drugs, as I was left to feel the full consequences of acting out my sexual fantasies.

I told a fellow AA about my sexual compulsion, and he encouraged me to take a First Step inventory of my behavior, so that I could discover for myself whether I belonged there. I did, and continued to go to AA meetings. I did the same thing later in SCA.

Sharing about my exhibitionism in AA meetings, I was eventually told where and when I could find an SCA meeting. It took a year, but I finally went to the SCA meeting. I knew from my very first meeting that if I was going to be able to stop exposing myself, it would be the result of attending SCA.

I wrote a sexual recovery plan (SRP), got a sponsor and a home group, and regularly attended a few meetings a week. But after a few years, while my fellows achieved recovery, I was still unable to claim even 24 hours of adherence to my SRP. I stayed, because I had nowhere else to go.

After a year in SCA, I finally decided to be honest. I told my home group of my failure to achieve even a day of sexual sobriety. They were surprised, but supported me unconditionally. I resolved to continue talking about my progress, thinking perhaps they could help me see what I was doing wrong. My new willingness to align my will with that of my Higher Power let me see that active sexual compulsion was not to be my destiny.

My Higher Power wanted me to live a happy and useful life. I let go of control and took the opportunities to recover as they presented themselves. An important lesson was not to get so caught up in my problems that I missed appreciating a child's laughter, the scent of a rose, or the beauty of a sunset. I began to enjoy my recovery and the fellowship of SCA.

When I shared my Fourth Step inventory with my sponsor, he said the standard, "You're just like everybody else in SCA; no better and no worse. Go ahead and get back in there with the rest of them." Because he didn't want to hurt me, it took him a month and a half to tell me what I needed to know that he was "shocked and appalled" at the shallowness of my values. He let me know that I belonged in the meetings, and that I was to let him know if someone said otherwise and he would take care of it. No one else can see it, but after that I began to see my name on the chair in which I sit. I belong.

Working on my Fourth Step earned me a breakthrough. I began to see my part in the continued failure to get more than 24 hours of sexual sobriety together. I worked on staying in the present. My meetings were safe, and I did not act out while attending them, or while going to coffee afterward. Gradually, I expanded the safety zone around the meeting locations from two blocks to two miles. Then it became the entire city. My frequency of slips decreased. By working on these 24 hours, I was able to knit together over three and a half years of sexual sobriety. Even after the slip that ended the three and a half years, I knew I could achieve sexual sobriety again, and I did.

Many of my friends and acquaintances have died from HIV/AIDS, suicide or alcohol-related illnesses. When the number of “deceased” contacts in my phone list reached 50, I quit counting. But I began to cherish my life, and that of others around me. I became more tolerant of troublemakers, and for the most part, quit taking criticism so seriously. I could thank them for bringing attention to my defects of character.

I received and was able to accept an offer of help to go back to college and finish my two-year degree. At that point, the horizon opened up, and I was able to dream. The question that had never come up before surfaced: What do I want to do? It had always been, “What do I have to do to survive?”

I had always been noncommittal as a result of my sexual compulsion’s demands. I lost the ability to predict my future, because I never knew where my episodes of acting out would take me. Now, with a clearer future, I am able to make and keep my commitments. So many of life’s lessons involved my lack of a commitment. The result was that vulgar, poverty-stricken life I once lived.

I went back to college, got two degrees, and was licensed in landscape architecture. Along the way, I entered into a relationship that has lasted for twenty years. I now know what it is like to form and maintain a deep and abiding relationship. The difference from my days of acting out is that I can now commit to a course of action. I may not always fulfill every commitment, but I make them in good faith and follow through on them.

I could always forfeit my license if I return to acting out my sexual fantasies, but that is less likely to happen now. When I arrived in SCA, I seemed to be getting fitted for my exhibitionist's trench coat. My destiny then was clear. But now, the life ahead is full of options, because of the abundance of abilities and therefore, choices available to me. I work diligently at doing what my Higher Power wants me to do, and I look forward to the end of life, as one looks forward to bedtime after a long day's work.

The greatest defects of character I discovered in my Fourth Step - fear and selfishness - may still be there, but they no longer prevent me from living a happy, confident and useful life. The "Vision" portion of my SRP states that I want to be a well-respected landscape architect in my community, to contribute ideas to society and to write. When I am working on fulfilling my vision, I have wind in my sails. I feel that I am going somewhere, and that vulgar, poverty-stricken life is far, far away.

Story #16 – *I Am Not Alone*

The day I was arrested was the worst day of my life, but I didn't realize then that it was only the beginning. I found it impossible to face my family and I was ashamed to leave my house. I fell into a depressed mental state. I thought of a hundred reasons why it would be better if I weren't around anymore, to never cause my family and friends more shame and embarrassment. My parents suggested I seek psychological help but I convinced them I was okay, but deep down I felt alone. How could anyone understand what I was going through? How would they judge me?

I remained this way for 6 months, until I was court-ordered to attend 52 Sexual Compulsives Anonymous meetings in 12 months. I had never heard of SCA before, nor could I imagine there was a 12-Step recovery program like this. I quickly jumped on to the sca-recovery.org website, located a meeting and began reading the information.

I was overjoyed when I first read the Opening Statement on the Welcome page that said, "Our primary purpose is to stay sexually sober and to help others to achieve sexual sobriety." This invitation was heartwarming to me and gave me hope to receive the help that I've needed all these years. I told my parents that this program was going to help me better myself and I was going to get as much out of it as I could. A Higher Power seemed to have led me in the right direction.

I attended my first meeting on March 15, 2013, the week after my court date. I was so nervous. I had never been to a 12-Step meeting and didn't know what to expect. I arrived 20 minutes early and took a seat by the door. I didn't make eye contact with anyone, afraid to show any signs of fear. But as people came in to the room, they greeted each other with hugs and smiles and people seemed genuinely happy to be there. I started to feel more and more comfortable as the atmosphere in the room became more welcoming. It was not the jailhouse meeting I had envisioned in my mind. The meeting began and everyone said the Serenity Prayer out loud in unity. I thought that was so cool.

As everyone introduced themselves, most said they were sexual compulsives, so when it was my turn, I said I was a sexual compulsive also. Even though I didn't fully understand what that meant, I somehow felt a big relief that I got to say it. We then each read a paragraph in the book Hope and Recovery, and as I read it, I felt as if I was reading a story about my life. My heart began pounding in my chest, wanting to burst out screaming, "Thank you, I'm in the right place!" When the sharing portion of the meeting began, I was the first to raise my hand. I didn't know what I could or couldn't say, but I felt the need to express my joy and appreciation for having found this program and to say how I hoped this program would help me be a better person. By the time I got to my car, I was shaking, out of exhilaration. I felt so thrilled that I was where I needed to be. When I got home, I told my parents everything that happened and they shared their joy along with me.

By the second week, I asked someone to be my sponsor. My sponsor asked me what I was looking to get out of the program and what I was willing to put in to the program. I thought I would be in this program for 12 months and then I wouldn't come back anymore, so I didn't want to attend multiple meetings weekly or take on any service commitments. I didn't know it yet, but my

Higher Power was about to put a challenge in front of me that was going to help adjust my thinking.

After three months my work schedule changed and I had to find a different meeting. It was a struggle for me because the mood was completely different in this meeting. There were no hugs or smiles and the tone of the meeting was very dry. People didn't seem to care. Every person in attendance was court-ordered, just like me, but many didn't seem eager to share. I could tell this had an effect on me because soon even I didn't want to share. I wasn't having the positive and pleasant experience that I was used to, so how could anyone feel comfortable enough to share? This group was in desperate need of support but no one seemed willing to be of service, not even me. I just didn't feel a part of this group. After a month and many discussions with my sponsor, I volunteered to be the literature person. I made it my goal to work hard at this commitment to the best of my abilities. I updated the script and purchased new binders, folders and envelopes to organize our literature and information. I also forced myself to help improve the atmosphere of the meeting. When people walked in, I greeted them and began small talk to lighten the mood. I welcomed newcomers and explained what they could expect from the meeting. A month later a new secretary was appointed and I volunteered to be the Intergroup representative.

I stepped up as Intergroup rep because I felt our meeting needed a voice to represent us. Since this program had already done so much for me, I felt willing to give back. During my five months in SCA, I had read all the literature, bought SCA's "little blue book," and had made updates to the Q&A Newcomers Guide and several other pamphlets. I decided to present the updated Q&A

guide at my first Intergroup meeting and their response was overwhelming. They appreciated the contribution I made and this gave me the motivation to look for other ways to be beneficial.

Eight months after I started SCA, I had completed all 52 meetings. The judge commended me on being ahead of schedule. I was no longer required to continue attending meetings, but I was now doing this for my own wellbeing. "This program is helping me; how can I stop now?" In March 2014, I volunteered to be the newcomer coordinator and the website coordinator. Since I've been in Intergroup, I have given my time in a variety of ways. I was given the opportunity to share at SCA's 40-year anniversary (Los Angeles) in 2013 and I was the literature person and a panelist in the 2014 convention. My sponsor has continued to support me through my ups and downs and encourages me to challenge myself and step out of my comfort zone. Thank goodness he was there for me, because soon I was going to need him more than ever.

About a year into program, I was dealt a hard blow. The girl I had a two-year relationship with, before I was arrested (she was underage), was now approaching her 19th birthday. I had always thought that when she turned 18, she would be knocking on my door and we would get married and live happily ever after. When the months went by and that didn't happen, I became very sad, but I always maintained hope. Then one day someone showed me a picture of her with another man. I told myself I was happy for her, but deep down, my heart was broken. I spoke to my sponsor and told him how hurt I felt. "We were supposed to be together forever," I said. "I was the one who got sent to jail, sent to community service and SCA, spent $30,000 in legal fees. I'm the one suffering. How could she brush me off like nothing?" I had even hoped that one day I could tell her all the great things I was doing in program and she and her family would be proud of me. But now I felt forgotten and used, and I wanted to quit the program. My sponsor was very understanding, and began telling me what a wonderful person I was. I began to cry. Looking back now, I see that time mends all things and as my favorite slogan states, "This too shall pass." It's been helpful for me to realize that I'm not alone and I can freely express what I'm going through and get support from those that really care and want to help strengthen me as I continue on this journey of life. My sponsor has been that strength for me.

In July 2014, my sponsor asked if I would be the secretary for the ISO convention. I saw it as a blessing and an honor to work side by side with my sponsor. For the next 7 months we diligently worked to put together a great convention. I'm very proud of the accomplishments I've made in my life with the help of this program.

For me, service has been the number one thing that has helped me maintain my sobriety. When I'm alone in my house with nothing to do, that's when I'm my most vulnerable. I need a healthy distraction to keep my mind focused. It's easy for me to be hard on myself and feel like I'm not good enough for anything, but when I work on these service commitments it gives me a sense of pride that I'm doing something good and helps me overlook the wrongs of my past.

Unfortunately, there are challenges I face daily, and my past still has a way of coming back to haunt me. A few years ago, my employer was made aware of my conviction and terminated me. I was in complete shock. I've sent more than 100 job applications and have had numerous interviews. However, the moment they run my background search, I am no longer a candidate. My addiction tells me to feel sorry for myself and act out because nobody cares about me. But that's not the type of person that I want to be anymore and I refuse to give up. I decided a long time ago that I was going to get the most out of this program. I've learned that this also means I need to give back all I can because it helps me in my recovery. These challenges have been set before me for a reason and I must be strong enough to face them. I will.

I am grateful that this fellowship accepts court-ordered individuals such as myself. I didn't want to seek help when I needed it, but when I was required to attend meetings, I had no choice. I thank my Higher Power for looking out for my best interests. This program continues to help me develop into the person that I aspire to be. I am better now mentally and emotionally than when I first came into program, thanks in large part to my welcoming fellowship brothers and sisters. I have had a great support group, which include my parents and my new girlfriend. My father has said he is proud of me. He said he has always tried to motivate me to do certain things in my life to help me be a better person, but the work that I've done in this program was all from me. As we hugged, I felt a surge of joy and emotion that I hadn't felt in a long time. Even as I write these words it brings tears to my eyes, because I never thought I could make him proud of me again.

This is a wonderful 12-Step program, regardless of where you come from or how you get here. We're a fellowship and "our primary purpose is to stay sexually sober and to help others to achieve sexual sobriety." I love my family; I love my life and I love this fellowship that brought me back from deep despair. If you're reading these words, please remember, you are a good person, you can make a difference in your life, you can change, and you are worth it! And remember, you are not alone.

Story #17 – *Finding my Voice*

My early-childhood introduction to sexual behavior resulted in an obsession that plagued me for four decades. It was not emotionally safe for me to express unpleasant emotions, so I learned to suppress my feelings, or medicate them with masturbation and images or fantasy. I did not experience much appropriate, affectionate touch from my father, and my mother was very unpredictable during my infancy and childhood. I never knew if she would be a source of nurture and care or fear and pain. She became enmeshed with me when I was older, and shared things inappropriate for my age. While I was touch-deprived and craved emotional connection from guys, I was also terrified of their attention. It was much safer to read or watch things that, over time, morphed into romance novels and porn.

The guys I interacted with fell into one of two categories: either I was fascinated (obsessed) with them but they weren't interested in me romantically, or they liked me but I didn't like them in that way. I flirted and said suggestive things and led them on, but had no intention of being physical with them. I was much more comfortable having the advantage, using my sexuality to manipulate and control. I enjoyed the "hit" I got from interacting this way and knowing I held the power.

You see, I viewed all guys as either a potential partner or a piece of furniture. Rather than seeing them as human beings with feelings and needs, in my mind men deserved to be used and mistreated. While I didn't know it at the time, this was due to a deeply embedded sexualized rage I held against all men.

I got "high" from my compulsive sexual behaviors and couldn't stop, and they were getting worse. The more I medicated uncomfortable emotions with sexual thoughts or behaviors, the more I turned to that over and over, and the more edgy or risky they had to get in order to successfully numb out those pesky feelings. I wasn't even fully aware that I was nearly constantly escaping into fantasy. It was like breathing.

I'd always had a fascination with sex-related things, and I channeled a lot of emotional energy into masturbation. However, after I got married, I was surprised at how difficult it was for me to be comfortable in my body or enjoy being sexual with my husband. I thought sex was supposed to happen like I'd seen or read it, with all the human imperfections edited out. Sex with a real person was scary and unpredictable. And when it didn't happen like I'd seen or imagined, I just checked out mentally into fantasy where it felt safer.

Sometimes I needed it to be completely dark during sex. Other times I felt less inhibited, but not because I was comfortable in my own skin and able to gratefully enjoy my husband's loving touch, like I can now. In active addiction, I felt less inhibited because I was using sex like a drug to get high. A type of binge-purge pattern developed, where I would behave more boldly and try edgy things to increase the high, only to feel guilty, used, degraded, and humiliated after sex. Often it would be weeks before I would attempt to be sexual again.

By the time my second child was born, I was shut down emotionally and sexually – even though my husband and I deeply loved each other, and we got along great. What was worse, on the rare occasions when I DID feel a desire to be sexual, my head and my body were often NOT in sync. My husband's touch did not produce what we hoped it would. I felt a ton of shame, confusion, and despair.

We went to two different marriage counselors trying to find out what was wrong, but they were both baffled. Normally, lack of sexual desire is a fruit of fighting in the partnership, but that wasn't the case for us. They had no clue how to help us. Other methods of trying to address the problem included taking antidepressants and different methods of birth control. I tried blaming my husband's porn use for my lack of desire. I even purchased erotic how-to literature and a variety of paraphernalia. In retrospect, I see how that fed my sex addiction and further objectified me. At first, I thought the problem was low libido. But now I know I was a sex addict.

I now understand that I lacked intimacy. Now I know that when I feel emotionally safe and connected with my partner, loving sexual behavior flows naturally from that space. But we didn't know that at the time. I didn't know that in order to have closeness and connection with myself I needed to be aware of my feelings and needs. I didn't know that there were many ways to connect with others, including intellectually, emotionally, experientially, physically, and spiritually. And I certainly didn't know how to combine those for a healthier sexuality!

In recovery, I heard that to be intimate means to let go of control, to learn to trust myself and others, and to have faith in a power greater than myself. I could NOT do that. Sex didn't mean love to me. It meant power. I couldn't let go of the source of my sense of power – controlling things and people, including controlling whom I let touch me how and when.

I didn't have a voice back then. I was very out of touch with what I liked, what I needed, what I wanted. Instead of owning my true power, I held onto the illusion of power and control by compulsively avoiding sexual contact, while simultaneously being mentally obsessed with it.

It was horrible to live like that! My husband felt rejected, and I felt confused and hopeless. I craved loving touch and closeness and connection. Yet I feared it. I had this confusing, "Come here – go away" attitude in all of my relationships. I was isolated and depressed. I was deeply lonely, even though I had a spouse, four wonderful children, and plenty of friends. I spent days crying and could barely get out of bed. I couldn't receive love. It got to the point where everything felt so dark and miserable and hopeless that I started thinking about ending my life. And then, one day, I got fed up with my husband's behavior and went online to research Twelve Step fellowships that start with the letter "S" so I could "help" him.

That's when I found out about intimacy avoidance and compulsive sexual avoidance (sexual anorexia). I wept with joy and relief as I saw that others knew what I was suffering from, and it helped me find hope and healing. I learned, to my great surprise, that I was a sex addict. Since my acting out looked different than my partner's, I had not seen it for what it was. But it fit.

So, I dedicated time to my recovery. I had the "gift of desperation," because I wanted to want to live. I started attending recovery meetings and collecting phone numbers of people whose shares I related to. Over time, I started having one-on-one conversations with them outside the meetings. I started helping during the meetings by reading things or leading meetings.

Another thing I did was to start putting my feelings into words. When I first heard grown people (especially men) in meetings describing how they were FEELING, I thought it was weird! "What's sex addiction got to do with feelings?" I wondered. But I learned that my compulsive sexual behaviors served to distract or numb me from unpleasant feelings. In order to be sober from intimacy avoidance in all its forms, I had to actually feel my emotions, and find healthier ways of coping with them. At first, it was a huge undertaking, which felt foreign and scary. I had to rely on "feelings charts" with faces to help me determine and express my emotions.

Now I am learning to welcome and accept all my emotions, asking for help, and allowing trustworthy people to support me in my difficult feelings. I can hold space for other people's intense feelings, and I can invite loving connection with many different wonderful people in my life. I am learning to let go of trying to control others, or trying to control my sexuality. I focus on cultivating a partnership with my Higher Power and allowing healing and growth and a change in perspective. All of these have had a tremendously positive effect on my sexuality.

As part of the First Step, I started doing things to nurture myself daily, and allowing others to nurture me. You see, sex is supposed to be nurturing! I had never thought of it that way or experienced that before. Sex was something I used like a drug to get high, or as a weapon to have power and control over someone. There was nothing loving about that!

I started doing small nice things for myself, which brought me comfort and sparked joy. I started believing I was worth being treated with gentleness and respect and tenderness, because I was treating myself like that. That's Step One: admitting I needed help and beginning to let that help in.

I began to practice healthy sensuality, which I consider part of Step Two. I started allowing myself to enjoy pleasant smells such as certain foods or the earth after a rain; to notice things that felt good on my fingers or toes like hand lotion or walking barefoot in a puddle; to see things that pleased me, such as art or nature. I became more fully alive, more sensual, and more connected to the world around me. In this state of wonder, awe, and openness, I can be more embodied and aware, detecting small changes in my body faster and easier. I'm learning what it feels like in my body, mind, and spirit when I'm connected to a Power greater than myself. I can receive and understand guidance, nudges, information, and awareness. It definitely surprised me that practicing sensory awareness brought me to the belief that I can be restored to sane thinking, but it has!

As my recovery progressed, I started learning that in order to let go of control and be in the moment sexually, I needed to have confidence that I could speak up in those moments if something felt uncomfortable in any way. Practicing speaking up for myself in non-sexual situations helped make this possible in a sexual setting. I also allow myself to explore sharing my feelings and needs in a way that invites connection with others, instead of making demands, trying to convince people of things, letting people walk all over me, or isolating.

Today, I am no longer shut down sexually, nor do I use sex as a drug or a weapon. My sexuality is more integrated into my whole being than it has ever been, and is a source of giving, creativity, love, light, and life. My sexuality and my spirituality are intertwined. I can express appreciation, love, and faith through tender, respectful sexual touches that honor my partner and myself and our Higher Power.

I no longer lack intimacy in my life, and I have closeness and connection with many wonderful people. I have a great network of supportive program friends of all genders and from a variety of backgrounds. I am no longer fearful of men. In fact, today some of my favorite people are men whose recovery I respect and whose friendship I'm deeply grateful for. I can be with my uncomfortable emotions and accept support in working through the traumatic ones. I am getting to know myself, speaking up for myself and stating what I need. I am cultivating a close, personal relationship with my Higher Power learning how to listen to my intuitive guidance. I can do many things that a few years ago were impossible. I owe all of that to recovery.

Story #18 – *The Promises Came True*

I grew up in a small town where I was related by blood or marriage to half the population. It was a difficult place to have any kind of privacy, but I learned to keep secrets early on. By the time I was seven years old, I realized I was strongly attracted to other boys, and I knew I could not let anyone know that. At twelve, I became obsessed with a classmate at school. I fantasized about him for five years until I graduated from high school. All that time I knew he had no interest in me, and I could never tell him how I felt about him. My teenage years were spent in a state of despair over my unfulfilled desire, and I spent most of my free time locked up in my room reading and listening to music.

I was in college in the mid-1960s, not a safe time to be openly gay. I didn't know how to meet other gay men. In my third year, I became obsessed with another straight boy, just as I had done in high school. I sank back into darkness, hiding my secret desire, feeling isolated and alone. That obsession lasted another five years and established a pattern of attraction to unavailable men that has been consistent throughout my life.

After college, I moved to Los Angeles. The Stonewall riots had happened while I was still closeted, avoiding sex out of fear and a misplaced sense of fidelity, and saving myself for someone who would never be available to me. In L.A., I joined the Gay Liberation Front where I had my very first sexual encounter with another member. Through him I discovered the gay bars, and decided to get as much sexual pleasure as I could to make up for all my earlier deprivation.

Throughout the 1970s, I was a barfly. Before the Internet and hook-up apps, the only places gay men could find each other were the bars, the baths, and public venues. I was in the bars every night. I made many conquests. I made friends, had lots of sex, and lived a life that was quite different from anything I had known before. I was carefree and pleased with myself. Everyone I knew was caught up in the same hedonistic whirlwind, and I thought nothing of it. My bouts of sexual excess were interlaced with a series of infatuations with people who were out of my reach and they fueled even more sexual excess.

An intense sexual fling with one person soon turned into something altogether different. He was a compulsive gambler. I moved in with him and became his enabler, providing him with money so he could pursue his own addiction. We were both employed, earning good wages. He would typically lose his entire paycheck, and then cajole me into giving him half of mine. If I resisted, he would devise ways to get his hands on my money by forging checks, stealing my credit cards, and using my identity to get credit. I was always on the hook for debts he created. Our relationship lasted for seventeen years.

AIDS blindsided us in the early 1980s. All the close friends I had made during the past decade died, leaving me alone with a compulsive gambler, the endless impoverishments he created, and hopeless fantasies about unavailable people. I tried many times to escape the relationship. I would move, and he would track me down and persuade me to come back. We often couldn't pay our rent and were evicted several times. He fostered my belief that I could not function without him. He kept me close because I was his source of money. I was very unhappy. My distress about my situation fed my own addiction, and I began to act out sexually more and more to relieve my pain.

One night I picked up someone on the street. He wanted me to pay him to have sex. He was attractive, so I agreed, and a whole new world opened up for me. Paying for sex seemed to free me from the bondage of attachment and obligation I so often felt with willing sexual partners. I always thought I had to please the other person. I felt I owed them something just for being willing to have sex with me. With a hustler, there was no responsibility. We would agree on a price for a specific service. When we were done, I could just drop him off on a street corner. The transaction seemed to provide a power that I didn't have in any other area of my life.

But I was wrong. It was just another trap for me. Though I have fond memories of some of my sexual experiences with hustlers, most were degrading. Hustlers tend to provide as little as possible for as much money as they can get. And then there were the drugs. I didn't use drugs myself, but I was always buying them for hustlers. The drugs were bait to help me get what I wanted. I was still as much of a people pleaser as I had always been. I couldn't stop doing it, chasing those occasional exhilarating experiences I had in my early pursuits.

Every day I would leave work, cruise the streets, pick up hustlers multiple times for quickies in the car parked in some dark corner of the city, continue until the wee hours of the morning, catch a few hours' sleep, go to work, usually late, drink a whole pot of black coffee to stay awake, and repeat the pattern the next night. After a week or so of this, I was so exhausted that I had to sleep in for a few days. Then I would start the cycle all over again. This went on for almost a decade.

My partner knew only a fraction of what I was doing. If he got money from me to gamble away, he didn't seem to care what I did. (Interestingly, I always managed to put aside just enough for my hustlers.) But he noticed that I was looking unhealthy. With his constant need for money, he was afraid of losing his source. He explored various group meetings looking for a mark - someone he could borrow money from. One night he wandered into an SCA meeting. The next day he said, "I know where you need to be."

It took him about six months to coax me into going to a meeting with him. I knew my life was insane, but I didn't think the group would help. Even though I was deeply depressed; even though hustlers had robbed me four times, once at knifepoint; even though I couldn't resist the nightly cruising; I didn't believe I was sexually compulsive. Still, I was beginning to feel the ill effects of my actions. I knew I needed something, so I allowed him to drag me to a meeting.

At my very first meeting, another person told "my story." We had both been doing the exact same things, and in recovery he had gotten some relief from it. Reading *The Characteristics* cinched it for me. I took a copy home and read them over and over. They were like an outline for my biography. *The Characteristics* persuaded me to come back, and soon I was attending a meeting every night. Nightly meetings became a habit for me for the next several years.

Many people in SCA were helpful and supportive. One person became something of a mentor and taught me a great deal about the 12 Steps. I read my first 4th Step inventory to him, and we often talked on the phone. The great service he did for me was to help me get free of my partner. We had a long talk that made me realize I was keeping the relationship going. As an enabler, I perpetuated the sick game we had been playing for years. I was furious that day. I did not want to see my part in it. I wanted to continue playing the helpless victim, shifting all the responsibility for my unhappiness onto another person. Yet after that talk, it became surprisingly easy for me to break the spell and get that person out of my life.

During my time in SCA, I've held many service positions. Service is one of the greatest tools of the program and being of service as a sponsor is, for me, the greatest tool of all. Sponsoring provides as much benefit to me as it does to the person I sponsor. I've worked the Steps various times with my own sponsors and in Step study groups. Every time I go through them, I learn something new about myself that provides insight into the problems I deal with.

I now have years of continuity with people in the program, and those relationships have enriched my life in ways I never anticipated. All the Promises have come true for me during my time in the program, and they came about even without my noticing the changes as they occurred. It's easy for me to see changes in others, but difficult to see them in myself. I came to SCA through sheer luck, and I often say that I got very few things I initially wanted from this program, but I got many things I needed, even though I didn't know I needed them.

My sexual recovery plan is quite simple. Years ago, when we were putting together the first SCA recovery book, I submitted my plan to the organizing committee. It is included in the book and lists the four things on which I count my time in sobriety. As of this writing, I have 32 years of abstinence from the items listed on my plan. I'm clear that abstinence is not recovery. It is only a tool. I continue to work on bringing integrity into my life, and the work I have done in SCA is my primary method for doing that.

During the years of the AIDS crisis our meetings were packed. We were all afraid of the disease. We wanted to get a handle on our sexual behavior so that we could survive the scourge. There were so many people in the fellowship then that have since moved on. Only a handful of old timers remain who remember the energy of those early meetings. I regret losing contact with so many members who have left the fellowship, but I have seen that newcomers still have a vital need for the relief the program offers. Newcomers are the lifeblood of the program. They remind us of who we were and how far we've come. It's fascinating to see the changes manifested in them as they discover the gifts of this program.

Story #19 – *Happy, Joyous and Free of Co-dependency*

For most of my early life, I assumed I was growing up in a "normal" family. There wasn't much obvious drama in our family. Mom and Dad had their differences from time to time, and they sometimes had too much to drink at night, but no gaping wounds jumped out to mar my tender childhood. I grew up the youngest of 4 boys, in a household where matters such as drinking were never discussed. Later, well into my adulthood and after I had begun recovery, my recollections started to change. I realized that my parents were alcoholics of varying degrees, both had extra-marital affairs, and that there was a much deeper animosity between Mother and Father than I had been aware of.

I was shy. I had a narrow circle of close friends but I felt socially awkward; not good at sports, smaller than everyone else in my class, and therefore bullied sometimes. I was slow to mature: I didn't reach my adult height until I entered college. I was slow to hit puberty. I took a girl to the junior prom, but only because she invited me.

I remained shy and backward during college, and never went out on a single date. I didn't have sex with anyone, and couldn't even self-identify as gay, though I found myself secretly attracted to boys and not so much to girls. Other than masturbation, my sex life remained virtually non-existent until I was 25, when I moved to New York City. There I was quickly introduced to gay life, particularly the nightlife and disco scene. This is where I was able to come out as openly gay and have my first gay sexual experiences. Within 2 years, I had met my first serious boyfriend and we quickly settled down into a domestic partnership.

Our life together seemed happy, especially during the early years. We were monogamous and I didn't feel any sense of deprivation being so. I was doing well in my chosen field, so we lived "large" - plenty of expensive vacations, dining out, ballet subscriptions, Broadway shows, conspicuous spending, and charitable giving. My partner stopped working as a lawyer early on, and I volunteered to support him, allowing him time to choose another vocation. He had a history of depression and anxiety, which he self-medicated with alcohol. We both remained in denial about his alcoholism for many years. This was the beginning of my upward trajectory of co-dependence.

We were monogamous for many years, though I found myself increasingly drawn toward the idea of having sex with others. Things changed rapidly after my partner met and fell in love with another man in the 22nd year of our relationship. This quickly developed into a long-distance relationship between him and his new friend, who lived on the west coast. I was fully aware of this situation, and it made me feel justified in wanting to have sex with others.

Perhaps it was no coincidence that my first-ever visit to a gay bathhouse took place the same weekend the two of them spent together in another city. I began to frequent bathhouses, particularly if my partner was visiting his boyfriend. They alternated visits with each other several times a year. I was occasionally invited along, but felt like the extra wheel.

Five years into this new situation, things deteriorated for me. My partner's boyfriend turned up on our doorstep, unemployed, while I was out of town. He quickly got another job, but he stayed in our home, which added to my partner's anxiety. My company, a major Wall Street firm, went under. These two events led to a sharp increase in household alcohol consumption, and to my partner's first suicide attempt - overdosing on anxiety medication. He survived, but it triggered a pattern of acute alcoholism, which led to frequent emergency room and hospital detox stays, psychiatric clinics, and rehab.

He blamed his illness on my sexual infidelities, his boyfriend continued to live with us, and our home life further deteriorated. I sought refuge elsewhere, and added booth stores to my list of acting out places. Whenever I got the chance, I would "go out for a walk," which inevitably led me to those spots where I would spend an hour or more voraciously seeking sex.

Finally, after a failed 6-month attempt at couples counseling, my compulsion became unmanageable and I was bingeing. I was working the midnight-8 am shift, which gave me the opportunity to leave the house extra-early so I could stop at the baths for an hour or two before work. I never told my partner I was doing this, though he learned enough to make him permanently suspicious of me. He and his boyfriend usually started their drinking at 4 pm, falling asleep well before 10 pm. That's when I would leave the apartment. I had stopped caring about safe sex and had become fatalistic about the potential consequences. I was afraid to get HIV tested for more than 2 years, hoping somehow to postpone having to hear the inevitable result. When I finally did go to my doctor, bingo - I had won the booby prize.

Between work, the baths and the booth stores, I was a pretty busy boy. My apps compulsion quickly became unmanageable. I was on them morning, noon, and night, especially at night when I was at work, often alone in a large office full of hundreds of unoccupied seats. I found it frustrating that most of the people I intrigued with wanted to hook up right away, at my place. This was impossible since I was at work in an office with security cameras. Very few potential hookups wanted to wait until 8 am, when I could leave the office and visit them. And of course, I could never "host," given my home situation.

Often, my frustration level reached the point where I would go back to the baths at 8:30am, on my way home. If my partner asked about my late arrival, I would explain it as a gym visit. Eventually he stopped asking. There is nothing sadder than being at a bathhouse on an early weekday morning, desperately trying to get laid. The few people still there were passed out from whatever drugs they had taken. It was mostly slim pickings, which made me all the more desperate to go back there that night, and recapture my fantasy.

This was the state of my life when I was finally diagnosed as HIV-positive. I was spending all my time either at work, intensely toning my body at the gym, or seeking sex. I felt trapped in my household relationship, which was now in name only. I still paid all the bills, and was afraid to admit that I couldn't maintain that high level of spending on a lifestyle we could no longer afford. It seemed as if there was no way out, no hope at all.

I had been seeing a therapist for nearly 5 years, but stopped when I realized that I was constantly lying about my sexual activities. It seemed absurd, but I was too ashamed to admit what I was really doing, so I started seeing a sex therapist and finally told the truth. I got into a group therapy, as well as an individual one. My therapist strongly recommended that I start attending 12-Step meetings, which I initially resisted. My partner had been compelled to attend AA meetings during his two rehabs, and he had strong negative reactions to it, complaining that 12-Step was a fraud and "too churchy."

But I finally took the plunge and went to my first SCA meeting: the Friday Beginner's. I immediately "compared and despaired" when I heard people share what seemed to be impossibly long day counts. Still, I made myself go back again, at first just to please my therapist. I soon began listening to shares, meeting people at fellowship, and taking service jobs such as Literature Rep at a beginner's meeting. Gradually, some of these other addicts - strangers to me when I first came into the rooms - became friends, and were very understanding and supportive when I told them about my "no way out" situation.

One thing that made me feel I was in the right place in these early meetings was the reading of *The Characteristics*. Some of them spoke to me right away. As my recovery progressed, I began to appreciate them even more. The 2nd Characteristic – "Compulsive sex became a drug, which we used to escape from feelings such as anxiety, loneliness, anger and self-hatred, as well as joy" - described my acute acting out period. I was trying to numb out, to not to think about my problems, and desperately trying to find a connection, anything but the burdensome one at home. The more sex I had, the more I wanted. Even when I was having sex, I was thinking about how soon I would get the next trick.

The 5th Characteristic – "Because of our low self-esteem, we used sex to feel validated and complete" - exactly described my quest for more and more anonymous, unsafe sex. I wanted people to esteem me, mainly as a sex toy, because I felt abused and constantly shamed in my home life. The 7th Characteristic – "Sex was compartmentalized instead of integrated into our lives as a healthy element" - also told my story. I was a "functional addict" going to the baths on the way to and from my night job.

After briefly working with an interim sponsor, I met another SCA member who became my sponsor and remains so to this day. He helped me get started with the Steps, something I wasn't keen about during the first few months. I later joined a Step-writing group, and found that very helpful. I worked them slowly but surely, sharing with my fellows, while providing and receiving support. I completed the 12th Step during my 4th year in SCA.

I started taking risks, but not the kind I used to take. I got into an SCA show - my first time ever appearing on stage. I made program calls, attended different meetings, and read some program literature. I also stepped up my service commitments: chairing meetings, doing treasury, becoming a sponsor, and later working with Intergroup and SCA's International Service Organization (ISO).

Early in my recovery, there was the 800-pound gorilla in the room I dreaded to confront: extricating myself from my increasingly untenable home situation, which was carrying me to the brink of bankruptcy. I had been so afraid and ashamed of my co-dependency relationship with my partner and his boyfriend that I would blush, even when I talked about it in the rooms or in fellowship. It gradually dawned on me that I could never experience the benefits of recovery unless I took action. I had been getting encouragement from people in the fellowship and from my therapist, but it took months before I felt ready to take the needed actions. Just before i moved out, I shared in the rooms that I needed a place to live, and got help the same day from a program friend who had a spare bedroom.

Eventually I got into a new relationship with someone who had long-term sobriety. I hadn't expected this, but once we started dating, the prospect of spending our lives together seemed so natural. We are now happily living together - no more co-dependency, no more deception, just pure honesty, respect, and love. We are great friends as well as lovers. I have paid off all my debts, and am happy to live on my modest financial means. I lost my job a year ago and decided to retire. I am lucky in that we are able to make ends meet on our respective incomes. Life isn't perfect, and never will be. Trials will inevitably come our way, but I feel that we will be able to face them squarely and with some serenity, as we continue to recover together. I am content with who I am.

Story #20 – *The Gift of My Arrest*

I was born and raised in the state of Washington. My parents were, for the most part, loving, hardworking people; but I remember my house as being an unhappy place for much of the time. My parents often fought about money, although it seemed to me like we had plenty of it. My mom seemed frustrated most of the time. To this day I'm not really sure why. She would get very angry with me over little things I did wrong. If I got myself or my clothes dirty while playing, she would usually beat me. Mom liked to use a belt, but often a coat hanger or shoe worked for her as well. I tried so hard not to make her mad, but I couldn't help it. Cleanliness was her obsession, and she was never satisfied.

When I was 9 or 10 years old, I had a best friend from down the street. He and I went everywhere, exploring the woods behind our neighborhood and building secret forts out of found wood and anything else we could find. He came from an even more abusive home than mine. I was very afraid of his father. His parents were always beating him. Often, I was sent home when he got in trouble, which seemed daily. One day at a sleepover at my house, he introduced me to sex. I had a vague knowledge of sex, but I wasn't aware that boys could do it together. My friend seemed to know everything about it, and he taught it all to me. I was an eager pupil. It seemed fun to break the rules and do secret, taboo things. It didn't take long before sex took up all our time together. Playing catch, riding bikes, and playing with action figures were all replaced with sexual exploration. This began to affect my relationships with other boys. Soon the only way I wanted to interact with other boys was through sex. Sometimes this worked but mostly it had embarrassing repercussions.

When I was 12, my dad asked my mom for a divorce. The family was ripped apart and my mom, baby sister, and I moved to a small town in California to live with my grandparents. I was very shy, and not knowing anyone in my new school, I kept to myself and tried not to let anyone see that I was different. My sexual experiences were my secret, both shameful and exciting. My former neighbor and I still got together when I visited my dad, having more and more sex until we were 16 years old.

When I was 16, my friend asked me if I'd had sex with any girls. I laughed it off, thinking he was joking. I said, "Of course not, I'm gay." It was the first time I'd said it out loud. He broke my heart by utterly rejecting me. He said I was sick and going to hell. I made a decision right then to never again tell anyone my true nature. I had many friends in high school, but kept them at a distance. They were really more acquaintances than friends. I was a very popular kid that no one really knew.

After high school I went away to the state college, placing me as far away from home, and specifically from my mother, as I could get. Once there, I was determined to be different. I was tired of the closet and I thought I would come out. What I wanted more than anything was a boyfriend. I figured if I just had a boyfriend all my troubles would be over. But instead of coming out, I stayed more isolated than ever. I made plenty of friends in college, but again, no one knew the real me. I spent what little spare time I had at highway rest stops just north of the campus, at the local nude beach, and in campus restrooms.

I wrote messages on the walls of restroom stalls. First, I would write a message with my right hand. Then, using my left hand to disguise my handwriting, I would pretend to be someone else who was agreeing to meet me. I thought this would attract attention and turn a relatively innocent ordinary campus restroom into a cruisy tearoom. It never actually worked as I had hoped.

In my junior year I finally came out to my friends, classmates, and professors. It was, of course, not a surprise to anyone who knew me. In a way it made my loneliness worse, because I soon realized that simply coming out wasn't going to get me a boyfriend (which was my ultimate goal). With every date that ended in failure, I was driven deeper and deeper into dangerous, desperate, and lonely public sex with strangers. While completing my student teaching, I finally met a man and started dating. After three dates, we had sex. I was so excited - this was it. Finally, another man validated me. He would love me and that would be enough for both of us. I needed his love because I didn't love myself at all.

I tried to stay faithful to him but it wasn't long before I was back at the rest stops, the local adult bookstore arcade, the campus locker room, and any other place I could find to have sex. Once during this period, as I was driving home for my grandmother's 80th birthday party, I stopped at every rest stop on the 800-mile trip home. At one of these stops, I engaged sexually with a much older man. I wasn't attracted to him, but that didn't matter. It was thrilling having sex in a restroom stall while other men came in and out, using the restroom, oblivious to what we were doing. When I finally got to the party, six hours late, I had missed my favorite meal, which she had prepared especially for me. I was so ashamed, but I played it off as terrible traffic when we spoke the next morning.

When I finished my education, I applied for teaching jobs in LA, where my boyfriend lived. I lived with my grandmother that summer. While I was there, I brought several strangers to her house after she fell asleep. It wasn't until I was working on my fourth Step in SCA that I realized how inappropriate and wrong it had been to endanger my grandmother by bringing strangers into her house. At the time, in my addiction, it seemed completely reasonable and kind of exciting.

At the end of that summer, I moved to California to start my teaching job. I confessed to my boyfriend about having sex outside of our relationship, and he broke it off with me immediately. I was heartbroken, but I knew I deserved it. After a few months I found an adult bookstore arcade where men had sex. There I met a man with whom I had an almost 10-year relationship. I was faithful to him until my spring break, when I visited a friend at another campus. Her school was still in session, so while my friend was in class, I visited just about every men's room on that huge campus. I couldn't get enough sex. I even had unprotected sex in the library. I had sunk to a new low. I had always used condoms before when having sex but this time I guess I didn't care.

This behavior went on and on for ten more years, until one day it finally happened. I always knew it could happen, but I had gotten away with public sex hundreds of times, so I never thought I'd get caught. On Saturday, March 15th, at 3pm, I was arrested in a public restroom near the beach. I was photographed, finger printed, and asked if I intended to kill myself. They took my belt and shoelaces. They didn't have room for me in the misdemeanor holding cell, so they put me in with men arrested for felonies. After getting booked for lewd conduct, I was taken to a cell with four cots. Three guys were lying on cots so I took the fourth one. After what seemed like forever, the cell door opened and they put another guy in with us. He was acting really weird, like he was "on something..." He kept pounding on the door for the deputy. Finally, they came to get him out. Minutes later the door opened again, and this time we were all told to come outside the cell. A deputy questioned me about the fifth man. I guess they were looking for his drugs. Standing in the hallway the deputy told me to take off my clothes. I did as he said. When I got to my underwear I stopped because I had an erection. He told me to remove them. I was humiliated even more. Looking back on it now, it should have been clear to me at that moment that I was a sex addict. Here I was on the worst day of my life, in jail, and I was getting aroused by the cop. Stark naked, we were all paraded down the hall back to our cell. We were allowed to get dressed again only when we were back inside the cell. It was eight hours before my boyfriend came to get me out.

That Monday I went back to work as if nothing had happened, but inside I was terrified that someone at school would find out and fire me. I was suicidal. Between classes I'd close the classroom door after the last student had walked out. Then I'd vomit into the trashcan, clean up as best I could, and open the door to greet my next class. This went on for months. During this time, I started going to a therapist to help me cope with the anxiety and depression around my legal troubles and the possibility that my teaching credential would be revoked. After a long legal process and a short suspension from teaching, I was able to keep my job and my credential.

One day in a therapy session, I was very tired. I kept yawning. My therapist asked me why I was so tired. I told her I'd been up almost all night reading the police report about my arrest and going over the penal code they charged me with. I told her I was trying to figure out how I might go back to a public restroom and legally pick somebody up for sex. She told me I was a sex addict. I couldn't believe what I had just heard. I was angry and in denial. She told me to go check out a Sexual Compulsives Anonymous meeting at the gay and lesbian center. Very reluctantly, I went to my first meeting. I introduced myself and went back for three months without saying a word other than, "My name is Jason and I'm sexually compulsive." I didn't even know what that meant, but I just kept saying it.

Near the end of my third month of attending meetings once a week, I went to fellowship with a couple of the guys from the meeting. I shared my story, all of it. I got a sponsor that night and immediately started going to three, sometimes four, meetings a week. I began sharing what was going on with me. With the help of my sponsor, I wrote a sexual recovery plan. I got out of my toxic relationship and moved into a new house.

That was seven years ago. Today I have 389 days of sobriety on my plan and I'm working my ninth Step. Since I started program, I've gone back to graduate school to get a master's degree. I'm currently being considered for promotion. I got my life back because of this program. I've had a few healthy relationships while in program. I'm single today, but I've learned I have a lot of work to do on myself before I'll be ready to date again. I still struggle with online pornography, but I'm not out there putting myself in legal jeopardy in public restrooms and bookstores. I'm not having sex with strangers, and I'm now respecting my body. Life isn't perfect, but thanks to a loving God of my understanding, the Steps, and truly close friends who know and understand me, life is good.

I will keep coming back because I believe that this program works if I work it. I have seen it work for my fellows, and I've seen it work for me too. Today I have nothing but gratitude for the officers who arrested me on that day seven years ago because I can see that God did through them what I could not do for myself. That arrest was the miracle that started my journey of recovery.

Story #21 – *Losing Fantasy and Finding My Self*

I have craved more of everything as long as I can remember. I wanted to be held more; I wanted more food, more attention just more, more, more!

In my conservative Christian family, sex was something that was never talked about. Physical affection was only expressed behind closed doors. This was incredibly confusing for me because I was abused sexually starting at 3 years old. This continued throughout my childhood, by various perpetrators, until my teenage years. I would disappear into my imagination when I was being abused, envisioning myself as a princess in a fairytale. I would turn my perpetrator into the handsome prince. I found safety in my imagination; escape into fantasy was my protection. In school I learned that I not only had to lie to teachers and children about the sexual abuse, I also couldn't tell them I wanted to be a princess. They all thought I was a boy, but inside I secretly knew I was a girl.

Throughout grade school I numbed myself with food. I gained weight and was ridiculed by my classmates and family. As I entered adolescence, I became painfully aware of my sexual attraction to boys. I had long given up the fantasy of being a princess and wanted desperately to fit the mold of a good Christian man. I was taught that homosexuality was a damnable sin. With all this inward stress I found relief in masturbation. At first it seemed to quench the pain that was boiling inside me, but without any tools for coping with sexuality or the pain of being an overweight 13-year-old, I became depressive. I thought if I could just lose weight the pain would go away, so I learned to purge my food and quickly lost weight. Between masturbation and purging, I was in a constant state of numbness.

As a teenager I added drugs and alcohol to my numbing vices. I started having sex with many girls to prove to my peers I was straight. At 15 years old I would get drunk and secretly go out in my small town and seduce older men. I don't remember ever enjoying sex, but I enjoyed the attention and the warmth. I tried to disappear into my imagination whenever I was with an older man, fantasizing about my body being that of a woman. The second the sex was over I would run home and cry myself to sleep in shame.

When I went away to college my drug use increased drastically and my life started to unravel. It was at this time also that it became clear to me that the feelings I had were not those of a gay man but those of a transgender woman. This was an emotional bombshell, and I used it as an excuse to numb even more. Eventually the pain became too great and I agreed with my gender counselor to enter into a drug rehab. I was 20 years old. This was my introduction to the Twelve Steps of Alcoholics Anonymous and the beginning of my journey of emotional sobriety.

I put down the drugs and alcohol, but in early sobriety my eating disorder came back with a fury. I was in early medical transition from male to female and I desperately wanted something to numb my pain and fear. I had stopped having sex, but I spent hours obsessing over male friends. I created entire fantasies about the possible relationships I could have with these men.

I finally reached a point where the pain from my bulimia became so great that I was willing to get help. Just like with drugs and alcohol, I learned that if I was willing to go to any lengths and practice the Twelve Steps, I could find freedom. And so I did, and for 5 years my life soared. By the time I was 27 I had made many advancements in my education, career and friendships. I was surrounded by people in recovery from alcohol and eating disorders. I was living and working in Los Angeles. With the help of many gay and transgender people in my meetings, I was able to walk through the many scary steps of my medical transition and multiple medical procedures. Throughout this, though, I continued to live out my romantic fantasies with cisgender heterosexual male friends, which often included extremely blurred boundaries. We flirted and there were lots of sexual innuendos, but the second I shared my romantic feelings, they would shut down. I often heard the phrase "But I'm not gay." I felt insane, but held on to my romanticized idea of forbidden love, living in the fantasy of "someday..." This was my pattern over the next few years. I would believe I was in love with one guy, with no physical relationship. Then after months of no sex I would meet a stranger in a drug store or at a gas station and have sex with them. One time I heard "I usually beat up trans girls with my buddies… no one can ever know." I had great anxiety and fear during these encounters, but kept going back to it. Sometimes I even tried to convince myself that I enjoyed it, but I always felt deep shame.

Recovery from my eating disorder started to slip. Slowly and insidiously, it crept back into my life. I kept this a secret from my sober friends. In truth I was trying to keep it a secret from myself. I thought, "If I just ignore it maybe it doesn't exist." I was also exhibiting erratic emotional ups and downs. My work started to suffer. My therapist told me I needed to address my love and sex addiction. "But how could I be a sex addict?" I thought. "I regularly go six months without sex!" I told myself it was all just residual emotional trauma from my sexual abuse. I found a new therapist who told me what I wanted to hear. I also was constantly fighting the inner belief that I was unlovable as a trans woman.

I spent years in therapy addressing my trauma. I did deep therapeutic work and learned many deeply valuable things about my life experience. I attempted to go to fellowships for sex and love addiction, but found the hetero-normative model of relationships to be untranslatable to my trans experience. I also found the stigma around sex and masturbation to be incredibly shaming. I had experienced enough shame in my Christian upbringing, so I walked out of those meetings with resentments and gave myself permission to do whatever I wanted.

Then I found someone who I believed was my soul mate. He told me he loved everything about me. The things I thought were the least desirable, he praised. He was rich and wanted to take care of me. He was my prince charming! When I found out he had another girlfriend in a foreign country, I was devastated, but I held on to the belief that he would choose me. After a couple of months, he boarded a flight to see the other girl and our short-lived relationship was over.

I quickly spiraled out of control with my eating disorder and dropped to a low weight. The people in my life grew deeply concerned. I couldn't function in my day-to-day life and was institutionalized by my family for depression. After a month, all the while continuing in my eating disorder, I developed a friendship with a man in the institution. I longed for him and believed I was in love with him. He did not reciprocate my feelings. I lost any hope of recovery and lost my desire to live.

After a lifetime of suicidal ideation, I decided I needed to kill myself and escape my spiritual hell.

After a near-death experience and permanent damage to my body, I found the willingness once again to go to any lengths to get recovery from my eating disorder. I ignored the romantic obsession that had driven me to the brink of suicide. I held on to the dream that one day I would find my prince charming and he would save me.

I found recovery through multiple fellowships and the Twelve Steps. I was restored to a healthy weight. I developed a comfort in my own skin that I had never known. After a year in recovery, I decided to start dating. Men in the world were expressing attraction to me and I was told by all my friends to try using dating apps. Right away I was hooked. I found an endless stream of men that wanted to meet me. I liked the attention. I always started by explaining that I wanted to date, not just a one-night stand. I filtered out all the guys that led with sexual messages, and I went on dates, lots of dates, sometimes two a day. I spent all my time getting ready with hair and makeup, manicure and pedicure, and waxing. All my energy went into dating. But the same thing kept happening, over and over. After one or two dates we would have sex, and then they would distance themselves from me   responding with one-word texts or disappearing altogether. I swore off the apps multiple times, but I always ended up back on them. Feeling desperate for attention, I began to respond to the guys that led with sexual messages. Sometimes I would just skip all conversation and just get sexual. I would have phone sex or send pictures or videos and masturbate.

Afterward I would feel complete shame and block their number. So, I tried swearing off apps again.

I started to feel desperate, and a friend shared with me her experience with Sexual Compulsives Anonymous. She had been working her plan for over three years and seemed to have a fulfilling romantic life. She was extremely sex positive and identified as queer as well. I tried my first meeting and it was there that I heard about the third column on the sexual recovery plan the creative activities and practices that brought people closer to their Higher Power. With all my years in different Twelve Step programs, I had never heard so much focus on using creativity as a tool. People talked about taking a dance class at 60 years old and healing their "little kids" that were never allowed to dance. I related. Another person talked about how they were an artist and unable to focus on their art when they were in their addiction. Part of their recovery was practicing their art and they were amazed at what a powerful experience it was. I saw so many LGBTQ+ individuals sharing their experience, strength and hope, and I wanted what they had.

Over the course of the next year, I randomly went to SCA meetings, but I always got there late and left early. I didn't want to create a "plan" like I heard people talking about. I wasn't willing to commit to the program. I still wanted to try to do it my own way. I found myself becoming more and more demoralized by my behavior. I saw my sexual acting out and romantic obsession interfering with my work and friendships. I regularly left my work and went to the bathroom to masturbate. I left social gatherings to meet guys. Even when I was with people, I found myself unable to focus because I was so obsessed with checking my dating apps or texting. After every sexual encounter I always found the same dark feelings of shame. It was one demoralizing experience after another. One night after a particularly shameful sexual encounter with a stranger it became painfully clear that every low point in my life had been preceded by a romantic obsession or an incredibly shameful sexual experience. I wanted to do anything to protect the recovery I had found with my alcohol and eating disorder. It was clear to me that I had to be willing to surrender and go to any lengths to get sober.

With tears in my eyes, I went to an SCA meeting and raised my hand when it was time to share. I found a temporary sponsor and set a time to meet to put together a plan. I was willing to try anything at this point. I just wanted some relief.

Once we created a plan with bottom line behaviors, I wanted to stay away from I felt a little safer. I didn't feel so alone. My sponsor recommended I try the Beginner's meeting, and when I walked in, I was welcomed by a large group of LGBTQ+ folks I felt safe with. When it came time for announcements the literature rep of the meeting said he needed someone to take his service position. The only thing I had to do was to be willing to show up every week. I could do that, so I volunteered.

I related to people who shared in every meeting I went to. I developed friendships and joined people for dinner after the meeting. After a couple of months, I met a man who possessed a peacefulness that I wanted for myself. I asked him to be my permanent sponsor and we started working the Steps. Every week when we met, I felt something powerful. I felt relief. He and I refined my plan and I accumulated days and then months of sobriety. After 60 days on my plan and with the support of my sponsor, I attempted to use a dating website. I found the way I was fetishized and hyper-sexualized by men really demoralizing and I decided I wasn't ready. I put all my energy into work and recovery. I found myself looking forward to my meeting and the friends I had made there. I saw my quality of life increasing. After a year of being on my plan and in recovery I started to talk to a guy I had met on a dating site a couple year prior and we went out on a date. My sponsor suggested bookending a tool he found incredibly useful. So, I texted my sponsor before the date and committed to not having any sexual interaction with the guy. After the date I texted my sponsor about how the date was and that I did exactly what I committed to. A couple of weeks later I told my sponsor that I wanted to have sex with that same guy. We talked about it and he suggested I check in after, have fun and take my Higher Power with me into the experience. I did just that and I had an enjoyable time at first. But some things he said about my trans identity during sex made me uncomfortable and triggered past experiences. I found myself dissociating, but I didn't stop. I left the experience and called my sponsor. I asked if it was "bad" that I didn't stop and that I felt triggered. He said, "I don't like to think in terms of bad or good. I like to just ask myself if this is working for me or something that would be helpful to put down." I liked that it took the shame away. We chatted about the things that had come up for me. He let me cry and supported me. I asked him if this meant that I should stop having sex. He first told me he couldn't make that decision for me, but reminded me that the only way to heal around sexuality is to develop new behaviors and experiences around it. We talked about what that might look like as a transgender woman in today's world. We didn't come to any conclusions that night. But

I was able to go to sleep that night feeling supported and "safe" with sex in a way I had never known.

Over the past 5 years I have seen my life open up in a way I could not have imagined possible. I have worked the Steps and had multiple service positions. I started sponsoring a man and I got to watch the miracle of the program unfold in his life. It has reinforced my faith in the practice of recovery. I have had ups and downs. I came into the rooms looking for instructions on how to find the man/relationship of my dreams, and I have been given a pretty awesome relationship with myself. Today I have the ability to show up and have meaningful connections, both in romance and friendships. My life is far from perfect, but it is far better than when I walked into the rooms of Sexual Compulsives Anonymous.

Story #22 – *The Best Valentine's Gift Ever*

I was surprised when I was asked to write my story for the SCA text. That's kind of the way my disease works. Let me explain what I mean. I identify as sexually compulsive and anorexic. The anorexic part doesn't just manifest in having a lack of sex in my life. It plays out in how I think of myself: insignificant and unworthy. Thanks to over 20 years in SCA, my first thoughts on such things as being asked to share my SCA journey are no longer my only thoughts hence, the writing of this story.

On the surface, I might appear to be a program unicorn. I am a woman, a woman of color, basically straight (I'd say 1 on the Kinsey scale), who was a virgin when I started the program. One might wonder why on earth I started a program that at the time was dominated by white gay men having acting-out sex?

The answer is that God did for me what I could not do for myself. Like many people in SCA, I came via another fellowship. At the time, I had lost a large amount of weight and was dealing with my brand-new 20-something body. So, when the office delivery guy asked me out on a date, I was ecstatic. He was so cute! After our first chaste movie date, I became obsessed. Would he be "the one?" At the very least, would he be the one I'd lose my virginity to?

What it was Like

It was Valentine's Day 1997. That morning, "my guy" gave me a cup of coffee. I gave him a sample of expensive men's cologne. For the rest of the day all I could think about was when we'd go out again and if I would sleep with him, or if not, how far I would go. The work I was supposed to be doing piled up on my desk.

That afternoon, exasperated by the work I wasn't doing and trying not to pick up extra food, I called my sponsor. Her words surprised me. "There's a meeting tonight at the Gay and Lesbian Center at 6pm. There will be a lot of men in it. Go in and sit down..."

Note that she didn't tell me what fellowship the meeting was for! Like a good sponsee, I did as I was told. As I walked into that crowded, standing-room-only space filled with largely white men, I wondered why my sponsor had sent me there. A few men moved aside and pointed to a seat that someone had just given up for me. As I made my way to that seat the qualifier, a gay white man in a business suit who was probably twice my age was talking about all the time he wasted cruising guys on his lunch hour. His despondent tone describing how an hour lunch turned into two, then three, struck a spark of recognition in me. "Oh," I thought, "I do the same thing on the internet..."

It was true. My nights after work - times when I should have been doing homework for grad school or cleaning up my apartment - would often be hijacked by erotic fiction online. My drug of choice was fan fiction - although at the time the term wasn't well known. One story would turn into two, then five, ten... By the time I would manage to break away from the computer the evening time would have turned into early morning. I also spent time writing my own erotic fan fiction. These practices often made me late for my job, and put me behind on my schoolwork.

Reading and writing this stuff was an out-of-body experience for me. The psychological term is probably dissociative. Just like the way I had been using food, the stories numbed me out to my feelings and fears about myself and my life. Later I would confess to my first SCA sponsor that I wouldn't even realize I was aroused until I turned the computer off.

Anyway, that single epiphany on February 14th, 1997, is one that I consider to be a gift from God. Because of it I was able to see myself and my compulsive behavior mirrored in people who were, on the surface, very different from me. One of the sayings in the program is try to "relate to the feelings, not the facts." It's good advice. I related to the sense of powerlessness, the self-loathing over what was happening, and later, the sense of unworthiness for love and affection that so many people spoke about. Although I did check out other 12-Step programs around sex, the term "sexually compulsive" made the most sense to me. I wasn't addicted to sex - I wasn't having any. However, was I compulsively using sexual things "to escape from feelings such as anxiety, loneliness, anger and self-hatred, as well as joy" (from Characteristic 3).

If I hadn't had that immediate reaction to the qualifier that day, I suspect *The Characteristics* would have convinced me to stay. Those characteristics spoke of issues with fantasy and masturbation, and seeking oblivion. I related to many of them, but if I had to pick one it would be Characteristic Six: "We tried to bring intensity and excitement into our lives through sex, but felt ourselves growing steadily emptier." This was clearly a part of what drove my addiction to erotica. I didn't believe I was capable of ever having a real sexual relationship with another human being, so I dove into a fantasy world to try and feel and express some kind of sexuality. The problem was that as soon as

I stopped reading, the reality of my life came roaring back in a painful contrast that made me feel even worse.

What Happened

I have stayed in SCA ever since that day in 1997, but I didn't take to it immediately. I had a tendency to run out of the rooms as soon as the meetings were over. I think I felt a bit intimidated by all these older white guys who seemed very sophisticated and urbane to me. That had more to do with my own low self-esteem than anything about them. Luckily, the one thing I was willing to do was raise my hand and share. Doing so let people in the rooms learn about who I was. Despite how different the facts of my story were, people would come up to me and tell me they related to my shares. Those interactions reinforced the idea that I was in the right place.

Eventually, I became willing to accept an invitation to fellowship after a meeting. Socializing is one of the tools in SCA, and it is an invaluable one in my recovery. Through fellowship I learned how to connect to people in a social setting - something I had always felt awkward about. Fellowship led me to get involved in an SCA holiday show, which led to me getting my first sponsor. That led to me doing a written First Step and coming up with a sexual recovery plan.

Until that point, I had been trying to create my own plans. My best thinking had me trying to cut everything sexual out of my life, a typical move for someone who is a sexual and social anorexic. After going over my history with my sponsor, a gay white male, he determined that cutting out all of my sexual outlets was detrimental to my recovery. Instead, we looked at what was killing me the fastest. Together we worked out a plan that had limits on how much time I could spend online. The plan included being accountable to others by having to make two phone calls and bookending the time.

It took months for me to accumulate time on my new plan. I had a lot of slips. However, one of the things I discovered is that sometimes a phone call would alleviate the desire to go online. I learned that oftentimes what I needed was not sexual. It was an emotional connection to another human being. Doing so often got me in touch with the feelings and fears I was trying to escape.

Over time I started to be able to separate my emotional needs from my sexual ones. One of things that my first sponsor taught me was that sometimes, like a cranky child, I was simply fighting the need to just go to sleep! The slogan HALT - Hungry, Angry, Lonely, Tired - is still one of favorites and something I have to watch out for.

I also learned that there are two ways to deal with FEAR. The first way: "F*** Everything and Run" - was how my sexually compulsive self dealt with fear. Everything from worry about a project deadline, to having to go to work at a job I didn't love, to not wanting to face the dishes in the sink, could send me to the computer or make me think that I "really needed" to masturbate. Not masturbating before work, or when I had plans to be somewhere at a certain time, became the second item on my plan.

Using this acronym for fear is how I learned to deal with my feelings: FEAR=Face Everything And Recover. Facing fears by making those phone calls, journaling about them, praying, and sharing at meetings became the tools I picked up instead of the compulsive sexual escapism I came in with. Voicing my fears somehow made it easier to do the things I was afraid of. As such, after a couple of years on my plan, I began to explore dating.

By this point in my recovery, I had gotten a different sponsor - my first one had moved away - and was doing Step work and working through a book on sexual anorexia. I was working on my Third Step and turning my will and my life over to the care of God as I understood God. For me that meant being willing to believe that some appropriate guy would think I was worth dating. Eventually I had my first real sexual relationship.

What It's Like Now

It's now some 23 years later. I have worked all of the 12 Steps in SCA and, as the 11th Step suggests, my spiritual life now includes prayer and meditation on a regular basis. This was not the case before the program.

I have sponsored people as well, which is also a part of the 12th Step. I've mostly sponsored other women, but I've also sponsored gay men. You see, despite being a woman, a person of color, and straight, my sexual anorexia, online fantasy addiction, and misuse of masturbation made me not a unicorn, but just a regular horse in the stable of sexual compulsives.

I'd like to say that through SCA I was able to find my perfect partner and we're living happily ever after, but that's not my story. Life has taken many twists and turns, including surviving a cancer diagnosis. What is my story is that through using the tools of SCA and working the Steps for most of my adult life is not a barren world of make-believe sex happening in online erotica. Instead, I can look back over my life and recall having relationships and experiencing healthy sexuality. Even relationships that didn't end well have become a positive experience to look back at. Because of them I now know what it's like to be in love, to get my heart broken, to try again, and to be the one who walks away. In short, I have been able to experience a full life with sexuality and intimacy as a part of it.

More importantly, I've learned to love and accept myself as a person worthy of having these things in my life. Most importantly of all, I've learned that not having a life partner doesn't mean I'm not lovable or less worthy of love than people who are partnered. I am grateful that I can honestly say this: If I don't end up with a life partner, I'm still capable of having love and intimacy with friends, family, and with myself. Because of SCA, that statement isn't an intellectual rationale. It's a lived experience. The best Valentine's Day gift I've ever gotten was not a cup of coffee or even a teddy bear - it is the gift of this program.

Story #23 – *My Story and My Truth*

I was first violently assaulted while still in my mother's womb. She didn't want a child, so she tried to abort me on her own. She then married my father, who was an alcoholic and a sex addict. He acted out sexually from the moment of my conception until the day my mother left him after finding him in bed with another woman.

As a single mother, raising a child interfered with her plans. Those had shifted from pursuing her education to engaging in her sex addiction. Since I was in the way, she relinquished custody of me to her parents.

My grandparents were now raising me, and my grandfather was my primary care provider. He was also a known pedophile. We lived in a small house, and I had no crib, so I slept in my grandfather's bed. From day one, I was sexualized and molested by my grandfather as he taught me "The Lord's Prayer."

I was 5 years old when my mother re-entered my life with a new husband, a man she had known only for one week before they married. He was a charmer! In our first encounter, he kicked me with a steel-toed boot and broke my tailbone, and in our second meeting, he smacked me hard and fractured my eardrum. He continued the emotional, physical, and sexual abuse over the next 12 years.

When my mother took me back from my grandparents, we moved across town into a newly developed neighborhood. I had no friends and was very lonely. I craved kindness and would do anything for companionship. We had an elderly neighbor who lived next door, and he would offer me wheelbarrow rides in exchange for my performing a sexual act. This arrangement continued into my adolescence.

I was very shy, and spent most of my time trying to be invisible. The molestation at home continued, as did the daily physical beatings. The beatings were so severe that I was sometimes unable to walk or to attend school for weeks at a time. I grew even more isolated from the outside world.

Life became a virtual nightmare as the chaos spun out of control. I was getting into trouble at school, unable to focus in class. I became a proverbial loner in every way, spending endless hours alone. At age 8, while playing in an abandoned church, I was attacked and brutally raped by the paperboy and left there like a piece of garbage at the altar. I remember trying to tell my mother about the rape and the frequent molestation at home. Her response was to wash my mouth out with soap while scolding me for "using that kind of language."

As a pre-teen, I started stealing, lying, and cutting the bottom of my feet until they bled. I cut myself to recall the daily pain I was feeling. By age 11, I wanted to die: I did not want to kill myself, I just wanted to evaporate into thin air. The pain was unbearable, and I had no safe place and nowhere to turn. I began to masturbate frequently, which seemed to relieve my pain, if only for a moment. It became my only relief, and I continued masturbating after being caught, severely shamed, and punished.

I became intensely interested in boys in junior high school, but the only experiences I ever had were with sexually and physically abusive men. I had no idea how to have a schoolgirl crush or a non-sexual friendship. I was unable to cope, and I expressed my cry for help through teenage rebellion. I got into trouble with the law, and I also found alcohol, which helped mask the daily pain I was experiencing.

When I turned 14, I began using makeup and dressing up to make myself appear older. I lied about my age and was able to pass as an 18-year-old. I began to pursue, attract, and easily seduce older men.

When I was old enough to drive, I started looking for acting-out places outside my hometown places where nobody knew me. My behavior became increasingly risky. Once, under the influence of alcohol, I left a party with a stranger who beat and sexually assaulted me.

Because I had become so defiant, trying to stand up to my abusive stepfather, I was kicked out of the house and had to live on my own at age 17. I moved to Los Angeles, where I was alone and without friends. After losing my job and being without food or shelter, I became desperate, so I married a man I was dating, merely on a dare. I knew little about this person, and he quickly became violent after I flushed his drugs down the toilet. He slit my throat, brutally beat me, and promised to finish me off. I got the marriage annulled, but out of fear of having to return to live with my parents, I soon married again.

This second husband was an overbearing, controlling misogynist and sex addict. He would leave in the middle of the night to hook up with other women. I felt betrayed and trapped, not wanting to admit I had made yet another mistake. To cope with the pain, I did what I knew best and had sex with another man within the first six months of my marriage. I continued to act out throughout the relationship, with only brief periods of monogamy.

By the mid-1970s, I already had two children and was left alone for days by their father. When my daughter was two years old, I met a man who approached me and just wanted to talk. He was kind and very complimentary. I had never felt special to anyone before. This relationship became sexual and continued on a casual basis for over ten years.

Once I realized I could get the attention I felt I deserved from other men by merely having sex with them, my acting out quickly escalated out of control. I had no boundaries on my acting out, and no one was off-limits. I had many men in my life at one time: those I had been sexual with, those I was currently having sex with, and those I was planning to be sexual with. My husband frequently caught me. I was taking more and more risks and putting myself in increasingly embarrassing sexual situations. The men I became involved with became progressively more dangerous. One attempted to sell me into a white sex slavery ring.

In the early '80s, I read a book on co-dependency. There was a resource list in the back of the book with suggestions on how to find help. Among the suggestions were a list of 12-Step programs and recommendations on how to seek psychotherapy. This discovery began my recovery journey.

I had no health insurance and very little money. I went to women's clinics and therapy offices and told my story in hopes of finding a therapist who would help me figure out how to stop acting out. The therapists I met with shed tears as I sat there and told my story, disassociated from it with a smile on my face. I was told repeatedly that my issues were too complicated for them to handle until I was finally given the name of someone to call. She is still my therapist today.

I began attending all the 12-Step programs listed in the co-dependency book, but none of them seemed to address my issues. At each meeting I attended, I eventually hooked up with men in the group and had sex with them. Naturally, I was then too ashamed to return to that group. I also attended groups that focused on sex addiction but found them too restrictive or limited only to men.

After 2 years of trying to find a group that "fit my needs," I desperately searched for a 12-Step program where no one knew me where I could have a fresh start. Purely by accident, I wandered into an SCA meeting. There were only gay men in the rooms, and I instantly felt safe. There was only one other woman there, and I initially looked at her as a threat. But we have since bridged that gap and become close.

The first time I heard *The Characteristics* read aloud in a meeting, I knew I was in the right place. The guys didn't like having a woman in the rooms, and they often told me that they did not need a reminder of their mothers at the meeting. But I had to stay. I had nowhere else to go. My life and my health had deteriorated so much that my doctor told me if I didn't change the course I was on I would die within 6 months. For 9 months, I attended 2-3 meetings per week, while continuing to act out daily. I finally got a sponsor, whom I still have today. I wrote a sexual recovery plan with my sponsor and started getting time on my plan, but struggled to stay sober.

Late in the evening of July 8, 1989, I was on my way home after lying about where and with whom I had been when my car broke down on the freeway. There were no cell phones or call boxes, so I was stuck on the roadside, alone and scared. I stood outside my car to avoid being hit by the semi-trucks that were barreling past my car only inches away. At that moment, I realized that my life was truly unmanageable and that I needed to work the program more thoroughly.

I began to work the Steps with my sponsor and stayed close to the program as if my life depended on it, which it did. I took on sponsees and continued to attend meetings regularly. I started doing service work, sharing at meetings, participating in outreach, going to fellowship, and attending SCA retreats and conferences. I also co-hosted an SCA convention. Most of the SCA members at my meetings knew my story, and I started to gain some self-esteem, which I had never felt in my life. I remained in therapy and, with the therapist's help, told my parents my truth about their abuse and how it contributed to my addiction. I enrolled in school and got my master's degree in 2000, which was the first time I had achieved what I wanted, and I felt successful. I had taken back my life, and the promises of the program were coming true. I no longer had to pretend I was someone else: there was one story and one truth, and it was mine.

Today I am in an 18-year healthy, committed relationship, and I just celebrated over 31 years of sobriety in SCA.

Story #24 – *Breaking the Cycle of Addiction*

I'm a recovering sex and love addict. That means I use anonymous sex and addictive love as drugs to cope with life. Both my parents were products of the great depression, WWII, and the cold war. I learned from them at an early age that life is a terrifying ordeal to be overcome through willpower and sheer self-determination, or to be avoided in the shelter of diversions or protection by others. Whenever I failed myself or others failed me, I was thrown into an emotional state that became overwhelming and intolerable. Temporary relief only came through the rush of an orgasm or the fantasy of a potential lover. Eventually sex and love addiction as tools for survival grew until I was living only to search for anonymous sex and unrequited love.

My dad was always away at work and my mom filled his absence by enveloping me as surrogate spouse. She pulled me out of school early almost every day to be her shopping companion and I slept next to her every night until the age of 14. This abandonment by my dad and enmeshment by my mom later led to a desperate need to find a relationship, no matter how dysfunctional, in order to avoid sleeping alone. I filled my father's absence by hanging around with the gardener that came twice a week. We became very close and he provided the male attention I was missing from my dad. Unfortunately, he used this trust to molest me every week between ages 5 and 7. Eventually I learned to masturbate on my own. I did it all day by rubbing my pants under the desk in class and instead of doing homework or sleeping at night.

I wasn't masturbating so frequently because it felt good. I was masturbating because it relieved uncomfortable feelings that felt overwhelming: dread of the outside world, fear of not being enough, and terror of losing my dad's protection. One of my earliest memories is from age 6, when my father had his heart attack. While paramedics treated him, I searched for keys to the gun cabinet and confirmed there were bullets in the drawers. I knew that neither my mom nor I could ever cope on our own, and without him we'd be living on the streets. The world was just too scary and I prepared to "get it over with" rather than be slowly torn apart by the demons outside. Masturbation provided relief from these fears and kept me away from the gun cabinet. For years, it was a life raft from suicide, until it turned into an anchor that almost pulled me under. My grades soon suffered, leading to pressure from my parents. The more they pressured me, the more I masturbated and the more my grades dropped. The lower my grades dropped, the greater my fear of failure and facing the outside world.

At age 7, a teacher noticed what I was doing and gave me a humiliating reprimand in front of the whole class. The school called my parents and kicked me out of second grade because I disturbed the other students by masturbating. My parents sent me to a therapist, who said anything I told him would be kept confidential. When I told him about the gardener, all hell broke loose. My mom and I started a game of cat and mouse - she getting ever more invasive to catch me masturbating, and I getting ever more creative in finding ways to do it. My mom started drinking and screamed every night over the dinner table about the gardener and my behavior. I felt like an outcast, responsible for all the pain I had caused my family. Over the next 10 years through 5 different schools, my addiction progressed with corresponding consequences and shame. I'd pray to God that things wouldn't go wrong: then they'd get even worse. In time I concluded either there was no God, or I was bad and he really had it out for me. This was later reinforced when I came out and was rejected by my parents, scorned by my straight friends, and condemned for being gay.

By age 11, I had started to practice what I had learned by regularly fondling an 8-year-old. Molestation by an adult at such an early age had fused into my prematurely developed sexuality an invasive need for power and disregard for boundaries. This conflation of power with sex was to form the foundation of years of addictive behavior.

By age 12, I had discovered pornography. I masturbated instead of studying, and pursued my classmates for sexual experimentation. My grades were abysmal and I was finally expelled for soliciting other boys for sex.

At 15, I discovered tearooms at the local mall, unaware of police surveillance. On Christmas Eve I was arrested for soliciting an officer while shopping with my dad. I wouldn't tell them my name and I didn't yet have a driver's license for ID. They were going to take me to jail when I pointed out my father. One cop read me my Miranda rights while 10 feet away the other told my dad I was arrested in a public restroom. By this time, my mom's drinking was around the clock. When we got home, she screamed, "You're a pervert, you're a pervert! I wish you had never been born!" After I got my driver's license, I used my innate radar for sexual activity to find every local tearoom. The utter humiliation of my arrest hadn't deterred me from public sex. Like a typical addict, I just decided to manage the risk by looking for cops to avoid another arrest.

When I got to college, I disappeared into sex in local restrooms. As a result, my grades were non-existent and I was asked to leave. I was expelled from 3 other colleges over the next 5 years because of my addiction. Suicide seemed like the only way out of this never-ending mess. I had stopped believing in God long ago. Hanging out the window of my top floor apartment, in desperation I pleaded “If there is a God, please let me know I’m not alone and there’s hope. Please God take me out of this pain!”

Suddenly incredible warmth suffused my entire being. My tears stopped abruptly and all the pain literally disappeared from my body. The room seemed to glow, making every color or detail exquisitely light and clear. I felt totally secure, like a small brick anchored in my own little spot in an endless wall of life. The sense of belonging was incredible, as if I was a tiny little part of something vast and unlimited, wanted, loved, and totally accepted. Startled, I observed the room with almost detached curiosity. The effect lingered, then the lightness and colors slowly returned to normal. However, the pain was completely gone and my body retained a sense of fulfillment and peace. I wondered what had happened and couldn’t connect it to my prayer in the window, as I didn’t really believe in God at that time. I discounted it as some freak of nature, a hallucination created out of the self-preservation instinct in my mind.

Around this time, I fell in love with a boy I met in a tearoom. We only spent a week together, but he completed me in a way I’d never experienced before. There was an emotional passion, way more powerful than casual sex, which created an overriding desire for more. Just like an alcoholic after his first drink, I craved the intensity, abandon, and immersion of love addiction from the very start. I wanted more of that intoxicating feeling, and decided the only way to get it was to find a permanent supply by securing a boyfriend. If I was to be a failure at education and life, at least I could find emotional shelter from my pain and self-hatred in the warm embrace of a partner. By this time, my parent's marriage was in shambles from my mom's alcoholism. I urgently needed to find something outside my home and family to feel safe and secure.

I started going to gay bars every night of the week in a desperate search for a relationship. I would seek out any stranger across the room whose physical looks resembled my mental image of the perfect lover. Then I would project onto this person all the other characteristics my fantasy lover would have: smart, fun, loving, successful, and dynamite in bed. In my mind, if he looked perfect then everything else would be perfect also. I would then have an overwhelming emotional reaction to my fantasy, imbuing the stranger with enormous power. If he reciprocated my interest, I felt powerful and "enough;" all my defects and self-hatred disappeared in the magnetism of his attraction. If he didn't reciprocate and ignored me, I felt powerless and lacking; my self-worth imploded and all the shame-demons of past failure swooped in and engulfed me in a hopeless despair, sure that I'd never find love.

If no one at the bar responded, I would switch to another bar, working my way down to the dive bar where the prospects were desperate. If I still couldn't find anyone, I'd cruise the gay alley, eventually perusing the hustlers for sheer expediency. Thinking I'd find the love of my life in a cruisy bar, back alley, or dark bathhouse is the great delusion of sex and love addiction.

Occasionally, I'd meet someone interested in a relationship after we had had sex. However, the minute I found out they really wanted me, the attraction went away. Other times I'd keep dating them to have regular access to sex. I was desperate to avoid sleeping alone and needed my bed occupied every night of the week.

Over the next several years I had three other boyfriends. They all came from alcoholic families and were a perfect fit for my love addiction. The more enmeshed and chaotic the relationship became, the more we acted out our fear of abandonment and losing the relationship through the intensity of our sex. The unmanageability became intolerable, but I couldn't leave because the pain of withdrawal was worse than the pain in the relationship. Only when things got unbearably insane, like when my boyfriend's dad killed someone in an alcoholic rage, was I finally able to leave.

One night I picked up a hustler in a park and proceeded to start having sex in the car. Suddenly, the police were at the window banging on the door. We were still clothed, but they handcuffed me anyway and took me off to jail. Sitting in the holding cell was a humiliating experience, wondering whom I could trust with my phone call and ashamed at how they'd probably react.

Finally, one Friday night, I'd had enough and was straddling the windowsill ready to jump. I was crying profusely and vaguely remember pleading to God to show me some sign that I wasn't alone and some reason not to push off. A short time later there was a knock at the door and it was my best friend from high school.

My friend spent the night so I wouldn't jump and the next day accompanied me to my first SCA meeting on Saturday, September 14th 1985. When they read *The Characteristics*, I felt like someone had been looking over my shoulder all my life. Here was a group of people that clearly knew exactly what I'd been going through. I didn't understand the program but felt that if they'd so clearly outlined the problem then maybe they had a solution.

They said to get a sponsor so I asked someone because I didn't think he'd reject me. My sponsor said the first word in Step One was "We." He said I couldn't do this alone and needed to go to meetings and make outreach calls. He wanted all his sponsees to join him for fellowship and at first, I thought I was way too busy to make such a drastic time commitment. However, I kept noticing how many evenings I was acting out while all my newfound friends were at the meeting. There's nothing lonelier than sitting in a bathhouse, looking at the clock, and realizing that everyone's having fun at fellowship without you. Eventually I agreed to attend meetings and fellowship every day of the week.

My sponsor suggested I make outreach calls to other members throughout the day. Ours is a disease of isolation. I avoided making calls because it was much easier to isolate in my addiction. I avoided answering calls because they'd usually ask how I was doing and I didn't want to talk about it. If I was acting out, I was afraid to tell them for fear they'd judge me worse than I was already judging myself. Eventually, I got in the habit of calling and developed a circle of support.

My sponsor also asked me to write a sexual recovery plan to get honest about the behaviors in my addiction. After some discussion about my most glaring issues we came up with a list of 11 activities that were plaguing my life.

I went through a bargaining phase with a vengeance. I'd dance around the edges of my sex plan, redefining my bottom lines, until finally I'd fall into a slip that couldn't be rationalized away. Deep inside I wanted to manage the consequences of my addiction while still enjoying it. I thought the program was about acquiring the power to control my behavior. I didn't realize that I couldn't control it and had to let go.

The agony of acting out all day no matter how much I worked my program was to continue for years. I acted out on the way to a meeting. I acted out on the way from a meeting. I even went to a hospital inpatient treatment program for 5 weeks, where I learned much about sexual addiction, childhood trauma, and alcoholic family systems. However, when I got home, I found that having that self-knowledge availed me nothing. Knowing how I got here didn't give me the power to act differently on the information.

After 5 years in program, I disappeared into a 3-month binge that ended when I finally hit bottom in an abandoned tenement surrounded by the refuse of my sexual compulsion. I realized there was no middle-of-the-road solution and my life was impossible. I felt I would rather die than face life without acting out, and I'd rather die than act out again. There was nowhere to go. The choice was going back to meetings and working the program as if my life depended on it, or check off the planet any way possible.

In the past I had submitted to working my program in order to control my disease. Now I admitted that I'd never control the disease and that I had to let go before it killed me. I was completely deflated and ready to give up on running my own recovery. From this place of humility, God finally started to grace me with some sobriety one day at a time. I started alternating ever-longer intervals of sobriety followed by ever-shorter periods of acting out. I also learned that the best way to stay sober was to help others stay sober. It worked for me whenever my sobriety was tested and all other program tools failed.

Once I stopped acting out, my issues around love addiction were no longer being medicated by sex. I started working with a new sponsor who had much recovery around love addiction. I learned that love addiction is about avoiding or recreating the abandonment and enmeshment from our childhood. I'd be unavailable in relationships so I couldn't get hurt, or be attracted to unavailable men and try to make them love me. I'd be dependent in relationships to heal my pain, or be attracted to needy men and try to fix their problems. Either extreme was an attempt to resolve old grief. I know now it is also a spiritual disease. I got my sense of power and security from others by trying to be their Higher Power or by making them mine.

Love addiction was much harder to let go of than compulsive sex. First, it was way more painful. Withdrawal from sex was uncomfortable, but withdrawal from an addictive relationship felt like every cell in my body was burning with fire. Second, it was much easier to identify a slip in sex addiction than in love addiction. I either paid for sex or I didn't; I watched porn or not. With love addiction the blurry lines between intimacy and intensity, care and codependency, vulnerability and enmeshment, abandonment and boundaries were difficult to discern. Eventually I adopted "reality by consensus." If my sponsors and peers said the same thing about my relationship, then it had to be true, no matter how much it didn't make sense to me.

After abstaining from relationships for a period of time, my sponsor and I developed a dating action plan to learn how to integrate intimacy in my life as a healthy element. I learned that healthy relationships grow in stages, and that each stage involves a different set of skills and level of surrender. Most important was to trust my Higher Power that my needs would be met. I prayed to God to make me a more capable of healthy intimacy, and then took action on my dating plan to grow and make myself available for that possibility. Over time, my dating experiences got more intimate and meaningful. I found that who I attracted and was attracted to was a reflection of my growth in recovery. I came to see that God put partners in my life as an opportunity to learn and expand my capacity to love. I stopped asking, "Is he the One?" and focused instead on what I could contribute to, rather than take from, the relationship.

My connection to a Higher Power has really grown over time. As a child I had concluded that either God didn't exist or he was vengeful and punishing. When I first worked Step Two, I wrote a "want ad" for God that was the opposite of everything I knew.

I made an effort to act as if it was true, but no matter how hard I tried I couldn't trade my fear for faith.

I had surrendered much in my recovery, but I was still hanging on to enough control over life to make myself miserable. I discovered that whenever I turned it over, things came out better than my limited mind could have foreseen. I found the most powerful use of prayer was to ask for God's will for me, instead of what I wanted from God. Most of all, I came to trust in the Steps as tools for living to get me out of the way, so God's love could come into my life.

I have received many gifts from the program, but perhaps the most meaningful was healing my family relationships. Before SCA, I never had an intimate conversation with my dad and was brutal enemies with my mom. After they came to my inpatient treatment for sexual addiction, my dad started going to a 12-Step program for family members. I went to meetings with him and he came to meetings and SCA retreats with me. We did an intervention on my mom's drinking, and she went to treatment and got sober by working a program. We did our Ninth Step amends with each other and worked our programs together. Both my parents came to SCA meetings to give me a sobriety cake in the first few years of my recovery. Over time we have built deep intimate relationships I never had as a child.

My Higher Power has kept me sexually sober through the death of my parents, Stage 4 cancer, and many other challenges. I was recently graced with 30 years of sobriety on my sexual recovery plan. That sobriety has allowed me to survive 33 years with an AIDS diagnosis without reinfection and I am currently asymptomatic. My partner and I just celebrated 23 years in a monogamous, loving relationship where intimacy is the norm; conflict is the exception.

Today, I still work the Steps because I'm still human. The process of surrender never ends. I'm graced with a daily reprieve as long as I work my program and see what I can contribute rather than take.

Each time I reach out to a newcomer, and every time someone I've touched passes it on to countless others I'll never meet, we come home to the limitless source of love and compassion that started it all. We know for a moment the sense of belonging that resides deep inside where we're all part of the vast and unlimited tapestry that is the universe of love in the mind of God.

Story #25 – *Protector Tormentor*

"My throat gets really tight, like I can't get my voice out." That's how someone described the feeling of telling painful secrets. I feel that way now, as I tell you mine.

I am 5 years old, standing by the side of a swimming pool. Suddenly I am beneath the water and sinking quickly. Large arms bring me back up and place me back on the cement. I am crying, scared that I am in trouble. Later, as I lay alone in the back of our station wagon, I hear girls' voices giggling. "Look, there's a little boy in there and he's in his underwear."

I am 7, and one winter afternoon, I am with my brothers outside our front door. We have been playing in the snow. The living room is full of relatives. My father opens the door and tells us that before we can come in, we have to strip to our underwear. We are cold and wet. Furtively looking to see if anyone is on the street, we strip down and rush inside and up the stairs, avoiding eye contact with anyone inside. For me, there was no arguing with my father. His rage was unpredictable. Punishment could be a strong slap, his belt, or the silent treatment. To survive family dinners, I learned, with a camera-like view, to observe and not argue.

At 7 it's my older brother who runs alongside me and teaches me how to ride a bicycle. Later, in his room he listens and answers the questions I am afraid to ask my parents, including where babies come from. It is in his room that my brother breaks the news that my pet rabbit is not as my father has told me, getting better at the veterinarian's, but dead from the weed killer my father used on the lawn. I cry for quite a long while. This and when one of my dogs died are two of the only times I allowed myself to cry.

I am 8 and my older brother introduces me to ejaculation. I walked in on him on top of my younger brother. Later, my younger brother explained that every time our brother "rubbed up and down" on him, he received a popular comic book. I told my older brother he could do it with me, and he didn't have to give me a comic book. I didn't volunteer altruistically to protect my younger brother. I was envious of the attention. Soon it was my turn. My older brother became my protector and tormentor. For the next 5 years, I returned to his room, wanting to feel special, noticed, important. When he was sexualizing me, my body did not react. I felt like I was watching what was going on from outside my body.

When I was 10, I asked my dad for his help for a school report due the following day. Angry, he asked why I had waited to start until the night before. Frightened, I said I didn't know and burst into tears. He stood inches away from me, never touching me, and told me to stop crying, that boys don't cry. When I stopped crying, he told me to go wash my face and that he would help me. That night we stayed up late and finished the report. He also became my protector and tormentor.

At 13, I started to masturbate. In my masturbation fantasies a gang of tough kids from school forced me to strip to my underwear and masturbate as they watched and laughed. By 16, in high school when no one else was home, I was going out into the backyard, stripping to my underwear and masturbating. Each time I did it, I told myself it was too dangerous and that I would get caught. Each time I promised myself I'd never do it again, yet the adrenaline rush pushed me to continue.

At 17, I went on a 7-week summer trip organized by my school's youth group. I felt great at being away from home, but also lonely and feeling like an outsider. I struggled with starting to experience my attraction to guys and not trusting anyone to talk with. At one point, quite upset, I considered just walking away from the tour group. I imagined I was the only one with these confused feelings. Streaking – running naked through a public place - was occurring that summer. I streaked several times. Everyone in the group cheered me on. I felt the adrenaline surge and was happy for the release.

My first day at college, I met my roommate. He shared he was gay, and I said I was also. This was the first time I had said this. I wanted to be his new best friend, meet all his friends, and hang out together. He didn't say no, but it was clear it wasn't going to happen.

In the student union a table of gay guys congregated while a history teacher held court. My roommate wouldn't join and said it was better to keep a low profile on campus. He didn't approve of teachers mixing with students. I was introduced to the nightlife of the local gay disco and the ease of hook ups. The guys who invited me home were older, which was fine with me. They had their own places and weren't worried about roommates or parents. I enjoyed talking and cuddling and managed through the sex. One night, I invited myself home with a gifted songwriter guitarist. As I held him, I felt like I was flying. I know I scared him when I described the vivid imagery I was seeing. I must have sounded like I was on something. I was high on being with someone I was attracted to. He allowed me to stay, but I was never invited to return.

I often spent the night with the history teacher. He introduced me to many interesting people and I gained entry to upscale parties. He cooked supper and breakfast. I thought myself so mature to have all this in exchange for offering my body to someone to whom I secretly had no attraction.

After college, I got a place of my own. When I shared with a friend about my family, he suggested I attend a 12-Step group for adult children of alcoholics. Though my father didn't drink, his unpredictability and my mother's silent enabling mirrored an alcoholic family. I attended meetings for several months. One evening, I wandered out of a meeting room and saw a notice for an SCA meeting in an adjoining room. When I entered, people were sharing about the sexual risks they had taken and their lack of fulfillment. I was home.

I shared my story with a sponsor - grateful someone wanted to listen. I worked the Steps. I joined a group for male survivors of sexual abuse and started individual therapy. After a few months, the therapist asked if I was ready to end the secret. He suggested I invite my parents to therapy. I was worried that my father might become violent. My mother said she didn't need to come, but my father came for two sessions. He said that if he had known what my brother was doing, he would have stopped it. I responded that my dad's behavior had kept me from talking. My father never owned any responsibility and said that I was exaggerating my stories of punishment. Gratefully, my younger brother, privately to me, corroborated my recollections.

In spite of my dad's denial, the secret shame was out. Slowly, I was able to feel safe around my dad. I am glad I was able to talk about things with him. The Serenity Prayer has guided me. "God, grant me the serenity to accept the things I cannot change." I am not going to change my father's view of the past or mother's choice to ignore his actions. "The courage to change the things I can." I learned my older brother was asked to leave a high-level position after a staffer reported sexual harassment. She had submitted to him sexually with the promise of advancement, which never materialized - similar to the many unrealized promises he made to me. I can now see that he was not my protector, but a highly manipulative con man that preyed upon my vulnerability through physical and emotional seduction. "And the wisdom to know the difference." With the support of my therapist and sponsor, I have severed all contact with him.

I was in a relationship and in recovery, but I still struggled with healthy sexuality. In order to be sexual, I played out an unspoken fantasy on my internal screen, alternating between victimizing another and being victimized. I increasingly compartmentalized my feelings. I started going outside our relationship and the relationship ended. I hadn't been able to turn the volume down on my internal movie. I had a few more multi-year relationships. Sometimes I tried sharing parts of my scenario and asking for my partner's participation. I was asking them to be with a different person than the one I had represented myself to be.

After being boxed up for months or even years at a time, my masturbation scenario resurfaced, stronger and more aggressive each time. No real partner can compete with the unsustainable adrenaline surge of my scenarios. In recovery, I am working on recapturing what it means to be fully present, to choose to be with another person, and to enjoy sex without needing to leave my body.

I am now attending SCA meetings regularly. I have always journaled, but now I try to check in with my feelings daily. I do a guided morning meditation. I have incorporated a body scan meditation, which is helpful when I am confused or distressed by what I am feeling. Masturbation is not disallowed from my life. For today, I am working on releasing my internalized tormentor and creating a gentle, nurturing, spiritual, loving self, and welcoming in my Higher Power.

Story #26 – *Regaining My Integrity*

I am a 66-year-old married man. I was 62 when I came into "S" recovery, still unaware that I was a sexually compulsive sex and love addict.

I grew up in a very dysfunctional home. My maternal grandparents were alcoholic, my paternal grandparents were fanatically religious and absent, and my mother had been sexually molested by my grandfather and was alcoholic. My father was alcoholic as well as emotionally and physically abusive. My parents were divorced by the time I was 6 and my father disappeared from the scene for 8 years, reappeared only long enough to sow more chaos, then promptly disappeared again. My mother, my brother, my sister, and I moved frequently until I was 20. A parade of men, some violent and dangerous and all dysfunctional in some way, trooped through our lives, and I concluded that men will always abandon you. My mother went from being an army wife to being an exotic dancer and barmaid, a technical proofreader, and a bar owner. But she was also chronically unemployed, depressed, and a raging alcoholic.

Ours was a highly sexualized household with blurred or non-existent boundaries. Early on I was exposed to my mother's sexual behavior, to dirty stories, to porn, to Polaroid pictures of my mother engaged in sex parties, to voyeurism, and to sex. The message I received from my mother's husbands and live-in boyfriends, from my older cousins, and even from my mother herself, was this: women exist to please men in a transactional way, and women should be emotionally manipulated into giving sex.

I learned to escape the chaos and to self-soothe through fantasy and compulsive masturbation. I had sexual contact with my sister and her friend, with my brother and male friends, and even with my mother. Desperate for affection, acceptance, and friendship, I initiated or accepted sex as part of the bargain.

I also learned that the risk of getting caught was both terrifying and powerfully seductive. As my sex addiction grew, my acting out escalated to explore ever more extreme, dangerous, and degrading ways of acting out. I was chasing the high that novelty and intensity offered in place of real intimacy. Only in recovery was I able to look back at the surprising and shocking extremes to which I'd gone and the degree to which I had eroded my morality, ethics, and character.

I have been on a life-long quest for intimacy, validation, and approval. For as long as I can remember I haven't really felt okay or good enough. I have a core belief that once someone really gets to know me, they will dislike me, reject me, or abandon me. I am a narcissistic egomaniac with an inferiority complex. I have sought validation and approval through two main avenues: external accomplishment and sexual intimacy.

Groucho Marx once said, "Sincerity is the key to success. Once you can fake that, you've got it made." I learned to apply this lesson at school, at work, and in seduction. While I worked hard and earnestly applied myself, I also found that flattery, manipulation, and the appearance of empathy were effective tools to help me succeed. I also learned that accomplishment and success were best achieved not by depending on anyone else, but through isolation, competition, and the manipulation of others. I became pretty good at putting up facades. The same was true with seduction: I became good at presenting myself as the type of gentle, empathetic, respectful, and caring man women were seeking. I was so good at faking it that I even fooled myself.

I identify with all 14 of the SCA characteristics of sexual compulsivity. I particularly resonate with number 12, which states, in part: While constantly seeking intimacy with another person, I found that the desperate quality of my need made true intimacy with anyone impossible… I believed sexual intimacy was true intimacy. To me, sex seemed to be the ultimate acceptance. I rushed into sex and relationships before someone could really get to know me. I married the first woman who would have me, who seemed to accept me for who I was. After my divorce I pursued success and sexual relationships with a vigorous, desperate urgency. I nearly remarried several times. I recklessly got a woman pregnant, resulting in an abortion for her and a vasectomy for myself. As my addiction progressed, I stepped over line after line, and my integrity and moral condition deteriorated as a result. I rushed my current wife to the altar before she could get to really know me. As passion cooled in our relationship, my compulsive acting out and cheating returned and escalated, growing more and more risky and extreme to get the same high.

Finally, having been caught one more time, I determined I had two choices: I could enter therapy and this fellowship, or I could get divorced. I joined this group, intending to just go through the motions in order to keep my wife from leaving me. When I started attending, I didn't believe I really had a problem. Fortunately, for me, I was eventually relieved of this notion.

I am thankful for the therapist I found, who continues to give me not only emotional support but practical, useful tools and advice for improving my life. He is the person who recommended this program and meetings.

My sexual recovery program gives me clarity and tools for living life in better, more fulfilling ways. Being retired and financially secure, I am fortunate to not have a lot of the pressures and challenges many others face. This doesn't mean I am stress-free, but I'm learning to handle stressors in better ways.

For example, when my wife was triggered recently and was lashing out at me, my abandonment issues got triggered and I was tempted to be defensive. In panic, I was tempted to blow up my relationship to escape my uncomfortable feelings. However, I was able to use several tools I have learned in my program. I reminded myself to "live in the pause," to procrastinate, and to reach out to friends and confidants in the program. I was able to weather the storm and act rather than react. Things calmed down.

Through the program's principles of rigorous honesty and my intention to do the next right thing, I am rehabilitating my character and regaining my integrity. I better understand my behaviors and have begun to accept responsibility for past misdeeds while being relieved of most of the destructive burden of shame. As a result, I feel better about myself, and I behave better. I find that positive attitudes and behaviors tend to reinforce each other.

I tend to be negative, fearful, and pessimistic. The program has given me a "bigger plate" so that I have room for helpings of gratitude alongside the servings of stress, loneliness, boredom, and fear that life dishes out. I aspire to express my gratitude, not only to help my own mental outlook, but also to help my wife and other people I care about.

I recently read a fortune cookie that said, “To be successful, admire and emulate others who are successful.” To a large extent, that is also a gift of this program, and what I try to do – to learn from and take inspiration and hope from the examples, wisdom, and support of others in this program.

Through this program I have come to realize that sexual intimacy isn’t the only form of intimacy available to me. Meetings, service, support, and friendships with others in the program help me find and nurture healthy, intimate, non-sexual relationships.

I am thankful for working (and reworking) the 12 Steps, along with the advice and support of the men who help me work them productively. I am grateful for the program tools I employ as needed, including program literature, sponsorship, journaling, and meditation. Last, but foremost, I am grateful to my wife for giving me the chance to redeem myself. She has given me hope for a better, more fulfilling, and genuinely intimate relationship. She has been my strongest, most loyal and caring supporter. She deserves far better treatment than I have given her. I have caused her such pain and resentment that the fate of our relationship is still uncertain. However, without this program there would be no hope at all. We would be divorced. It is thanks to this program and to those my Higher Power works through, that I now have a future with hope – The hope that I can give my wife the love, the caring, and the intimacy that I should have been giving her all along.

Story #27 – *Up from the Tombs*

On March 9, 2009, my world came crashing down around me. There was a knock on my door. Two detectives from the New York Police Department entered my apartment and told me they had received a tip that I had a tremendous amount of child pornography on my computer. They were right. I was arrested and spent a night and most of the next day in a jail known colloquially as "The Tombs..."

As I entered a cell occupied by several other men, a disheveled gentleman (whom I assumed was homeless) came up to me with an apple in his hand and said, "Buddy, you look like you could use this." My ego, which had been steadily deflating from the very moment the police entered my apartment, was shattered. I knew then that, regardless of whom this person was, he was kind to me at a time when I felt totally undeserving of any kindness.

The day after my release, I found out I had lost my job. My apartment (which was provided by my employer) needed to be surrendered. I lost the esteem of my coworkers, and I thought I had lost the love of my family. Most importantly, I lost much of my identity. I identified myself by the work I did. What was left over from that identity was a space occupied by my addictive behavior; my life consisted of doing my job or looking at porn. There was little else.

Fortunately, my employer insisted that I see a social worker as part of an exit strategy. She recommended I see a therapist. I took that suggestion to heart and began seeing a therapist who specialized in treating sex addicts and individuals suffering from post-traumatic stress syndrome.

In the first session with the therapist, she told me she would see me for my sex addiction, but only if I was willing to attend a 12-Step program for sex addiction. She gave me a list of local "S" meetings, and cautioned me to be honest about why I was in the rooms.

My first "S" meeting was in another fellowship. It was a small meeting, located in the basement of an Upper West Side church, and consisted of fewer than ten people. As I told my story I could see people stare at me. I could feel their disbelief; these supposed peers, and their desire to separate themselves from me.

I crossed that fellowship off my list and went to my first SCA meeting. It was the Friday Beginner's Meeting, located in the LGBTQ Center in the West Village. I got there early, and an individual named Tommy came up to me and said "Welcome," and began to explain the meeting format. He warned me that it was a large meeting and that "beginners" were given a special time to share after the social break. But he also said that I could raise my hand to share at any time during the meeting.

As people began arriving, the room changed from being a quiet, safe place with only one other person to a busy gathering of 60 people. I wanted to leave but I felt surrounded and stuck in place. As the meeting progressed, I listened to the 12 Steps and *The Characteristics* and then to a 20-minute-long share by a member of the fellowship. I have no recollection of what he said, but I felt a commonality. He hadn't come into SCA after being arrested for possession of child porn, but he did talk about putting himself at risk for arrest by having sex in public places. More importantly, he talked about an inability to stop his compulsive behaviors, despite making repeated attempts, until he started working the tools of SCA.

His earlier inability to stop was similar to my own: I had emptied my computer of all files containing child porn on numerous occasions, only to accumulate these images again and again over time.

During the social break, a few members of the fellowship came up to me and greeted me. I thought that after they heard what I had done, then, like people at the other fellowship, these members would shun me, too. Despite this, I did reveal why I was there, and during my share I admitted to being addicted to child pornography. Instead of being shunned, I heard, “Welcome,” and “Keep coming back” from members of the group. After the meeting, the meeting chair came up to me and invited me to join him and several members of the group for fellowship. I accompanied them to a vegan restaurant in the Village. When I went home that night, I tore up the rest of the list of S groups. I had found a place where I could begin to address my issues.

In that first year, I learned from other members that I was not the first person to come in to the fellowship with problems related to child pornography addiction. One member shared how a friend of his came into recovery but ultimately went to prison for his crimes. My own court case dragged on for a bit more than a year. Ultimately, I met with an assistant district attorney, and my attorney was able to arrange a plea deal for 10 years of probation and 20 years on the sex offender registry. The judge commended me for getting into therapy soon after my arrest, and said that he was impressed that I was attending a 12-Step program several times a week. He said that he hoped I would use my time on probation productively.

My recovery in SCA has not always been smooth. There have been times when I felt as if I was purposefully snubbed. Two people voiced that they wanted to kill me. One of them later pulled me aside and apologized. The other invited me to lunch so that I could explain why I should continue to live. After going through my story in detail, he paid for lunch, and we became friendlier.

I got an interim sponsor and began working the 12 Steps. I came to realize that I could not easily make amends to the thousands of children whose images I used for my own pleasure. My best amends was to singularly devote myself to my recovery and not repeat my past behaviors. I gave long shares (called qualifications in SCA New York) when asked. I did not hesitate to explain why I was in the rooms. I expressed my gratitude for not being incarcerated, yet shared my frustration over some of the things that my probation officers required of me. I tried to be of service to other recovering addicts, and I began volunteering for service positions within the fellowship.

I still sometimes feel alone in my recovery, but after a few minutes I realize that the part of me that still wants to act out with child porn wants me to isolate, wants me to blame others for not liking me, and ultimately wants me to do and feel anything that will justify my desire to look at child porn. The desire still pops up from time to time, but I have tools that work for me.

I do a First Step often. I recount my powerlessness over my addiction, and I recall the time I spent in a jail cell. I tell of how the loss of my job directly led to the loss of any self-esteem that I had managed to build during my 28-year career. I recall stories of my fellows who had been victims of childhood sexual abuse; who would share the pain they still feel from that abuse. I knew that, prior to recovery, when I had viewed images of children, I had not seen them as victims. Yet here in the rooms I was confronted with the pain of real flesh-and-blood victims. It was a rude awakening that I did not enjoy. It was deeply sobering to realize that my actions had consequences that extended far beyond my control. Each child whose image I had viewed was a victim. While I may not have directly abused that child, I had gotten something from viewing the image of that abuse. I was therefore complicit in it. My amends is to provide solace to my fellows wherever possible, even if the best way to do so is to remain silent. I try to be positive in my shares and continually express my gratitude for the gift of a recovery that takes place one day at a time.

Story #28 – *My Rock Bottom*

One of the first assignments from my sponsor was to write about hitting rock bottom. "Why on Earth would I want to do that," I asked him. He told me that writing it would help me explore the powerlessness and unmanageability of this hideous disease. I put if off for days, then had a dream that inspired me. The dream made me feel safe and loved, and when I woke up, I thought, "I can do this!" So, I sat quietly and put pen to paper.

In my dream I was holding a naked baby boy, who I knew symbolized me. We were on a log flume and he pooped himself. I held him over the side and tried to wash him off, but he slipped out of my arms and into the water. I jumped in to rescue him. I quickly bathed him and we got back in. I held him tight and I felt a tremendous amount of love. Then I awoke. I'm finally ready to take care of the little boy inside me, I thought, to bathe away the past and to hold on tight for the ride. I am in God's will and his love.

Tuesday Oct.12

I went to my doctor for a routine physical, having turned 40 the previous summer. The doctor caught me off guard when he asked if I wanted an HIV test. I said sure, knowing that my acting out that summer had included crystal meth, unprotected sex and prostitutes. As my blood was drawn, I told the nurse I was nervous because I had been unsafe. He said, "Don't worry. You know, if you are positive, you'll be fine. The meds are much better now. I've been positive for about 20 years." I looked at him and smiled. I took a few deep breaths as he filled the vile with my blood. I left and went about my day, not telling my husband I'd been tested.

Later that day I smoked pot, which was my daily routine - smoke and take the dog for a walk. I had been more or less stoned for the past 20 years. I walked my dog to our favorite park. It was a beautiful day and I was looking for divine intervention. I have a guardian angel - a dear friend who passed away a few years back. I said a little prayer to her. "Can you help me out? Please make me negative." I heard a little voice in my head say, "Too late sweet baby." That was not the answer I was looking for.

So, I asked God, as I had perhaps 10 other times that day, "Please God, make me negative." I expected something, a warm feeling or a booming voice from above. Nothing came, just the sounds of dogs barking and LA humming behind me. I felt alone and scared. I shook if off and continued with my walk.

Wednesday Oct. 13

I'm at the park again with my dog and a couple of dog-walking friends. The phone rang; it was my doctor's office. I was expecting the nurse, but this time it was my doctor's voice. He sounded serious. "We received your test results back. The HIV test came back positive."

I froze. My friends were just a few feet away. I motioned I had to take the call and walked away. The doctor went on. "It is possible that this could be a false positive. It's unlikely but it does happen. We've sent out for a second test to confirm. It will come back Friday." Friday was two days away.

"What am I supposed to do?" I asked. "How will I tell my husband? What should I do when I leave this park? I don't want to tell him until we are sure. I don't want him to worry." "Well," said the doctor, "I think you should stay calm."

I knew at this point I would have to conjure up the biggest lie in the history of my life, and tell my husband a story that would hide my behavior. I'm the victim here, I thought. Protect yourself, hide the shame, and bury the truth. Everything will be fine. There is still a chance… just 2 days.

I left the park and compartmentalized the news. I closed this file as tightly as I could, but by this point the filing cabinet had tipped over, spilling its ugly truths all over the place, revealing all the destruction and chaos of my life. I used pot again when I got home, but it just made things worse, amplifying my quiet torment. We had dinner with our best friend. I sat at the table and went through the motions, completely detached, hearing myself having conversation and wine and dinner, knowing that the course of my life, my husband's life, and our friend's life was about to change.

I decided to savor every moment with my husband over the next two days. It was like there was a huge magnifying glass on our world. Every detail, every glance, touch, every kiss was going to change. Soak it all in, I told myself. Savor it, remember it, because it's all about to crash and burn around you.

I had a horrible nightmare that night. I dreamed I was in a lake filled with dead bodies, some fresh and some rotten with decay. I was trying to swim across a lake filled with death.

Thursday Oct. 14

This morning over coffee my husband told me, “You were yelling in your sleep last night.” I told him about my dream. He hugged me, “It’s just a dream, honey.” I poured us some more coffee and shrugged it off.

I went about my day just trying to hold it together. All day long I would go over to my husband for hugs and kisses, which he sweetly returned. Savor these moments, I thought, and figure out this lie. Don’t tell him what you’ve done. Hide the shame and bury the truth. You can’t tell him the truth. Savor these last moments of this life, this double life, this life full of lies and sickness.

I had nightmares again. This time I was walking alone at night and masses of undead HIV zombies were coming at me, grabbing me, biting into my neck, tearing huge chunks of flesh off my body, clawing, bleeding, infecting me. I’m dying. I woke up screaming, sitting up in bed. My husband stroked my hair telling me “It’s okay, everything is okay, go back to sleep.” I fell back into restless sleep.

Friday Oct. 15

I got up and did my best to act “normal,” just waiting for the phone to ring. I got ready and left for work.

The call came later that afternoon while at a supermarket checkout. I answered as upbeat as I could. It was the confirmation call. I am HIV positive. I am in the lake, zombies everywhere, being torn apart. I scream silently as the smiling checker rings up my order. I told myself, Close the file. Deal with this later. Figure out the lie. Hide the truth. But how?

I got home from work and my husband was getting ready for the gym. He asked if I wanted to go. I just looked at him. "Are you okay?" he asked. "No, we need to talk." I told him that I'd had an HIV test and it came back positive. I told him part of the truth – that I had cheated and had unsafe sex.

He was shocked. Everything was unraveling before me. The wreckage of my life - OUR life - hung in the silence between us. I watched a tear roll down his face. He looked at me and I will never forget his eyes. They were so full of sorrow, betrayal, confusion and love. Those beautiful blue eyes, so lost in tears.

My God, what have I done? I broke his heart. I destroyed something so pure. For years I thought my actions were mine alone, isolated and hidden, and that if no one was being hurt, then it was fine. ADDICTION IS A LIAR.

I felt as if a black hole, a vortex, opened up and sucked all the joy from my life. It was pulling me down and drowning me in shame, truth, fear, broken promises and lies. Crushing me with guilt, self-deceit, confusion, anger and worthlessness. Complete self-loathing, self-destruction. Solitude. I did this to myself.

I could not stop crying. I had to go outside for some air. I burst into our backyard, gulping the night air, and all I could do was scream. I went into the garage and I screamed and yelled - visceral, guttural moans I have never heard come from my body. I am not sure how long this went on but at some point, I realized how hysterical I was and I feared for my life. I thought, you deserve to die. And a moment later I thought I don't want to die. I screamed "God help me please!" I took deep breaths and calmed myself. I found some paper towels, blew my nose and dried my face.

I went back inside to the bathroom and I took a look in the mirror. I did not know the person looking back. Who is this sick, broken, twisted liar? I looked away and down at my hands, at my wedding ring, which I had taken off so easily in the past.

What have I done? I could not completely grasp the ramifications, nor did I want to. I got a big glass of water, took a Xanax and went to bed in the guest room. I waited for it to numb, to help me escape. But there was no escape. No matter where you go there you are.

I spent the next week trying to figure out an answer to how I could have done this. My doctor suggested I see a therapist, so I went and told him my story in all its horrific glory. I was getting all worked up and ranting and crying. I asked, "How could I do this? I don't understand how a smart, logical, successful person could be so self-destructive..."

He told me about OCD and that sometimes the compulsion is sex. He then gently said, "You're an addict, don't you see? You've hit rock bottom." Those words hung in the air…addict… rock bottom. "What am I supposed to do?" I asked. "That's up to you," he replied. Typical therapist answer. "I want to fix this," I said.

He explained that there is no "fix," but there is recovery through a 12-Step program called SCA. He suggested I attend at least three meetings a week, and he handed me a yellow three-fold pamphlet. I agreed, and made an appointment with him for the following week.

I left feeling exhausted. I looked down at the pamphlet as I walked down the hall to the elevator. Sexual Compulsives Anonymous, huh? Screw that. I'm not one of those people. I'm not an addict and what's the point anyway? Then I heard another voice in my head, a loud clear voice that said, "You are going and you're finding a meeting tonight."

So, I went, that Tuesday night in the fall of 2010. There were only about six people in the room. I was handed *The Characteristics Most of Us Seem to Have in Common* to read as part of the meeting. Damn! That was me in print. I told these men "I have hit bottom and there is only one way for me to go and that's up. I can't let this addiction destroy what little I have left to live for." I was welcomed and encouraged to "keep coming back" and "it works if you work it!"

There were so many tears that week and the crushing pain of a life lost. Two lives lost. I had no idea if SCA would work for me, but I had to believe it would. I had nothing else to lose. I attended four meetings that week and got a sponsor. I began the journey of working the 12 Steps. I admitted I was powerless over sexual compulsion and that my life had become unmanageable. I started working my First Step and I began to get my answers to how this all happened. Sexual compulsion had kept me in bondage and consumed me. I assumed for years I was in control of my life and I was managing the duplicity and chaos. How far from the truth was that? Working the 12 Steps did not change who I was. It revealed who I was.

Through the Steps I uncovered and shared terrible secrets, and along the way I found an immense amount of integrity and willingness. I cleaned the wreckage of my past, made amends, gave forgiveness and found forgiveness for myself. I prayed like crazy, and I now carry the message. And most importantly, I know that a power greater than myself has restored me to sanity. I have recently celebrated 10 years on my sexual recovery plan and am still married, for 23 years. We've survived the storm and thrive now in honesty, integrity and unconditional love.

I owe my life to SCA. It really does work if you work it. Keep coming back.

Chapter 30: Endpiece

Reminders

Slow scares me
There's no rush to thrill me then
There's no heady dopamine release to ease the pain of uncertainty
To build a foundation seems boring to me
Because I've rushed headlong into things, traditionally
But where has it gotten me?

So now I write my stories as part of my day
Leave the fantasies for my screenplays
And try to let myself breathe before I send that text
Try to relax before I feel people-pleasing closing in
Try to refrain from explaining before I owe an explanation

My heart aches with longing
Wanting so badly to connect
Realizing that the desperate quality of my need can ironically push others away
The panic I feel about not being able to control how things will be
Leaves me playing both sides of the court
Trying to capture something that hasn't begun yet

And it leaves me feeling stupid
So I'll try to keep being gentle with myself
And remind myself I love myself
And remind myself I am worthy exactly as I am
I am passionate
I am a romantic
These things are great gifts
And I am learning how to wield them
No pearls before swine
And I don't need to open my heart before she's earned it